Frommer's®
Bermuda 2004

POSTCARDS FROM

You can relax, swim and snorkel at Jobson's Cove, one of Bermuda's many secluded beaches. See chapter 6. © Bob Krist Photography.

P9-EEK-738

Old-fashioned carriages transport you around Bermuda in style. See chapter 3.
© J. Barry O'Rourke/Corbis.

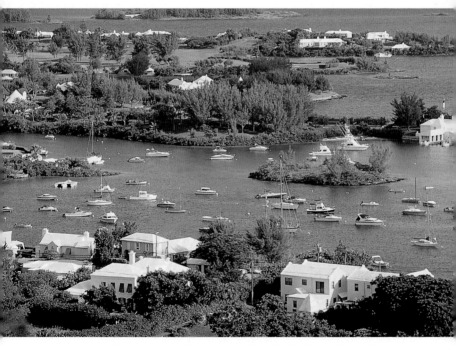

To take in an incredible panorama of Bermuda and the Atlantic Ocean, climb to the top of Gibbs Hill Lighthouse, the oldest cast-iron lighthouse in the world. Springtime visitors may be lucky enough to see migrating whales beyond the shore reefs.
© M. Timothy O'Keefe Photography.

The pool, golf course, and ocean views from the Fairmont Southampton Princess. See chapter 4 for a complete review of the resort. © *Howard Millard/The Viesti Collection.*

Horseshoe Bay Beach, in Southampton Parish, is one of Bermuda's finest places to soak up the sun. See chapter 6. © Robert Holmes Photography.

Bermuda is one of the world's top golf destinations. See chapter 6 for reviews of the top courses. © Jay Thomas/International Stock.

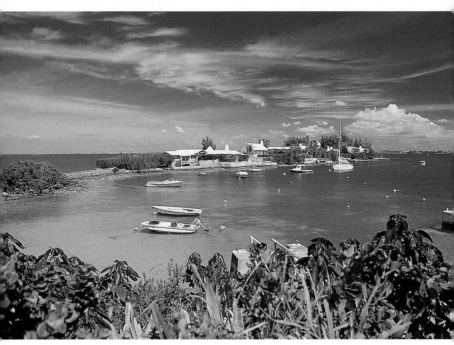

With its crystal waters and many small islands, Bermuda is a great destination for sailing and boating. See chapter 6 for details. © Bob Krist Photography.

You may catch a Bermuda businessman in Bermuda shorts in warm weather. © *Catherine Karnow Photography.*

In the Crystal Caves, you can take a guided tour through a network of subterranean lakes, caves, and caverns, which house dramatic stalagmite and stalactite formations. © Bob Krist Photography.

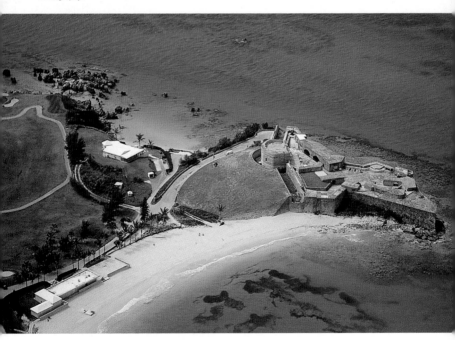

Absorb some of Bermuda's history at Fort St. Catherine, built in the 17th century in St. George's Parish. © Bob Krist Photography.

If it's too crowded at lovely Horseshoe Bay Beach, take one of the trails that wind through the park nearby to discover several other secluded cove beaches. © *Kindra Clineff Photography.*

Frommer's®

Bermuda

2004

by Darwin Porter & Danforth Prince

Here's what the critics say about Frommer's:

"Amazingly easy to use. Very portable, very complete."
— *Booklist*

"Detailed, accurate, and easy-to-read information for all price ranges."
— *Glamour Magazine*

"Hotel information is close to encyclopedic."
— *Des Moines Sunday Register*

"Frommer's Guides have a way of giving you a real feel for a place."
— *Knight Ridder Newspapers*

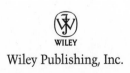

WILEY

Wiley Publishing, Inc.

About the Authors

A native of North Carolina, **Darwin Porter** was a bureau chief for the *Miami Herald* when he was 21, and later worked in television advertising. A veteran writer, he's the author of numerous bestselling Frommer's Travel Guides, notably to England, France, Germany, Italy, and the Caribbean. Working with Darwin is **Danforth Prince,** formerly of the Paris bureau of the *New York Times.* Both of these journalists discovered Bermuda during their various spring break "College Weeks" and have been frequent visitors ever since.

Published by:

Wiley Publishing, Inc.

111 River St.
Hoboken, NJ 07030

ISBN 0-7645-3733-4
ISSN 1069-3572

Editor: Amy Lyons
Production Editor: Tammy Ahrens
Cartographer: Elizabeth Puhl
Photo Editor: Richard Fox
Production by Wiley Indianapolis Composition Services

For information on our other products and services or to obtain technical support, please contact our Customer Care Department within the U.S. at 800-762-2974, outside the U.S. at 317-572-3993 or fax 317-572-4002.

Wiley also publishes its books in a variety of electronic formats. Some content that appears in print may not be available in electronic formats.

Manufactured in the United States of America

5 4 3 2 1

Contents

8 Island Strolls   188

9 Shopping   200

10 Bermuda After Dark   214

Appendix: Bermuda in Depth   220

Index   236

List of Maps

An Invitation to the Reader

In researching this book, we discovered many wonderful places—hotels, restaurants, shops, and more. We're sure you'll find others. Please tell us about them, so we can share the information with your fellow travelers in upcoming editions. If you were disappointed with a recommendation, we'd love to know that, too. Please write to:

Frommer's Bermuda 2004
Wiley Publishing, Inc. • 111 River St. • Hoboken, NJ 07030

An Additional Note

Please be advised that travel information is subject to change at any time—and this is especially true of prices. We therefore suggest that you write or call ahead for confirmation when making your travel plans. The authors, editors, and publisher cannot be held responsible for the experiences of readers while traveling. Your safety is important to us, however, so we encourage you to stay alert and be aware of your surroundings. Keep a close eye on cameras, purses, and wallets, all favorite targets of thieves and pickpockets.

Frommer's Star Ratings, Icons & Abbreviations

Every hotel, restaurant, and attraction listing in this guide has been ranked for quality, value, service, amenities, and special features using a **star-rating system.** In country, state, and regional guides, we also rate towns and regions to help you narrow down your choices and budget your time accordingly. Hotels and restaurants are rated on a scale of zero (recommended) to three stars (exceptional). Attractions, shopping, nightlife, towns, and regions are rated according to the following scale: zero stars (recommended), one star (highly recommended), two stars (very highly recommended), and three stars (must-see).

In addition to the star-rating system, we also use **seven feature icons** that point you to the great deals, in-the-know advice, and unique experiences that separate travelers from tourists. Throughout the book, look for:

Finds	Special finds—those places only insiders know about
Fun Fact	Fun facts—details that make travelers more informed and their trips more fun
Kids	Best bets for kids and advice for the whole family
Moments	Special moments—those experiences that memories are made of
Overrated	Places or experiences not worth your time or money
Tips	Insider tips—great ways to save time and money
Value	Great values—where to get the best deals

The following **abbreviations** are used for credit cards:

AE	American Express	DISC	Discover	V	Visa
DC	Diners Club	MC	MasterCard		

Frommers.com

Now that you have the guidebook to a great trip, visit our website at **www.frommers.com** for travel information on more than 3,000 destinations. With features updated regularly, we give you instant access to the most current trip-planning information available. At Frommers.com, you'll also find the best prices on airfares, accommodations, and car rentals—and you can even book travel online through our travel booking partners. At Frommers.com, you'll also find the following:

- Online updates to our most popular guidebooks
- Vacation sweepstakes and contest giveaways
- Newsletter highlighting the hottest travel trends
- Online travel message boards with featured travel discussions

What's New in Bermuda

Even some diehard fans compare Bermuda to certain beauty queens—beautiful but dull. We prefer to think of it as "tranquil." If you're looking for exotic local color or sizzling rum- and reggae-filled nights, look farther south to the Caribbean. But if you need to escape the stress and strain of daily life, look to Bermuda.

This quiet island is one of the best places in the world for a honeymoon or a celebration of any romantic occasion. The joint may not be jumping, but it's the most relaxing—and safest—of the foreign islands off the American coast. Bermuda offers a relatively hassle-free environment where you can concentrate on your tan, minus the annoyance of aggressive vendors and worries about much crime. If you're into sunning and swimming, it doesn't get much better than Bermuda between May and September. Pink sand and turquoise seas—it sounds like a corny travel poster, but it's for real. As Mark Twain said, "Sometimes a dose of Bermuda is just what the doctor ordered."

Frankly, Bermuda is predictable, and its regular visitors wouldn't have it any other way. The tiny island chain has attracted vacationers for decades, and there aren't many secrets left to uncover. But those sandy pink beaches remain just as inviting as ever, no matter how many times you return.

Even to friends of Bermuda who make an annual pilgrimage to the island, the Bermudians can be a bit smug. They know their island is more attractive than Chicago, New York, Los Angeles, or Miami, and they're not above reminding you. Bit of an imperial attitude, isn't it? Exactly.

Some critics claim that Bermuda has become Americanized. Look again. That's true of islands much farther south, such as The Bahamas, but Bermuda remains stoically Bermuda. The island and its population steadfastly adhere to British customs, even if, at times, that slavish devotion borders on caricature. (The afternoon tea ritual is pleasant enough, but the lawyers' and judges' powdered wigs are a bit much—those things must get hot in a semitropical climate!) Some visitors find all the British decorum rather silly on a remote island that's closer to Atlanta than to London. But many others find the stalwart commitment to British tradition colorful and quaint, enhancing the unique charm of the lovely, wonderful place that is Bermuda.

If you're looking for some of the best golf in the world, Bermuda is your mecca. It has the scenery, the state-of-the-art courses, and the British tradition of golfing excellence. Even the most demanding player is generally satisfied with the island's offerings.

If you're a sailor, you'll find the waters of Bermuda reason enough for a visit. Better yet, reason enough to be alive. The farther you go from shore, of course, the greater the visibility. Discovering a hidden cove, away from the cruise-ship crowds, can make your day.

If you hate driving on the left side of the road, that's fine with Bermudians. You *can't* drive—they won't rent you a car. Bike around, or hop on a scooter and zip from one end of the island to the other.

We could go on and on with reasons for you to come to Bermuda, from exploring natural wonderlands to playing on choice tennis courts with gentle sea breezes and warm sunshine. But we'll end here with a couple of warnings: Demanding foodies will find better dining on other islands, such as Martinique—although Bermuda has made much culinary progress of late. And if you want nightlife, glittering casinos, and all that jazz, head for San Juan. There is some nightlife in Bermuda, if you enjoy nursing a pint in a pub. It's always wise to bring along some good company (or a good book) to ensure a blissful night here.

Locals will always tell you, "If you want change, go to The Bahamas. We stay the same in Bermuda." Defying local wisdom, we've come up with some developments.

PLANNING YOUR TRIP   The good news for most travelers is that prices have remained fairly stable in Bermuda. Following a tremendous drop-off in tourism in the aftermath of the September 11, 2001, terrorist attacks, the visitor count to Bermuda fell way down, although it gradually came back in 2003.

Shops, restaurant owners, and hoteliers have been reluctant to raise prices with such a downturn in their economy. British visitors will find that the pound remains fairly stable against the U.S. dollar. Unless conditions change, they can anticipate no sudden shocks when the final tab arrives. See chapter 3 for more information.

ACCOMMODATIONS   The year 2004 or early 2005 will see the debut of the $250-million, 100-hectare (250-acre), five-star **Tucker's Point Club,** which will become the most exclusive, deluxe hotel ever to open on Bermuda's shores. It is being built on the site of the long famous Castle Harbour Hotel, which was demolished to make way for this spectacular new property. Its lucky guests will be coddled in comfort.

One of Bermuda's latest hotels, on an island where a new hotel opening is rare, is the boutique hotel called **The Wharf Executive Suites Hotel,** 1 Harbour Rd. (*©* **441/232-5700**), catering primarily to the business traveler but also most suitable for vacationers as well. Lying a 7-minute ferry ride from Hamilton's harbor, it features studio suites with kitchenettes. See chapter 4 for more information.

DINING   New hotels are rare in Bermuda, but the opening of new restaurants—or else their discovery— are far more frequent. A pub-cum-restaurant, **Beethoven's,** has opened at the Clocktower Building at the Royal Naval Dockyard (*©* **441/234-5009**). Two Swiss chefs serve a finely honed Swiss and Mediterranean cuisine in a historic setting. Dishes are well prepared and beautifully presented.

A first-class resort, The Reef, is attracting attention to its **Clubhouse Dining Room,** 56 South Shore Rd. (*©* **441/238-0222**). Its menu of top-rated Bermudian and international dishes is changed daily, based on the shopping for market-fresh ingredients.

The Port Royal Golf Course, has seen the opening of **Greg's Steakhouse,** Middle Road, Port Royal (*©* **441/234-6092**), specializing in some of the island's best beef as well as seafood, especially fresh Bermuda rockfish.

One of the island's more recent restaurant openings is **Barracuda Grill,** 5 Burnaby Hill (*©* **441/292-1609**), in the heart of the city of Hamilton. In a modern setting with contemporary art, you can enjoy some of the capital's seafood dishes, the menu based in part on what the local fishermen caught that day.

The restaurant owned in part by actor Michael Douglas, Ariel Sands Hotel, has blossomed out with a new restaurant **Aqua,** 34 Shore Rd. (© **441/236-1010**), serving a Bermudian, international, and Italian cuisine, and doing so fairly well. The chefs here roam the world for inspiration, and you're likely to be tempted by everything from Cajun-styled mahimahi to a Mexican loin of veal filled with black beans and spring onions and served with a cucumber salsa. See chapter 5 for more information.

SIGHTSEEING   To celebrate the role that African slaves played in the formation of Bermuda, the **African Diaspora Heritage Trail** has been launched. Thirteen sites have been identified, including the site of the landing of the slave ship, **Enterprise.**

Free brochures are available at tourist offices for those wanting to take this trail, documenting black cultural history. See chapter 7 for more information.

AFTER DARK   The latest "hot spot" is the **Café Lido/"The Deep"** at the Elbow Beach Hotel in Paget Parish, 60 South Shore Rd. (© **441/ 234-9884**). Sheltering 250 "dancing fools," it is a first-rate club with a venue for dancing and entertainment. Another one of Bermuda's leading clubs is the new **Ozone Nightclub & the Lucky Strike Casino** in the Emporium Building, 69 Front St. (© **441/292-4978**), in Hamilton. A modern, trendy club, it is known for its special-effects lighting and extensive recorded music. See chapter 10 for more information.

The Best of Bermuda

If you've decided that Bermuda sounds like the perfect place to relax, feel free to start unwinding right now, because we've done all the legwork for you. Below you'll find our carefully compiled lists of the best that Bermuda has to offer, from beaches and dive sites to resorts, restaurants, and sightseeing—and nearly everything else you'll want to see and do.

1 The Best Beaches

Your first priority on your Bermuda vacation probably will be to kick back at the beach. But which beach? Hotels often have private stretches of sand, which we've described in each accommodation review (see chapter 4, "Where to Stay"). There are many fine public beaches as well. Here's our Top-10 list, arranged clockwise around the island, beginning with the southshore beaches closest to the City of Hamilton. See chapter 6, "Fun in the Surf & Sun," for a map.

- **Elbow Beach** (Paget Parish): The pale pink sand stretches for almost a mile at Elbow Beach, one of the most popular beaches in Bermuda. At least three hotels sit on its perimeter. Because protective coral reefs surround it, Elbow Beach is one of the safest beaches on the island for swimming. Around Easter, it tends to be packed with college students who invade Bermuda for College Weeks. See p. 141.

- **Astwood Cove** (Warwick Parish): At the bottom of the steep, winding road that intersects with South Shore Road, this beach is so remote that it's rarely overcrowded. Come here when you want to be alone. The trees and shrubbery of Astwood Park

provide a verdant backdrop. See p. 142.

- **Warwick Long Bay** (Warwick Parish): This popular beach, on the south side of South Shore Park, features a half-mile stretch of sand against a backdrop of scrubland and low grasses. Despite frequent winds, an offshore reef keeps the waves surprisingly small. Less than 60m (200 ft.) offshore, a jagged coral island appears to be floating above the water. There is excellent snorkeling here— the waters are clear and marine life comes in close to shore. See p. 143.

- **Chaplin Bay** (Warwick and Southampton parishes): At the southern extremity of South Shore Park, straddling the boundary of two parishes, this small but secluded beach almost completely disappears during storms and particularly high tides. An open-air coral barrier rises from the water, partially separating one half of the beach from the other. See p. 144.

- **Horseshoe Bay** (Southampton Parish): This is Bermuda's most famous beach, and it's one of the best for families. Unlike most island beaches, Horseshoe Bay has a lifeguard on duty from May to

September. The **Horseshoe Bay Beach Cafe** (© **441/238-2651**) offers complete facilities, including watersports equipment rental. See p. 144.

- **Church Bay** (Southampton Parish): If you like to snorkel, this southwestern beach is for you. The relatively calm waters, sheltered by offshore reefs, harbor a variety of marine life. Sunbathers love the unusually deep, pink sands of this beach. See p. 144.
- **Somerset Long Bay** (Sandys Parish): The waters off this beach are often unsafe for swimming, but its isolation will appeal to anyone who wants to escape the crowds. With about a quarter-mile of sand, the crescent-shaped beach is ideal for strolling. The undeveloped parkland of Sandys Parish shelters it from the rest of the island. See p. 145.

- **Shelly Bay** (Hamilton Parish): On the north shore, you'll discover calm waters and soft, pink sand—and you'll want for nothing else. This beach is well known among beach buffs, but it's rarely overcrowded and there's always a spot in the sun just waiting for you. See p. 145.
- **Tobacco Bay** (St. George Parish): A popular stretch of pale pink sand, this is the most frequented beach on St. George's Island. It offers lots of facilities, including equipment rentals and a snack bar. See p. 145.
- **John Smith's Bay** (Smith's Parish): The only public beach in Smith's Parish is long and flat. It boasts the pale pink sand for which the south shore is famous. There's usually a lifeguard on duty from May to September—a plus for families. There are toilet and changing facilities on-site. See p. 146.

2 The Best Outdoor Pursuits

See chapter 6, "Fun in the Surf & Sun," for details on arranging any of these activities.

- **Golf:** Known for its outstanding courses, Bermuda attracts the world's leading golfers (and those who'd like to be). Over the years, such luminaries as President Eisenhower, President Truman, and the Duke of Windsor have hit the island's links. Rolling, hummocky fairways characterize the courses. Many avid golfers come to Bermuda to "collect courses," or play them all. Some holes, such as Port Royal's notorious 16th, are "from hell," as golfers say: Both the tee and the hole are high on cliff edges, with the rich, blue sea a dizzying 30m (100 ft.) below. See "The Best Golf Courses," below, for our top picks.

- **Boating & Sailing:** Yachters around the world agree: Bermuda is one of the world's top boating destinations. Many people forget that Bermuda isn't one island, but an archipelago, with all kinds of nooks and crannies waiting to be discovered. With the fresh wind of the Atlantic blowing in your hair, you can embark on your own voyage of discovery, exploring Great Sound and its islets, including Long Island and Hawkins Island. Tiny, secluded beaches beckon you to put down anchor and relax awhile. If you're a novice, try Mangrove Bay; it's protected and safer than some of the more turbulent seas. See "More Fun in the Water" in chapter 6.
- **Diving:** If you're happiest under the sea, Bermuda has what you're

Bermuda

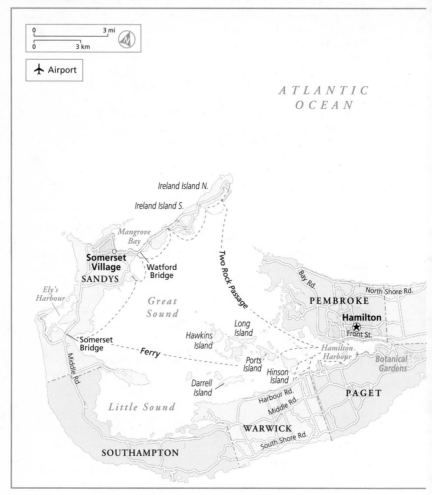

looking for. That includes the wrecks of countless ships, underwater caves, rich reefs, and, during most of the year, warm, gin-clear waters. All around the island you'll find a kaleidoscope of coral and marine life that's the most varied in this part of the world. Many scuba experts consider Bermuda one of the safest and best places to learn the sport. Seasoned divers will not be disappointed either—Bermuda has

terrific diving areas for experts. Depths begin at 7.5m (25 ft.) or less, but can exceed 24m (80 ft.). Some wrecks are in about 9m (30 ft.) of water, which puts them within the range of snorkelers. See "The Best Dive Sites," below, and "Scuba Diving," in chapter 6.

- **Biking:** You can't rent a car on Bermuda, so you might as well hit the road on two wheels. Most of the island isn't great cycling terrain, because the roads are narrow and the traffic heavy. We suggest that you head for the Railway Trail, the island's premier bike path. The paved trail, which follows the former route of Bermuda's railway line, runs almost the entire length of the island. See "Other Outdoor Pursuits: Biking, Horseback Riding & Tennis," in chapter 6.

- **Horseback Riding:** Guiding a horse through the dune grass and oleander, especially at South Shore

Park, is an experience you won't want to miss. Because this sport is restricted to supervised trails on Bermuda, it can be all the more memorable—you'll have the gorgeous seascapes all to yourself. Horseback-riding centers guide you on trail rides through the best of the countryside, and to beautiful hidden spots along the north coast. See "Other Outdoor Pursuits: Biking, Horseback Riding & Tennis," in chapter 6.

3 The Best Dive Sites

The following are some of the most exciting shipwreck and coral-reef dives. See chapter 6, "Fun in the Surf & Sun," for more information about dive outfitters.

- **The** *Constellation:* This 60m (200-ft.), four-masted schooner, which wrecked en route to Venezuela with a cargo of glassware, drugs, and whiskey in 1943, lies in 9m (30 ft.) of water off the northwest side of the island, about 13km (8 miles) west of the Royal Naval Dockyard. The true story of this ship inspired Peter Benchley to write *The Deep.* See "The Diving Sites," in chapter 6.

- **The** *Cristóbal Colón:* The largest known shipwreck in Bermuda's waters is this 144m (480-ft.) Spanish luxury liner; it ran aground in 1936 on a northern reef between North Rock and North Breaker. It lies in 9m to 17m (30 ft.–55 ft.) of water. See "The Diving Sites," in chapter 6.

- **The** *Hermes:* This 50m (165-ft.) steamer ship rests in some 24m (80 ft.) of water about 1.6km (1 mile) off Warwick Long Bay on the south shore. It foundered in 1985. The *Hermes,* the *Rita Zovetta,* and the *Tauton* (see below) are Bermuda favorites because of the incredible multicolored variety of fish that populate the waters around the ships. You'll have a chance to see grouper, brittle starfish, spiny lobster, crabs, banded coral shrimp, queen angels, tube sponge, and more. See "The Diving Sites," in chapter 6.

- *L'Herminie:* A first-class, 60-gun French frigate, *L'Herminie* was 17 days out of its Cuban port, en route to France, when it sank in 1838. The ship lies in 6m to 9m (20 ft.–30 ft.) of water off the west side of the island, with 25 cannons still visible. See "The Diving Sites," in chapter 6.

- **The** *Marie Celeste:* This paddle wheeler sank in 1864. Its 4.5m- (15-ft.-) diameter paddle wheel, off the southern portion of the island, is overgrown with coral standing about 17m (55 ft.) off the ocean floor. See "The Diving Sites," in chapter 6.

- **The** *North Carolina:* One of Bermuda's most colorful and well-preserved wrecks, this English sailing barkentine foundered in 1879 and now lies in about 12m (40 ft.) of water off the western portion of the island. The bow, stern, masts, and rigging are all preserved, and all sorts of vibrant marine life call the wreck home. See "The Diving Sites," in chapter 6.

- **The** *Rita Zovetta:* A 180m (360-ft.) Italian cargo ship, lying in 6m to 21m (20 ft.–70 ft.) of water off the south side of the island, the *Rita Zovetta* ran aground off St. David's Island in 1924. It's a favorite with underwater photographers because of the kaleidoscope of fish that inhabit the area. See "The Diving Sites," in chapter 6.

- **South West Breaker:** This coral-reef dive off the south shore, about 2.5km (1½ miles) off Church Bay, has hard and soft coral decorating sheet walls at depths of 6m to 9m (20 ft.–30 ft.). See "The Diving Sites," in chapter 6.

- **Tarpon Hole:** Near Elbow Beach, off the south shore, this dive's proximity to the Elbow Beach Hotel makes it extremely popular. The honeycombed reef—one of the most beautiful off the coast of Bermuda—is known for its varieties of coral: yellow pencil, elkhorn, fire, and star. See "The Diving Sites," in chapter 6.

- **The *Tauton:*** This popular dive site is a British Royal Mail steamer that sank in 1914. It lies in 4m to 12m (10 ft.–40 ft.) of water off the north end of the island and is home to numerous varieties of colorful marine life. See "The Diving Sites," in chapter 6.

4 The Best Golf Courses

All four of these courses are 18 holes.

- **Belmont Golf & Country Club** (Warwick Parish): Scotsman Emmett Devereux designed this par-70, 5,282m (17,331-ft.) course in 1923. It has been challenging golfers ever since, especially on its par-5 11th hole, a severe dogleg left with a blind tee shot. Trade winds play havoc with the listed lengths. Critics complain that the layout is "maddening," yet they continue to return for new challenges. The grass is dense thanks to a modern irrigation system. See p. 155.

- **Fairmont Southampton Golf Club** (Hamilton Parish): This is a par-54, 2,454m (8,052-ft.) course, with elevated tees, strategically placed bunkers, and an array of water hazards to challenge even the most experienced golfer. One golfer said of this course, "You not only need to be a great player, but have a certain mountaineering agility as well." See p. 156.

- **Port Royal Golf Course** (Southampton Parish): This public course ranks among the best on the island, public or private; in fact, it's one of the greatest public courses in the world. Jack Nicklaus apparently agrees—he's fond of playing here. Robert Trent Jones designed the par-71, 6,003m (19,695-ft.) course along the ocean. The 16th hole is the most famous in Bermuda; photos of it have appeared in countless golf magazines. The hole is situated on a dramatic oceanside cliff with stunning views—one wrong hit from the club and your ball will go flying into the ocean below. Greens fees are relatively reasonable. See p. 156.

- **St. George's Golf Club** (St. George Parish): One of the island's newest courses—and one of its best—this par-62, 3,697m (12,129-ft.) course was designed by Robert Trent Jones. Within walking distance of historic St. George, it lies on a windy headland at the northeastern tip of Bermuda. Although you'll enjoy panoramic vistas, your game is likely to be affected by Atlantic winds. The greens are the smallest on the island, at no larger than 7.2m (24 ft.) across. See p. 157.

5 The Best Tennis Facilities

- **The Fairmont Southampton** (Southampton Parish): This is Bermuda's premier destination for avid players. Its tennis court complex is not only the largest on the island, but also is maintained in state-of-the-art condition. The deluxe hotel, one of the finest on Bermuda, offers 11 Plexipave courts. The courts are somewhat protected from the north winds, but swirling breezes may affect your final score. See p. 158.

- **Government Tennis Stadium** (Pembroke Parish): Although Bermuda has been known as the

The Baffling Bermuda Triangle

The area known as the Bermuda Triangle encompasses a 2,414,016 sq. km (1.5-million-sq.-mile) expanse of open sea between Bermuda, Puerto Rico, and the southeastern shoreline of the U.S. This bit of the Atlantic is the source of the most famous, and certainly the most baffling, legend associated with Bermuda.

Tales of the mysterious Bermuda Triangle persist, despite attempts by skeptics to dismiss them as fanciful. Below are three of the most popular. Can they be true? See what you think:

- In 1881, a British-registered ship, the *Ellen Austin,* encountered an unnamed vessel in good condition sailing aimlessly without a crew. The captain ordered a handful of his best seamen to board the mysterious vessel and sail it to Newfoundland. A few days later, the ships encountered each other again on the high seas. But to everyone's alarm, the crewmen who had transferred from the *Ellen Austin* were nowhere to be found—the ship was completely unmanned!

- Another tale concerns the disappearance of a merchant ship, the *Marine Sulphur Queen,* in February 1963. It vanished suddenly and without warning, and no one could say why. The weather was calm when the ship set sail from Bermuda, and everything onboard was fine—the crew never sent a distress signal. In looking for explanations, some have theorized that the ship's weakened hull gave way, causing the vessel to descend quickly to the ocean floor. Others attribute the loss to more mysterious forces.

- The most famous of all the legends concerns an incident in 1945. On December 5, five U.S. Navy bombers departed from Fort Lauderdale,

tennis capital of the Atlantic since 1873, players often complain that the trade winds around the island affect their game, especially near the water. That's why many prefer inland courts, such as those at this government-owned stadium. It offers three clay and five Plexicushion courts (three illuminated for night play). The facility, which is north of the City of Hamilton, requires players to wear proper tennis attire. On-site you'll find a pro shop, a ball machine, and a pro offering private lessons. See p. 159.

6 The Best Day Hikes

- **The Bermuda Railway Trail** (Sandys Parish): Stretching for about 34km (21 miles), this unique trail was created along the course of the old Bermuda Railway. It served the island from 1931 to 1948 (cars weren't allowed on the island until the late 1940s). Armed with a copy of the *Bermuda Railway Trail Guide,* available at visitor centers, you can follow the route of the train known as "Rattle and Shake." Most of the trail still winds along a car-free route, and you can travel as much (or as little) of it as

Florida, on a routine mission. The weather was fine; no storm of any kind threatened. A short time into the flight, the leader of the squadron radioed that they were lost, and then the radio went silent. All efforts to establish further communication proved fruitless. A rescue plane was dispatched to search for the squadron—but it, too, disappeared. The navy ordered a search that lasted 5 days, but there was no evidence of any wreckage. To this day, the disappearance of the squadron and the rescue plane remains a mystery as deep as the waters of the region.

How do those who believe in the Bermuda Triangle legend account for these phenomena? Some contend that the area is a time warp to another universe; others think the waters off Bermuda are the site of the lost kingdom of Atlantis, whose power sources still function deep beneath the surface. Still others believe that laser rays from outer space are perpetually focused on the region, or that underwater signaling devices are guiding invaders from other planets, and that these aliens have chosen the site for the systematic collection of human beings for scientific observation and experimentation. (Smacks of *The X-Files*, doesn't it?) Some, drawing upon the Book of Revelation, are fully persuaded that the Bermuda Triangle is really one of the gates to Hell (in this version, the other gate lies midway between Japan and the Philippines, in the Devil's Sea).

No matter what your views on these mysteries, you're bound to provoke an excited response by asking residents what they think about it. On Bermuda, almost everyone has an opinion about the island's biggest and most fascinating legend.

your stamina allows. See p. 158 and 195.

• **From the Royal Naval Dockyard to Somerset** (Sandys Parish): A 6.4km (4-mile) walk leads from the dockyard, the former headquarters of the British navy on Bermuda, to Somerset Island. Along the way you'll cross a beautiful nature reserve, explore an old cemetery, view the Royal Naval Hospital, where thousands of yellow fever victims died in the 19th century, and be rewarded with a sweeping panoramic view of Great Sound. Sandy beaches along the route are perfect for pausing from your hike to stretch out on the sand or take a dip in the ocean. See "Walking Tour 3: Sandys Parish," in chapter 8.

• **Spittal Pond Nature Reserve** (Smith's Parish): This 24-hectare (60-acre) sanctuary is the island's largest nature reserve, home to both resident and migratory waterfowl. You can spot some 25 species of waterfowl from November to May. Scenic trails and footpaths cut through the property. Explore on your own or take a guided hike offered by the Department of Agriculture. See p. 179.

7 The Best Sailing Outfitters

Bermuda is one of the Atlantic's major sailing capitals. Many sail-yourself boats are available for rent to qualified sailors, and kayaks, paddleboats, boards, and more are available for everyone. If you'd like to sail on a larger craft, the outfitters will provide you with a captain. Here are some of the best outfitters:

- **Blue Hole Water Sports** (Grotto Bay Beach Hotel, Hamilton Parish; ✆ 441/293-2915): Here you'll find a large selection of watercraft, including Sunfish, Boardsailers, kayaks, Paddle Cats, and Sun Cats. Rentals are available for up to 8 hours. See p. 153.
- **Pompano Beach Club Watersports Centre** (Southampton Parish; ✆ 441/234-0222): This is the best outfitter in this tourist-laden parish. Open from May to late October, it offers a variety of equipment, including the O'Brien Windsurfer, a popular windsurfer suitable for one person on the intermediate or advanced level. Its fleet also includes vessels that hold one or two people: Dolphin paddleboats, Buddy Boards, Aqua-Eye viewing boards, Aqua Finn sailboats, and kayaks. These can be rented for up to 4 hours. See p. 153.
- **Somerset Bridge Watersports** (Somerset Parish; ✆ 441/234-0914): This is the best place to rent a Boston whaler sailboat, which can hold three or four passengers. It's an ideal craft for exploring the archipelago's uninhabited islands. This outfitter rents 4m (13-ft.) whalers and a 30-hp, 5m (15-ft.) Open Bowrider, a speedcraft often used to pull water-skiers, which accommodates four. See p. 153.

8 The Best Views

Bermuda is incredibly scenic, with lovely panoramas and vistas unfolding at nearly every turn. But not all views are created equal. Below are some of our personal favorites. See chapter 7, "Seeing the Sights," for additional suggestions.

- **Scaur Hill Fort Park:** From Somerset Bridge in Sandys Parish, head for this fort atop the parish's highest hill. Walk the fort's ramparts, enjoying the vistas across Great Sound to Spanish Point. You can also gaze north to the dockyard and take in the fine views of Somerset Island. On a clear day, a look through the telescope reveals St. David's Lighthouse, 23km (14 miles) away on the northeastern tip of the island. After enjoying the fantastic views from the fort, you can stroll through the fort's 9 hectares (22 acres) of beautiful gardens. See p. 169.
- **Gibbs Hill Lighthouse:** For an even better view than the one enjoyed by Queen Elizabeth II (see below), climb the 185 spiral steps of the lighthouse. Built in 1846, it's the oldest cast-iron lighthouse in the world. From the top, you can relish what islanders consider the single finest view in all of Bermuda—a panorama of the island and its shorelines. You can, that is, if the wind doesn't blow you away—be sure to hang on to the railing. In heavy winds, the tower actually sways. See p. 173.
- **Warwick Long Bay:** This stretch of pristine pink sand is a dream beach of the picture-postcard variety. It backs up to towering cliffs and hills studded with Spanish

bayonet and oleander. A 6m- (20-ft.-) high coral outcrop, rising some 60m (200 ft.) offshore and resembling a sculpted boulder, adds variety to the stunning beachscape. See p. 182.

9 The Best Historic Sights

See "The Best Places to Experience Old Bermuda," below, for a description of the Royal Naval Dockyard.

- **Fort St. Catherine** (St. George Parish): This fort—with its tunnels, cannons, and ramparts—towers over the beach where the shipwrecked crew of the *Sea Venture* first came ashore in 1609 (becoming Bermuda's first settlers). The fort was completed in 1614, and extensive rebuilding and remodeling continued until the 19th century. The audiovisual presentation on St. George's defense system helps you better understand what you're seeing. See p. 187.

- **Scaur Hill Fort Park** (Sandys Parish): Fort Scaur and Fort St. Catherine were part of a ring of fortifications that surrounded Bermuda. Built by the British navy, the fort was supposed to protect the Royal Naval Dockyard from an attack that never materialized. During World War II, U.S. Marines were billeted nearby. Overlooking Great Sound, the fort offers views of some of the island's most dramatic scenery. See p. 168.

- **St. Peter's Church** (St. George Parish): This is the oldest Anglican house of worship in the Western Hemisphere. At one time virtually everyone who died on Bermuda was buried here, from governors to criminals. To the west of the church lies the graveyard of slaves. This is the site of the original church, which colonists built in 1612. A hurricane destroyed the church in 1712, but some parts of the interior survived. It was rebuilt on the same site in 1713. See p. 185.

- **Verdmont** (Smith's Parish): This 1770s mansion is on property once owned by William Sayle, founder and first governor of South Carolina. Filled with portraits, antiques, and china, the house offers a rare glimpse into a long-faded life of old-fashioned style and grace. Resembling a small English manor house, it's the finest historic home in Bermuda. See p. 179.

10 The Best Places to Experience Old Bermuda

Although much of Bermuda is modern, the first settlers arrived in 1609. The following places provide insights into the old, largely vanished Bermudian way of life. See chapter 7, "Seeing the Sights," for more details.

- **The Back Streets of St. George** (St. George Parish): Almost every visitor to the island has photographed the 17th-century stocks on King's Square in historic St. George. But it's in the narrow back alleys and cobblestone lanes, such as Shinbone Alley, that you'll really discover the town's old spirit. Arm yourself with a good map and wander at leisure through such places as Silk Alley (also called Petticoat Lane), Barber's Lane Alley (named for a former slave from South Carolina), Printer's Alley (where Bermuda's first newspaper was published), and Nea's Alley (former stamping ground of the Irish poet Tom Moore). Finally, walk through Somers Garden and head up the steps to Blockade Alley. On the hill is the aptly named Unfinished Cathedral. See "Walking Tour 2: Historic St. George Town," in chapter 8.

- **The Royal Naval Dockyard** (Sandys Parish): Nothing recaptures the maritime spirit of this little island colony more than this sprawling complex of attractions (with a multimillion-dollar cruise-ship dock) on Ireland Island. Britain began building this dockyard in 1809, perhaps fearing attacks on its fleet by Napoleon or greedy pirates. Convicts and slaves provided much of the construction labor, and the Royal Navy occupied the shipyard for almost 150 years. It closed in 1951, and the navy has little presence here today. The Maritime Museum—the most important museum on the island—and other exhibits on Bermuda's nautical heritage give you a good feel for a largely vanished era. See p. 172.

- **St. David's Island** (St. George Parish): Though most of Bermuda looks pristine and proper, you'll still find some vestiges of rustic maritime life on St. David's. Some St. David's islanders never even bother to visit neighboring St. George, and to some locals, a trip to the West End of Bermuda would be like a trip to the moon. St. David's Lighthouse has been a local landmark since 1879. To see how people used to cook and eat, drop by Dennis's Hideaway (see below, under "Bermuda's Best-Kept Secrets").

11 Bermuda's Best-Kept Secrets

- **Dining at Dennis's Hideaway** (St. George Parish; ✆ 441/297-0044): At his small home on remote St. David's Island, Dennis Lamb is an unforgettable host. He personifies the eccentricity of his fellow islanders. Not only will Dennis feed you shark hash, mussel pie, and other hard-to-find seafood dishes, but he'll also give you some insight into how life was lived on Bermuda long ago. When he's not tending his pots, cleaning fish, or throwing food to one of his yapping dogs, he might also share his philosophy of life with you. No ties allowed. Call ahead for a reservation. See p. 138.

- **Escaping to a Remote Natural Setting** (Smith's Parish; ✆ 441/234-1831). Bermuda still has some oases that aren't overrun with visitors. Such a place is the **Heydon Trust,** along Somerset Road, a sanctuary for migratory birds. It's a true walk through nature, with flowering bushes and citrus orchards. See p. 180.

- **Spelunking in Crystal Caves** (Hamilton Parish; ✆ 441/293-0640): A spelunker's paradise, Bermuda has the highest concentration of limestone caves in the world. They form one of the island's major natural wonderlands. Their surreal formations took millions of years to come into being, and the great stalactites and stalagmites have a Gothic grandeur. The best caves are Crystal Caves at Bailey's Bay. Discovered in 1907, these caves house crystal-clear Cahow Lake. See p. 172.

12 The Best Resorts for Honeymooners & Other Lovers

Bermuda has long been one of the newlyweds' favorite destinations. Its hotels, from deluxe resorts to guesthouses, attract lovers of all kinds looking for a little peace, solitude, and seclusion.

Although some couples seek out small housekeeping cottages and guesthouses, most prefer a package offered by one of the splashy resort hotels. The following resorts not only feature romance, but also some of the best deals around.

Note: It's a good idea to consult a travel agent for help in getting the best bargain. Before you call any of these hotels directly, see our "Package Tours" section in chapter 2, "Planning Your Trip to Bermuda." For full hotel reviews, see chapter 4, "Where to Stay."

- **Elbow Beach Hotel** (Paget Parish; ✆ **800/223-7434** in the U.S., or 441/236-3535): This hotel promises "marriages made in heaven." Its Romance Packages include daily breakfasts, plus a candlelit dinner for two in your room on the first night. Upon departure, newlyweds receive a copy of the *Elbow Beach Cookbook.* See p. 78.
- **The Fairmont Southampton** (Southampton Parish; ✆ **800/441-1414** in the U.S., 800/268-7176 in Canada, or 441/238-8000): The island's most luxurious hotel does everything it can to attract honeymooners seeking lots of activities, from watersports to nighttime diversions (other than those in the honeymoon suite). Its honeymoon packages, which start at 4 days and 3 nights, include breakfast and dinner on a MAP (Modified American Plan) "dine-around plan" (dinner and breakfast are included in the hotel rate, but you can dine in any of the two Princess resorts' restaurants), a bottle of champagne, a basket of fruit, admission to the exercise club, and even a special-occasion cake, plus a souvenir photo and a watercolor print by a local artist. See p. 72.

- **Grotto Bay Beach Hotel** (Hamilton Parish; ✆ **800/582-3190** in the U.S., 800/463-0851 in Canada, or 441/293-0188): This resort, which actively caters to honeymooners, features everything from midnight swims at a private beach to cozy lovers' nests with private balconies overlooking the ocean. The honeymoon packages include romantic dinners and arrangements for cruises and walking tours, as well as optional champagne, fruit, and flowers. See p. 82.
- **Harmony Club** (Paget Parish; ✆ **888/427-6664**): If you shun the big splashy resorts that attract a lot of families with children, head to this small, couples-only all-inclusive resort. Guests are housed in romantic Queen Anne–style buildings in a setting of formal gardens and gazebos. Dinners are served by candlelight on fine china and crystal. Honeymoon packages are available. See p. 84.
- **Sonesta Beach Resort** (Southampton Parish; ✆ **800/766-3782** in the U.S., or 441/238-8122): You'll find champagne chilling in your room when you arrive—and it just gets better from there. To set the mood, the staff will arrange an introductory horse-and-buggy ride in the old Bermuda tradition. The following day, they'll lend you a motor scooter for getting around. The sports director offers one free tennis or scuba lesson. The hotel is right on the beach, and also boasts a fully equipped, professionally staffed health spa. Honeymooners can dance to live music at the Boat Bay Club and Lounge, with its views of moonlit Boat Bay. See p. 73.

13 The Best Places to Stay with the Kids

Bermuda is more kid-friendly than any other place we know in the Caribbean or The Bahamas. It's a safe, clean environment in a politically stable country. Nearly all Bermuda hotels go the extra mile to welcome families with children, but these are our top choices. Turn to chapter 4, "Where to Stay," for full reviews.

- **The Fairmont Southampton** (Southampton Parish; ℂ **800/ 441-1414** in the U.S., 800/ 268-7176 in Canada, or 441/238-8000): From June through Labor Day, this hotel features the best children's program in Bermuda. Children under 17 stay free; and if the parents choose the MAP (breakfast and dinner included in the rates), kids also get free meals. With its many sports facilities, including two freshwater pools and 11 tennis courts, this Princess is definitely for families who enjoy the sporting life. The former Touch Club has been redesigned as Lenny's Loft, a social center for children's activities. From Lenny's Loft, kids are taken on excursions around the island. See p. 72.
- **Grotto Bay Beach Hotel** (Hamilton Parish; ℂ **800/582-3190** in the U.S., 800/463-0851 in Canada, or 441/293-0188): With its excellent summer children's program, this hotel attracts many families. It sits on 8.5 tropically landscaped hectares (21 acres), so guests usually don't mind its relative isolation across from the airport. The swimming pool has been blasted out of natural rock,

and there are subterranean caves to explore. Beachside barbecues and other activities make this a lively place. See p. 82.

- **Elbow Beach Hotel** (Hamilton Parish; ℂ **800/223-7434** or 441/ 236-3535): This longtime family favorite, on one of the best beaches in Bermuda, allows children under 13 to stay free when sharing a room with their parents. It also offers a year-round "Family Value Package" which grants very low rates for four people (usually two children and two parents) with buffet breakfast, 4 hours of babysitting, 1 hour paddleboat rental, 2 hours of tennis, and free passes to the zoo and aquarium all thrown in to the deal. Call the hotel or ask a travel agent for details. See p. 78.
- **Sonesta Beach Resort** (Southampton Parish; ℂ **800/766-3782** in the U.S., or 441/238-8122): This luxurious resort offers one of the best family packages on the island. A maximum of four people, including two children, can take advantage of the 4-day, 3-night packages; children eat free, and a second guest room is provided at 25% off the regular rate. A "Just Us Kids" activities program for ages 5 to 12 is held daily during the summer, with pizza parties, unlimited free ice cream, and children's games, among other diversions. The "Just Us Little Kids" program entertains the 2- to 4-year-olds with a wading pool, playroom, ice-cream parties, and other activities. See p. 73.

14 The Best Hotel Bargains

- **Granaway** (Warwick Parish; ℂ **441/236-3747**): This former private home from 1734 is a virtual picture postcard cliché of

Bermudian charm, with its pink walls and whitewashed roof. Opening onto views of Great Sound, it has been handsomely converted to receive guests—even the former slave quarters are now comfortable. See p. 101.

- **Astwood Cove** (Warwick Parish; ✆ **800/637-4116** in the U.S., or 441/236-0984): This place is definitely a good buy in pricey Bermuda. For families seeking a self-contained studio or suite apartment with a fully equipped kitchenette and a private porch or patio, this is a great choice. You prepare your own meals and use the hotel's English bone china and wine glasses. Studio apartments have sofa beds that can accommodate a third person. See p. 95.

- **Salt Kettle House** (Paget Parish; ✆ **441/236-0407**). The name is not the only thing charming

about this informal and secluded 2-centuries-old cottage. It's a real discovery, and bargain hunters eagerly seek it out, preferring it to the glitz of the megaresort hotels. You can swim in the nearby cove, retiring to your waterside cottage at night. See p. 101.

- **Rosemont** (City of Hamilton, Pembroke Parish; ✆ **800/367-0040** in the U.S., 800/267-0040 in Canada, or 441/292-1055): A collection of housekeeping cottages near the Hamilton Princess, Rosemont has long been a family favorite, offering a central location at a good price. The site offers panoramic views of Hamilton Harbour and the Great Sound. Guests often prepare their own meals. See p. 97.

15 The Best Restaurants

Admittedly, you don't come to Bermuda for grand cuisine. That said, there are quite a few places to enjoy a memorable meal.

- **Aqua** (Devonshire Parish; ✆ **441/236-1010**): In the Ariel Sands Hotel, this is a new restaurant, owned in part by actor Michael Douglas. It's quickly become one of the island's best, with its savory blend of Bermudian and international recipes. Expect everything from Cajun cookery to Indian-style tandoori dishes. See p. 135.

- **The Norwood Room** (Hamilton Parish; ✆ **441/236-5416**): The students may be the chefs at this restaurant located in a hotel training school, but the cuisine served here is among the finest in Bermuda; each dish is prepared with care. Of course, a master chef of the Caribbean oversees the action, and the service from the in-training staff is the island's finest. See p. 120.

- **Black Horse Tavern** (St. George Parish; ✆ **441/297-1991**): When you crave good, hearty food served in a casual atmosphere, this is the place to come. Islanders fill most of the tables at night, ordering shark hash or curried conch. See p. 137.

- **La Coquille** (Pembroke Parish; ✆ **441/292-6122**): This is one of the island's most sophisticated French restaurants and it enjoys a faithful following. Right in the heart of Bermuda, the international staff serves delectable French-inspired Mediterranean cuisine. See p. 122.

- **Lobster Pot & Boat House Bar** (City of Hamilton, Pembroke Parish; ✆ **441/292-6898**): If you don't find the local foodies at the restaurants we discuss above, they'll surely be at this local favorite, enjoying some of the island's best regional dishes. Black rum and sherry peppers are the secret ingredients in the fish chowder, and baked fish and lobster are sure to tempt you. See p. 127.

- **Newport Room** (at The Fairmont Southampton, Southampton Parish; ℂ **441/238-8000**): Part of the resort complex, this nautically decorated restaurant attracts an upscale crowd, especially yachters. The glistening teak decor makes it the most expensively furnished restaurant in Bermuda, and the French cuisine is worthy of the decor. The rack of lamb with mixed-nut crust is the stuff of which memories are made. See p. 114.

- **Tamarisk Dining Room** (at Cambridge Beaches, Sandys Parish; ℂ **441/234-0331**): This is an elegant enclave at the western tip of Bermuda. Housed in one of the island's premier accommodations, it offers excellent service and a frequently changing menu of impeccably prepared international cuisine. For your main course, you can't do better than juicy tenderloin of beef with grain mustard and blanched garlic sauce. The wine cellar is up to the high standards of the menu. See p. 109.

- **Tom Moore's Tavern** (Hamilton Parish; ℂ **441/293-8020**): The Irish poet Tom Moore reportedly was a frequent visitor to this restaurant, which dates from 1652 and overlooks Walsingham Bay. The menu, however, is no relic—it's quite innovative. Duck is a specialty, as is Bermuda lobster; but who can forget the quail in puff pastry stuffed with foie gras? See p. 136.

- **Waterlot Inn** (at The Fairmont Southampton Princess, Southampton Parish; ℂ **441/238-8000**): In a historic inn and warehouse, this restaurant serves the island's most famous Sunday brunch, but it's also an ideal choice for dinner. Everybody from Eleanor Roosevelt to Mark Twain has praised the Mediterranean cuisine. See p. 114.

Planning Your Trip
to Bermuda

In this chapter, you'll find everything you need to plan your trip, from when to go to how to land the best package deals. Getting to Bermuda is easier than ever, thanks to more frequent flights from such gateway cities as New York, Boston, and Washington. We've also included information on several cruise lines that sail to the island from spring until late autumn.

1 Visitor Information

Some of your best sources of information may be relatives, friends, or colleagues who have been to Bermuda, so ask around. For information sources once you're in Bermuda, see "Orienting Yourself: The Lay of the Land," in chapter 3, "Getting to Know Bermuda."

THE BERMUDA DEPARTMENT OF TOURISM

IN THE UNITED STATES To receive a visitor information packet about Bermuda before you go, call © **800/237-6832** (800/BERMUDA); www.bermudatourism.com.

To speak to a travel representative, contact the **Bermuda Department of Tourism** office at 205 E. 42nd St., New York, NY 10017 (© **212/818-9800**); or 245 Peachtree Center Ave. NE, Suite 803, Atlanta, GA 30303 (© **404/524-1541**).

IN CANADA Contact the **Bermuda Department of Tourism** at 1200 Bay St., Suite 1004, Toronto, ON, Canada M5R 2A5 (© **416/923-9600**).

IN THE UNITED KINGDOM Contact the **Bermuda Department of Tourism** at 1 Battersea Church Rd., London SW11 3LY (© **020/8410-8188**).

TRAVEL AGENTS

Travel agents can save you plenty of time and money by hunting down the best package deal or airfare. For the time being, most travel agents charge you nothing for their services—they're paid through commissions from the airlines and other agencies. However, most airlines have cut commissions, and increasingly, agents are finding they have to charge customers fees. Some unscrupulous agents may only offer you the travel options that bag them the juiciest commissions. Shop around and ask hard questions. The best way to use a travel agent is to make preliminary decisions using this guide, and go into your meeting as a smart and informed consumer.

If you decide to use a travel agent, make sure the agent is a member of the **American Society of Travel Agents (ASTA),** 1101 King St., Alexandria, VA 22314 (© **703/739-2782;** www.astanet.com). To receive a copy of the free booklet *Avoiding Travel Problems,* send ASTA a self-addressed, stamped envelope.

Tips Your Own Personal "Weblet"

The Bermudian government remains committed to attracting more and more visitors. Its latest offering is to arrange a personalized Bermuda mini-guidebook for potential visitors. Within minutes of hanging up the phone, Internet-connected **800/BERMUDA** callers receive a personalized "weblet" that gives specific, detailed information on hotels and activities based on information supplied by the caller. Your weblet's search engines allow you to supply personal criteria and receive a selection of hotels and restaurants designed to appeal to your taste and pocketbook. Special-interest buttons can be pressed for data on golf, honeymoon packages, nightlife, and sports facilities.

---

2 Entry Requirements & Customs

ENTRY REQUIREMENTS

U.S. and **Canadian** citizens do not officially need a passport to enter Bermuda, but we strongly recommend that you carry one whenever you travel to a foreign country.

Bermuda Immigration authorities require U.S. citizens to have at least one of the following items in their possession: a birth certificate (or a certified copy of it accompanied by a photo ID), a U.S. naturalization certificate, a valid passport, a U.S. Alien Registration card, or a U.S. reentry permit. Go with the passport.

Canadian citizens must have either a birth certificate (or a certified copy), a Canadian certificate of citizenship, or a valid passport plus proof of Landed Immigrant status.

Bermuda Immigration authorities require visitors from the **United Kingdom** and **Europe** to show a valid passport. All visitors must have a return or onward ticket in addition to their valid passport or original birth certificate.

Any traveler staying in Bermuda longer than 3 weeks must apply to the **Chief Immigration Officer** in person, at the Government Administration Building, 30 Parliament St., Hamilton HM 12, Bermuda (© 441/295-5151), for an extended stay. You will be asked to fill out an Immigration Application for an extended stay, which then will or will not be approved by authorities.

OBTAINING A PASSPORT

The websites listed here provide downloadable passport applications as well as the current fees for processing passport applications. For an up-to-date country-by-country listing of passport requirements around the world, go the "Foreign Entry Requirement" Web page of the U.S. State Department at **http://travel.state. gov/foreignentryreqs.html**.

For Residents of the United States: Whether you're applying in person or by mail, you can download passport applications from the U.S. State Department website at **http://travel. state.gov**. For general information, call the **National Passport Agency** (© 202/647-0518). To find your regional passport office, either check the U.S. State Department website or call the **National Passport Information Center** (© 900/225-5674); the fee is 55¢ per minute for automated information and $1.50 per minute for operator-assisted calls.

For Residents of Canada: Passport applications are available at travel agencies throughout Canada or from the central **Passport Office,** Department of Foreign Affairs and International

Trade, Ottawa, ON K1A 0G3 (© **800/567-6868;** www.dfait-maeci. gc.ca/passport).

For Residents of the United Kingdom: To pick up an application for a standard 10-year passport (5-yr. passport for children under 16), visit your nearest passport office, major post office, or travel agency or contact the **United Kingdom Passport Service** at © **0870/521-0410** or search its website at www.ukpa.gov.uk.

For Residents of Ireland: You can apply for a 10-year passport at the **Passport Office,** Setanta Centre, Molesworth Street, Dublin 2 (© **01/ 671-1633;** www.irlgov.ie/iveagh). Those under age 18 and over 65 must apply for a €12 3-year passport. You can also apply at 1A South Mall, Cork (© **021/272-525**) or at most main post offices.

For Residents of Australia: You can pick up an application from your local post office or any branch of Passports Australia, but you must schedule an interview at the passport office to present your application materials. Call the **Australian Passport Information Service** at © **131-232,** or visit the government website at www.passports.gov.au.

For Residents of New Zealand: You can pick up a passport application at any New Zealand Passports Office or download it from their website. Contact the **Passports Office** at © **0800/225-050** in New Zealand or

04/474-8100, or log on to www. passports.govt.nz.

CUSTOMS
WHAT YOU CAN BRING INTO BERMUDA

Visitors may bring into Bermuda duty-free apparel and articles for their personal use, including sports equipment, cameras, 200 cigarettes, 1 quart of liquor, 1 quart of wine, and approximately 20 pounds of meat. Other foodstuffs may be subject to duties. All imports may be inspected on arrival. Visitors entering Bermuda may also claim a duty-free gift allowance.

WHAT YOU CAN TAKE HOME FROM BERMUDA

Returning **U.S. citizens** who have been away for at least 48 hours are allowed to bring back, once every 30 days, $800 worth of merchandise duty-free. You'll be charged a flat rate of 4% duty on the next $1,000 worth of purchases. Be sure to have your receipts handy. On mailed gifts, the duty-free limit is $100. With some exceptions, you cannot bring fresh fruits and vegetables into the United States. For specifics on what you can bring back, download the invaluable free pamphlet *Know Before You Go* online at **www.customs.gov.** (Click on "Travel," then "Know Before You Go! Online Brochure.") Or contact the **U.S. Customs Service,** 1300 Pennsylvania Ave., NW, Washington, DC 20229 (© **877/287-8667**) and request the pamphlet.

Tips **Planning Pointer**

Before leaving home, make copies of your most valuable documents, including the inside page of your passport that has your photograph. Also copy your driver's license, airline ticket, hotel vouchers, and any other pertinent documents. You should also make copies of the prescriptions for any medications you take. Leave one copy at home, place one copy in your luggage, and carry the original with you. The information on these documents is extremely valuable if your possessions are lost or stolen.

For a clear summary of **Canadian** rules, write for the booklet *I Declare,* issued by the **Canada Customs and Revenue Agency** (© 800/461-9999 in Canada, or 204/983-3500; www.ccra-adrc.gc.ca). Canada allows its citizens a C$750 exemption, and you're allowed to bring back duty-free one carton of cigarettes, 1 can of tobacco, 40 imperial ounces of liquor, and 50 cigars. In addition, you're allowed to mail gifts to Canada valued at less than C$60 a day, provided they're unsolicited and don't contain alcohol or tobacco (write on the package "Unsolicited gift, under $60 value"). All valuables should be declared on the Y-38 form before departure from Canada, including serial numbers of valuables you already own, such as expensive foreign cameras. Note: The $750 exemption can only be used once a year and only after an absence of 7 days.

U.K. citizens returning from **a non-EU country** such as Bermuda have a customs allowance of: 200 cigarettes; 50 cigars; 100 cigarillos; 250 grams of smoking tobacco; 2 liters of still table wine; 1 liter of spirits or strong liqueurs (over 22% volume); 2 liters of fortified wine, sparkling wine or other liqueurs; 60cc (ml) perfume; 250cc (ml) of toilet water; and £145 worth of all other goods, including gifts and souvenirs. People under 17 cannot have the tobacco or alcohol allowance. For more information, contact HM Customs & Excise at © 0845/010-9000 (from outside the U.K.,

020/8929-0152), or consult their website at www.hmce.gov.uk.

The duty-free allowance in **Australia** is A$400 or, for those under 18, A$200. Citizens can bring in 250 cigarettes or 250 grams of loose tobacco, and 1,125 milliliters of alcohol. If you're returning with valuables you already own, such as foreign-made cameras, you should file form B263. A helpful brochure available from Australian consulates or Customs offices is *Know Before You Go.* For more information, call the **Australian Customs Service** at © **1300/363-263,** or log on to www.customs.gov.au.

The duty-free allowance for **New Zealand** is NZ$700. Citizens over 17 can bring in 200 cigarettes, 50 cigars, or 250 grams of tobacco (or a mixture of all three if their combined weight doesn't exceed 250g); plus 4.5 liters of wine and beer, or 1.125 milliliters of liquor. New Zealand currency does not carry import or export restrictions. Fill out a certificate of export, listing the valuables you are taking out of the country; that way, you can bring them back without paying duty. Most questions are answered in a free pamphlet available at New Zealand consulates and Customs offices: *New Zealand Customs Guide for Travellers, Notice no. 4.* For more information, contact **New Zealand Customs,** The Customhouse, 17–21 Whitmore St., Box 2218, Wellington (© **04/473-6099** or 0800/428-786; www.customs.govt.nz).

3 Money

Time is money, and because Bermuda is less than 2 hours from most cities on the U.S. East Coast, the savings begin even before you land on the island. A 4-day, 3-night vacation in Bermuda can actually include 4 days of vacation for the price of 3 nights' accommodations. An 8:30am flight from New York gets you to Bermuda in time for lunch, with the whole afternoon to play.

The variety of accommodations—there are luxury resort hotels, small hotels, intimate guesthouses, and cottage colonies—allows visitors to indulge their preferences and tastes regardless of budget.

Hotel costs also depend on what time of year you travel. If you're seeking major discounts—sometimes as much as 60% off high-season rates—try visiting during the off season. (For more information, see "When to Go," below.) Off-season rates, which we've listed in this guide, are a bonanza for cost-conscious travelers—though you're not guaranteed that it'll be warm enough to truly enjoy the beach.

Travel agents sometimes offer special packages, which can represent a substantial savings over regular hotel rates for families, golfers, tennis players, honeymooners, and others; for more information, see "Booking a Travel Package," later in this chapter.

Dining out is an expensive undertaking. In the top places, you can end up spending as much as $80 per person for a meal, excluding wine. Even moderate to expensive restaurants charge $25 to $50 per person. Any dinner under $25 per person is considered inexpensive. You might want to investigate the package plans that most of the large resorts offer, which include meals. For details on meal plans, see "Rates & Reservation Policies" in chapter 4, "Where to Stay." Other ways to reduce dining costs are to pack picnic lunches, or to have your main meal in the middle of the day, at a pub. To cut costs even more, families and others planning to stay for a week or more might opt for a housekeeping unit (efficiencies and apartments are available), a cottage with a kitchenette, or even a condominium (some are rented like timeshare units).

In figuring your budget, be sure to consider transportation costs. Getting around the island isn't always easy, and because rental cars are not available, you'll have to rely on local transportation. With the exception of taxis, which are very expensive, public transportation is efficient and inexpensive. Options include the simple and comprehensive bus system, ferries, and bicycle or motorbike rentals; see "Getting Around," in chapter 3, "Getting to Know Bermuda," for complete details. Once you reach a particular parish, many attractions are accessible on foot.

In general, athletic and cultural activities—such as tennis, riding, guided tours, museums, and attractions—are good values. Golfers will find that greens fees are comparable to or less than fees at other destinations.

If you find the idea of unknown or extra costs intimidating, you might

The Bermuda, U.S. & Canadian Dollars & the British Pound

The Bermuda Dollar is tied at a constant rate to the U.S. dollar, and is valued on an equal basis: BD$1 = US$1. At the time of this writing, the British pound trades at an average of US$1 = 63 pence, and the Canadian dollar trades at an average of US$1 = C$1.50. The chart below gives a rough approximation of conversion rates you're likely to find at the time of your trip. Rates fluctuate, so be sure to confirm the rate before you make any serious transactions.

US$/BD$	UK£	C$	US$/BD$	UK£	C$
.25	.16	.38	50.00	31.50	75.00
1.00	.63	1.50	60.00	37.80	90.00
5.00	3.15	7.50	70.00	44.10	105.00
10.00	6.30	15.00	80.00	50.40	120.00
20.00	12.60	30.00	90.00	56.70	135.00
30.00	18.90	45.00	100.00	63.00	150.00
40.00	25.20	60.00			

What Things Cost in Bermuda	BD$/US$
Average 15-minute taxi ride	12–15
Bus from the City of Hamilton to Ireland Island	4.50
Local telephone call	.20
Double room at Elbow Beach Hotel (expensive)	375
Double room at Rosemont (moderate)	164
Double room at Salt Kettle House (inexpensive)	110
Lunch for one at Tamarisk Dining Room Inn (expensive)	24
Lunch for one at Wickets Brasserie & Cricket Club (inexpensive)	18
Dinner for one at Ascots (expensive)	36
Dinner for one at La Trattoria (moderate)	30
Dinner for one at The Beach (inexpensive)	16
Bottle of beer in a bar	5
Coca-Cola in a cafe	2.50–4
Cup of coffee in a cafe	2–3.50
Glass of planter's punch in a restaurant	5–7
Roll of ASA 100 color film, 36 exposures	6–7
Admission to Bermuda Maritime Museum	7.50

consider a package tour, where everything will be arranged for you. That way, you'll know the cost of your vacation before leaving home. For more information, see "Packages for the Independent Traveler," later in this chapter.

CURRENCY

Legal tender is the Bermuda dollar (BD$), which is divided into 100 cents. It's pegged through gold to the U.S. dollar on an equal basis—BD$1 equals US$1.

U.S. currency is generally accepted in shops, restaurants, and hotels. Currency from the United Kingdom and other foreign countries is usually not accepted, but can be easily exchanged for Bermuda dollars at banks and hotels.

It's a good idea to exchange at least some money—just enough to cover airport incidentals and transportation to your hotel—before you leave home,

so you can avoid lines at airport ATMs (automated teller machines). You can exchange money at your local American Express or Thomas Cook office or your bank. If you're far away from a bank with currency-exchange services, American Express offers travelers checks and foreign currency, though with a $15 order fee and additional shipping costs, at www.american express.com or ☎ 800/807-6233.

ATMS

The easiest and best way to get cash away from home is from an ATM. These machines are plentiful in Bermuda. The **Cirrus** (☎ 800/424-7787; www.mastercard.com) and **PLUS** (☎ 800/843-7587; www.visa.com) networks span the globe; look at the back of your bank card to see which network you're on, then call or check online for ATM locations at your destination. Be sure you know your personal identification number

(PIN) before you leave home and be sure to find out your daily withdrawal limit before you depart. Also keep in mind that many banks impose a fee every time a card is used at a different bank's ATM, and that fee can be higher for international transactions (up to $5 or more) than for domestic ones (where they're rarely more than $1.50). On top of this, the bank from which you withdraw cash may charge its own fee. To compare banks' ATM fees within the U.S., use www. bankrate.com. For international withdrawal fees, ask your bank.

You can also get cash advances on your credit card at an ATM. Keep in mind that credit card companies try to protect themselves from theft by limiting the funds someone can withdraw outside their home country, so call your credit card company before you leave home.

TRAVELER'S CHECKS

Traveler's checks are something of an anachronism from the days before the ATM made cash accessible at any time. Traveler's checks used to be the only sound alternative to traveling with dangerously large amounts of cash. They were as reliable as currency, but, unlike cash, could be replaced if lost or stolen.

These days, traveler's checks are less necessary because most cities have 24-hour ATMs that allow you to withdraw small amounts of cash as needed. However, keep in mind that you will likely be charged an ATM withdrawal fee if the bank is not your own, so if you're withdrawing money every day, you might be better off with traveler's

checks—provided that you don't mind showing identification every time you want to cash one.

You can get traveler's checks at almost any bank. **American Express** offers denominations of $20, $50, $100, $500, and (for cardholders only) $1,000. You'll pay a service charge ranging from 1% to 4%. You can also get American Express traveler's checks over the phone by calling ✆ **800/221-7282;** Amex gold and platinum cardholders who use this number are exempt from the 1% fee. AAA members can obtain checks without a fee at most AAA offices.

Visa offers traveler's checks at Citibank locations nationwide, as well as at several other banks. The service charge ranges between 1.5% and 2%; checks come in denominations of $20, $50, $100, $500, and $1,000. Call ✆ **800/732-1322** for information. **MasterCard** also offers traveler's checks. Call ✆ **800/223-9920** for a location near you.

If you choose to carry traveler's checks, be sure to keep a record of their serial numbers separate from your checks in the event that they are stolen or lost. You'll get a refund faster if you know the numbers.

CREDIT CARDS

Credit cards are safe way to carry money, they provide a convenient record of all your expenses, and they generally offer good exchange rates. You can also withdraw cash advances from your credit cards at banks or ATMs, provided you know your PIN. If you've forgotten yours, or didn't even know you had one, call the

---

(*Tips* Small Change

When you change money, ask for some small bills or loose change. Petty cash will come in handy for tipping and public transportation. Consider keeping the change separate from your larger bills, so that it's readily accessible and you'll be less of a target for theft.

number on the back of your credit card and ask the bank to send it to you. It usually takes 5 to 7 business days, though some banks will provide the number over the phone if you tell them your mother's maiden name or some other personal information. Your credit card company will likely charge a commission (1% or 2%) on every foreign purchase you make, but don't sweat this small stuff; for most purchases, you'll still get the best deal with credit cards when you factor in things like ATM fees and higher traveler's check exchange rates.

All major U.S. credit cards, including American Express, Diners Club, MasterCard, and Visa are commonly accepted in Bermuda.

MONEYGRAMS
Sponsored by American Express, **Moneygram** (© **800/926-9400;** www.moneygram.com) is the fastest growing money-wiring service in the world. Funds can be transferred from one individual to another in less than 10 minutes, throughout the world.

An American Express phone representative will give you the names of four or five offices near you. (You don't necessarily have to go to an American Express office; in small communities, wiring locations are often pharmacies or convenience stores.) Acceptable forms of payment include cash, Visa, MasterCard, or Discover, and occasionally, a personal check. Service charges collected by American Express are $40 for the first $500 sent, with a sliding scale of commissions for larger sums. Included in the transfer is a 10-word telex-style message. The deal also includes a free 3-minute phone call to the recipient. Funds are transferred within 10 minutes, and they can then be retrieved by the beneficiary at the most convenient location when proper ID, and in some cases, a security code established by whomever provides the funds, is presented.

4 When to Go

THE WEATHER
A semitropical island, Bermuda enjoys a mild climate; the term "Bermuda high" has come to mean sunny days and clear skies. The Gulf Stream, which flows between the island and North America, keeps the climate temperate. There's no rainy season and no typical month of excess rain. Showers may be heavy at times, but the skies clear quickly.

Being farther north in the Atlantic than the Bahamas, Bermuda is much cooler in winter. Springlike temperatures prevail from mid-December to late March, with the average temperature ranging from the low 60s°F to 70°F (16°C–21°C). Unless it rains, winter is fine for golf and tennis but not for swimming; it can be cool, and you may even need a sweater or a jacket. Water temperatures in winter are somewhat like the air temperature, ranging from about 66°F (19°C) in January to 75°F (24°C) through March. Scuba divers and snorkelers will find Caribbean waters appreciably warmer in winter. From mid-November to mid-December and from late March to April, be prepared for unseasonable spurts of spring or summer weather.

In summer, the temperature rarely rises above 85°F (29°C). There's nearly always a cool breeze in the evening, but some hotels have air-conditioning. And local water temperatures can be as high as 86°F (30°C) during the summer—warmer than many inshore and offshore Caribbean waters.

As a result, Bermuda's off season is the exact opposite of that in the Caribbean. It begins in December and lasts until about March 1. In general, hotels offer low-season rates—with discounts ranging from 20% to 60%—during this time. This is the time to go if you're traveling on a tight budget. During autumn and winter, many hotels also offer discounted package deals. Some hotels close for a couple of weeks or months at this time.

A look at the official chart of temperature and rainfall will give you a general idea of what to expect during your visit.

Bermuda's Average Daytime Temperatures & Rainfall

	Jan	Feb	Mar	Apr	May	June	July	Aug	Sept	Oct	Nov	Dec
Temp. (°F)	65	64	64	65	70	75	79	80	79	75	69	65
Temp. (°C)	19	18	18	19	21	24	30	27	30	24	21	19
Rainfall (in.)	4	5	4.6	3	3.9	5.2	4	5.3	5.3	6	4.5	3.9

THE HURRICANE SEASON

This curse of the Caribbean, the Bahamas, and Bermuda lasts officially from June to November, but don't panic—more tropical storms pound the U.S. mainland than Bermuda. It's also less frequently hit than islands in the Caribbean. Satellite forecasts are generally able to give adequate warning of any really dangerous weather.

If you're concerned, you can call the nearest branch of the National Weather Service (it's listed under the U.S. Department of Commerce in the phone book). Radio and TV weather reports from the National Hurricane Center in Coral Gables, Florida, will also keep you posted.

To receive automated information about climate conditions in Bermuda, you can also contact the information service associated with the Weather Channel. It costs 95¢ per query and works like this: Dial ℂ **800/WEATHER** and listen to the recorded announcement. When you're prompted, enter the account number of a valid Visa or MasterCard. After the card is approved, punch in the name of any of 1,000 cities worldwide whose weather is monitored by the Weather Channel—in the case of Bermuda, the city is Hamilton.

⌒ **Fun Fact** **Getting Sucked In: The Official Word on the Bermuda Triangle**

In response to a flood of concern from travelers about the possibility of getting sucked into the so-called Bermuda Triangle and disappearing forever, the U.S. Board of Geographic Names has recently issued an official statement: "We do not recognize the Bermuda Triangle as an official name and do not maintain an official file on the area. The 'Bermuda or Devil's Triangle' is an imaginary area located off the southeastern Atlantic coast of the United States, which is noted for a high incidence of unexplained losses of ships, small boats, and aircraft. The apexes of the triangle are generally accepted to be Bermuda, Miami, and San Juan. In the past, extensive but futile Coast Guard searches prompted by search and rescue cases such as the disappearances of an entire squadron of TBM Avengers shortly after take-off from Fort Lauderdale, or the traceless sinking of Marine Sulphur Queen in the Florida Straits, have lent credence to the popular belief in the mystery and the supernatural qualities of the Bermuda Triangle."

HOLIDAYS

Bermuda observes the following public holidays: New Year's Day (Jan 1), Good Friday, Easter, Bermuda Day (May 24), the Queen's Birthday (first or second Mon in June), Cup Match Days (cricket; Thurs and Fri preceding first Mon in Aug), Labor Day (first Mon in Sept), Christmas Day (Dec 25), and Boxing Day (Dec 26). Public holidays that fall on a Saturday or Sunday are usually celebrated the following Monday.

BERMUDA CALENDAR OF EVENTS

January & February

Bermuda Festival. Throughout January and February, island-wide events abound. They include golf and tennis invitationals, an international marathon, a dog show, open house and garden tours, and the Bermuda Festival, a 6-week international festival of the performing arts, held in the City of Hamilton. It features drama, dance, jazz, classical, and popular music, as well as other entertainment by the best international artists. Some tickets for the festival are reserved until 48 hours before curtain time for visitors. For details and a schedule for the 2004 festival, contact **Bermuda Festival,** P.O. Box HM 297, Hamilton HM AX, Bermuda (© **441/295-1291;** www.bermuda festival.com).

The Bermuda International Marathon, with international and local runners, takes place the third weekend in January. For further information and entry forms, contact the **International Race Weekend Committee,** Bermuda Track and Field Association, P.O. Box DV 397, Devonshire DV BX, Bermuda (© **441/236-6086;** www.bermuda tracknfield.com).

Golden Rendezvous. Mature travelers 50 years of age or older can enjoy specially designed cultural activities throughout the month of February during this Golden Rendezvous month. With mature travelers averaging the longest vacation stays, Bermuda offers special happenings in February including tours. For more information, call © **441/292-0023.**

March

Bermuda College Weeks. At least 10,000 students flock here every year—so it may not be the best time for the rest of you to come. These weeks began as Rugby Weeks in 1933, when teams from Ivy League schools came to compete against British or Bermudian teams. "Where the boys are," to borrow the popular song title, led to "where the girls are," and a tradition was born.

The Department of Tourism issues a College Week Courtesy Card to those who have a valid college ID card. The Courtesy Card is a passport to a week of free island-wide beach parties, lunches, boat cruises, dances, and entertainment, courtesy of the Bermudian government. Dates coincide with U.S. college vacations. Contact a Bermuda Department of Tourism office (see "Visitor Information," earlier in this chapter) to obtain a list of events.

Home and Garden Tours. Each spring, the Garden Club of Bermuda lays out the welcome mat at a number of private homes and gardens. A different set of houses, all conveniently located in the same parish, is open every Wednesday during this event. The program usually includes a total of 20 homes, many of them dating from the 17th and 18th centuries. The Bermuda Department of Tourism Office (© **800/BERMUDA;**

www.bermudatourism.com) provides a complete listing of homes
and viewing schedules. The tours
run from the end of March to
mid-May.

April

Beating Retreat Ceremony. The
Bermuda Regiment and massed
pipes and drums (a military band
and a Corps of Drums) create an
event that combines a marching
band concert and a parade. The
ceremony's roots are in the 17th
century, when British soldiers
were stationed on the island and a
roll of drums called them back to
their garrisons at nightfall. It's
presented once or twice per month,
rotating among the city of Hamilton, St. George, and the Royal
Naval Dockyard. The ceremony
usually takes place once or twice a
month, from April to July, and
in September and October. The
Bermuda Department of Tourism Office (© **800/BERMUDA;**
www.bermudatourism.com) supplies exact times and schedules.

Peppercorn Ceremony. His Excellency the governor collects the
annual rent of one peppercorn for
use of the island's Old State House
in St. George. Mid- to late April.
For information and the exact date,
call © **800/223-6106.**

Agriculture Exhibit. Held over 3
days in late April at the Botanical
Gardens in Paget, this event is a
celebration of Bermuda's agrarian
and horticultural bounty. In addition to prize-winning produce,
the Agriculture Exhibit provides a
showcase for local arts and crafts.
For more information, contact
the **Department of Agriculture
and Fisheries,** P.O. Box HM
834, Hamilton HM CX, Bermuda
(© 441/236-4201), or the **Bermuda
Department of Tourism** (© **800/
223-6106**).

International Race Week. Every
year, during late April and early May,
this yachting event pits equivalent
vessels from seven classes of sailing
craft against one another. Yachting
enthusiasts around the world follow
the knockout, elimination-style
event with avid interest. The Marion
to Bermuda race (see below) takes
place in June.

Other sailing contests are scheduled for alternate years. The world's
most famous wind-driven contest,
the Newport-to-Bermuda Race,
falls next in June 2004. The record
to date: a 56-hour transit.

Unfortunately for spectators, the
finish lines for the island's sailing
races usually lie several miles offshore. Afterward, boats are often
moored in Hamilton Harbour; any
vantage point on the harbor is good
for watching the boats come in.
Even better: Head for any of the
City of Hamilton's harborfront
pubs, where racing crowds celebrate
their wins (or justify their losses)
over pints of ale.

For information on all sailing
events held off the coast of
Bermuda, contact the **Sailing Secretary,** Royal Bermuda Yacht Club,
P.O. Box HM 894, Hamilton HM
DX, Bermuda (© **441/295-2214**),
or (for races originating off the U.S.
coast) the **New York Yacht Club,**
37 W. 44th St., New York, NY
10036 (© **212/382-1000**).

May

**Bermuda Heritage Day and
Month.** Bermuda Heritage Month
culminates on **Bermuda Day,**
May 24, a public holiday that's
Bermuda's equivalent of Independence Day. Bermuda Day is punc-
tuated with parades through
downtown Hamilton, dinghy and
cycling races, and the Bermuda
Half-Day Marathon (open only to
island residents). For the rest of the

month, a program of cultural and sporting events is presented (the schedule will be available at the tourist office). In addition to the Bermuda Department of Tourism Office (© 800/BERMUDA; www.bermudatourism.com), any hotel in town can fill you in on the events planned for the year's biggest political celebration.

June

Queen's Birthday (first or second Mon in June; contact the Bermuda Department of Tourism Office at © 800/BERMUDA or www.bermudatourism.com for exact times and schedules). The Queen's birthday is celebrated with a parade down Front Street in the City of Hamilton.

Marion to Bermuda Race. This 1,038km (645-mile) race from Marion, MA to Bermuda will be in mid June. See the entry for "International Race Week," under April, above, for details on international sailing events. For more information, call © 441/295-2214; www.marionbermuda.com.

August

Cup Match and Somers Days. Also known as the Cup Match Cricket Festival, this annual event celebrates the year's bounty with Bermuda's most illustrious cricket match. It's often compared to American Thanksgiving. Cricketers from the East End (St. George's Cricket Club) play off against those from the West End (Somerset Cricket Club), with lots of attendant British-derived protocol and hoopla. Tickets cost about $10; they're available at the gate on match day. The event is held on Thursday and Friday before the first Monday in August. For more information, call © 800/223-6106.

September

Labor Day. This public holiday, held on the first Monday in September, features a host of activities; it's also the ideal time for a picnic. The high point is a parade from Union Square in the City of Hamilton's Bernard Park.

Marine Science Day. Lectures, hands-on demonstrations, and displays for adults and children mark this day devoted to the study of the sea. Hosted by the **Bermuda Biological Station.** Call © 441/297-1880 for more information.

October

Match Racing. For Match Racing, pairs of identical sailing vessels, staffed by a rotating roster of teams from throughout the world, compete in elimination-style contests. For details on international sailing events, see the entry for "International Race Week," under April, above.

November

The Opening of Parliament. A traditional ceremony, with a military guard of honor, celebrates the opening of Parliament by His Excellency the governor, as the Queen's personal representative. In anticipation of the entry of MPs into Parliament at 11am, crowds begin gathering outside the Cabinet Building around 9:30 or 10am. Spectators traditionally include lots of schoolchildren being trained in civic protocol, as well as nostalgia buffs out for a whiff of British-style pomp. For more information, call © 800/223-6106.

Guy Fawkes Day. A small annual celebration with a mini-fair marks this day. The celebration starts with the traditional burning of 17th-century British traitor Guy Fawkes' effigy at the Keepyard of the Bermuda Maritime Museum, Royal

Naval Dockyard, at 4:30pm. November 5.

Seniors Rugby World Cup. Former international rugby players, who have recently retired from the international stage, compete with Bermudians at the Bermuda National Sports Club (© 441/ 236-6994). Mid-November.

Remembrance Day. Bermudian police, British and U.S. military units, Bermudians, and veterans' organizations participate in a small parade in remembrance of all who have given their lives in battle. November 11.

Invitation Tennis Weeks. More than 100 visiting players vie with Bermudians during 2 weeks of matches. Unlike Wimbledon— this event's role model—virtually everyone buys tickets at the gate. For information, contact the **Bermuda Lawn Tennis Association,** P.O. Box HM 341, Hamilton HM BX, Bermuda (© 441/296-0834; www. blta.bm).

December

Bermuda Goodwill Tournament. Pro-amateur foursomes from international golf clubs play more than 72 holes on four of Bermuda's eight courses. Anyone who wants to compete must pass the sponsors' stringent requirements and may appear only by invitation. Spectators are welcome to watch from the sidelines free. For more information, contact the **Bermuda Goodwill Golf Tournament,** P.O. Box WK 127, Warwick WK BX, Bermuda (© 441/ 295-9972). Early December.

5 Planning an Island Wedding or Honeymoon

GETTING MARRIED ON BERMUDA

Couples who would like to get married on Bermuda must file a "Notice of Intended Marriage" with the Registry General, accompanied by a fee of $205 (in the form of a bank draft or money order, not a personal check). Make out the draft to "The Accountant General" and mail or deliver it in person to the **Registry General,** Government Administration Building, 30 Parliament St., Hamilton HM 12, Bermuda (© 441/297-7709). Bermuda Department of Tourism offices in Atlanta, Boston, Chicago, and New York (see "Visitor Information," earlier in this chapter) distribute "Notice of Intended Marriage" forms, or you can contact the Bermuda Tourist Office (© 800/ **BERMUDA**) and a form will be mailed to you. If either of the prospective marriage partners has been married before, that person must attach a photocopy of the final divorce decree to the "Notice of Intended Marriage."

Once the Registry General receives the "Notice of Intended Marriage," it will be published, including names and addresses, in any two of the island's newspapers. Assuming that there is no formal objection, the registry will issue the license 15 days after receiving the notice. Airmailing your completed notice to Bermuda takes 6 to 10 days, so plan accordingly. The marriage license will be sent to you and will be valid for 3 months.

HIRING A WEDDING CONSULTANT

Many hotels can help make wedding arrangements—reserving the church and clergy, hiring a horse and buggy, ordering the wedding cake, and securing a photographer. Bermuda weddings range from simple ceremonies on the beach to large-scale extravaganzas at the Botanical Gardens. Other popular sites include churches and yachts.

Fun Fact **Have Your Cake & Eat It, Too**

Custom dictates that Bermudians have two wedding cakes: a plain pound cake covered with gold leaf for the groom, and a tiered fruit cake covered with silver leaf and topped with a miniature cedar tree for the bride. The tiny tree is planted on the day of the wedding to symbolize the hope that the marriage will grow and mature like the tree. The rest of the first tier of the bride's cake is frozen until the christening of the first child.

Wedding consultants can discuss your options with you and arrange all the details. **The Wedding Salon,** 76 Spanish Point Rd., #10, Pembroke HM 02, Bermuda (© **919/217-4395;** fax 919/266-2182; www.bermuda weddingsalon.com), operates its planning office in North Carolina. After a contractual agreement is made, the office puts customers in contact with their Bermuda consultant. **The Bridal Salon,** Parkside Building, 3 Park Rd., Suite 7, Hamilton HM 09, Bermuda (© **888/253-5585** or 441/292-2025; fax 441/296-2070; www.bridalsuite bermudaweddings.com), arranges wedding packages that range in cost from $1,000 to $15,000.

Some hotels—including the Elbow Beach Hotel, the Sonesta Beach Resort, and both of the Fairmont Princess hotels—will arrange weddings; see chapter 4, "Where to Stay," for contact information. If you're staying at a small hotel, it's better to go through a wedding consultant to plan your wedding.

HONEYMOONING ON BERMUDA

Bermuda attracts more than 23,000 honeymooners and second honeymooners each year, with good reason: It offers an ideal environment for couples, whether they prefer an active schedule or a relaxing one. Many of Bermuda's hotels, from luxurious resorts to intimate cottage colonies, offer honeymoon packages. Typically, these include airfare, accommodations, meal plans, champagne upon arrival, flowers in your room, and discounts at local attractions and restaurants. See "The Best Resorts for Honeymooners & Other Lovers," in chapter 1, "The Best of Bermuda," for the best packages. For other options, consult your travel agent or call the hotels listed in chapter 4, "Where to Stay," directly and inquire about honeymoon packages.

6 Travel Insurance

Although close to the United States, a visit to Bermuda is, in essence, "going abroad." You can encounter all the same problems in Bermuda that you would in going to a more remote foreign destination. Therefore, it's wise to review your insurance coverage, especially concerning lost luggage or medical insurance.

Check your existing insurance policies and credit-card coverage before you buy travel insurance. You may already be covered for lost luggage, cancelled tickets or medical expenses. The cost of travel insurance varies widely, depending on the cost and length of your trip, your age, health, and the type of trip you're taking.

TRIP-CANCELLATION INSURANCE Trip-cancellation insurance helps you get your money back if you have to back out of a trip, if you have to go home early, or if your travel supplier goes bankrupt. Allowed reasons for cancellation can range from sickness to natural disasters to the State Department declaring your destination unsafe for travel. (Insurers usually won't cover vague fears, though, as many travelers discovered who tried to cancel their trips in October 2001 because they were wary of flying.) In this unstable world, trip-cancellation insurance is a good buy if you're getting tickets well in advance—who knows what the state of the world, or of your airline, will be in 9 months? Insurance policy details vary, so read the fine print—and especially make sure that your airline or cruise line is on the list of carriers covered in case of bankruptcy. For information, contact one of the following insurers: **Access America** (© 866/807-3982; www. accessamerica.com); **Travel Guard International** (© 800/826-4919; www.travelguard.com); **Travel Insured International** (© 800/243-3174; www.travelinsured.com); and **Travelex Insurance Services** (© 888/457-4602; www.travelex-insurance.com).

MEDICAL INSURANCE Most health insurance policies cover you if you get sick away from home—but check, particularly if you're insured by an HMO. With the exception of certain HMOs and Medicare/Medicaid, your medical insurance should cover medical treatment—even hospital care—overseas. However, most out-of-country hospitals make you pay your bills up front, and send you a refund after you've returned home and filed the necessary paperwork. And in a worst-case scenario, there's the high cost of emergency evacuation. If you require additional medical insurance,

try **MEDEX International** (© 800/527-0218 or 410/453-6300; www.medexassist.com) or **Travel Assistance International** (© 800/821-2828; www.travelassistance.com; for general information on services, call the company's Worldwide Assistance Services, Inc., at © 800/777-8710).

LOST-LUGGAGE INSURANCE On domestic flights, checked baggage is covered up to $2,500 per ticketed passenger. On international flights (including U.S. portions of international trips), baggage is limited to approximately $9.05 per pound, up to approximately $635 per checked bag. If you plan to check items more valuable than the standard liability, see if your valuables are covered by your homeowner's policy, get baggage insurance as part of your comprehensive travel-insurance package or buy Travel Guard's "BagTrak" product. Don't buy insurance at the airport, as it's usually overpriced. Be sure to take any valuables or irreplaceable items with you in your carry-on luggage, as many valuables (including books, money and electronics) aren't covered by airline policies.

If your luggage is lost, immediately file a lost-luggage claim at the airport, detailing the luggage contents. For most airlines, you must report delayed, damaged, or lost baggage within 4 hours of arrival. The airlines are required to deliver luggage, once found, directly to your house or destination free.

7 Health & Safety

STAYING HEALTHY

If you need medical attention while on Bermuda, finding a doctor or getting a prescription filled is no real problem. See "Drugstores" under "Fast Facts: Bermuda," in chapter 3, "Getting to Know Bermuda," for addresses of pharmacies. In an emergency, call

King Edward VII Hospital, 7 Point Finger Rd., Paget Parish (© 441/236-2345), and ask for the emergency department. For less serious medical problems, ask someone at your hotel for a recommendation.

Limit your exposure to the sun, especially between the hours of 11am

> **Tips   Daily Life in Bermuda**
>
> Here are some miscellaneous Bermuda survival tips: Know that ATMs only dispense Bermuda dollars, and that buses only accept coins. Also, don't get caught in the City of Hamilton's rush-hour traffic, which is Monday to Friday from 8:30 to 9am and 5 to 6pm.

to 2pm and during the first few days of your trip. Use a sunscreen with a high protection factor and apply it liberally. Remember that children need more protection than adults do.

As you travel around Bermuda on a scooter, on bike, or on foot, it's always wise to carry along some bottled water to prevent dehydration.

WHAT TO DO IF YOU GET SICK AWAY FROM HOME

In most cases, your existing health plan will provide the coverage you need. But double-check; you may want to buy **travel medical insurance** instead. (See the section on insurance, above.) Bring your insurance ID card with you when you travel.

If you suffer from a chronic illness, consult your doctor before your departure. For conditions like epilepsy, diabetes, or heart problems, wear a **Medic Alert Identification Tag** (℃ 800/ 825-3785; www.medicalert.org), which will immediately alert doctors to your condition and give them access to your records through Medic Alert's 24-hour hot line.

Pack **prescription medications** in your carry-on luggage, and carry prescription medications in their original containers, with pharmacy labels—otherwise they won't make it through airport security. Also bring along copies of your prescriptions in case you lose your pills or run out. Don't forget an extra pair of contact lenses or prescription glasses. Carry the generic name of prescription medicines, in case a local pharmacist is unfamiliar with the brand name.

Contact the **International Association for Medical Assistance to Travelers (IAMAT)** (℃ 716/754-4883 or 416/652-0137; www.iamat.org) for tips on travel and health concerns in the countries you're visiting, and lists of local, English-speaking doctors. The United States **Centers for Disease Control and Prevention** (℃ 800/311-3435; www.cdc.gov) provides up-to-date information on necessary vaccines and health hazards by region or country.

If you get sick, consider asking your hotel concierge to recommend a local doctor—even his or her own. You can also try the emergency room at a local hospital; many have walk-in clinics for emergency cases that are not life-threatening. You may not get immediate attention, but you won't pay the high price of an emergency room visit.

THE SAFE TRAVELER

Bermuda has a low to moderate crime rate. Incidents of serious violent crime are infrequent, but petty thefts and assaults do occur. Valuables left in hotel rooms (occupied and unoccupied) or left unattended on beaches are vulnerable to theft. Criminals often target transportation systems and popular tourist attractions. Examples of common crimes include pick pocketing, theft of unattended baggage and items from rental motorbikes, and purse snatchings (often perpetrated against pedestrians by thieves riding motorbikes).

Travelers should exercise caution when walking after dark or visiting out-of-the-way places on the island, as they can be vulnerable to crime, and because narrow and dark roadways can contribute to accidents. There have been incidents of verbal, and sometimes physical, assault against both locals and tourists have been reported. Petty drug use is frequent and open. Gang activity, including assaults and arson, has been reported in the area as well. There have been several assaults and thefts in the area of Pitts Bay Road from the Hamilton Princess Hotel into the town of Hamilton, and the back roads of Hamilton are often the setting for assaults, particularly after the bars close.

The loss or theft abroad of a U.S. passport should be reported immediately to the local police and the nearest U.S. embassy or consulate. U.S. citizens can refer to the Department of State's pamphlet, *A Safe Trip Abroad,* for ways to promote a more trouble-free journey. This publication and others, such as *Tips for Travelers to the Caribbean,* are available by mail from the Superintendent of Documents, U.S. Government Printing Office, Washington, DC 20402, via the Internet at www.access.gpo.gov/su_docs, or via the Bureau of Consular Affairs home page at http://travel.state.gov.

8 Specialized Travel Resources

TRAVELERS WITH DISABILITIES

Bermuda is not a great place for persons with disabilities who are not planning to stay on-site at a resort. Getting around the islands is a bit difficult even for the agile, who must rely on motorbikes, bicycles, and buses. It is difficult to walk with a cane outside the town of St. George and City of Hamilton, because most roads don't have sidewalks or adequate curbs. When two vehicles pass, you are often crowded off the road.

Taking taxis to everything you want to see can be a very expensive undertaking. Unfortunately, the public buses are not geared for passengers in wheelchairs. However, you can ask your hotel to check on the availability of volunteer buses operated by the Bermuda Physically Handicapped Association (no phone). It occasionally runs buses with hydraulic lifts. You can also call the tourist office and request a schedule for such transportation; make arrangements as far in advance as possible.

Before you go, you can seek information from the Bermuda chapter of the **Society for Accessible Travel and Hospitality** (www.sath.org). Visitors planning to bring a guide dog to Bermuda must obtain a permit in advance from any Bermuda Department of Tourism office.

The most accessible hotels in Bermuda are Elbow Beach Hotel, the Sonesta Beach Resort, the Fairmont Hamilton Princess, and The Fairmont Southampton.

Organizations that offer assistance to travelers with disabilities include the **Moss Rehab Hospital** (www.mossresourcenet.org), which provides a library of accessible-travel resources online; the **Society for Accessible Travel and Hospitality** (© 212/447-7284; www.sath.org; annual membership fees: $45 adults, $30 seniors and students), which offers a wealth of travel resources for all types of disabilities and informed recommendations on destinations, access guides, travel agents, tour operators, vehicle rentals, and companion services; and the **American Foundation for the Blind** (© 800/232-5463; www.afb.org), which provides information on traveling with Seeing Eye dogs.

For more information specifically targeted to travelers with disabilities, the community website **iCan** (www.icanonline.net/channels/travel/index.cfm) has destination guides and several regular columns on accessible travel. Also check out the quarterly magazine *Emerging Horizons* ($15 per year, $20 outside the U.S.; www.emerginghorizons.com); **Twin Peaks Press** (© **360/694-2462;** http://disabilitybookshop.virtualave.net/blist84.htm), offering travel-related books for travelers with special needs; and *Open World Magazine,* published by the Society for Accessible Travel and Hospitality (see above; subscription: $18/yr., $35 outside the U.S.).

TIPS FOR BRITISH TRAVELERS WITH DISABILITIES

The **Royal Association for Disability and Rehabilitation (RADAR),** unit 12, City Forum, 250 City Rd., London, ECIV 8AF (© **020/7250-3222;** fax 020/7250-0212; www.radar.org.uk), publishes holiday "fact packs," three in all, which sell for £2 each or all three for £5. The first one provides general information on planning and booking a holiday, insurance, finances, and useful organization and holiday providers. The second outlines transportation available abroad and equipment for rent. The third deals with specialized accommodations.

GAY & LESBIAN TRAVELERS

Think twice before planning a holiday on Bermuda. Although many gays live in and visit Bermuda, the colony is rather repressive to homosexuals. Displays of affection by same sex couples will be frowned on at public beaches and most hotel pools, restaurants, or attractions. If you want really happening gay beaches, bars, and clubs, head for South Miami Beach, Key West, Puerto Rico, or U.S. Virgin Islands, a series of islands that are much more accepting of homosexual relationships.

For most of its existence, Bermuda had harsh penalties against male homosexuals, making sex between consenting legal age males a crime subject to imprisonment. Lobbying against such a harsh measure, The Bermuda Human Rights Alliance, a Bermuda gay and lesbian group, helped to bring about a repeal of the criminal code. Since an assembly vote in the Bermuda Parliament, sex between men over the age of 18 is now legal.

If you're contemplating a visit, point your browser to **www.gaybermuda.com**, a comprehensive website geared to gay travelers to Bermuda.

SENIOR TRAVELERS

Mention the fact that you're a senior citizen when you make your travel reservations. Although all of the major U.S. airlines except America West have cancelled their senior discount and coupon book programs, many hotels still offer discounts for seniors. In most cities, people over the age of 60 qualify for reduced admission to theaters, museums, and other attractions, as well as discounted fares on public transportation.

Though much of the island's sporting and nightlife activity is geared toward more youthful travelers, Bermuda has much to offer seniors. The best source of information for seniors is the Tourism Office (see "Visitor Information," earlier in this chapter). If you're staying in a large resort hotel, the activities director or concierge is another excellent source.

Members of **AARP** (formerly known as the American Association of Retired Persons), 601 E St. NW, Washington, DC 20049 (© **800/424-3410** or 202/434-2277; www.aarp.org), get discounts on hotels, airfares, and car rentals. AARP offers members a wide range of benefits, including *Modern Maturity* magazine and a monthly newsletter. Anyone over 50 can join.

Many reliable agencies and organizations target the 50-plus market. **Elderhostel** (© **877/426-8056;** www.elderhostel.org) arranges study programs for those aged 55 and over (and a spouse or companion of any age) in the U.S. and in more than 80 countries around the world. Most courses last 5 to 7 days in the U.S. (2 to 4 weeks abroad), and many include airfare, accommodations in university dormitories or modest inns, meals, and tuition.

Recommended publications offering travel resources and discounts for seniors include: the quarterly magazine *Travel 50 & Beyond* (www.travel50andbeyond.com); *Travel Unlimited: Uncommon Adventures for the Mature Traveler* (Avalon); *101 Tips for Mature Travelers,* available from Grand Circle Travel (© **800/221-2610** or 617/350-7500; www.gct.com); *The 50+ Traveler's Guidebook* (St. Martin's Press); and *Unbelievably Good Deals and Great Adventures That You Absolutely Can't Get Unless You're Over 50* (McGraw Hill).

FAMILY TRAVEL

If you have enough trouble getting your kids out of the house in the morning, dragging them thousands of miles away may seem like an insurmountable challenge. But family travel can be immensely rewarding, giving you new ways of seeing the world through smaller pairs of eyes.

Bermuda is one of the best vacation destinations for the entire family. Toddlers can spend blissful hours in shallow seawater or pools geared just for them, and older children can enjoy boat rides, horseback riding, hiking, and snorkeling. Most resort hotels offer advice for families with kids (including help in finding a babysitter), and many have play directors and supervised activities for various age groups.

Outside the town of St. George and City of Hamilton, walking with a baby stroller is difficult—most roads don't have sidewalks or adequate curbs. It is extremely dangerous to carry a baby on a motorbike or bike, as baby seats are not provided. Buses, taxis, and ferries are the safest ways to travel around Bermuda with a baby.

Refer to chapter 4 for some recommendations of "Family-Friendly Accommodations," and to chapter 5 for our pick of "Family-Friendly Restaurants."

You can find good family-oriented vacation advice on the Internet from sites like the **Family Travel Network** (www.familytravelnetwork.com); **Traveling Internationally with Your Kids** (www.travelwithyourkids.com), a comprehensive site offering sound advice for long-distance and international travel with children; and

---

Value **Zero Cost Lodging**

Elder Travelers, 1615 Smelter Ave., Black Eagle, MT 59414 (www.eldertravelers.com), aids those who are more than 50 years old, like to travel and to meet people, but may not have the funds or desire to stay in hotels. Their stated purpose is to provide members with "zero cost lodging" anywhere in the world, as senior "guests" are hooked up with counterpart "hosts," who provide lodging in the destination that the guest is traveling in. For $40 annually, you'll receive an informative newsletter, which provides links to the best travel sites worldwide. You can enroll in the guest and host database and find more information on this unique group at www.eldertravelers.com.

Family Travel Files (www.thefamily
travelfiles.com), which offers an
online magazine and a directory of
off-the-beaten-path tours and tour
operators for families.

FOR BLACK TRAVELERS

Agencies and organizations that provide resources for black travelers
include: **Rodgers Travel** (© 215/
473-1775; www.rodgerstravel.com), a
Philadelphia-based travel agency with
an extensive menu of tours in destinations worldwide, including heritage
and private group tours; the **African-
American Association of Innkeepers
International** (© 877/422-5777;
www.africanamericaninns.com),
which provides information on
member B&Bs in the U.S., Canada,
Bermuda, and the Caribbean; and
Henderson Travel and Tours
(© 800/327-2309 or 301/650-5700;
www.hendersontravel.com), which
has specialized in trips to Africa
since 1957.

The Internet offers a number of
helpful travel sites for the black traveler.
Black Travel Online (www.black
travelonline.com) posts news on

upcoming events and includes links to
articles and travel-booking sites. **Soul of
America** (www.soulofamerica.com) is a
more comprehensive website, with
travel tips, event and family reunion
postings, and sections on historically
black beach resorts and active vacations.
For more information, check out the
following collections and guides: For
more information, check out the
following collections and guides: *Go
Girl: The Black Woman's Guide to
Travel & Adventure* (Eighth Mountain Press), a compilation of travel
essays by writers including Jill Nelson
and Audre Lorde, with some practical
information and trip-planning advice;
Travel and Enjoy Magazine (© 866/
266-6211; www.travelandenjoy.com;
subscription: $24/yr.), which focuses
on discounts and destination reviews.

STUDENT TRAVEL

The Bermuda Department of Tourism
offers Spring Break programs for
sports teams from the mainland, as
well as Spring Break Arts Programs.
Inquire with the tourism office for
details (see "Visitor Information" earlier in this chapter).

9 Planning Your Trip Online

SURFING FOR AIRFARES

The "big three" online travel agencies,
Expedia.com, Travelocity.com, and
Orbitz.com sell most of the air tickets
bought on the Internet. (Canadian
travelers should try expedia.ca and
Travelocity.ca; U.K. residents can go
for expedia.co.uk and opodo.co.uk.)
Each has different business deals with
the airlines and may offer different
fares on the same flights, so it's wise to
shop around. Expedia and Travelocity
will also send you **e-mail notification**
when a cheap fare becomes available
to your favorite destination. Of the
smaller travel agency websites, **Side
Step** (www.sidestep.com) has gotten
the best reviews from Frommer's

authors. It's a browser add-on that
purports to "search 140 sites at once,"
but in reality only beats competitors'
fares as often as other sites do.

Also remember to check **airline
websites,** especially those for low-fare
carriers such as Southwest, JetBlue,
AirTran, WestJet, or Ryanair, whose
fares are often misreported or simply
missing from travel agency websites.
Even with major airlines, you can
often shave a few bucks from a fare by
booking directly through the airline
and avoiding a travel agency's transaction fee. But you'll get these discounts
only by **booking online:** Most airlines
now offer online-only fares that even
their phone agents know nothing

Frommers.com: The Complete Travel Resource

For an excellent travel-planning resource, we highly recommend Frommers.com (www.frommers.com). We're a little biased, of course, but we guarantee that you'll find the travel tips, reviews, monthly vacation giveaways, and online-booking capabilities thoroughly indispensable. Among the special features are our popular **Message Boards,** where Frommer's readers post queries and share advice (sometimes even our authors show up to answer questions); **Frommers.com Newsletter,** for the latest travel bargains and insider travel secrets; and **Frommer's Destinations Section,** where you'll get expert travel tips, hotel and dining recommendations, and advice on the sights to see for more than 3,000 destinations around the globe. When your research is done, the **Online Reservations System** (www.frommers.com/book_a_trip) takes you to Frommer's preferred online partners for booking your vacation at affordable prices.

about. For the websites of airlines that fly to and from your destination, go to "Getting There: Flying to Bermuda," below.

Great **last-minute deals** are available through free weekly e-mail services provided directly by the airlines. Most of these are announced on Tuesday or Wednesday and must be purchased online. Most are only valid for travel that weekend, but some (such as Southwest's) can be booked weeks or months in advance. Sign up for weekly e-mail alerts at airline websites or check mega-sites that compile comprehensive lists of last-minute specials, such as **Smarter Living** (smarterliving.com).

For much more about airfares and savvy air-travel tips and advice, pick up a copy of *Frommer's Fly Safe, Fly Smart* (Wiley Publishing).

SURFING FOR HOTELS
Shopping online for hotels is much easier in the U.S., Canada, and Bermuda than it is in the rest of the world. Also, many smaller hotels and B&Bs—especially outside the U.S.—don't show up on websites at all. Of the "big three" sites, **Expedia** may be the best choice, thanks to its long list of special deals. **Travelocity** runs a close second. Hotel specialist sites **hotels.com** and **hoteldiscounts.com** are also reliable. An excellent free program, **TravelAxe** (www.travelaxe.net), can help you search multiple hotel sites at once, even ones you may never have heard of.

10 The 21st-Century Traveler

INTERNET ACCESS AWAY FROM HOME
Travelers have any number of ways to check their e-mail and access the Internet on the road. Of course, using your own laptop—or even a PDA (personal desk assistant) or electronic organizer with a modem—gives you the most flexibility. But even if you don't have a computer, you can still access your e-mail and even your office computer from cybercafes.

WITHOUT YOUR OWN COMPUTER
It's hard nowadays to find a city that *doesn't* have a few cybercafes. Although

there's no definitive directory for cybercafes—these are independent businesses, after all—three places to start looking are at **www.cyber captive.com**, **www.netcafeguide.com**, and **www.cybercafe.com**.

Most major airports now have **Internet kiosks** scattered throughout their gates. These kiosks, which you'll also see in shopping malls, hotel lobbies, and tourist information offices around the world, give you basic Web access for a per-minute fee that's usually higher than cybercafe prices. The kiosks' clunkiness and high price means they should be avoided whenever possible.

To retrieve your e-mail, ask your **Internet Service Provider (ISP)** if it has a Web-based interface tied to your existing e-mail account. If your ISP doesn't have such an interface, you can use the free **mail2web** service (www.mail2web.com) to view (but not reply to) your home e-mail. For more flexibility, you may want to open a free, Web-based e-mail account with **Yahoo! Mail** (mail.yahoo.com). (Microsoft's Hotmail is another popular option, but Hotmail has severe spam problems.) Your home ISP may be able to forward your e-mail to the Web-based account automatically.

If you need to access files on your office computer, look into a service called **GoToMyPC** (www.gotomypc.com). The service provides a Web-based interface for you to access and manipulate a distant PC from anywhere—even a cybercafe—provided your "target" PC is on and has an always-on connection to the Internet (such as with Road Runner cable). The service offers top-quality security, but if you're worried about hackers, use your own laptop rather than a cybercafe to access the GoToMyPC system.

WITH YOUR OWN COMPUTER

Major Internet Service Providers (ISP) have **local access numbers** around the world, allowing you to go online by simply placing a local call. Check your ISP's website or call its toll-free number and ask how you can use your current account away from home, and how much it will cost.

Most business-class hotels throughout the world offer dataports for laptop modems, and a few thousand hotels now offer high-speed Internet access using an Ethernet network cable. You'll have to bring your own cables either way, so **call your hotel in advance** to find out what the options are.

USING A CELLPHONE IN BERMUDA

The three letters that define much of the world's **wireless capabilities** are GSM (Global System for Mobiles), a big, seamless network that makes for easy cross-border cellphone use throughout Europe and dozens of other countries worldwide. In the U.S., T-Mobile, AT&T Wireless, and Cingular use this quasi-universal system; in Canada, Microcell and some Rogers customers are GSM, and all Europeans and most Australians use GSM.

If your cellphone is on a GSM system, and you have a world-capable phone such as many (but not all) Sony Ericsson, Motorola, or Samsung models, you can make and receive calls across civilized areas on much of the globe, from Andorra to Uganda, and certainly Bermuda. Just call your wireless operator and ask for "international roaming" to be activated on your account. Unfortunately, per-minute charges can be high.

World-phone owners can bring down their per-minute charges with a bit of trickery. Call up your cellular operator and say you'll be going abroad for several months and want to "unlock" your phone to use it with a local provider. Usually, they'll oblige. Then, in Bermuda, pick up a cheap, prepaid phone chip at a mobile phone store and slip it into your phone. (Show your phone to the salesperson, as not all phones work on all networks.) You'll get a local phone number—and much, much lower calling rates.

Otherwise, **renting** a phone is a good idea. While you can rent a phone from any number of overseas sites, including kiosks at airports and at car-rental agencies, we suggest renting the phone before you leave home. That way you can give loved ones your new number, make sure the phone works, and take the phone wherever you go— especially helpful when you rent overseas, where phone-rental agencies bill

in local currency and may not let you take the phone to another country.

Two good wireless rental companies are **InTouch USA** (℃ 800/872-7626; www.intouchglobal.com) and **Road Post** (℃ 888-290-1606 or 905/272-5665; www.roadpost.com). Give them your itinerary, and they'll tell you what wireless products you need. InTouch will also, for free, advise you on whether your existing phone will work in Bermuda; simply call ℃ **703/ 222-7161** between 9am and 4pm EST, or go to http://intouchglobal.com/travel.htm.

11 Getting There: Flying to Bermuda

From North America's East Coast, you can be in Bermuda in approximately 2 hours. From London, England, the trip takes about 7 hours.

BY PLANE

American Airlines (℃ 800/433-7300; www.aa.com) flies nonstop, twice a day from New York's JFK Airport. Departures coincide with dozens of connecting flights from elsewhere in North America.

Delta (℃ 800/241-4141; www.delta.com) offers daily nonstop service from Boston and Atlanta. The Boston flight departs in the morning (around 9am). The Atlanta flight leaves around 11am—late enough to allow connections from most of the other cities in Delta's vast network.

Continental Airlines (℃ 800/ 525-0280; www.continental.com) offers nonstop service from New Jersey's Newark Airport. Departures are each day.

US Airways (℃ 800/428-4322; www.usairways.com) offers nonstop flights from Philadelphia and Boston year-round, plus nonstop flights from New York (La Guardia) from April 6 to October 6.

Air Canada (℃ 800/268-7240 in Canada, 888/247-2262 in U.S.; www.aircanada.ca) offers daily nonstop

flights from Toronto, with frequent connections into Toronto from virtually every other city in Canada. The flight departs around 9am, permitting convenient connections from Montreal and Quebec City. The airline also offers a nonstop flight from Halifax on Saturday at noon.

The airline of choice from the United Kingdom is **British Airways** (℃ 0845/773-3377; www.britishairways.com). It flies from London's Gatwick Airport about three times a week, year-round. No other airline flies nonstop between Britain and Bermuda.

Most airlines offer the best deals on tickets booked at least 14 days in advance, with a stopover in Bermuda of at least 3 days. You might need to stay over on a Saturday night to keep fares down. Airfares fluctuate according to the season but tend to remain competitive among the companies vying for a piece of the lucrative Bermuda run.

Peak season (summer) is the most expensive time to go; low season (usually from mid-Sept to early Nov until mid-Mar) sees less expensive fares. The airlines that fly to Bermuda seldom observe a shoulder (intermediate) season. Because most aircraft flying from North America to

> **Tips Packing Tip**
>
> Bermuda is more formal than most resort destinations, so men planning to dine at upscale restaurants should be sure to pack a jacket and tie.

Bermuda are medium-sized, there's space for only two classes of service: first class and economy.

American Airlines offers round-trip flights from New York to Bermuda that, with restrictions that include the requirement of a 3-day delay between outbound and return legs of the trip, start at $473 round-trip from Monday through Thursday. Passengers are charged a supplement of about $22 per leg of the trip for trips that originate in either New York or Bermuda on a Friday, Saturday, or Sunday. Round-trip business class fares (the equivalent of first class travel on some other airlines), regardless of the season, cost $1,408.

GETTING THROUGH THE AIRPORT

With the federalization of airport security, security procedures at U.S. airports are more stable and consistent than ever. Generally, you'll be fine if you arrive at the airport **1 hour** before a domestic flight and **2 hours** before an international flight; if you show up late, tell an airline employee and he or she will probably whisk you to the front of the line.

Bring a **current, government-issued photo ID** such as a driver's license or passport, and if you've got an E-ticket, print out the **official confirmation page;** you'll need to show your confirmation at the security checkpoint, and your ID at the ticket counter or the gate. (Children under 18 do not need photo IDs for domestic flights, but the adults checking in with them need them.)

Security lines are getting shorter than they were during 2001 and 2002, but some doozies remain. If you have

trouble standing for long periods of time, tell an airline employee; the airline will provide a wheelchair. Speed up security by **not wearing metal objects** such as big belt buckles or clanky earrings. If you've got metallic body parts, a note from your doctor can prevent a long chat with the security screeners. Keep in mind that only **ticketed passengers** are allowed past security, except for folks escorting disabled passengers or children.

Federalization has stabilized **what you can carry on** and **what you can't.** The general rule is that sharp things are out, nail clippers are okay, and food and beverages must be passed through the X-ray machine—but that security screeners can't make you drink from your coffee cup. Bring food in your carry-on rather than checking it, as explosive-detection machines used on checked luggage have been known to mistake food (especially chocolate, for some reason) for bombs.

Travelers in the U.S. are allowed one carry-on bag, plus a "personal item" such as a purse, briefcase, or laptop bag. Carry-on hoarders can stuff all sorts of things into a laptop bag; as long as it has a laptop in it, it's still considered a personal item. The Transportation Security Administration (TSA) has issued a list of restricted items; check its website (www.tsa.gov/public/index.jsp) for details.

FLYING FOR LESS: TIPS FOR GETTING THE BEST AIRFARE

Passengers sharing the same airplane cabin rarely pay the same fare. Travelers who need to purchase tickets at the last minute, change their itinerary at a moment's notice, or fly one-way often get stuck paying the premium rate. Here are some ways to keep your air-fare costs down.

- Passengers who can book their ticket **long in advance,** who can **stay over Saturday night,** or who **fly midweek** or **at less-trafficked hours** will pay a fraction of the full fare. If your schedule is flexible, say so, and ask if you can secure a cheaper fare by changing your flight plans.
- You can also save on airfares by keeping an eye out in local news-papers for **promotional specials** or **fare wars,** when airlines lower prices on their most popular routes. You rarely see fare wars offered for peak travel times, but if you can travel in the off-months, you may snag a bargain.
- Search **the Internet** for cheap fares (see "Planning Your Trip Online," above).
- **Consolidators,** also known as bucket shops, are great sources for international tickets, although they usually can't beat the Internet on fares within North America. Start by looking in Sunday news-paper travel sections; U.S. travel-ers should focus on the *New York Times, Los Angeles Times,* and *Miami Herald.* For less-developed destinations, small travel agents who cater to immigrant commu-nities in large cities often have the best deals. *Beware:* Bucket shop tickets are usually nonrefundable or rigged with stiff cancellation penalties, often as high as 50% to 75% of the ticket price, and some put you on charter airlines with questionable safety records.

Several reliable consolidators are worldwide and available on the Net. **STA Travel** is now the world's leader in student travel, thanks to their purchase of Council Travel. It also offers good fares for travelers of all ages. **Flights.com** (© 800/TRAV-800; www.flights.com) started in Europe and has excellent fares worldwide, but particularly to that continent. It also has "local" websites in 12 countries. **Fly-Cheap** (© 800/FLY-CHEAP; www.1800flycheap.com) is owned by package-holiday megalith MyTravel and so has especially good access to fares for sunny destinations. **Air Tickets Direct** (© 800/778-3447; www.air ticketsdirect.com) is based in Montreal and leverages the cur-rently weak Canadian dollar for low fares; it'll also book trips to places that U.S. travel agents won't touch, such as Cuba.

- Join **frequent-flier clubs.** Accrue enough miles, and you'll be rewarded with free flights and elite status. It's free, and you'll get the best choice of seats, faster response to phone inquiries, and prompter service if your luggage is stolen, your flight is canceled or delayed, or if you want to change your seat. You don't need to fly to build frequent-flier miles—**frequent-flier credit cards** can provide thousands of miles for doing your everyday shopping.
- For many more tips about air travel, including a rundown of the major frequent-flier credit cards, pick up a copy of *Frommer's Fly Safe, Fly Smart* (Wiley Publishing).

12 Cruising to Bermuda

Cruise ships tie up at three harbors in Bermuda: St. George in the East End, the Royal Naval Dockyard in the West End, and Hamilton Harbour at the City of Hamilton. While the cruise experience isn't for everyone, it's very appealing to some people, and is cer-tainly a carefree, all-inclusive vacation.

Ships from the East Coast of the United States reach Bermuda in a little over a day. You'll spend a few full days (usually 3) moored at the island, exploring during the day and returning to the ship at night. It's convenient and comfortable—like having a luxury hotel and restaurant that travels with you.

Of course, that's also its major disadvantage. Most cruisers don't get to know the real Bermuda as well as those who stay in hotels ashore. For instance, cruise-ship passengers generally eat all their meals aboard the ship—mainly because they've already paid for the meals as part of their cruise price—and so they miss out on sampling Bermuda's cuisine. They also rarely get to meet and interact with Bermudians the way land-based visitors do.

Seven-day cruises out of New York usually spend 4 days at sea, with 3 days in port. Most cruise ships arrive in the traditional port of the City of Hamilton, the capital of Bermuda and its chief commercial and shopping center. If shopping is more important to you than sightseeing, be sure that your cruise ship docks here. Once you're ashore, head to Front Street for shopping, or get your bearings by taking the walking tour that we describe in Chapter 8, "Island Strolls."

If you're more interested in historic Bermuda, make sure that your ship is scheduled to anchor at St. George, at the eastern tip of the island. With its narrow lanes and old buildings and streets, St. George has been called the Bermudian equivalent of Colonial Williamsburg. Your ship will probably offer a guided tour of the town as a shore excursion; we've provided a self-guided tour in chapter 8 if you'd rather explore on your own. St. George has become more of a shopping destination than it used to be, but this still isn't the primary place to come for shopping. Depending on the cruise line, its schedules, and the current tides, some cruise ships dock at both St. George and the City of Hamilton while in Bermuda. Ships often plan to dock at St. George, but find that they cannot do so because of the tides.

It's not too likely that you'll disembark at Somerset, which is at the western end of the island and farthest from many of Bermuda's attractions. The West End has its own charm and sightseeing appeal; it is home of the Royal Naval Dockyard, one of the island's major attractions. In a shopping mall at the dockyard, you'll find craft stores and museums.

WHICH CRUISE LINE IS FOR YOU?

If you decide that a Bermuda cruise is right for you, you'll need to choose your cruise line. Some lines want their passengers to have a totally action-filled vacation—one filled with activities from sunup to sundown. Others see time at sea as a period of tranquillity and relaxation, with less emphasis on organized activities. The cruise lines listed here offer regularly scheduled Bermuda sailings. See the section that follows for tips on getting a good deal on the price.

- **Carnival Cruise Lines** (© **800/ 327-9501** or 305/599-2200; www.carnival.com) is the world's largest cruise line, although Bermuda doesn't figure heavily into its itineraries. Its *Carnival Legend* sails from Baltimore on 6-day Bermuda trips visiting King's Wharf at anchorage in Bermuda. *Carnival Pride* sails from New York on 7-day trips to Bermuda. Both vessels spend most of their time in the Caribbean but offer these summer trips. If you watch the TV, you know by now that these are the party ships of the Caribbean, colorful, jumbo-sized resorts with the flash of Vegas.

- **Celebrity Cruises** (*©* **800/327-6700** or 305/539-6000; www.celebrity-cruises.com). Noted for modern, state-of-the-art, large-but-not-mammoth cruise ships, and for exceptional cuisine and service, Celebrity is unpretentious but classy. It's several notches above mass market but still competitively priced. Cabins are roomy and well equipped, and the decor in general is elegantly modern, eschewing the glitz of some competitors. Celebrity attracts a broad range of passengers, including families drawn by the line's children's programs. Its *Zenith* and *Horizon* both sail 7-night Bermuda itineraries from New York between May and October. They spend 2 nights in St. George and 2 nights in the City of Hamilton. Runs from other East Coast cities are interspersed throughout the season.

- **Norwegian Cruise Line** (*©* **800/327-7030** or 305/436-4000; www.ncl.com). NCL offers affordable (sometimes downright cheap) down-to-earth cruises. The *Norwegian Majesty* makes Bermuda runs from Boston between April and October, allowing 4 days of "shore leave" in St. George. The *Norwegian Majesty* was "stretched" a whole new midsection length, gaining more than 33m (110 ft.) in size with an additional 220 new cabins added. There's a lot more deck space and a new casino and swimming pool, too. NCL's ships offer a great roster of activities and sports, both of the active and spectator variety. The ship even has sports bars with links to ESPN, so you won't miss the big game. NCL's latest innovation is what they call "Freestyle Cruising." As part of this concept, passengers are no longer assigned a dining time; instead they can eat at any time, in whichever dining room they choose, with whomever they choose, every night. Dinner dress code is "resort casual," with occasional dress-up nights that are completely optional. Not surprisingly, NCL tends to attract a somewhat younger, laid-back crowd. Most passengers are couples aged 25 to 60, with a fair number of honeymooners. Families with kids tend to show up during holidays.

- **Royal Caribbean Cruises, Ltd.** (*©* **800/327-6700;** www.rccl.com). Royal Caribbean sails its 1,600-passenger *Nordic Empress* on Bermuda runs from New York between May and October. The ship, built in 1990, has compact but well-designed cabins and a wide variety of entertainment, including a casino, a health spa, a children's program, and much more. Its onboard atmosphere is a little more high-energy than Celebrity and Princess, and roughly comparable to NCL. Stopovers include 2 days in St. George and 2½ days in Hamilton Harbour. You can find all walks of life on a Royal Caribbean cruise. The common denominator: passengers looking for fun and action in an attractive setting. Most passengers are couples, but there also tend to be plenty of families and singles on board as well. Overall, passengers are active, social, and looking for a good time, no matter what their age.

HOW TO GET THE BEST DEAL ON YOUR CRUISE

Cruise lines operate like airlines, setting rates for their cruises and then selling them in a rapid-fire series of discounts, offering almost whatever it takes to fill their ships. Because of this, great deals come and go in the blink of an eye, and most are available only through travel agents.

If you have a travel agent you trust, leave the details to him or her. If not, try contacting a travel agent who specializes in booking cruises. Some of the most likely contenders include the following: **Cruises, Inc.,** 1415 NW 62 St., Suite 205, Fort Lauderdale, FL 33009 (© **800/854-0500** or 954/958-3700; www.cruiseinc.com); **Cruises Only,** 1011 E. Colonial Dr., Orlando, FL 32803 (© **800/CRUISES** or 407/ 898-5353; www.cruisesonly.com); **The Cruise Company,** 10760 Q St., Omaha, NE 68127 (© **800/289-5505** or 402/339-6800; www.thecruise company.com); **Kelly Cruises,** 1315 W. 22nd St., Suite 105, Oak Brook, IL 60523 (© **800/837-7447** or 630/ 990-1111); **Hartford Holidays Travel,** 129 Hillside Ave., Williston Park, NY 11596 (© **800/828-4813** or 516/ 746-6670; www.hartfordholidays. com); and **Mann Travel** and **Cruises American Express,** 4400 Park Road, Charlotte, NC 28209 (© **800/ 849-2301** or 704/556-8311; www. travelcruises.com).

A FEW MONEY-SAVING TIPS

- **Book early:** You can often receive considerable savings on a 7-day cruise by booking early. Ask a travel agent or call the cruise line directly.
- **Book an inside cabin:** If you're trying to keep costs down, ask for an inside cabin (one without a window). They're often the same size and offer the same amenities as the more expensive outside cabins. If you're planning on using the space only to sleep, who needs a window?
- **Take advantage of senior discounts:** The cruise industry offers some discounts to seniors (usually defined as anyone 55 or older), so don't keep your age a secret. Membership in AARP, for example, can net you substantial discounts; always ask your travel agent about these types of discounts when you're booking.
- **Don't sail alone:** Cruise lines base their rates on double occupancy, so solo passengers usually pay between 150% and 200% of the per-person rate. If you're traveling alone, most lines have a program that allows two solo passengers to share a cabin.

13 Booking a Travel Package

Before you start your search for the lowest airfare, you may want to consider booking your flight as part of a package that includes accommodations. It's often possible to save serious money by going this route.

Package tours are not the same as escorted tours. They are simply a way to buy airfare and accommodations at the same time. For popular destinations like Bermuda, they are a smart way to go, because they save you a lot of money. In many cases, a package that includes airfare, hotel, and transportation to and from the airport costs less than the hotel alone would have if you had booked it yourself. That's because tour operators buy packages in bulk and resell them to the public at a cost that drastically undercuts standard rates.

Packages vary widely. Some offer a better class of hotels than others. Some offer the same hotels for lower prices. Some offer flights on scheduled airlines, while others book charters. In some packages, your choice of accommodations and travel days may be limited. Some packages let you choose between escorted vacations and independent vacations; others allow you to add on a few excursions or escorted day trips (also at lower prices than you could locate on your own) without booking an entirely escorted tour. Each destination usually has one or two packages

> **Tips   A Timesaving Tip**
>
> Shopping around for the right package can be time-consuming. To speed up the process, contact **TourScan Inc.,** P.O. Box 2367, Darien, CT 06820 (© **800/962-2080** or 203/655-8091; fax 203/655-6689; www.tourscan.com). It provides a computerized list of hotel and air package deals to Bermuda, The Bahamas, and the Caribbean. This organization usually has a range of offerings. Its twice-yearly *Island Vacation Catalog* contains complete details; the price ($4) is refunded if you book a tour. If you decide to take a tour, you can book it through TourScan or use any travel agent.

that are cheaper than the rest because they buy in even greater bulk. If you spend the time to shop around, you can save in the long run. Use the reviews in this guide to choose your hotel wisely.

RECOMMENDED PACKAGE TOUR OPERATORS

One good source of package deals is the airlines themselves. Most major airlines offer air/land packages, including **American Airlines Vacations** (© **800/321-2121;** http://aav1.aavacations.com), **Delta Vacations** (© **800/221-6666;** www.deltavacations.com), **US Airways Vacations** (© **800/455-0123** or 800/422-3861; www.usairwaysvacations.com), **Continental Airlines Vacations** (© **800/301-3800;** www.coolvacations.com), and **United Vacations** (© **888/854-3899;** www.unitedvacations.com).

Online Vacation Mall (© **800/839-9851;** www.onlinevacationmall.com) allows you to search for and book packages offered by a number of tour operators and airlines. The **United States Tour Operators Association**'s website (www.ustoa.com) has a search engine that allows you to look for operators that offer packages to a specific destination. Travel packages are also listed in the travel section of your local Sunday newspaper. **Liberty Travel** (© **888/271-1584;** www.libertytravel.com), one of the biggest packagers in the Northeast, often runs full-page ads in Sunday papers. Or check ads in national travel magazines such as *Arthur Frommer's Budget Travel Magazine, Travel & Leisure, National Geographic Traveler,* and *Condé Nast Traveler.*

14 Recommended Reading

Most of the books listed below have been printed in Bermuda. Thus, while they're readily available on the island, they may be hard to find in the United States and elsewhere.

THE MYSTERIOUS BERMUDA TRIANGLE

Many writers have attempted to explain the Bermuda Triangle. None has sufficiently done so yet, but all of the books make good reads for those of us intrigued by this tantalizing mystery.

The best of the lot is *The Bermuda Triangle Mystery Solved* (Prometheus Books) by Larry Kusche. It's a good read even though it doesn't "solve" the mystery. A mass market paperback, *Atlantis: Bermuda Triangle* (Berkley Pub Group) by Greg Donegan also digs into the puzzle, as does another paperback, *The Mystery of the Bermuda Triangle* (Heineman Library) by Chris Oxlade.

ART & ARCHITECTURE

For Bermuda style, both inside the house and outside, two books lead the pack: *Bermuda Antique Furniture and Silver,* published by Bermuda

National Trust, and *Architecture Bermuda Style,* by David R. Raine, issued by Pompano Publications.

DIVERS, HIKERS & SHIPWRECKS

Daniel Berg has written the finest book on the shipwrecks of Bermuda—a great choice for a diver to read before actually going under the water. It's called *Bermuda Shipwrecks: A Vacationing Diver's Guide to Bermuda's Shipwrecks* (Aqua Explorers).

Divers might also like to pick up a copy of *Marine Fauna and Flora of Bermuda* (John Wiley & Sons, Inc.), edited by Wolfgang Sterrer. Another good book for divers is *Diving Bermuda* (AquaQuest Publications, Inc.), part of the Aqua Quest Diving Series, this one authored by Jesse Concelmo and Michael Strohofer. It is the most up to date of all the sports guides to Bermuda, having come out in the spring of 2002.

Getting to Know Bermuda

Settling into Bermuda is relatively easy. First-timers soon learn that Bermuda isn't one island, as is commonly thought, but a string of islands linked by causeways and bridges—at least the 20 or so that are inhabited. The other islands can be reached by boat.

Bermuda is a prosperous island characterized by neat, trim houses that are a source of great pride to their owners. There won't be a casino at your megaresort—Bermuda has no casinos—and you'd better have your fill of Big Macs before you leave home. There are some fast-food joints, but nothing like those on the U.S. mainland, or even in The Bahamas. There's a sense of order in Bermuda, and everything seems to work efficiently, even when the weather's hot.

1 Arriving

BY PLANE

Planes arrive at the **Bermuda International Airport,** Kindley Field Road, St. George (© **441/293-2470**), 14.5km (9 miles) east of the City of Hamilton and about 27km (17 miles) east of Somerset at the far western end of Bermuda.

The flight from most East Coast destinations, including New York, Raleigh/Durham, Baltimore, and Boston, takes about 2 hours. Flights from Atlanta take 2½ hours; from Toronto it's less than 3 hours.

After clearing Customs (see "Entry Requirements & Customs," in chapter 2, "Planning Your Trip to Bermuda," for details), you can pick up tourist information at the airport before heading to your hotel. Because you aren't allowed to rent a car in Bermuda, and buses don't allow passengers to board with luggage, you must rely on a taxi or minivan to reach your hotel.

LEAVING THE AIRPORT BY TAXI OR MINIVAN

More than 600 taxis are available on Bermuda, and cabbies meet all arriving flights. Taxis are allowed to carry a maximum of four passengers. If you and your traveling companion have a lot of luggage, you will need the taxi to yourselves.

Including a tip of 10% to 15%, it costs about $30 to reach a destination in the City of Hamilton. The fare to St. George is about $30; to Tucker's Town, $25. To the southshore hotels, the charge is likely to be $26 to $33. To the West End, the charge is more than $45. Fares go up 25% between midnight and 6am, as well as all day on Sundays and holidays. Luggage carries a surcharge of 25¢ per piece. A meter determines the fare. Expect to pay about $4 for the first 1.5km (1 mile) and $3 for each additional 1.5km (1 mile).

There are several authorized taxi companies on the island, including **C.O.O.P.** (© **441/292-4476**), **Radio Cabs** (© **441/295-4141**), and **Sandys** (© **441/234-2344**).

It's cheaper for a party of four or more to call a minivan and split the cost, than to take two taxis (because usually only 2 people with luggage can fit into each taxi). Arrange for a minivan before you arrive by contacting **Bermuda**

Did You Know?

- More than 23,000 couples honeymoon on Bermuda each year.
- Bermudians imported the idea of moon gates—large rings of stone used as garden ornaments—from Asia centuries ago. Walking through a moon gate is supposed to bring good luck.
- This mysterious island inspired William Shakespeare's 1610 play, *The Tempest*.
- Somerset Bridge is the world's smallest drawbridge. At only 22 inches wide, the opening is just large enough for a ship's mast to pass through.
- Bermuda has more golf courses per square kilometer than any other place in the world; there are eight of them on the island's approximate 34 sq. km (54 sq. miles).
- Sir Brownlow Gray, the island's former chief justice, played the first game of tennis in the Western Hemisphere on Bermuda in 1873.
- With the arrival of spring comes the blossoming of Bermuda's Easter lilies, first brought to the island from Japan in the 18th century.
- Bermuda has no billboards: There is a ban on outdoor advertising and neon signs.

Hosts, 2 Kindley Field Rd., St. George CR 04 (© **441/293-1334**). This outfit can arrange to have a bus waiting for your flight. If you're part of a party of two people, you can ask a waiting bus at the airport if it has room to take on two extra passengers. Trips cost about $25 per person to the farthest hotel. Bermuda Hosts can provide transportation for golfers and can arrange sightseeing tours.

BY CRUISE SHIP

This is the easiest way to arrive in Bermuda. The staff presents you with a list of tour options long before you arrive in port, and almost everything is done for you, unless you opt to make your own arrangements (although an independent taxi tour is far more expensive than an organized tour). Most passengers book shore excursions at the same time they reserve their cruise.

Depending on your ship, you will probably arrive either in the City of Hamilton (best for shopaholics) or St. George (best for architecture and history buffs). A few ships also dock at the Royal Naval Dockyard on Bermuda's West End. Whatever port you dock at, you can avail yourself of the waiting taxis near your ship, or rent a moped or bicycle (see "Getting Around," later in this chapter) and do some touring and shopping on your own. For more information about cruising to Bermuda, see p. 43.

2 Orienting Yourself: The Lay of the Land

For administrative purposes, the islands of Bermuda are divided into **parishes,** all named for shareholders of the original 1610 Bermuda Company. From west to east, they are:

SANDYS PARISH

In the far western part of the archipelago, Sandys (pronounced *sands*) Parish encompasses the islands of **Ireland, Boaz,** and **Somerset.** This parish (named for Sir Edwin Sandys, a major shareholder of the 1610 Bermuda Company) centers in Somerset Village, on Somerset Island. Sandys Parish is often called Somerset.

Some visitors to Bermuda head directly for Sandys Parish and spend their entire time here; they feel that the far western tip, with its rolling hills, lush countryside, and tranquil bays, is something special and unique. (This area has always stood apart from the rest of Bermuda: During the U.S. Civil War, when most Bermudians sympathized with the Confederates, Sandys Parish supported the Union.) Sandys Parish has areas of great natural beauty, including **Somerset Long Bay,** the biggest and best public beach in the West End (which the Bermuda Audubon Society is developing into a nature preserve), and **Mangrove Bay,** a protected beach in the heart of **Somerset Village.** Try a walk around the old village; it's filled with typically Bermudian houses and shops. On Somerset Road is the **Scaur Lodge Property,** whose waterfront hillside is open daily at no charge.

If you want to be near the shops, restaurants, and pubs of the City of Hamilton, you may want to stay in a more central location and visit Sandys Parish on a day trip. However, the parish's isolation is part of its charm for those who prefer tranquillity and unspoiled nature to shopping or lingering over an extra pint in a pub. This is the perfect parish for couples seeking privacy and romance.

An advantage of staying here is that Sandys has several embarkation points for various types of sea excursions. The parish also boasts some of the most elegant places to stay in Bermuda. You can commute to the City of Hamilton by ferry, although it's a bit time consuming, especially if your days on Bermuda are limited.

SOUTHAMPTON PARISH

Southampton Parish (named for the third earl of Southampton) is a narrow strip of land opening at its northern edge onto Little Sound and on its southern shore onto the Atlantic Ocean. It stretches from Riddells Bay to Tucker's Island, and is split by Middle Road.

If dining at waterfront restaurants and staying at big resort hotels is part of your Bermuda dream, then Southampton is your parish; it's the site of such famed resorts as The Fairmont Southampton Princess and the Sonesta Beach Resort. Southampton is also the best place to stay if you plan to spend a great deal of time on the island's fabled pink, sandy beaches. Among Southampton's jewels is **Horseshoe Bay,** one of Bermuda's most attractive public beaches, with changing rooms, a snack bar, and space for parking.

Southampton lacks the intimacy and romance of Sandys, but it has a lot of razzle-dazzle going for it. It's the top choice for a golfing holiday. If you like to sightsee, you can easily occupy 2 days just exploring the parish's many attractions. It also has more nightlife than Sandys—although not as much as the City of Hamilton.

Tips **Visitor Information on the Island**

You can get answers to most of your questions at the Visitors Service Bureau locations at the **Ferry Terminal,** Hamilton (✆ **441/295-1480**); **King's Square,** St. George (✆ **441/297-1642**); and the **Royal Naval Dockyard** (✆ **441/234-3824**). The offices are open Sunday to Friday from 9am to 5pm.

Bermuda's Parishes

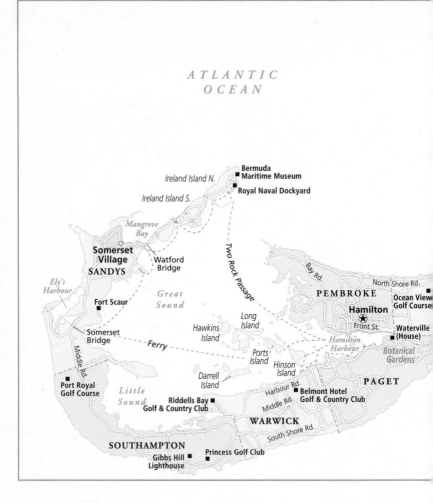

WARWICK PARISH

Named in honor of the second earl of Warwick, this parish lies in the heart of Great Bermuda Island. Like Southampton, it is known for its long stretches of rosy sand. Along the south shore is **Warwick Long Bay,** one of Bermuda's best public beaches. Warwick also offers parklands bordering the sea, winding country roads, two golf courses, and a number of natural attractions. This area is the best on the island for horseback riding, which is the ideal way to see pastoral Bermuda up close.

Warwick is a great choice for visitors seeking cottage or apartment rentals (where you can do some of your own cooking to cut down on the outrageous expense of food). The parish is not strong on restaurants; one of its disadvantages is that you have to travel a bit if you like to dine out. Nightlife is also spotty—just about the only action you can find after dark is in hotel lounges. This parish is for tranquillity-seekers, but because of its more central location, it doesn't offer quite the seclusion Sandys does.

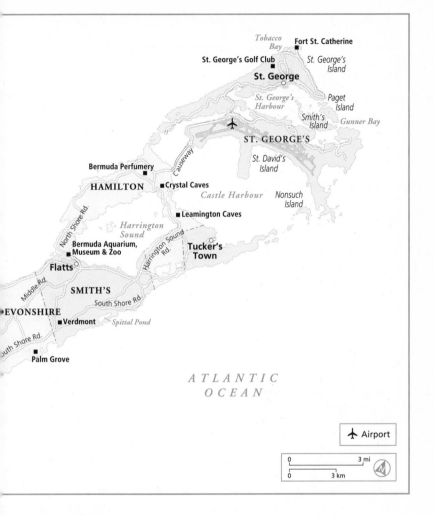

Tobacco Bay
Fort St. Catherine
St. George's Golf Club
St. George's Island
St. George
St. George's Harbour
Paget Island
Smith's Island
Gunner Bay
ST. GEORGE'S
Bermuda Perfumery
Causeway
HAMILTON
Crystal Caves
St. David's Island
Castle Harbour
Nonsuch Island
Leamington Caves
Harrington Sound
North Shore Rd.
Harrington Sound Rd.
Bermuda Aquarium, Museum & Zoo
Tucker's Town
Flatts
Middle Rd.
SMITH'S
South Shore Rd.
•EVONSHIRE
Verdmont
Spittal Pond
outh Shore Rd.
Palm Grove

ATLANTIC OCEAN

✈ Airport

0   3 mi
0   3 km

PAGET PARISH

Paget Parish lies directly south of the capital City of Hamilton, separated from it by Hamilton Harbour. Named after the fourth Lord Paget, it has many residences and historic homes and it's also the site of the 15-hectare (36-acre) **Botanical Gardens.** But the southshore beaches—the best in the chain of islands—are what draw visitors here in droves. In spring, the Elbow Beach Hotel is the center of most College Week (spring break) activities. Paget Parish is also the site of **Chelston,** on Grape Bay Drive, the official residence of the U.S. consul general. Situated on 5¾ hectares (14½ acres) of landscaped grounds, it's open only during the Garden Club's Home and Garden Tours in the spring (see "Bermuda Calendar of Events," in chapter 2, "Planning Your Trip to Bermuda," for details).

This is one of the best parishes to stay in—it has many excellent accommodations, including Elbow Beach Hotel. It's close enough to the City of Hamilton for an easy commute, but far enough away to escape the hordes. Because public transportation is all-important (you can't rent a car), Paget is a good place to situate yourself; it has some of the best and most convenient ferry connections and bus schedules. There are docks at Salt Kettle, Hodson's, and Lower Ferry; you can even "commute" by ferry to Warwick Parish or Sandys Parish to the west. Paget's relatively flat terrain, rural lanes, and streets lined with old mansions make this an ideal place for biking. Hikers will find many small trails bordering the sea.

If you don't like big resort hotels, you can find many rental cottages and several little guesthouses here. Unlike Warwick, Paget has a number of dining choices. Elbow Beach offers the most, but other fine options include Fourways Inn and Paraquet Restaurant. Most of the parish's nightlife centers on Elbow Beach.

There are no major disadvantages to staying in Paget. You will find over-crowded beaches during spring break, though, and congestion in the City of Hamilton in the summer, when many cruise ships arrive.

PEMBROKE PARISH

This parish (named after the third earl of Pembroke) houses one-quarter of Bermuda's population. It is home to the **City of Hamilton,** Bermuda's capital and its only full-fledged city. The parish opens at its northern rim onto the vast Atlantic Ocean and on its southern side onto Hamilton Harbour; its western border is on Great Sound. The City of Hamilton is the first destination that most cruise ship passengers will see.

This parish is not ideal for those seeking a tranquil holiday. Pembroke Parish, already packed with the island's greatest population density, also attracts the most visitors. The little city is especially crowded when cruise ships are in the harbor and travelers pour into the stores and restaurants. Yet for those who like to pub-crawl English style, shop until they drop, and have access to the largest concentration of dining choices, Pembroke—the City of Hamilton in particu-lar—is without equal on Bermuda.

Whether or not you stay in Pembroke, try to fit a shopping (or window-shopping) stroll along Front Street into your itinerary. The area also boasts a number of sightseeing attractions, most of which are easily accessible on foot (a plus because you don't have to depend on taxis, bikes, or scooters—which can get to be a bit of a bore after a while). Nightlife is the finest on the island. Don't expect splashy Las Vegas–type revues, however; instead, think restaurants, pubs, and small clubs.

DEVONSHIRE PARISH

Lying east of Paget and Pembroke parishes, near the geographic center of the archipelago, Devonshire Parish (named for the first earl of Devonshire) is green and hilly. It has some housekeeping (self-catering) apartments, a cottage colony, and one of Bermuda's oldest churches, the **Old Devonshire Parish Church,** which dates from 1716. Three of Bermuda's major roads traverse the parish: the aptly named South Shore Road, Middle Road, and North Shore Road. As you wander its narrow lanes, you can, with some imagination, picture yourself in the parish's namesake county of Devon, England.

Golfers flock to Devonshire to play at the **Ocean View Golf Course.** Along North Shore Road, near the border of Pembroke Parish, is **Devonshire Dock,** long a seafarer's haven. In fact, during the War of 1812, British soldiers came to Devonshire Dock to be entertained by local women. Today, fishers still bring in grouper and rockfish, so you can shop for dinner if you're staying at a nearby cottage with a kitchen.

Tips Finding an Address

The island chain of Bermuda doesn't follow a rigid system of street addresses. Most hotels, even in official government listings, don't bother to include an address, although they do include post-office boxes and zip codes. Bermudians just assume that everybody knows where everything is, which is fine if you've lived on Bermuda all your life. But if you're a first-time visitor, get a good map before setting out—and don't be shy about asking directions. Most people are very helpful.

Most of the establishments you'll be seeking are on some street plan. However, some places use numbers in their street addresses, and others—perhaps their neighbors—don't. The actual building number is not always important, because a building such as a resort hotel is likely to be set back so far from the main road that you couldn't see its number anyway. Look for signs with the name of the hotel rather than the street number. Cross streets will also aid you in finding an address.

Devonshire has a number of unspoiled nature areas. The **arboretum** on Montpelier Road is one of the most tranquil oases on Bermuda. This open space, created by the Department of Agriculture, Fisheries, and Parks, is home to a wide range of Bermudian plant and tree life, especially conifers, palms, and other subtropical trees. Along South Shore Road, west of the junction with Collector's Hill, is the **Edmund Gibbons Nature Reserve.** This portion of marshland, owned by the National Trust, provides living space for a number of birds and rare species of Bermuda flora.

Devonshire is one of the sleepy residential parishes, known for its hilly interior, beautiful landscape, and fabulous estates bordering the sea. There's little sightseeing here; all those stunning private estates aren't open to the public, so unless you get a personal invite, you're out of luck. But the parish is right in Bermuda's geographic center, so it's an ideal place to base yourself if you'd like to explore both the West End and the East End. There are two major drawbacks: With a few notable exceptions, the parish has very few places to stay and almost no dining choices.

SMITH'S PARISH

Named for Sir Thomas Smith, this parish faces the open sea to the north and south. To the east is Harrington Sound; to the west, bucolic Devonshire Parish.

The parish encompasses **Flatts Village,** one of the island's most charming parish towns (take bus no. 10 or 11 from the City of Hamilton). It was a smugglers' port for about 200 years and served as the center of power for a coterie of successful "planter politicians" and landowners. Flatts Village's government was second in importance to that of St. George, which was Bermuda's capital at the time. People gathered at the rickety Flatts Bridge to "enjoy" such public entertainment as hangings; if the offense was serious enough, victims were drawn and quartered here. From Flatts Village, you have panoramic views of both the inlet and Harrington Sound. At the top of McGall's Hill is St. Mark's Church, based on the same designs used for the Old Devonshire Parish Church.

Most visitors view Smith's Parish as a day trip or a half-day trip, although the parish does have places to stay, such as the Pink Beach Club and Cottages. Dining choices are extremely limited, however, unless you stick to the hotels. Again, if you're seeking lots of nighttime diversion, you'll have to go to another parish. Because the **Spittal Pond Nature Reserve** is here, many nature lovers prefer Smith's to the more populated parishes. Basically, Smith's Parish is for the visitor who wants serenity and tranquillity but not at the celestial prices charged at the "cottages" of Sandys.

HAMILTON PARISH

Not to be confused with the City of Hamilton (which is in Pembroke Parish), Hamilton Parish lies directly north of Harrington Sound, opening onto the Atlantic. It's bordered on the east by St. George and on the southwest by Smith's Parish. Named for the second marquis of Hamilton, the parish surrounds Harrington Sound, a saltwater lake stretching some 10km (6 miles). On its eastern periphery, the parish opens onto Castle Harbour.

The big attractions here are the **Bermuda Aquarium,** the **Crystal Caves,** and **Leamington Caves.** Scuba diving and other water sports are also very popular in the area.

Around **Harrington Sound,** the sights differ greatly from those of nearby St. George (see below). You'll find activities like fishing, swimming, sunfish sailing, and kayaking at Harrington Sound, but it doesn't offer the historical exploration that St. George does. Some experts believe that Harrington Sound was a prehistoric cave that fell in. Harrington Sound's known gateway to the ocean is an inlet at Flatts Village (see "Smith's Parish," above). However, evidence suggests that there are underwater passages as well—several deep-sea fish have been caught in the sound.

For the best panoramic view of the north shore, head for **Crawl Hill,** the highest place in Hamilton Parish, just before you come to Bailey's Bay. Crawl is a corruption of the word *kraal,* which is where turtles were kept before slaughter. **Shelly Bay,** named for one of the passengers of the *Sea Venture,* is the longest beach along the north shore.

At Bailey's Bay, **Tom Moore's Jungle** consists of wild woods. The poet Tom Moore is said to have spent many hours writing verse here under a calabash tree (which is still standing). The jungle is now held in private trust, so you must obtain permission to enter it. It's much easier to pay your respects to the Romantic poet by going to Tom Moore's Tavern (see "Hamilton Parish" in chapter 5, "Where to Dine").

Although the parish has some major resorts, such as Grotto Bay Beach Hotel, most visitors come here for sightseeing only. We have to agree: Hamilton is a good place to go exploring for a day or half-day, but you're better off staying elsewhere. If you stay here, you'll spend a great deal of your holiday time commuting into the City of Hamilton or St. George. Bus no. 1 or 3 from the City of Hamilton gets you here in about an hour.

ST. GEORGE PARISH

At Bermuda's extreme eastern end, this historic parish encompasses several islands. The parish borders Castle Harbour on its western and southern edges; St. George's Harbour divides it into two major parts, **St. George's Island** and **St. David's Island.** A causeway links St. David's Island to the rest of Bermuda, and St. George's is also linked by road. Many parish residents are longtime sailors and fishers. St. George Parish also includes **Tucker's Town** (founded in 1616 by Gov. Daniel Tucker), on the opposite shore of Castle Harbour.

Settled in 1612, the **town of St. George** was once the capital of Bermuda; the City of Hamilton succeeded it in 1815. The town was settled 3 years after Sir

---

(Tips **Finding Your Way**

We've included bulleted maps throughout this book to help you locate Bermuda's accommodations, restaurants, beaches, and sights. There's also a handy full-color foldout map in the back of the book.

The Bermuda Department of Tourism publishes a free *Bermuda Handy Reference Map.* The tiny pocket map, distributed by the tourist office and available at most hotels, includes an overview and orientation map of Bermuda, highlighting its major attractions, golf courses, public beaches, and hotels. (It does not, however, pinpoint individual restaurants unless they are attached to hotels.) On the other side is a detailed street plan of the City of Hamilton, indicating all its major landmarks and service facilities, such as the ferry terminal and the post office. There's also a detailed map of the Royal Naval Dockyard, the West End, and the East End, plus tips on transportation—ferries, taxis, buses—and other helpful hints, such as a depiction of various traffic signs. For exact locations of Visitors Service Bureau locations where you can pick up a copy of the *Bermuda Handy Reference Map,* see the "Visitor Information on the Island" box, above.

George Somers and his shipwrecked party of English sailors came ashore in 1609. (After Admiral Somers died in Bermuda in 1610, his heart was buried in the St. George area, while the rest of his body was taken home to England for burial.) Founded by Richard Moore, of the newly created Bermuda Company, and a band of 60 colonists, St. George was the second English settlement in the New World, after Jamestown, Virginia. Its coat of arms depicts St. George (England's patron saint) and a dragon.

Almost 4 centuries of history come alive here. Generations upon generations of sailors have set forth from its sheltered harbor. St. George even played a role in the American Revolution: Bermuda depended on the American colonies for food, and when war came, supplies grew dangerously low. Although Bermuda was a British colony, the loyalties of its people were divided, because many Bermudians had relatives living on the American mainland. A delegation headed by Col. Henry Tucker went to Philadelphia to petition the Continental Congress to trade food and supplies for salt. George Washington had a different idea. He needed gunpowder, and a number of kegs of it were stored at St. George. Without the approval of the British Bermudian governor, the parties struck a deal. The gunpowder was trundled aboard American warships waiting in the harbor of Tobacco Bay under cover of darkness. In return, the grateful colonies supplied Bermuda with food.

Although St. George still evokes a feeling of the past, it's actively inhabited. When cruise ships are in port, it's likely to be overrun with visitors. Many people prefer to visit St. George at night, when they can walk around and enjoy it in relative peace and quiet. You won't be able to enter any of the sightseeing attractions, but they're of minor importance. After dark, a mood of enchantment settles over the place: It's like a storybook village.

Would you want to live here for a week? Probably not. Once you've seen the glories of the town of St. George—which you can do in a day—you're inconveniently isolated at the easternmost end of Bermuda for the rest of your stay. Several chains, including Club Med, have tried and failed to make a go of it here. Accommodations are extremely limited, although there are a number of restaurants (many of which, frankly, are mediocre). For history buffs, no place in Bermuda tops St. George. But as a parish to base yourself in, you might do better in the more centrally located and activity-filled Pembroke or Southampton parishes. As for nightlife in St. George, you can always go to a pub on King's Square.

BERMUDA IN A NUTSHELL: SUGGESTED SIGHTSEEING ITINERARIES FOR 1 TO 5 DAYS

You may be eager to start exploring right away, especially if your time is short. Below is a suggested itinerary for the first 5 days. A week's visit will let you break up your sightseeing trips with time on the beach, boating, or engaging in some of the island's other outdoor pursuits, such as golf or scuba diving. Hitting the beach is the first priority for most visitors—but you don't need us to tell you how to schedule your time in the sun!

If You Have 1 Day

If you have only 1 day for sightseeing, we suggest you spend it in the historic former capital of **St. George,** a maze of narrow streets with quaint names: Featherbed Alley, Duke of York Street, Petticoat Lane, Old Maid's Lane, and Duke of Kent Street. You can spend a day exploring British-style pubs, seafood restaurants, shops (several major City of Hamilton stores have branches here), old forts, museums, and churches. You can even see stocks, a ducking stool, and a pillory, all used generations ago to humiliate wrongdoers.

And what would a day in Bermuda be without time spent on the beach? **Elbow Beach** and **Warwick Long Bay** are among the most appealing spots. The no. 7 bus will take you there from St. George.

If You Have 2 Days

Spend **Day 1** as indicated above. Devote **Day 2** to sightseeing and shopping in the City of Hamilton. If you're staying in Paget or Warwick, a ferry from either parish will take you right into the city. For many visitors, the City of Hamilton's shops are its most compelling attraction. Try to time your visit to avoid the arrival of cruise ships; on those days, the stores and restaurants in the city can really get crowded. You can obtain a schedule of cruise ship arrivals and departures from the tourist office.

If you took our advice and went to the beach yesterday, try a different one today. After all, Bermuda isn't just about sightseeing and shopping—it's about those marvelous pink sands, too.

If You Have 3 Days

Spend **Days 1 and 2** as outlined above. On **Day 3,** take the ferry from the City of Hamilton across Great Sound to Somerset. Carry your cycle on the boat—you'll need it later (see "Getting Around," below, for details on rentals). You'll disembark at the western end of Somerset Island in Sandys Parish, where you'll find the smallest drawbridge in the world. It's easy to spend an hour walking around Somerset Village. Then head west on foot or on bicycle until you reach Somerset Long Bay beach, along the northern rim of the island.

Sandys Parish has several places for lunch (see chapter 5, "Where to Dine"). The **Somerset Country Squire Tavern,** a typical village inn near the Watford Bridge ferry stop at the western end of the island, is one of the best.

After lunch, hop on your bicycle and cross Watford Bridge to **Ireland Island,** home of the **Royal Naval Dockyard** and the **Maritime Museum.** On your way back to Somerset Bridge and the ferry back to the City of Hamilton, you might take the turnoff to Fort Scaur; from **Scaur Hill,** you'll have a commanding view of Ely's Harbour and Great Sound. If you don't want to go through Somerset again, the ferry at Watford Bridge will also take you back to the City of Hamilton.

If You Have 4 or 5 Days

Spend **Days 1 through 3** as outlined above. Make **Day 4** a beach day. Head for **Horseshoe Bay beach,** in Southampton Parish, in the morning. Spend most of your time there, exploring hidden coves in all directions. Have lunch right on the beach at a concession stand. In the afternoon, visit **Gibbs Hill Lighthouse.** After a rest at your hotel, sample some Bermudian nightlife.

On **Day 5,** conclude your stay with an excursion to **Flatts Village,** which lies in the eastern sector of Smith's Parish. Explore the **Bermuda Aquarium, Natural History Museum & Zoo;** and consider an undersea walk (see the "A Look Under Bermuda's Waters" box in chapter 6, "Fun in the Surf & Sun").

Have lunch at the **Inlet Restaurant,** in the Palmetto Hotel, then visit **Elbow Beach.** After relaxing over afternoon tea at one of the hotels, arrange to see a show—perhaps gombey dancing, if it's scheduled—in the evening.

3 Getting Around

Driving is on the left, and the national speed limit is 32kmph (20 mph) in the countryside, 24kmph (15 mph) in busier areas. Cars are limited to one per resident family—and visitors are not allowed to rent cars at all. You'll rely on taxis, bikes, motorized bicycles called "putt-putts," and maybe even a romantic, colorful, fringe-topped surrey.

BY TAXI

Dozens of taxis roam the island, and virtually every hotel, restaurant, and shop is happy to call one for you. The hourly charge is $30 for one to four passengers. A luxury tour van accommodating up to six passengers costs $42 an hour. If you want to use one for a sightseeing tour, the minimum is 3 hours.

BY MOTORBIKE

Bermuda is the only Atlantic island that restricts car ownership to local residents. Part of the reason for this is the notoriously narrow roads, which have small or nonexistent shoulders and hundreds of blind curves. Add frequent rainfall and the British custom of driving on the left, and there would be traffic chaos if newcomers were allowed to take to the roads in rented cars.

The resulting dependence on cabs and rented motor scooters, mopeds, and bicycles is simply a fact of Bermudian life that newcomers quickly accept as part of the island's charm. Although not having a car at your disposal is inconvenient, the island's tourist brochures make it seem just wonderful: A happy couple

Tips Taxi Touring Tip

When a taxi has a blue flag on its hood (locals call the hood the "bonnet"), the driver is qualified to serve as a **tour guide.** The government checks out and tests these drivers, so you should use them if you plan to tour Bermuda by taxi. "Blue-bonnet" drivers charge no more than regular taxi drivers.

For a radio-dispatched cab, call **C.O.O.P.** (© 441/292-4476).

bicycling or mopeding around Bermuda on a sunny day, slowly putt-putting across the islands.

What the brochures don't tell you is that the roads are too narrow, and Bermudians—who are likely to own cars, and pay dearly for the privilege—feel that the road is theirs. Sometimes it starts raining almost without warning, but the skies usually clear rapidly, and the roads dry quickly. During inclement weather, scooter riders are likely to be edged close—sometimes disturbingly close—to the shoulder; in the aftermath of rainstorms, they'll almost certainly be splattered with water or mud. Many accidents occur on slippery roads after a rain, especially involving those not accustomed to using a motor scooter.

Who should rent a moped or scooter, and who should avoid them altogether? Frankly, the answer depends on your physical fitness and the time of day. Even the most stiffly starched might find a wind-whipped morning ride from the hotel to the beach or tennis courts invigorating and fun. Dressed to the nines for a candlelit dinner, you'd find the experience horrifying. And although the putt-putters can be a lot of fun during a sunny day, the machines can be dangerous and capricious after dark—and, of course, when you've had too many daiquiris. Not everyone is fit enough. Visitors on mopeds have a high accident rate, with at least some of the problems related to driving on the left.

Considering the hazards, we usually recommend that reasonably adept sports enthusiasts rent a moped for a day or two. For evening outings, we firmly believe that a taxi is the way to go.

What are the requirements for renting a motorbike? You must be 16 or older. Some vehicles are big enough for two cozy adults. Helmets are required, and rental companies must provide them. Know in advance that on a hot day, they're uncomfortable. But, what the heck—you'll be at the beach soon enough.

What's the difference between a moped and a motor scooter? Many visitors rent one or the other and never really understand the difference. They're basically alike, with equivalent maximum speeds and horsepower. Mopeds have larger wheels than scooters, and subject riders to fewer shocks as they traverse bumps in the road. Most (but not all) mopeds are designed for one rider; scooters accommodate either a single passenger or two passengers riding in tandem.

There are quite a few gas stations (called "petrol stations"). Once you "tank up" your motorbike, chances are you'll have plenty of gas to get you to your destination; for example, one tank of gas in a motorbike will take you from Somerset in the west to St. George in the east.

Among the rental companies listed below, there's a tendency toward price-fixing. Rental fees across the island tend to be roughly equivalent, and shopping around for a better deal is usually a waste of time. Mopeds for one rider rent for $45 for the first day, $65 for 2 days, $78 for 3 days, and $119 for 7 days. Scooters for two riders cost $53 to $62 for 1 day. You must pay with a major credit card; it serves as a deposit in case of damage or theft. You must also purchase a one-time insurance policy for $18. The insurance is valid for the length of the rental.

You can rent mopeds and scooters at **Wheels** (© 441/292-2245), which has two locations on Front Street in the City of Hamilton; one at Flatts Village; and at the following resorts: the Fairmont Hamilton Princess, the Sonesta Beach Resort, Grotto Bay Hotel, the Stonington Beach Resort, White Sands Hotel & Cottages, and Horizons and Cottages. You'll find comparable prices at **Concord Cycle Shop,** at The Fairmont Southampton Princess (© 441/238-3336).

Island-Hopping on Your Own

Most first-time visitors think of Bermuda as one island, but in fact it's a small archipelago. Many of the islands that make up the chain are uninhabited. If you're a bit of a skipper, you can explore them on your own. With a little guidance and the proper maps, you can discover small islands, out-of-the-way coral reefs, and hidden coves that seem straight from the old Brooke Shields B-movie, *The Blue Lagoon*.

For this boating adventure, rent a Boston whaler with an outboard engine. The name of these small but sturdy boats reveals their origins: New Englanders once used them in their pursuit of Moby Dick. It's important to exercise caution, remembering that the English found Bermuda in 1612 only after the *Sea Venture*, en route to the Jamestown Colony, was wrecked off the Bermuda coast.

In the East End, you can explore Castle Harbour, which is almost completely surrounded by islands, forming a protected lake. If you stop to do some fishing, snapper is your likely catch. (Visitors who rent condos or apartments often take their quarry back to their kitchenette to prepare it for dinner.) To avoid the often-powerful swells, drop anchor on the west side of Castle Harbour, near Castle Harbour Golf Club and Tucker's Town. Then head across Tucker's Town Bay to Castle Island and Castle Island Nature Reserve. In 1612, Governor Moore ordered the construction of a fort on Castle Island, the ruins of which you can see today.

In the West End, begin your exploration by going under Somerset Bridge into well-protected Ely's Harbour. To the north, you can visit Cathedral Rocks before making a half-circle to Somerset Village; from here, you can explore the uninhabited islands off Mangrove Bay.

You can rent a 4m to 4.5m (13-ft.–15-ft.) Boston whaler—and pick up some local guidance—at **Blue Hole Water Sports,** Grotto Bay Beach Hotel, Hamilton Parish (✆ **441/293-2915**). Prices begin at $65 for 2 hours, $110 for 4 hours, and $165 for 8 hours. Rates do not include gas.

Oleander Cycles Ltd., Valley Road, P.O. Box 114, Paget Parish (✆ **441/236-5235**), rents only scooters. A first day rental for a single seater is $35; $45 for double. Subsequent days have price reductions depending on the length of rental. There is an additional $20 charge for deposit and another $20 for insurance. There are also locations on Gorham Road in the City of Hamilton (✆ **441/295-0919**), and at Middle Road in Southampton (✆ **441/234-0629**). All locations are open daily from 8:30am to 5:30pm. Rentals require a $20 deposit.

Eve's Cycle Livery, 114 Middle Rd., Paget Parish (✆ **441/236-6247**), rents a variety of scooters; they cost $42 to $60 for the first day, and $181 to $250 for 7 days, depending on the model, with successively lower prices for each additional day.

BY BICYCLE

Looking for a more natural means of locomotion than a putt-putt? You can rent bikes at most cycle liveries (see "By Motorbike," above), but for cyclists who don't work out 6 hours a day, pedaling a bike up Bermuda's steep hills can be a bit of a challenge. Prices start from $15 a day, depending on your steed's brand name and degree of stylishness. **Eve's Cycle Livery,** 114 Middle Rd., Paget Parish (© **441/236-6247**), offers one of the best rental deals on the island. Named after the legendary matriarch who founded the company more than 40 years ago, Eve's rents men's and women's pedal bicycles (usually 10- to 12-speed mountain bikes, well suited to the island's hilly terrain). They go for $20 for the first day, $15 for the second day, and $10 for the third day. The shop is a 10-minute taxi ride (or a leisurely 20-min. cycle) west of the City of Hamilton. As with motorbiking, exercise caution because roads are narrow and often slippery, and scooter riders and left-hand driving can make things confusing. See "Biking," in chapter 6, "Fun in the Surf & Sun," for more details.

BY BUS

You can't rent a car. Taxis are expensive. Horse-drawn carriages aren't really a viable option. You may not want to ride a bicycle or a motorbike. What's left for getting around Bermuda? Buses, of course.

The bus network covers all major routes, and nearly all hotels, guesthouses, and restaurants have bus stops close by. There's even a do-it-yourself sightseeing tour by bus and ferry. Regularly scheduled buses go to most of the destinations that interest visitors in Bermuda, but be prepared to wait. Some buses don't run on Sundays and holidays, so be sure you know the schedule for the trip you want to make.

Bermuda is divided into 14 zones of about 3km (2 miles) each. The regular cash fare for up to three zones is $3. For more than three zones, it's $4.50. Children 5 to 16 pay $1 for all zones; children under 5 ride free. *Note:* You must have the exact change or tokens ready to deposit in the fare box as you board the bus. Drivers do not make change or accept bills. On the run from the City of Hamilton to the Royal Naval Dockyard (no. 7 or 8), the fare is $4.50 for adults, $1 for children.

You can purchase $4 tokens at branch post offices or at the **Central Bus Terminal** on Washington Street in the City of Hamilton, where all routes, except route 6, begin and end. The terminal is just off Church Street, a few steps east of City Hall. You can get there from Front Street or Reid Street by going up Queen Street or through Walker Arcade and Washington Mall.

If you plan to travel a lot, you might want to purchase a booklet of 15 tickets. A booklet of 14-zone tickets costs $26; of 3-zone tickets, $16. For children, 15 tickets cost $7, regardless of the number of zones. You can buy the booklets at post offices or the central bus terminal. You can also purchase passes that allow travel for 1 day to 1 month. A 1-day pass costs $11, a 1-week pass is $36, and a 1-month pass is $45.

For more information on bus service, call © **441/292-3854.**

In the east, **St. George's Mini-Bus Service** (© **441/297-8199**) operates a minibus service around St. George Parish and St. David's Island. The basic one-way fare is $2. Buses depart from King's Square in the center of St. George, and can be flagged down along the road. Service is year-round, daily from 7:30am to midnight.

Trolleylike **buses** that seat 60 serve the capital of Hamilton (the city) and the Royal Naval Dockyard. Passengers can get on and off throughout the day for a single fare of $10. The City of Hamilton trolley stops at the major points of interest, including the Botanical Gardens; the dockyard bus calls at the crafts market. Tickets are sold at most hotels, the City of Hamilton train station, and the Oleander cycle shop (see "By Motorbike" above). For bus routes, see the map on the inside back cover.

BY FERRY

One of the most interesting ways of getting around Bermuda is the government-operated ferry service. Ferries crisscross Great Sound between the City of Hamilton and Somerset; the one-way fare is $4. They also take the harbor route, from the City of Hamilton to the hotel-filled parishes of Paget and Warwick. The ride from the City of Hamilton to Paget costs $2.50. On all routes, children 5 to 16 pay $1, and children under 5 ride free. Motorbikes and bicycles are allowed on the City of Hamilton to Somerset run for $4.

For ferry service information, call © **441/295-4506** in the City of Hamilton. Ferry schedules are posted at each landing and are available at the Ferry Terminal, the Central Bus Terminal in the City of Hamilton, and most hotels.

BY HORSE-DRAWN CARRIAGE

Once upon a time, this was the only way a tourist could get around Bermuda. Before 1946 (when automobiles first came to the island), horses were the principal means of transportation. Today they are available only for those into the romance and nostalgia of yesteryear. They don't take you to any unusual places, instead they trot along routes that both the driver and horses know too well. You can book one of the four-wheeled rigs for a chauffeured tour of the island's midsection.

Drivers congregate on Front Street in the City of Hamilton, adjacent to the no. 1 passenger terminal near the cruise-ship docks. A single carriage (accommodating 1–4 passengers) drawn by one horse costs $30 for 30 minutes. An additional 30 minutes costs another $30. If the carriage picks you up, the cost is $40 for the first 30 minutes. For rides lasting more than 3 hours, the fee is negotiable. Contact **Terceira's Stables** at © **441/236-3014.**

 FAST FACTS: **Bermuda**

American Express The representative in the City of Hamilton, **Meyer Agencies,** 35 Church St. (P.O. Box 510), Hamilton HM 12 (© **441/295-4176**), provides complete travel service, traveler's checks, and emergency check cashing.

Banks The main offices of Bermuda's three banks are in the City of Hamilton. All banks and their branches are open Monday from 9:30am to 4pm, Tuesday to Friday from 8:30am to 4:30pm. Banks are closed Saturday, Sunday, and public holidays. Many big hotels will cash traveler's checks, and there are ATMs all around the island.

The **Bank of Bermuda Ltd.,** 6 Front St., Hamilton (© **441/295-4000**), has branches on Church Street, Hamilton; Par-la-Ville Road, Hamilton; King's Square, St. George; and in Somerset.

The **Bank of N.T. Butterfield & Son, Ltd.,** 65 Front St., Hamilton (© **441/295-1111**), has several branches, including locations in St. George and Somerset.

The **Bermuda Commercial Bank Ltd.** is at 43 Victoria St., Hamilton (© **441/295-5678**).

Bookstores **Bermuda Book Store (Baxters) Ltd.,** Queen Street, Hamilton (© **441/295-3698**), stocks everything that's in print about Bermuda, including titles on gardening, flowers, local characters, poets, and other topics; some books are available only through this store. There are also many English publications not easily obtainable in the United States, as well as a fine selection of children's books. You can also buy maps, prints, and that beach novel you forgot to bring. Open Monday to Saturday from 8am to 6pm.

Business Hours Most businesses are open Monday to Friday from 9am to 5pm. Stores are generally open Monday to Saturday from 9am to 5pm; several shops open at 9:15am. A few shops are also open in the evening, but usually only when big cruise ships are in port.

Car Rentals There are no car-rental agencies in Bermuda because visitors are not allowed to rent cars. For transportation information, see "Getting Around," earlier in this chapter.

Climate See "When to Go," in chapter 2, "Planning Your Trip to Bermuda."

Crime See "Safety," below.

Currency Exchange Because the U.S. dollar and the Bermuda dollar are on par, both currencies can be used. It's not necessary to convert U.S. dollars into Bermuda dollars. Canadian dollars and British pounds must be converted into local currency. For more information, see "Money," in chapter 2, "Planning Your Trip to Bermuda."

Customs For details on what you can bring into Bermuda and what you can carry home, see "Entry Requirements & Customs," in chapter 2, "Planning Your Trip to Bermuda."

Dentists For dental emergencies, call **King Edward VII Hospital,** 7 Point Finger Rd., Paget Parish (© **441/236-2345**), and ask for the emergency department. The hospital maintains lists of dentists on emergency call.

Doctors In an emergency, call **King Edward VII Hospital,** 7 Point Finger Rd., Paget Parish (© **441/236-2345**), and ask for the emergency department. For non-emergencies, ask the concierge at your hotel for a recommendation.

Documents Required See "Entry Requirements & Customs," in chapter 2, "Planning Your Trip to Bermuda."

Drinking Age See "Liquor Laws," below.

Driving Rules Visitors cannot rent cars. To operate a motor-assisted cycle, you must be age 16 or over. All cycle drivers and passengers must wear securely fastened safety helmets. Driving is on the left side of the road, and the speed limit is 32kmph (20 mph) in the countryside, 24kmph (15 mph) in busy areas.

Drug Laws Importation of, possession of, or dealing in unlawful drugs (including marijuana) is illegal in Bermuda; there are heavy penalties for infractions. Customs officers, at their discretion, may conduct body searches for drugs or other contraband goods.

Drugstores Try the **Phoenix Drugstore,** 3 Reid St. (© **441/295-3838**), open Monday to Saturday from 8am to 6pm, Sunday from noon to 6:30pm.

In Paget Parish, **Paget Pharmacy,** 130 Rural Hill Plaza (© **441/236-7275**), is open Monday to Saturday from 8am to 8pm, Sunday from 10am to 6pm.

The **Somerset Pharmacy,** 49 Mangrove Bay, Somerset Village (© **441/234-2484**), is open Monday to Saturday from 8am to 6pm, Sunday from noon to 2pm.

Electricity Electricity is 110 volts AC (60 cycles). American appliances are compatible without converters or adapters. Visitors from the United Kingdom or other parts of Europe need to bring a converter.

Embassies & Consulates The **American Consulate General** is at Crown Hill, 16 Middle Rd., Devonshire (© **441/295-1342**). It does not keep general business hours, but has hours for specific services. Call before you go to find out whether the service you need is available. It is closed on Thursday and Friday. The **Canadian Consulate General** (Commission to Bermuda) is at 1251 Avenue of the Americas, New York, NY 10020 (© **212/596-1600**). Britain doesn't have an embassy or consulate in Bermuda.

Emergencies To call the police, report a fire, or summon an ambulance, dial © **911.** The non-emergency police number is © **441/295-0011.** For Air-Sea Rescue, dial © **441/297-1010.**

Etiquette Well-tailored Bermuda shorts are acceptable on almost any occasion, and many men wear them with jackets and ties. On formal occasions, they must be accompanied by knee socks. Aside from that, Bermudians are rather conservative in their attitude toward dress— bikinis, for example, are banned more than 7.5m (25 ft.) from the water. Men are usually required to wear a jacket to dinner.

Eyeglass Repair **Argus Optical Company** (Henry Simmons, O.D.), Melbourne House, Parliament Street, Hamilton (© **441/292-5452**), works with prescription glasses and contact lenses. Hours are Monday to Friday from 9am to noon and 1 to 4:45pm.

Gasoline Mopeds take a mixture of oil and gas, and always have a separate pump at gasoline (petrol) stations. Honda scooters require regular unleaded gasoline. The typical touring biker needs about one refill per week. Both Honda scooters and mopeds are rented with full tanks. Gasoline stations are conveniently situated around the island, and gas for cycles costs $3 to $4 per liter.

Holidays See "When to Go," in chapter 2, "Planning Your Trip to Bermuda."

Hospitals **King Edward VII Memorial Hospital,** 7 Point Finger Rd., Paget Parish (© **441/236-2345**), has a highly qualified staff and Canadian accreditation.

Hot Lines Call © **441/236-3770** and you'll be connected to the Bermuda Psychiatric Hospital's outpatient clinic or (in the evening) St. Brendan's Hospital. Either can help with life-threatening problems, personal crises, or referral to a medical specialist.

Information For information before you go, see "Visitor Information," in chapter 2, "Planning Your Trip to Bermuda"; once you're on Bermuda, see "Orienting Yourself: The Lay of the Land," earlier in this chapter. For telephone directory assistance, call © **411.**

Legal Aid The U.S. consulate will inform you of your limited rights and offer a list of attorneys. However, the consulate's office cannot interfere with Bermuda's law-enforcement officers. The **Citizens' Emergency Center** of the Office of Special Consular Services in Washington, D.C. (© **202/ 647-5225**), operates a hot line that's useful in an emergency for U.S. citizens arrested abroad. The staff can also tell you how to send money to U.S. citizens arrested abroad.

Liquor Laws Bermuda sternly regulates the sale of alcoholic beverages. The legal drinking age is 18, and most bars close at 1am. Some nightclubs and hotel bars can serve liquor until 3am. Many bars are closed on Sunday.

Hard liquor is sold in specialty stores selling liquor, beer, and wine. Although it's legal for grocery stores to sell hard liquor, most limit their inventories to beer and wine. Alcohol can't be sold on Sunday. You can bring beer or other alcohol to the beach legally, as long as your party doesn't get too rowdy and you generally stay in one spot. The moment you actually *walk* on the beach or the streets with an open container of liquor, it's illegal. (The thinking behind this law is apparently that roaming gangs of loud, obnoxious drunks are more dangerous and disruptive than sedentary gangs of loud, obnoxious drunks.)

Mail Deposit regular mail in the red pillar boxes on the streets. You'll recognize them by the monogram of Queen Elizabeth II. The postage rates for airmail letters up to 10 grams and for postcards is 65¢ to the United States and Canada, 80¢ to the United Kingdom. Airmail letters and postcards to the North American mainland can take 5 to 7 days, to Britain possibly a little longer. Often visitors return home before their postcards arrive.

Newspapers/Magazines Bermuda has one daily newspaper, the *Royal Gazette.* Three weekly papers—the *Bermuda Sun,* the *Bermuda Times,* and the *Mid-Ocean News*—are issued on Friday. Major U.S. newspapers, including the *New York Times* and *USA Today,* and magazines such as *Time* and *Newsweek* are delivered to Bermuda on the day of their publication on the mainland. *This Week in Bermuda* is a weekly guide for tourists.

Passports See "Entry Requirements & Customs," in chapter 2, "Planning Your Trip to Bermuda."

Pets If you want to take your pet with you to Bermuda, you'll need a special permit issued by the director of the **Department of Agriculture, Fisheries, and Parks,** P.O. Box HM 834, Hamilton HM CX, Bermuda (© **441/ 236-4201**). The island has no quarantine facilities, so animals arriving without proper documents will be refused entry and will be returned to the point of origin. Some guesthouses and hotels allow you to bring in small animals, but others will not, so be sure to inquire in advance. Always check to see what the latest regulations are before attempting to bring a dog or other pet—including Seeing Eye dogs—to Bermuda.

Pharmacies See "Drugstores," above.

Photographic Needs If you want to buy a camera or film, or develop Kodak or Fuji film, try the City of Hamilton's leading camera store, **Stuart's,** 5 Reid St., near the corner of Queen Street (© **441/295-5496**). Film can be developed in-house in about 4 hours (sometimes within 1 hr., for a surcharge). Open Monday to Saturday from 9am to 5pm.

Police In an emergency, call © **911**; otherwise, call © **441/295-0011**.

Post Offices The **General Post Office,** 56 Church St., Hamilton (© **441/ 297-7866**), is open Monday to Friday from 8am to 5pm, Saturday from 8am to noon. Post office branches and the Perot Post Office, Queen Street, Hamilton, are open Monday to Friday from 8am to 5pm. Some post offices close for lunch from 11:30am to 1pm. Daily airmail service for the United States and Canada closes at 9:30am in Hamilton. See also "Mail," above.

Radio & TV News is broadcast on the hour and half-hour over AM stations 1340 (ZBM), 1230 (ZFB), and 1450 (VSB). The FM stations are 89 (ZBM) and 95 (ZFB). Tourist-oriented programming, island music, and information on activities and special events air over AM station 1160 (VSB) daily from 7am to noon.

The television channel, 10 (ZBM), is affiliated with America's Columbia Broadcasting System (CBS).

Restrooms The City of Hamilton and St. George provide public facilities, but only during business hours. In the City of Hamilton, toilets are at City Hall, in Par-la-Ville Gardens, and at Albouy's Point. In St. George, facilities are available at Town Hall, Somers Gardens, and Market Wharf. Outside of these towns, you'll find restrooms at the public beaches, the Botanical Gardens, in several of the forts, at the airport, and at service stations. Often you'll have to use the facilities in hotels, restaurants, and wherever else you can find them.

Safety Bermudians are generally peaceful people, not given to violence. To be sure, the island has experienced racial tensions in the past, but right now relations between white and black residents seem to be harmonious, as blacks assume a greater role in Bermuda's affairs.

Crimes against tourists, violent or otherwise, are rare, but don't be lulled into a false sense of security. Crime does exist in Bermuda, as it does in any society. Take care to protect your valuables, especially when you're at the beach. Lock your moped each time you leave it. If you bring very valuable items with you (this is not advisable), place them in your hotel safe and never leave them carelessly in your room.

Smoking Tobacconists and other stores carry a wide array of tobacco products, generally from either the United States or England. Prices vary but tend to be high. At most tobacconists you can buy classic cigars from Havana, but Americans must enjoy them on the island—they can't be taken back to the United States. Smoking in public places (such as restaurants) is generally permitted, but check before lighting up. Movie theaters set aside a section for nonsmokers.

Taxes Bermuda charges visitors a Passenger Tax before they depart from the island. For those who leave by air, the tax, collected at the airport, is $20 for adults or children (children under 2 are exempt). For those who leave by ship, the tax, collected in advance by the cruise-ship company, is $60 (children under 2 are exempt).

All room rates, regardless of the category of accommodation or the plan under which you stay, are subject to a government tax of 6% (for simple guesthouses) to 7.5% (for the large majority of Bermuda's conventional hotels).

Taxis See "Getting Around," earlier in this chapter.

Telephone/Telegrams/Telexes/Faxes Worldwide direct-dial phone, fax, and cable service is available at the **Cable & Wireless Office,** 12 Burnaby St., Hamilton, opposite City Hall (© **441/297-7022**). Hours are Monday to Friday from 9am to 5pm. Prepaid phone cards may be purchased and used island-wide, and calling cards may be used from selected call boxes.

Cable & Wireless, in conjunction with the Bermuda Telephone Co., provides international direct dialing (IDD) to more than 150 countries. Country codes and calling charges may be found in the Bermuda telephone directory. Telephone booths are available at the Cable & Wireless office, and customers can either prepay or buy cash cards in $10, $20, and $50 denominations. Cash-card phone booths are available at numerous locations around the island. Making international calls with cash cards can be a lot cheaper than using the phone at your hotel, which might impose stiff surcharges. To make a local call, deposit 20¢ (Bermudian or U.S.). Hotels often charge 20¢ to $1 for local calls.

Special phones at passenger piers in the City of Hamilton, St. George, and the dockyard will connect you directly with an AT&T, Sprint, or MCI operator in the United States, permitting you to make collect or calling-card calls.

Telephone Directory All Bermuda telephone numbers appear in one phone book, revised annually. The Yellow Pages list all the goods and services you are likely to need in the back.

Time Bermuda is 1 hour ahead of Eastern Standard Time (EST). Daylight savings time is in effect from the first Sunday in April until the last Sunday in October, as it is in the United States.

Tipping In most cases, a service charge is added to hotel and restaurant bills. In hotels, the charge is in lieu of tipping various individuals, such as bellhops, maids, and restaurant staffers (for meals included in a package or in the daily rate). Check for this carefully to avoid double tipping. Otherwise, a 15% tip for service is customary. Taxi drivers usually get 10% to 15%.

Tourist Offices See "Visitor Information," in chapter 2, "Planning Your Trip to Bermuda," and the "Visitor Information on the Island" box, earlier in this chapter.

Transit Information For information about ferry service, call © **441/ 295-4506**. For bus information, call © **441/292-3854**.

Useful Telephone Numbers On Bermuda, for time and temperature, call © **977-1**. To learn "What's On in Bermuda," dial © **974**. For medical emergencies or the police, dial © **911**. If in doubt during any other emergency, dial © **0** (zero), which will connect you with your hotel's switchboard or the Bermuda telephone operator.

Water Tap water is generally safe to drink.

Weather Call © **977** at any time for a forecast covering the next 24-hour period.

Where to Stay

Bermuda offers a wide choice of lodgings, from small, casual guesthouses to large, luxurious resorts. Facilities vary greatly in size and amenities within each category.

CHOOSING THE PLACE THAT'S RIGHT FOR YOU

Accommodations in Bermuda basically fall into five categories:

- **Resort Hotels:** These generally large properties are Bermuda's most lavish, offering many facilities, services, and luxuries—but also charging the highest prices, especially in summer. The lowest rates, usually discounted about 20%, are in effect from mid-November to March. The large resorts usually have their own beaches or beach clubs, along with swimming pools; some have their own golf courses. It's cheaper to choose the Modified American Plan (MAP) dining option (explained below under "Rates and Reservation Policies"), which includes breakfast and dinner, than to order all your meals a la carte. However, if you go the MAP route, you'll be confined to the same dining room every night and miss the opportunity to sample different restaurants.
- **Cottage Colonies:** This uniquely Bermudian option typically consists of a series of bungalows constructed around a clubhouse, which is the center of social life, drinking, and dining. The cottages, usually scenically arranged on landscaped grounds, are designed to provide maximum privacy and are typically equipped with kitchenettes for preparing light meals. In many of the cottage colonies, breakfast isn't available; you can go out, or buy supplies the night before and prepare your own meal. Most colonies have their own beaches or swimming pools.
- **Small Hotels:** This option might be just the right fit for those who hate megaresorts. Bermuda's small hotels offer the intimacy of upscale bed-and-breakfasts, but with considerably more facilities. At a small hotel, you might feel more connected to the island and its people. Another plus? They're often cheaper than the big resorts.
- **Housekeeping Units:** These cottage or apartment-style accommodations (often called efficiencies in the U.S.) usually occupy landscaped estates surrounding a main clubhouse. All of them offer kitchen facilities—perhaps a full, well-equipped kitchen, but at least a kitchenette where you can whip up snacks and breakfast. Most offer minimal daily maid service. Generally, housekeeping units are simpler and less expensive than cottage colonies.
- **Guesthouses:** These are Bermuda's least expensive accommodations. The larger guesthouses are old Bermuda homes in garden settings. Generally, they've been modernized and have comfortable guest rooms. Some have their own swimming pools. A number of guesthouses are small, modest places, offering breakfast only; you may share a bathroom with other guests. If you stay in a guesthouse, you may have to "commute" to the beach.

Another option is renting a **villa** or vacation home. Villa rentals are like renting someone's home. At some, you're entirely on your own; others provide maid service. Most are on or near a beach. This is generally an expensive option.

Private **apartments** offer fewer frills than villas or condos; the building housing the apartment may not have a swimming pool, or even a front desk. Apartments are available with or without maid service.

Cottages, or cabanas, offer the most independent lifestyle in the category of vacation accommodations—they're entirely self-catering. Some open onto a beach, and others surround a communal swimming pool. Most of them are fairly basic, consisting of a simple bedroom plus a small kitchen and bathroom. For the peak summer season, make cabana reservations at least 5 or 6 months in advance.

Several United States and Canadian agents can arrange these types of rentals. **Villanet,** 12600 SE 38 St., Ste. 202, Bellevue, WA 98006 (📞 **206/417-3444;** www.rentavilla.com), specializes in condos and villas. It can arrange bookings for a week or longer.

RATES & RESERVATION POLICIES

The rates that we've listed throughout this chapter are "rack rates"—the rates you'd be quoted if you walked in off the street. These are helpful largely for purposes of comparison. Especially at the big resorts, almost no one ever pays the rack rate. By booking a package deal that includes airfare, or just by asking for packages and discounts at the hotel when you make your reservation, you can usually do much better. At small hotels and guesthouses, the rates quoted here are much more likely to be accurate. Before you book anything, read the "Booking a Travel Package" section in chapter 2.

All room rates, regardless of meal plan, are subject to a 7.5% tax, which will be tacked onto your bill. A service charge (10%–15%) is also added to your room rate in lieu of tips; remember that the service charge does not cover bar tabs. Third-person rates (for those occupying a room with two other people) are lower, and children's rates vary according to their age. The rack rates we've listed in this chapter include tax and service charge unless otherwise noted. However, we strongly encourage you to confirm what the rates include when you reserve, to avoid any misunderstanding. Hotels usually quote you the full rate you'll pay upon checkout; they don't want misunderstandings either.

Bermuda's high season is spring and summer—the opposite of the Bahamian and Caribbean high season. Most of Bermuda's hotels charge high-season rates from March (Easter is the peak period) through mid-November. A few hotels have year-round rates, and others charge in-between, or "shoulder," prices in spring and autumn. If business is slow, many smaller places shut down in winter.

You may see some unfamiliar terms and abbreviations used to describe rate plans. **AP** (American Plan), sometimes called "full board," includes three meals a day. **MAP** (Modified American Plan), sometimes called "half-board," includes breakfast and dinner. **BP** (Bermuda Plan) includes full American or English

---

Tips **Planning Pointer**

The rack rates in this chapter include tax and service charges unless we note otherwise. To avoid any possible misunderstanding, be sure you understand what is included in the rates at your hotel when you make reservations.

breakfast. **CP** (Continental Plan) includes only continental breakfast (basically bread, jam, and coffee). **EP** (European Plan) is always cheapest—it includes only the room, no meals.

Note that prices aren't uniform in several of the larger, older resorts, which offer a wide range of rooms. For instance, one guest at the Elbow Beach Hotel might be paying a price that can be categorized as "moderate," whereas another might be booked at a "very expensive" rate—it all depends on your room assignment. So even if you can't pay $200 a night, it might be worth a call to see if a cheaper room is available.

Accommodations that are members of the Bermuda Hotel Association require 2 nights' deposit within 14 days of confirming a reservation; full payment 30 days before arrival; and notice of cancellation 15 days before scheduled arrival, or you'll forfeit your deposit. Some smaller hotels and other accommodations levy an energy surcharge; inquire about this when you make your reservations.

TIPS FOR SAVING ON YOUR HOTEL ROOM

- **Don't be afraid to bargain.** Get in the habit of asking for a lower price than the first one quoted. Most rack rates include commissions of 10% to 25% or more for travel agents, which many hotels will cut if you make your own reservations and haggle a bit. Always ask politely whether a less-expensive room is available, or whether any special rates apply to you. You may qualify for corporate, student, military, senior, or other discounts. Be sure to mention membership in AAA, AARP, frequent flyer programs, or trade unions, which may entitle you to special deals as well.
- **Rely on a qualified professional.** Certain hotels give travel agents discounts in exchange for steering business their way, so if you're shy about bargaining, an agent may be better equipped to negotiate discounts.
- **Dial direct.** When booking a room in a chain hotel, call the hotel's local line, as well as the toll-free number, and see where you get the best deal. A hotel makes nothing on a room that stays empty. The clerk who runs the place is more likely to know about vacancies than the person at the toll-free number, and will often grant deep discounts in order to fill rooms.
- **Consider a suite.** If you are traveling with your family or another couple, you can pack more people into a suite (which usually comes with a sofa bed) and thereby reduce your per-person rate. Remember that some places charge for extra guests and some don't.
- **Book an efficiency.** A room with a kitchenette allows you to grocery shop and eat some meals in. Especially during long stays with families, you're bound to save money on food this way.

LANDING THE BEST ROOM

Somebody has to get the best room in the house, and it might as well be you.

Always ask for a corner room. They're usually larger, quieter, and closer to the elevator. They often have more windows and light than standard rooms, and they don't always cost more.

When you make your reservation, ask if the hotel is renovating; if it is, request a room away from the renovation work. Many hotels now offer nonsmoking rooms; if smoke bothers you, by all means ask for one. Inquire, too, about the location of the restaurants, bars, and discos, which could all be sources of irritating noise. If you aren't happy with your room when you arrive, talk to the front desk. If the hotel has another room, the staff should be happy to accommodate you, within reason.

Tips **Dining at Your Hotel**

Chances are, you'll take more meals at your hotel in Bermuda than you would in other sunny destinations, such as Florida. Although you're generally out and about for lunch, many visitors don't like to hire an expensive taxi or take a bike or motorbike along Bermuda's narrow roads in search of a spot for dinner. Taxis are expensive and motorbikes can be a bit hazardous at night. Since you can't rent a car, you are often stuck for meals at your hotel, and therefore you might want to consider food options when deciding where to stay.

In many destinations, hotel restaurants aren't a big factor in selecting an accommodation. But because of transportation difficulties in Bermuda, especially at night, consider the cuisine served at a hotel before checking in. To help you out, we've added more details about hotel dining than you can find in most other guidebooks.

---

1 Resort Hotels

With their wealth of amenities, the big resort hotels can keep you so well occupied that you may not feel the need to leave the premises (but make sure you resist the pull of the resort and venture out!). The large hotels typically have their own beaches or beach clubs and swimming pools; some have their own golf courses. Most of these hotels also boast such luxury services and facilities as porters, room service, planned activities, sports facilities (such as tennis courts), shops (including bike shops), beauty salons, bars, nightclubs, entertainment, and taxi stands.

VERY EXPENSIVE
SOUTHAMPTON PARISH

The Fairmont Southampton ★★★ *Kids*   Sitting atop Bermuda's highest point, this resort is the largest and most luxurious property on the island. It overlooks the ocean, the bay, and its own good beach, located in front of the hotel. The hotel's beach is sheltered in a jagged cove, flanked by cliffs and studded with rocky outcroppings lashed by the tides. All aspects of the hotel more than justify its membership in "The Leading Hotels of the World." Often compared to its sibling, the Hamilton Princess, the Fairmont Southampton is located on the beach, whereas the Princess in the City of Hamilton is situated close to shops and attractions. We don't think it's the place for those who want an intimate, romantic hideaway; in fact, its biggest drawback is that it's a favorite with conventions and tour groups. Nonetheless, it and Elbow Beach are the finest choices for the well-heeled family who wants to stay at a place where virtually everything is on-site—from sports to beaches to a wide selection of dining.

The hotel is decorated in 18th-century English style, with well-upholstered furnishings. Baronial staircases connect the public rooms, situated on three floors. The plush guest rooms are arranged in wings that radiate more or less symmetrically from a central core. This design gives each luxurious room a private veranda with a sweeping view of the water. Rooms are generally spacious, with one king or two double beds. Bathrooms, which come with shower-tub combinations, tend to be modest. For those who can afford it, the choice spot here is the Entrée Gold floor, a hotel-within-a-hotel, pampering its guests in ultimate luxury on the top floor, offering an array of services from shoeshines to private check-ins. The Gold Floor offers complimentary continental breakfast, newspapers, and the use of a fax and VCR.

The cuisine is among the island's finest—we recommend several of the resort's restaurants even if you're not staying here (see chapter 5, "Where to Dine"). In a place this large, it's hard to keep an eye on quality, but the Southampton Princess does admirably well. This is a mammoth operation, but the hotel has wisely split its dining into smaller enclaves. The dining rooms include Windows on the Sound, a three-tiered palace reminiscent of Mayfair in the 1930s and New York's Rainbow Room; through 6m- (20-ft.-) high arched windows, you can see the islands of Great Sound. Other choices include Wickets Brasserie & Cricket Club, Newport Room, Rib Room Steak House, the Whaler Inn, and the Waterlot Inn. Nightlife is more staid here than at the Sonesta, and not every restaurant has a bar that's open to non-diners (the Waterlot Inn and the Whaler Inn do). Jasmine's Lounge has live music, usually a jazz combo, beginning at 8pm.

Guests who don't want to leave the premises enjoy a self-contained village of bars, restaurants, shops, and athletic facilities that are among the island's finest. Everyone's favorite pool is a re-creation of a Polynesian waterfall, with streams of heated water spilling from an artificial limestone cliff. You can swim here even during cold weather, thanks to the greenhouse above. A shuttle bus transports guests to and from various hotel facilities, and hotel ferries make runs along Little Sound into the City of Hamilton.

101 South Shore Rd. (P.O. Box HM 1379), Hamilton HM FX, Bermuda. © **800/441-1414** in the U.S., 800/268-7176 in Canada, or 441/238-8000. Fax 441/239-6916. www.fairmont.com. 593 units. Winter $189–$259 double, from $479 suite; summer $359–$459 double, from $689 suite. AE, DC, MC, V. Free private ferry from The Fairmont Hamilton Princess. **Amenities:** 6 restaurants; 4 bars; private beach club; outdoor pool; indoor pool; par-3, 18-hole golf course; 7 tennis courts; fitness center with spa facilities; dive shop; children's program in summer; concierge; moped rental; business services; salon; 24-room service; massage; babysitting; laundry; dry cleaning. *In room:* A/C, TV, dataport, minibar, coffeemaker, hair dryer, iron, safe.

Sonesta Beach Resort ⚡ *Kids*   This is the only major luxury resort on Bermuda with access to three beaches, including Church Bay, 5 minutes away by bike. Among full-service hotels, only Elbow Beach and the Southampton Princess outclass it. Built in the shape of a crescent, the resort sits on 10 hectares (25 acres) of prime seafront property, curving along the spine of a rocky peninsula whose jagged edges provide oceanviews. The resort features ample lengths of oceanside walkways. Those who seek Bermudian charm and character would probably prefer Cambridge Beaches resort, but spa goers, honeymooners, and watersports and beach buffs like this resort a lot. The Sonesta also caters to families, who gravitate to its wide selection of activities, including beaches, spacious rooms with private terraces, a large swimming pool, and even first-rate babysitters.

The circular bay in front, flanked by limestone cliffs and sandy beaches, was used long ago by gunpowder smugglers, and later by rumrunners, who loved its well-camouflaged entrance. Circled with palm-shaded cabanas and bars, the bay has a soft, sandy bottom and looks like a small corner of Polynesia transported to the Atlantic.

Bermuda's Hotels at a Glance

Hotel	Access for disabled	Directly beside the beach	On-site swimming pool	Restaurant on premises	Cable TV in bedroom	Fitness facilities	Access to golf nearby	On-site tennis courts	Convention facilities	Family-friendly	Childcare facilities	On-site spa facilities	Access to water sports	Accepts credit cards	Air-conditioned bedrooms	Live on-site entertainment	Wharf or marina facilities
Ariel Sands Beach Club		✓	✓	✓			✓	✓		✓	✓		✓	✓	✓	✓	
Astwood Cove			✓							✓				✓			
Aunt Nea's Inn at Hillcrest												✓	✓				
Cambridge Beaches		✓	✓	✓		✓	✓	✓	✓			✓	✓		✓	✓	✓
Clear View Suites & Villas	✓	✓	✓	✓	✓		✓	✓	✓	✓	✓		✓	✓			
Dawkin's Manor			✓	✓						✓			✓	✓			
Edgehill Manor			✓		✓					✓				✓			
Elbow Beach Hotel	✓	✓	✓	✓	✓	✓	✓	✓	✓	✓	✓	✓	✓	✓	✓	✓	
Fairmont Hamilton Princess	✓		✓	✓	✓	✓	✓	✓	✓	✓	✓	✓	✓	✓	✓	✓	✓
Fairmont Southampton Princess	✓	✓	✓	✓	✓	✓	✓	✓	✓	✓	✓	✓	✓	✓	✓	✓	✓
Fordham Hall					✓								✓	✓			
Fourways Inn			✓	✓	✓		✓		✓				✓	✓			
Garden House			✓		✓									✓			
Granaway	✓		✓		✓				✓	✓			✓	✓		✓	
Grape Bay Cottages					✓				✓	✓			✓	✓			
Greenbank Guest House									✓			✓	✓	✓		✓	
Greene's Guest House			✓		✓		✓		✓					✓			
Grotto Bay Beach Hotel	✓	✓	✓	✓	✓	✓	✓	✓	✓	✓	✓		✓	✓	✓	✓	✓
Hamiltonian Hotel & Island Club			✓		✓			✓		✓			✓	✓			
Harmony Club		✓	✓	✓		✓	✓						✓	✓	✓		
Horizons and Cottages			✓	✓			✓	✓		✓	✓			✓	✓		
Little Pomander Guest House	✓				✓		✓			✓			✓	✓	✓		
Loughlands			✓				✓	✓		✓					✓		
Marley Beach Cottages		✓	✓		✓		✓			✓			✓	✓	✓		
Marriott's Castle Harbour Resort	✓		✓	✓	✓	✓		✓	✓	✓	✓		✓	✓	✓	✓	

Bermuda's Hotels (cont.)	Access for disabled	Directly beside the beach	On-site swimming pool	Restaurant on premises	Cable TV in bedroom	Fitness facilities	Access to golf nearby	On-site tennis courts	Convention facilities	Family-friendly	Childcare facilities	On-site spa facilities	Access to water sports	Accepts credit cards	Air-conditioned bedrooms	Live on-site entertainment	Wharf or marina facilities
Mermaid Beach Club		✓	✓	✓					✓			✓	✓				
Munro Beach Cottages				✓		✓			✓	✓			✓	✓			
Newstead Hotel			✓	✓			✓	✓	✓	✓			✓	✓	✓	✓	✓
The Oxford House				✓					✓				✓	✓			
Palmetto Hotel & Cottages			✓	✓			✓		✓	✓		✓	✓	✓	✓	✓	✓
Paraquet Guest Apartments			✓	✓		✓			✓					✓			
Pink Beach Club & Cottages		✓	✓	✓			✓	✓	✓	✓	✓		✓	✓	✓	✓	
Pompano Beach Club		✓	✓	✓		✓	✓	✓	✓	✓	✓		✓	✓	✓	✓	
The Reefs		✓	✓	✓	✓		✓	✓	✓	✓	✓	✓	✓	✓	✓	✓	✓
Robin's Nest			✓		✓									✓			
Rosedon			✓		✓				✓				✓				
Rosemont			✓		✓				✓	✓			✓	✓			
Royal Heights Guest House			✓		✓				✓				✓	✓			
Royal Palms Hotel			✓	✓	✓				✓				✓	✓			
St. George's Club	✓	✓	✓	✓	✓		✓	✓	✓	✓	✓	✓		✓	✓	✓	
Salt Kettle House						✓			✓			✓		✓			✓
Sandpiper Apartments			✓		✓				✓				✓	✓			
Sonesta Beach Resort	✓	✓	✓	✓	✓	✓	✓	✓	✓	✓	✓	✓	✓	✓	✓	✓	
Stonington Beach Hotel		✓	✓	✓			✓	✓	✓	✓	✓		✓	✓	✓	✓	
Surf Side Beach Club		✓	✓	✓	✓		✓		✓	✓			✓	✓	✓		
Valley Cottages & Apartments			✓		✓		✓		✓				✓	✓			
Vienna Guest Apartments			✓		✓		✓						✓	✓			
Waterloo House			✓	✓			✓	✓				✓	✓	✓	✓		
Whale Bay Inn		✓			✓		✓							✓			
The Wharf Executive Suites				✓									✓	✓			✓

Bermuda Accommodations

✈ Airport

The Oxford House **31**
Paraquet Guest Apartments **21**
Pink Beach Club & Cottages **45**
Pompano Beach Club **3**
The Reefs **6**
Robin's Nest **39**
Rosedon **36**
Rosemont **35**
Royal Heights Guest House **8**
Royal Palms Hotel **38**
St. George's Club **43**
Salt Kettle House **28**
Sandpiper Apartments **13**

Sonesta Beach Resort **7**
Stonington Beach Hotel **23**
Surf Side Beach Club **14**
Valley Cottages & Apartments **15**
Vienna Guest Apartments **16**
Waterloo House **32**
The Wharf Executive Suites Hotel **27**

See also "The City of Hamilton Accommodations" map

Moments   Hanging Out with the Dolphins

The Fairmont Southampton runs the well-publicized **Dolphin Quest Interactive Program,** which offers in-the-water encounters with Atlantic bottlenose dolphins. In a .8 hectare (2-acre) holding pen that's 1m to 3.5m (4 ft.–12 ft.) deep and separated from the open sea with underwater netting, the hotel keeps seven dolphins. Four "Dolphin Experiences" are scheduled each day (year-round at 9 and 11am, and 2 and 4pm). Up to 10 swimmers (wearing bathing suits in summer, wet suits in winter) cavort in the water with the dolphins for just under 30 minutes. The price for adults is $105, for children under 16, $85. In winter, it's easy to get a slot, but in summer, there's so much demand that the hotel has a lottery. Is all this cruel to the dolphins? The staff is rigorous about protecting and caring for them; the overall atmosphere is playful and lighthearted; and the dolphins have a fairly large area to swim in. But we can't help worrying that continued contact with hordes of people and separation from their natural habitat must have something of a traumatizing effect on these beautiful animals.

At a multi-million dollar cost, the resort recently renovated its guest rooms and public areas. Rooms have private terraces, thick carpeting, high-quality light woods, louvered closets, and electronic locks. Bathrooms are generous in size, with tiled shower and tub areas. Some units open onto garden views, while more expensive units boast ocean or beach views. Some accommodations are set aside for nonsmokers and those with disabilities.

The hotel has three restaurants, including the elegant Lillian's, which serves northern Italian cuisine. There's also the bistro-style Longtail, and the Sea Grape, which offers alfresco dining overlooking Boat Bay. Lillian's and the Sea Grape are worthy choices even if you're not staying at the hotel. Overall, the food here is perfectly good, if not truly gourmet or as excellent as that at the Southampton Princess. You'll never go thirsty at the Sonesta—each restaurant has a bar. The one at the Longtail is particularly fun, with live entertainment—calypso, jazz, merengue, or at least a deejay—almost every night. There's also a jukebox and a row of big-screen TVs in Splits, the hotel's sports bar.

6 Sonesta Dr., Southampton Parish (P.O. Box HM 1070), Hamilton HM EX, Bermuda. © **800/766-3782** in the U.S., or 441/238-8122. Fax 441/238-8463. www.sonesta.com. 400 units. May–Aug $305–$425 double, from $465 suite; Apr and Sept–Nov 15 $275–$385 double, from $425 suite; Nov 16–Mar $150–$205 double, from $240 suite. Buffet breakfast $18 per person. Must pay for breakfast at check-in. Discount honeymoon and family packages available. AE, MC, V. Bus: 7. **Amenities:** 3 restaurants; 2 bars; outdoor swimming pool; indoor swimming pool; 6 tennis courts (2 lit for night play), full-time tennis pro; health club and spa; diving center for snorkelers and scuba divers; children's program (May 1–Labor Day); business services; salon; room service available until 11pm; babysitting; laundry; dry cleaning. *In room:* A/C, TV, minibar, iron, hair dryer, safe.

PAGET PARISH

Elbow Beach Hotel ★★★ *Kids*   Elegant and commanding, this is the best full-service resort on Bermuda, though it lacks the intimacy and local charm you'd find at a smaller place like The Reefs. The hotel complex opens onto Elbow Beach, where a prime strand of sand is reserved for hotel guests. Following a $42 million sprucing up—and that is one massive renovation—Elbow Beach reopened in 1999. The renovations added a decidedly upscale colonial English gloss to the hotel, with miles of expensive chintzes and piles of reproduction

The City of Hamilton Accommodations

Edgehill Manor **2**
The Fairmont Hamilton
  Princess **5**
Fordham Hall **7**
The Oxford House **8**
Rosedon **4**
Rosemont **3**
Royal Palms Hotel **1**
Waterloo House **6**

+■ Church
(i) Information
⊠ Post Office

The Spa Treatment

Sonesta Beach Resort, Southampton (☎ **800/766-3782** in the U.S., or 441/238-8122; www.sonesta.com) has the island's most comprehensive spa facilities. Designed in the European style, it offers health and fitness programs you'd find in an American spa, including a "Bermuda Shorts Cellulite Treatment"; deluxe facial care from Paris; and ancient forms of therapeutic and relaxing massage such as aromatherapy, reflexology, and Swedish massage. Some people check into the hotel as part of a 3-night, 4-day spa program The program, which is jointly operated with Bersalon of Bermuda (☎ **441/238-1226**), includes access to low fat, low calorie, and low sodium menu items, and a daily regime, as loosely or as rigidly structured as you want, of aerobics, massage, skin and body care, supervised exercise, mud treatments, and so on.

The facilities are also available to hotel guests and nonguests who want selected treatments (priced separately) rather than the full spa experience. The up-to-date accouterments include Universal gym equipment, saunas, steam baths, and massage rooms. The staff conducts daily exercise classes. Half- and full-day packages are available to nonguests. For after-workout pick-me-ups, there's a beauty salon adjacent to the health spa.

---

antiques. Elbow Beach appeals to vacationers, especially families, who like everything under one roof (or at least on-site). Another advantage is the proximity to the City of Hamilton, which is 10 minutes away by taxi. The resort sits on 20 hectares (50 acres) of gardens with its own .5km (¼-mile) pink-sand beach on the south shore. Long gone are the days when rowdy college students descended at Easter.

You can choose from a wide array of accommodations, from rooms with balconies overlooking the water to duplex cottages; from lanai rooms overlooking the pool and the Atlantic, to others that are surfside. Many guest room walls are draped in silk. Bathrooms are Italian marble, with shower-tub combinations, up-to-date plumbing, and touches of luxury like robes. The most spacious units are in low-rise buildings on terraces leading to the sands; the least desirable rooms open onto a heavily trafficked corridor on the lobby floor.

The cuisine here has never been better; the culinary "dream team" includes chefs who have worked at some of the grandest dining rooms of the world, from Atlanta's Ritz-Carlton to Wolfgang Puck's California restaurants. All guests, including those on MAP, may choose dinner at either of the hotel's two ocean-view restaurants or at a nightly outdoor theme party. The main dining room, the Seahorse Grill, is the most formal of the restaurants. At the beachfront Cafe Lido, the kitchen focuses on seafood with a Mediterranean accent. The resort also participates in a "dine around" program with several City of Hamilton restaurants; hotel guests can eat at participating restaurants and charge their meals to the resort.

60 South Shore Rd. (P.O. Box HM 455), Hamilton HM BX, Bermuda. ☎ **441/236-3535.** Fax 441/236-8043. www.mandarinoriental.com/bermuda. 244 units. Apr 10–Oct $375–$520 double, from $520 suite; off season $285–$390 double, from $350 suite. Packages available. Children under 18 stay free in parent's room. AE, DC, MC, V. Bus: 1, 2, or 7. **Amenities:** 4 restaurants; 5 bars; large swimming pool; golf putting green; 5 all-weather tennis courts (2 lit for night play); health spa with whirlpool; dive shop; watersports (including deep-sea

fishing, kayaking, and windsurfing); summer children's program (the best on island); moped rental; salon; 24-hour room service; babysitting; laundry; dry cleaning; executive suites. *In room:* A/C, TV, minibar, hair dryer, iron, safe.

PEMBROKE PARISH (CITY OF HAMILTON)

The Fairmont Hamilton Princess ★ This landmark luxury hotel launched Bermuda's tourist industry and is still going strong. Following a recent $15 million renovation, it is brighter and better than ever. Its sibling, the Fairmont Southampton, has better dining, grander facilities, and the advantage of being on a beach, but it is somewhat remote; the Hamilton Princess earns fans and devotees because it is more conveniently positioned for shopping and sightseeing. The hotel, which evokes a wedding cake, is near downtown Hamilton, on the edge of Hamilton Harbour. Elbow Beach (the closest beach), is a 20-minute taxi ride or 45-minute bicycle ride from the hotel. The easily accessible ferry delivers guests to the Fairmont Southampton, and sun lovers can get their fill at the sandy stretch there. The lack of a beach here doesn't keep the glitterati away: This is the hotel of choice for Hollywood and European movie stars, as well as the yachting set. Past visitors have included everyone from Mark Twain to Michael Jackson (quite a range!).

Opened in 1884 and named for Princess Louise (Queen Victoria's daughter), this Princess is far more staid than its cousin in Southampton (see above). It doesn't even attempt to offer the roster of activities available at Elbow Beach, so the young and the restless might want to book elsewhere. This is the flagship of the Princess Hotel chain, and it's certainly the one with the most history: British intelligence officers stationed here during World War II worked to crack secret Nazi codes.

Modern wings, pierced with row upon row of balconied loggias, surround the hotel's colonial core. The property was designed around a concrete pier that extends into the harbor, near a Japanese-style floating garden. In 1996, management renovated the well-decorated guest rooms and public salons, making a good property even better. Many of the spacious rooms have private balconies, which were designed "to create the feeling that you'd choose the same kind of bedroom if you owned a home here." Most of the tiled bathrooms are generous in size. Some 40% of the guests are repeat visitors.

The hotel has a wide array of bars and restaurants. For a review of Harley's, see chapter 5, "Where to Dine."

76 Pitts Bay Rd. (P.O. Box HM 837), Hamilton HM CX, Bermuda. © **800/441-1414** in the U.S., or 441/295-3000. Fax 441/295-1914. www.fairmont.com. 410 units. Apr–Nov $329–$369 double, from $459 suite; off season $229–$249 double, from $409 suite. AE, DC, MC, V. Frequent ferry service to and from the Southampton Princess, weather permitting. Bus: 7 or 8. **Amenities:** 2 restaurants; 2 bars; heated freshwater swimming pool; unheated saltwater swimming pool; access to golf, tennis, sailing, and white-sand beaches at the Southampton Princess; fitness center featuring an exercise room with extensive exercise equipment, massage area, saunas, and showers; water-aerobics classes; dive shop (an independent concessionaire); concierge; moped rental; business center; salon; 24-hour room service; babysitting; laundry; dry cleaning; executive suites. *In room:* A/C, TV, minibar, hair dryer, iron, safe.

Tips Package Deals

Refer to the "Booking a Travel Package" section of chapter 2 before you call these resorts yourself. Buying a package is the way to go; you can save hundreds of dollars over what you would pay by booking your hotel and airfare separately.

The Debut of Bermuda's Grandest Hotel

If work continues according to schedule, some time in 2004 or early 2005, the $250 million, 100-hectare (250-acre), five-star Tucker's Point Club will open at Tucker's Town, the most exclusive and private residential area of Bermuda.

The previous hotel that stood here, Castle Harbour Hotel, was shut down in 1999 for demolition. It was once the most famous hotel in Bermuda except for the Hamilton Princess. Castle Harbour opened on November 1, 1932, but over the decades fell into a perpetually money-losing operation.

Construction on the new resort started in 2002 and, if all goes well, it will be the number one luxury property on the island, with 108 suites for hotel guests in the new Rosewood Hotel and 44 private club residential accommodations "for the exceedingly affluent."

Tucker's Point Club will be under the management of Rosewood, which also operates such prestigious properties as The Mansion on Turtle Creek in Dallas and Caneel Bay at St. John in the U.S. Virgin Islands.

The amenities of Tucker's Point Club will rival those of the finest resorts in the Western Hemisphere. Here you will find a championship golf course, tennis, a beach club, and a state-of-the-art European spa and health club.

Tucker's Point Club's new 18-hole championship golf course, designed by Roger Rulewich, former Senior Designer for Robert Trent Jones, builds upon the beauty of the former Castle Harbour golf course. The course features newly designed holes and greens, contoured fairways and bunkers, and a new practice facility and driving range.

EXPENSIVE
HAMILTON PARISH

Grotto Bay Beach Hotel ★ *(Kids)*   This resort (named after its subterranean caves) is lushly planted with tropical fruit trees. A sandy but mediocre beach nearby offers a view of an unused series of railroad pylons, leading onto forested Coney Island across the bay. The beach is narrow, with rocky outcroppings, and unfortunately there are not a lot of other good beaches nearby. However, the nearby coastline is enchanting, with many natural caves and intimate coves. From the seaside, the airy public areas look like a modern version of a mogul's palace, with big windows, thick white walls, and three peaked roofs with curved eaves.

This recently restored resort appeals to young couples and families who don't need all the hustle and bustle and central location of a resort like Elbow Beach. Although it's unattractively located across from the airport, noise from planes is not a problem. The sprawling, 8.5-hectare (21-acre) property contains 11 three-story buildings with balconies and sea views (but no elevators). If your room is far from the main building, you may think you've been sentenced to Siberia (though there are secluded units that appeal to honeymooners). All accommodations are well furnished; the bathrooms are equipped with shower-tub combinations and are well-maintained. The children's programs and playground make this a good bet for families. There are also a lot of activities offered, including nature walks, twice-weekly "cave crawls," daily cave swims, organized activities for teenagers, scavenger hunts, communal croquet near the bar, fish feeding, and bridge competitions. The best rooms are directly on the beach, but they're at the bottom of a serpentine flight of about 30 masonry steps. That's no big deal for guests of average fitness, but those with limited mobility might opt for ocean-view, not oceanfront, rooms.

The on-site restaurants serve fair if unremarkable Continental cuisine, enlivened by fresh seafood. A multimillion-dollar renovation has perked up the look of all food and beverage outlets, including the Bayside Bar & Grill, the Rumhouse Bar, the Greenhouse Restaurant, the Palm Court, and the Hibiscus dining room, which now offers an outside patio allowing guests to dine alfresco. The lounge books live entertainment nightly, and there are a handful of other bars on the property. Afternoon tea is served every day, and there's a daily happy hour. Blasted out of natural rock, the swimming pool has a swim-up bar. Solitude, tranquillity, and friendly, personal service are the draws here.

11 Blue Hole Hill, Hamilton CR 04, Bermuda. ℂ **800/582-3190** in the U.S., 800/463-0851 in Canada, or 441/293-0188. Fax 441/293-2306. www.netlinkbermuda.com/grottobay. 201 units. Nov $150–$165 double; Dec1–Mar $130–$145 double; Mar 13–Apr 9 $150–$165 double; Apr 10–Oct $270–300 double; suites from $350 year-round. MAP (breakfast and dinner) $53 per person. AE, MC, V. Bus: 1, 3, 10, or 11. **Amenities:** 2 restaurants; 2 bars; outdoor freshwater pool; nearby golf course; 4 tennis courts (2 lit for night play), frequent tennis clinics; small health club; daily Jazzercise in the Rum House Lounge before breakfast; Jacuzzi; excursion boat; watersports center and dive shop; summer children's program; babysitting; laundry; dry cleaning. *In room:* A/C, TV, mini-fridge, coffeemaker, hair dryer, iron, safe.

2 Small Hotels

In direct contrast to the sprawling resorts are Bermuda's more intimate, informal, small hotels. Many have their own dining rooms and bars, and some even have their own beaches or beach clubs; all offer pools and patios.

VERY EXPENSIVE
SOUTHAMPTON PARISH

Pompano Beach Club ★   Right next to the Port Royal Golf Course, this seaside hotel is perched on a limestone hill, above a cove beach fringed with rocky outcroppings. From the terraced beach above the hotel's clubhouse, waist-deep water covers the clean, sandy bottom for the length of 2½ football fields before the deep water begins. It attracts couples of all ages who want privacy and tranquillity; golfers especially like this place.

The hillside villas scattered over the landscaped property have a balcony or terrace to take advantage of the oceanviews. If you can afford it, request the deluxe rooms at the top of the price scale (see below), as these accommodations often have wet bars and showers with oversize tubs. Some units are more spacious than others.

If you don't want to dine around at night, you can order meals on site in a dining room, with alfresco tables on a terrace.

36 Pompano Beach Rd., Southampton SB 03, Bermuda. ℂ **800/343-4155** in the U.S. and Canada, or 441/234-0222. Fax 441/234-1694. www.pompano.bm. 56 units. May 1–Oct 31 $430–$510 double, from $460 suite; Apr and Nov $340–$400 double, from $370 suite; off season $250–$290 double, from $270 suite. Packages available. Rates include MAP (breakfast and dinner). AE, MC, V. Hamilton ferry to Somerset. Bus: 7 or 8. **Amenities:** Restaurant; 2 bars; freshwater heated swimming pool; easy access to the government-owned Port Royal Golf Course; 4 all-weather tennis courts (2 lit); oceanfront fitness center; ocean and poolside Jacuzzi; Sunfish, paddle boat, Windsurfer and snorkeling equipment rentals; on-site moped rental; babysitting with 24-hr. notice; laundry. *In room:* A/C, TV, coffeemaker, mini-fridge, hair dryer, iron, safe.

The Reefs ★★ Not as refined, but also not as stuffy, as Horizons or Cambridge Beaches, this is one of the island's state-of-the-art inns, opening onto a private beach of pink-flecked sand surrounded by palm trees and jutting rocks. The Reefs was extensively renovated and vastly improved in late 2000 and early 2001. It boasts top-notch maintenance, first-class personal service, and unmatched ocean views. This "lanai colony" of salmon-pink cottages on Christian Bay spreads along a low coral ridge. The lanais are cheerfully decorated in rattan and bright island colors. All have private sun decks and ocean views. These mid-size accommodations have tasteful furnishings and small bathrooms with shower-tub combinations, separate dressing areas and dual basins. The Cottage Suites by the Reefs, the most desirable accommodations, is a series of one-, two-, or three-bedroom cottages built along the cliffs and hillside of the resort and featuring the privacy of a home with the luxuries and services of a resort. If you're looking for action, head over to the nearby Sonesta Beach Resort, or even consider checking into Elbow Beach or the Fairmont Southampton. But if you want a smaller place and more tranquillity, consider one of The Reefs' relaxing pink lanais.

The attentive staff of the plant-filled Ocean Echo, the more formal option, serves Continental and North American cuisine. The chefs concentrate on bringing out the food's natural flavors; they don't overpower your taste buds with extra sauces and gimmicks. If you want to let your hair down a bit, opt for Coconuts; there's no finer or more romantic spot in Bermuda for an alfresco sunset dinner than this beach terrace. The chefs draw inspiration from around the world—Thailand to the United States. See chapter 5 for a separate recommendation of the Clubhouse dining room and Coconuts. The kidney-shaped swimming pool sits on a ledge with an ocean view.

56 South Shore Rd., Southampton SN 02, Bermuda. ✆ **800/742-2008** in the U.S. and Canada, or 441/238-0222. Fax 441/238-8372. www.thereefs.com. 67 units. Apr 14–Nov 3 $318–$798 double, $518–$1,318 suite; off season $236–$496 double, $326–$806 suite. Rates include MAP (breakfast and dinner). AE, MC, V. Bus: 7. **Amenities:** 3 restaurants; 2 bars; pool; 3 golf courses nearby; 2 all-weather tennis courts; fitness center; complimentary kayaks and snorkeling equipment; moped and mountain-bike rental; babysitting; laundry; dry cleaning. *In room:* A/C, TV, dataport, fridge, hair dryer, iron, safe.

PAGET PARISH

Harmony Club ★ This is Bermuda's only all-inclusive hotel—you'll know exactly what your vacation will cost in advance. It's for couples only. However, the couple can be any combination of gender or age (over 18). Elbow Beach, the closest beachfront, is a 15-minute walk or a 5-minute scooter ride away. Named after the circa-1830 home of a 19th-century merchant that stood on the site, this hotel retains only a few vestiges of its original historic core, but tries to keep the friendly informality of a private home. It was renovated in 1997.

The accommodations, furnished in Queen Anne style, occupy a series of rambling pink-sided wings that encircle formal gardens with gazebos. Rooms near the road tend to be somewhat noisy. Units are generous in size, with sitting areas, double or king beds, oversize closets, and well-maintained private bathrooms with shower-tub combinations.

If you stay here, you'll eat all your meals here, because you're paying for an all-inclusive plan. The chefs are competent, if not dazzling. However, there's such a wealth and variety of food that you're almost certain to find something you like. Evening meals are served by candlelight on fine china and crystal in the Casuarina. A full English tea is served every afternoon; there are also weekly cocktail parties and entertainment 6 nights a week.

109 South Shore Rd., Paget PG BX, Bermuda. ℂ **888/427-6664** or 441/236-3500. Fax 441/236-2624. www.harmonyclub.com. 68 units. Nov 1–Apr 15 $278 double; Apr 16–Oct $358 double. Rates include all meals and drinks, activities. AE, DC, MC, V. Bus: 7 or 8. No children under 18 accepted. **Amenities:** Restaurant; bar; freshwater swimming pool; putting green; 2 tennis courts; whirlpool; Jacuzzis; sauna; moped rental next to hotel; laundry; dry cleaning. *In room:* A/C, TV, dataport, coffeemaker, hair dryer, safe.

Newstead Hotel ⋆   Long known as a favorite of older and more staid visitors, in 2000, this hotel poured $5 million into renovating its buildings and bringing its image up to date. The hotel originated in 1923 around the Edwardian home of Sir Richard and Lady Fairey. Shortly thereafter, it expanded to include another half-dozen buildings, each of which are tucked into a flowering garden at the edge of the harbor. Don't expect a sandy beachfront—swimming is conducted either within a heated swimming pool or from a pair of piers jutting out into the sheltered harbor. Evoking a country house that's supervised by a well-bred hostess, the ambience of this small hotel is dignified and refined—definitely not the place for hell-raisers. The property contains drawing rooms, a library, and lounges that are furnished, in part, with English antiques. Traditionalists prefer the old-fashioned bedrooms of the main house, but you can also opt for up-to-date comforts in the more contemporary modern buildings. Each accommodation features gleaming brass and lots of polished hardwoods. Most rooms have twin beds and tiled bathrooms with shower-tub combinations, complete with dressing area; newer units contain double sinks. The least desirable rooms in the main house (those opening onto the road in front of the house) have older-looking bathrooms and might be exposed to street noise. The most luxurious options are the modern poolside units, with furnished terraces, comfortable sitting rooms, and king-size beds.

The Rockfish Grill serves breakfast, lunch, and dinner from an a la carte menu in a setting that was newly configured. Less formal lunches and dinners (but not breakfasts) are served at Noah's, a casual dining spot overlooking Hamilton Harbour.

27 Harbour Rd. (P.O. Box PG 196), Paget PGBX, Bermuda. ℂ **800/468-4111** in the U.S. and Canada, or 441/236-6060. Fax 441/236-7454. www.newsteadhotel.com. 43 units. Apr–Oct $310–$375 double, $295–$465 suite; off season $250 double, $285–$365 suite. AE, MC, V. Ferry from Hamilton. **Amenities:** 2 restaurants; 2 bars; heated swimming pool; swimming in the harbor from a pair of private docks; somewhat out-of-shape putting green; 2 Har-Tru tennis courts; mini-gym; spa; salon; room service available only during mealtimes; babysitting; laundry. *In room:* A/C, TV, dataport, mini-fridge, coffeemaker, hair dryer, safe.

Stonington Beach Hotel ⋆   The Hospitality and Culinary Institute of Bermuda operates this offbeat place near Elbow Beach, one of the island's best beaches. Training ground or not, this is a good choice, with a gracious atmosphere and welcoming service, which is far superior to that of the better-known Harmony Club. Stonington is smart, neat, modern, and almost corporate-looking, but it lacks softness and a sense of tradition. Some employees are students, under the supervision of a professional international staff. The students are likely to be more helpful than many battle-trained, jaded veterans of the hotel field, but if you're looking for mistakes, you'll no doubt find them.

A lamp-lit drive leads up to the buff-colored facade, where you'll follow a stucco passageway to an inner octagonal courtyard. The accommodations are in four outlying buildings; a complete renovation was done in 1994. The rooms are comfortably spacious, equipped with a wide balcony or a patio offering ocean-views. Each has a ceiling fan and a love seat that can serve as an extra folding bed. The large bathrooms have shower and tub combinations. Steps cut from limestone lead through foliage to the hotel's sandy beach.

The library, with its glowing fireplace, is extremely inviting, as is the outdoor beach bar and the in-house restaurant, The Norwood Room (see chapter 5, "Where to Dine," for a full review). In the unlikely event that you don't like the food here, the hotel has a dinner-exchange program with four surrounding properties—so you won't be trapped in the same dining room every night if it doesn't suit you.

South Shore Rd. (P.O. Box HM 523), Hamilton HM CX, Bermuda. ℂ **800/457-4000** in the U.S. and Canada, or 441/236-5416. Fax 441/236-0371. www.stoningtonbeach.com. 64 units. Apr 16–Oct $375–$475 double; Nov–Apr 15 $250–$325 double. Rates include MAP (breakfast and dinner). AE, MC, V. Bus: 7. **Amenities:** 2 restaurants; bar; heated freshwater swimming pool; 2 tennis courts; access to a nearby fitness center; babysitting with advance notice; laundry; dry cleaning. *In room:* A/C, TV, mini-fridge, hair dryer, safe.

The Wharf Executive Suites Hotel ⭐   One of Bermuda's newest hotels— and a new hotel in Bermuda is a real rarity—is this boutique hotel that opened in 2002. It caters to the business traveler and the extended stay visitor. The location is on the harbor overlooking the city of Hamilton, which is reached by taking a 7-minute ferry ride. The management with some justification bills their offering as a "home away from home." No hotel can be that but this one tries admirably. The hotel is in a white-painted building offering studio suites equipped with kitchenettes and full suites with full kitchens. All bedrooms have executive work centers, including a desk and ergonomic chair, a two-line speakerphone, a high-speed internet connection, and a fax machine/printer/copier. A personalized concierge service is also provided. Rooms are spacious and furnished in a conservative, traditional style, each unit with a balcony overlooking Hamilton Bay. There is no restaurant on site, but a continental breakfast is served. The property was the former Palm Reef Hotel, and it's been totally renovated and refurbished, including new bathrooms with combination tub/showers.

1 Harbour Rd., Paget, PG BX Bermuda. ℂ **441/232-5700.** Fax 441/232-4008. www.bermudaresort hotels.com. 15 units. July 1–Oct 31 $225 double, $395 suite; Nov 1–Mar 1 $210 double, $370 suite. Rates include continental breakfast. AE, MC,V. **Amenities:** Laundry; dry cleaning. *In room:* A/C, TV, hair dryer, coffeemaker, kitchenette (studios), full kitchen (suites), iron, safe.

PEMBROKE PARISH (CITY OF HAMILTON)

Waterloo House ⭐   This is the favorite of business people in the City of Hamilton who appreciate the convenience of its location—on the harbor, not on a beach. It's more intimate and serene than its main competitor, the Hamilton Princess, but the Waterloo isn't as well maintained. Nonetheless, Waterloo still has its devotees, even if parts of it are in need of better maintenance and housekeeping. Two recent guests told us they stay here every year, and wouldn't think of checking into another hotel. There is a lot of charm to the place if you can overlook some flaws such as fabrics in need of renewal.

On the edge of Hamilton Harbour (on the outskirts of town), this enlarged and remodeled private home was built around 1910. Terraced gardens descend to the water in the Italian Riviera style; behind salmon-colored walls, the gardens contain palms, magnolias, poinsettias, urns overflowing with ivy, a splashing fountain, and white wrought-iron garden furniture shaded with fringed parasols. There are nooks for drinks and sunbathing around the property, and shade trees surround the swimming pool.

Inside, the drawing room has antique English furnishings and decorative tile floors. Rooms vary in size and decoration; each evokes the feeling of a country-house guest room. A newer wing offers small studios and twin-bedded units, though accommodations in the main unit have more character. The highest prices are for the five cottages, which have living and dining areas and refrigerators (though no kitchens). Cottage bathrooms are roomy and well maintained, with plenty of room for personal items. The tiled bathrooms in the newer wing are larger and better maintained, even though we still prefer the older unit for its quaint charm. All bathrooms feature shower and tub combinations.

The main dining room (reviewed in chapter 5, "Where to Dine") overlooks the terrace and harbor. On the lower terrace level is a bar lounge with Moorish arches, English armchairs, and hand-woven pillow covers. You can enjoy afternoon tea on the lawn at the water's edge.

Pitts Bay Rd. (P.O. Box HM 333), Hamilton HM BX, Bermuda. © **800/468-4100** in the U.S. and Canada, or 441/295-4480. Fax 441/295-2585. www.waterloohouse.com. 30 units. Apr–Nov $340–$380 double, $510–$780 suite; Dec–Mar $260–$362 double, $360–$630 suite. Rates include full breakfast; MAP (breakfast and dinner) $50 per person. AE, MC, V. Bus: 1, 2, 10, or 11. **Amenities:** Restaurant; bar; freshwater outdoor swimming pool; private dock; reciprocal relationship with Bermuda's best golf courses; privileges at the members-only Coral Beach and Tennis Club (tennis and squash) 6.5km (4 miles) from Hamilton, where the pink sands and protected waters create some of the best swimming conditions on the island; small fitness center; spa; business center with secretarial services; limited room service; laundry; dry cleaning; waterside barbecue area. *In room:* A/C, TV, fax, dataport, hair dryer, safe.

EXPENSIVE
PEMBROKE PARISH (CITY OF HAMILTON)

Rosedon ★ If you'd like a small local hotel with charm and character, in the City of Hamilton, Rosedon is for you. Those who want a megahotel with lots of facilities can check into the Hamilton Princess across the street. Otherwise, head for this stately 1906 mansion that has been successfully converted into an inn. The staff is helpful, polite, and personable. Although its rates are rather high for what it is—basically, an overblown guesthouse—it has its fans. Business travelers often stay here because of its proximity to the City of Hamilton.

Rosedon resembles a colonial-era plantation great house, with a pristine white exterior and royal blue shutters. Extensive gardens and lawns encircle the house. Look for the loquat tree (a small evergreen), a Bermuda trademark; other shrubs include hibiscus, banana plants, and bird of paradise. Once occupied by an English family, this was the first house in Bermuda with gaslights. The building has a formal entry hall and two antiques-filled lounges. A flagstone terrace with parasol-shaded tables surrounds the large, temperature-controlled pool.

The individually decorated, mid-size bedrooms have balconies or patios, along with small but neat bathrooms containing shower-tub combinations. The modern veranda accommodations in the rear are often preferred over rooms in the main house. Called lanai suites, the modern accommodations open onto the pool. The colonial-style bedrooms in the main house, however, have more island flavor and character.

The honor system prevails at the self-service bar. The full breakfast included in the rates is good and plentiful, with plenty of variety even if you stay a week. It can also be delivered to your room. There's afternoon tea, but no restaurant.

Pitts Bay Rd. (P.O. Box HM 290), Hamilton HM AX, Bermuda. © **800/742-5008** in the U.S. and Canada, or 441/295-1640. Fax 441/295-5904. www.rosedonbermuda.com. 47 units. Apr–Nov $214–$310 double; off season $160–$236 double. Extra person $30. Rates include full breakfast and afternoon tea. AE, MC, V. Free round-trip shuttle service to Stonington Beach, 10 min. away. Bus: 5. **Amenities:** Bar; heated outdoor swimming pool; access to tennis courts at South Shore Beach & Tennis Club; room service available 6am–9pm; babysitting; same-day laundry service. *In room:* A/C, TV, fridge, coffeemaker, hair dryer, iron, safe.

MODERATE
PEMBROKE PARISH (CITY OF HAMILTON)

Hamiltonian Hotel & Island Club   Set on a hill less than 1.5km (1 mile) northwest of the City of Hamilton, this is a quiet, relatively simple hotel that markets its rooms as timeshare units. Don't expect a particularly cozy reception— think of it as an anonymous getaway from the pressures of urban life, with no particular facilities for dining or partying. The one-bedroom accommodations are in four pink-sided, stone-roofed, apartment-style buildings. They're comfortable and well maintained, with average-sized bathrooms equipped with shower-tub combinations. Units don't have a full kitchen, but you can heat up food, and make toast or coffee—in other words, prepare yourself a snack.

Langton Hill (P.O. Box HM 1738), Hamilton HM GX, Bermuda. © 800/203-3222 in the U.S. or Canada, or 441/295-5608. Fax 441/295-7481. 32 units. Apr–Nov $156 double; off season $98 double. AE, MC, V. **Amenities:** Swimming pool on a plateau about 15 steps uphill from the rest of the complex; 3 tennis courts (2 lit for night play). *In room:* A/C, TV, fridge, coffeemaker.

3 Cottage Colonies

These accommodations are uniquely Bermudian. Each colony has a main club-house with a dining room, lounge, and bar, plus its own beach or pool. The cottage units, spread throughout landscaped grounds, offer privacy and some-times luxury. Most have kitchenettes suitable for preparing beverages and light snacks, but not for full-scale cooking.

If you were a travel agent working for Brooke Astor, Barbara Walters, and Goldie Hawn, you'd book them as follows: the aristocratic Astor into Cambridge Beaches; the media star Walters into Horizons; and the actress and producer Hawn into Ariel Sands. We hope that helps distinguish colony from colony.

VERY EXPENSIVE
SANDYS PARISH

Cambridge Beaches ★★★   The recently restored Cambridge Beaches attracts rich honeymooners, old-money families, and *Vanity Fair* couples who seek privacy, pampering, and plenty of facilities. The ambience is even more refined than that of the Horizons, and guests have access to five private palm-fringed beaches. If you're a first-time visitor, the clubby atmosphere may make you feel like an outsider. For snob appeal, Cambridge Beaches is numero uno in Bermuda (followed by Horizons). It's the natural choice for Saudi royalty. If your children are under 5, make sure they show up with a nanny—it's a house rule.

On a peninsula overlooking Mangrove Bay in Somerset, the colony's 10 hectares (25 acres) of semitropical gardens and green lawns occupy the entire western tip of the island. The colony centers around an old sea captain's house. The main lounges are tastefully furnished with antiques; the dominant feeling here is that of a country estate. Scattered throughout the gardens are nicely fur-nished cottages, some of which are nearly 300 years old. They have distinct Bermudian architectural features, with an added British starchiness. All of the cottages (some of which were once private homes) are conservatively furnished, and come with sun-and-breakfast terraces, generally with unobstructed views of the bay and gardens. A cottage can comfortably house four. The least expensive units have land rather than ocean vistas. Clad in marble, the bathrooms contain dual basin sinks and whirlpool tubs along with showers.

Dining is in the excellent and very pricey Tamarisk Dining Room (reviewed in chapter 5, "Where to Dine"), or on the terrace, where barbecues are sometimes held. There's also an informal lounge, the Port O' Call Pub, with nightly entertainment during the high season.

30 Kings Point Rd., Sandys Parish MA 02, Bermuda. ✆ **800/468-7300** in the U.S., 800/463-5990 in Canada, or 441/234-0331. Fax 441/234-3352. www.cambridgebeaches.com. 94 units. Apr 16–Oct $465–$650 double, $715–$770 suite, $1,275–$1,480 cottage for 4; off season $390–$542 double, $585–$635 suite, $1,065–$1,275 cottage for 4. Rates include MAP (breakfast and dinner). MC, V. Bus: 7 or 8. **Amenities:** 2 restaurants; 3 bars; 2 temperature-controlled pools; access to all golf courses of Bermuda, including nearby Robert Trent Jones–designed golf course, Port Royal; putting green; 3 tennis courts (1 lit for night play); exercise room and full-service European-style spa featuring whirlpool, massages, steam, sauna, and hair dressing, plus 50-odd types of skin, beauty, and relaxation treatments; watersports equipment and instruction including windsurfing, canoeing, kayaking, snorkeling, fishing (equipment is available), sailing, snorkeling trips, plus glass-bottom-boat excursions and fishing voyages and a full marina with Boston whalers and sailboats available for both self-piloted rentals and guided sailing excursions; 2 bonefishing flats adjacent to the colony; bicycle rental; moped rental; concierge; salon; room service available 7am–10pm; babysitting; laundry; dry cleaning. In room: A/C, TV upon request, fridge, hair dryer, iron, safe.

PAGET PARISH

Horizons and Cottages ★★★   This deluxe cottage colony sits atop a hill overlooking Coral Beach, a 10-minute walk away. The lack of a beach on the premises might be a serious drawback for some visitors, especially at these prices. Otherwise, you'll be a pampered darling here. Both of Bermuda's top cottage colonies—Cambridge Beaches and Horizons—are popular with a well-heeled crowd. Subdued sophistication characterizes both, though Horizons is perhaps a touch less snobbish. At Horizons, families with big bank accounts predominate in summer, and there's a mature repeat clientele in winter; trust-fund honeymooners show up year-round. Sometimes the atmosphere evokes a discreet house party, with fellow guests regularly being introduced. You might find more privacy, anonymity, and seclusion at Cambridge Beaches.

Horizons and Cottages have at their core a converted manor farm (ca. 1690), where the traditional ambience remains. A Relais & Châteaux member, Horizons is on a 10-hectare (25-acre) estate with terraced gardens and lawns. The reception rooms of the manor house have old Bermudian architectural details, as well as antiques from England and the Continent; several drawing rooms have open fireplaces.

All guest units are handsomely furnished with Italian terra-cotta tile floors, scatter rugs, traditional tray ceilings, and ceiling fans. They have separate dressing areas and private terraces overlooking the ocean. Some units are split-level. The generous tiled bathrooms come with oversize mirrors, and tub and shower combinations.

The main dining room, the Middleton Room (reviewed in chapter 5, "Where to Dine"), serves French *cuisine naturelle,* using all fresh products. The food, especially the tender steak and fresh seafood dishes, is exceptional for Bermuda, although the chefs at Cambridge Beaches seem to work more magic. Lunch is served on the terrace, which is transformed into an entertainment area in the evenings, with informal dancing and, at times, calypso music. Guests can also have lunch and dinner, by reservation, at Newstead and Waterloo House.

33 South Shore Rd., Paget PG04, Bermuda. ✆ **800/468-0022** in the U.S. and Canada, or 441/236-0048. Fax 441/236-1981. www.horizonscottages.com. 48 units. $440–$530 double; $570–$580 suite. Rates include MAP (breakfast and dinner). AE, MC, V. Bus: 2 or 7. **Amenities:** Restaurant; bar; heated freshwater swimming pool; 9-hole golf course; 18-hole putting green; 3 tennis courts; access to nearby Coral Beach & Tennis Club for more golf, tennis, squash and snorkeling gear, and health club and spa; bike and scooter rentals nearby; room service for some rooms—breakfast only; massage; babysitting; laundry. In room: A/C, fax, dataport, kitchenette for some rooms, hair dryer, safe, TV or minibar upon request.

> ## Kids Family-Friendly Accommodations
>
> **Elbow Beach Hotel** (p. 78)   Children stay free in their parents' room at this hotel, one of the best full-service resorts on the island. Your best bet is the "Family Value Package," which includes accommodations, transfers, daily breakfast buffet, and a host of activities and extras; inquire about it when you book.
>
> **The Fairmont Southampton** (p. 72)   This giant resort offers the best children's program on the island, including parties and reliable babysitting. Children under 17 stay free in a room with one or two adults, and receive complimentary breakfast and dinner daily.
>
> **Grotto Bay Beach Hotel** (p. 82)   A longtime family favorite, this hotel features a heavily discounted "Family Special" for two adults and two children under 16 spending at least 4 nights.
>
> **Rosemont** (p. 97)   Rosemont caters to families, and each of its units contains a kitchen. Some rooms can be joined together to accommodate larger broods. Babysitting can be arranged.
>
> **Royal Palms Hotel** (p. 98)   Although it can't compete with the big resorts in facilities, this longtime family favorite extends a cordial welcome. It's within walking distance of the City of Hamilton, so families can save on transportation. There's a freshwater pool, but the beach is a 10-minute ride or 30-minute walk away.
>
> **Sandpiper Apartments** (p. 95)   Families looking for a moderately priced vacation might check in here. Some units have living/dining areas with two double pullout sofa beds. Each unit has a kitchen where Mom and Dad can prepare simple meals to cut down on the high cost of dining out in Bermuda.
>
> **Sonesta Beach Resort** (p. 73)   Try to book into this stellar resort on a family package plan (consult a travel agent). Most rooms accommodate two parents and two kids, and there are plenty of activities and diversions for children, including unlimited free ice cream and pizza parties.

DEVONSHIRE PARISH

Ariel Sands Beach Club ★★   At the ocean's edge, with a sandy beach just a 2-minute walk away, secluded Ariel Sands is one of the best cottage colonies in Bermuda, though not quite in the platinum class of Cambridge Beaches and Horizons. This is a quiet place, popular with well-heeled families looking for a summer retreat. The grounds are nicely landscaped, with flowering trees, coconut palms, and one of the most original sculptures on the island—Seward Johnson, Jr.'s stainless-steel statue of Ariel, who dances like a water sprite on the surf.

One of Ariel's part-owners is the mother of actor Michael Douglas (and ex-wife of film legend Kirk Douglas), and the movie star contributed $5 million to the resort's recent refurbishment. It looks fresh, bright, and new—better than it has in years. In chilly weather, a double-hearth fireplace warms a reception lounge and bar area. The smallish rooms have private entrances. They're attractively decorated, with white walls, cool pastels, Bermudian flower paintings, straw matting on terra-cotta floors, and bentwood furniture; most have private porches. The art in many of the private and public rooms is based on themes from *The Tempest*, and guest rooms have names such as Miranda's Cabana, Sea Nymph, and Prospero. The mid-size bathrooms with shower-tub combinations are handsomely tiled and well maintained.

The first-class health spa offers such services as beachside massages, aromatherapy, skin and hair treatments, and a full exercise facility. Complete health and fitness appraisals are available, including programs devoted to nutrition, cardiac risk, and lifestyle health issues.

34 South Shore Rd., Devonshire (P.O. Box HM 334), Hamilton HM BX, Bermuda. (€) **800/468-6610** in the U.S., or 441/236-1010; call collect from Canada. Fax 441/236-0087. www.arielsands.com. 47 units. Apr–Oct $300–$900 double; Nov-Mar $210–$620 double. Rates include breakfast. AE, MC, V. Bus: 1. **Amenities:** Restaurant; bar; 1 freshwater and 2 saltwater pools; 2 tennis courts (both lit for night games); health club and spa; snorkeling equipment rental; moped rental; concierge; room service available at mealtimes only; babysitting with 24-hr. notice; laundry; dry cleaning. *In room:* A/C, TV, dataport, fridge, coffeemaker, hair dryer, iron, safe.

SMITH'S PARISH

Pink Beach Club & Cottages ★★   Two pretty rosy beaches surround this complex of pink cottages, and bay grape trees and hibiscus bushes grace the 6.5-hectare (16-acre) garden setting. This remote cottage colony, the largest on Bermuda, doesn't have the opulence or flair of Cambridge Beaches or Horizons, but it does attract an affluent international crowd. The staff, among the best on the island, includes people who have been with Pink Beach since it opened in 1947. The cottages range from studios—with a combination bedroom/sitting room, good-sized bathroom, and patio—to full units with a living room and terrace. Contemporary furnishings, fully equipped kitchens, and plush carpeting add to the allure. The bathrooms have combination tub and shower. If you can snare them, the very best accommodations, and the most luxurious, are a quartet of oceanfront suites. These are ideal for honeymooners or other couples, or even families seeking spacious accommodations. Sea Rock Cottage offers 17 junior suites, offering much of the same luxury as the oceanfront suites. Also on site is a series of recently completed condos located in five buildings, which form a half moon around the beach at the entry point to Tucker Town. With the completion of these new extensions, half of the club's accommodations will have been either refurbished or totally rebuilt around the turn of this century. The heart of the colony is the limestone clubhouse, with a natural-wood dining room where "backyard" vegetables and fresh seafood go into the international cuisine. Every table provides a view of the ocean, and occasionally of a celebrity diner. The food is nicely prepared, if not outstanding. The chefs strive for variety, but you might find dining here every night a bit monotonous. Breakfast here is a treat; request it the night before and a maid will serve you on your private terrace.

South Shore Rd. (P.O. Box HM 1017), Hamilton HM DX, Bermuda. (€) **800/355-6161** in the U.S. and Canada, or 441/293-1666. Fax 441/293-8935. www.pinkbeach.com. 94 units. Apr 15–Nov 15 $430–$750 double; off season $360–$495 double. Rates include MAP (breakfast and dinner). AE, MC, V. Closed Dec 15 to early Mar. Bus: 1. **Amenities:** Restaurant; bar; large freshwater pool; sun terrace; 2 championship golf courses 2 min. from hotel; 2 tennis courts; fitness center; spa services; watersports equipment; moped rental; salon; massage; babysitting; laundry; dry cleaning. *In room:* A/C, dataport, coffeemaker, hair dryer, iron, safe.

ST. GEORGE PARISH

St. George's Club ★   Far less stuffy than the cottage colonies listed above, this resort encompasses 7 hectares (18 acres) atop Rose Hill (off York St.). It features clusters of traditionally designed Bermudian one- and two-bedroom cottages. A family or two or three couples traveling together can share a cottage and bring the price down to a reasonable level. A shuttle bus takes guests to the beach club at Achilles Bay, about a 2-minute ride away, where the beach is sandy with some rocky outcroppings. The Atlantic waters are a bit turbulent in autumn and spring, but they calm during the summer. The complex functions primarily as a timeshare property; units are rented to the public when the owners are not using them. Cottages have private balconies or patios, comfortable living and dining areas, fully equipped kitchens, and bathrooms with sunken tubs (and showers) and marble vanities. Views are of the ocean, the pool, or the golf course.

The colony's elegant restaurant, Griffin's, is open to the public, and is among the finest dining rooms in the East End. Blackbeard's Hideout restaurant is also a popular rendezvous spot.

Rose Hill (P.O. Box GE 92), St. George GE BX, Bermuda. © **441/297-1200.** Fax 441/297-8003. www. stgeorgeclub.com. 71 units. Apr–Nov $275 cottage for up to 4, $375 cottage for up to 6; Dec–Mar $180 cottage for up to 4, $225 cottage for up to 6. AE, MC, V. Bus: 6, 8, 10, or 11. **Amenities:** 2 restaurants; 2 bars; 3 freshwater swimming pools (1 heated); adjacent Robert Trent Jones–designed 18-hole golf course (guests receive preferential tee times and reduced rates); 3 all-weather tennis courts (2 can be lit at night); watersports equipment; moped rental; babysitting upon request; laundry. *In room:* A/C, TV, fully equipped kitchen in majority of units, kitchenette in remaining units, iron.

MODERATE
HAMILTON PARISH

Clear View Suites & Villas   Adjacent to a grassy, rock-strewn patch of seafront, Clear View offers units that feature kitchenettes and a good deal of privacy. Midway between the City of Hamilton and St. George, it's a cluster of one- and two-story pink concrete buildings erected during the 1970s. Each holds two to six units decorated with pastel upholstery, tiled surfaces, and big windows. Units with sea views are more expensive. Bathrooms are tiled and well-kept with shower-tub combinations.

The centerpiece of the resort is a white-sided farmhouse that holds the restaurant, Landfall, which offers Bermudian cuisine, and a bar. You can swim in the ocean, but there's no beach—most guests head 1.5km (1 mile) west to the sands of Shelly Bay Beach. A small art gallery displays the works of local painters. Ruth Paynter (and her husband Gerald) arrange art classes that are popular among the island's community of retirees.

Sandy Lane, Hamilton Parish CR 02, Bermuda. © **800/468-9600** in the U.S. or Canada, or 441/293-0484. Fax 441/293-0267. 45 units. $195–$250 double. MAP (breakfast and dinner) $40 per person. AE, DC, MC, V. Bus: 10 or 11. **Amenities:** Restaurant; bar; 2 outdoor saltwater pools; tennis court; moped rental; conference facility; coin-op washers and dryers. *In room:* A/C, TV, kitchenette, fridge, coffeemaker.

4 Housekeeping Units

Housekeeping apartments, Bermuda's efficiency units, vary from modest to superior. Most have kitchens or kitchenettes and provide minimal daily maid service. Housekeeping cottages, which are air-conditioned and have fully equipped kitchens or kitchenettes, offer privacy and casual living on or close to a beach.

VERY EXPENSIVE
WARWICK PARISH

Mermaid Beach Club   Set beside a curvy shoreline that has both rocky cliffs and a sandy beachfront, this informal place avoids the stiff, snobby atmosphere of cottage colonies like Cambridge Villas and attracts couples of all ages who want to have a good time without having to dress up . . . ever. The complex consists of two-story cement-sided buildings, which are the outgrowth of a beach club founded in the 1940s. All units have patios or balconies overlooking the sea. Guest rooms are simple and summery, decorated with pastels and rattan furniture. The kitchenettes are fine for whipping up salads and sandwiches, but too small for anything more ambitious. Each room also has a clean bathroom with a shower-tub combination.

There's a nautical-theme main bar. You'll need a cab or moped to pick up groceries—a mini-mart in a Shell gas station is 15 minutes on foot or 2 minutes by moped from the hotel; a more substantial market is about an 8-minute moped ride away.

South Shore Rd. (P.O. Box WK 250), Warwick WK BX, Bermuda. © **800/441-7087** in the U.S. and Canada, or 441/236-5031. Fax 441/236-8325. 32 units, 22 with kitchenettes. Apr–Oct $299–$430 apt with kitchenette; off season $150–$260 apt with kitchenette. AE, MC, V. Bus: 7. **Amenities:** Bar; pool; bike-rental shop; babysitting; laundromat. *In room:* A/C, kitchenette is some units, coffeemaker.

PAGET PARISH

Fourways Inn ★ This posh little place feels like a secret hideaway. Pink-sided, airy, and stylish, the Bermudian cottages occupy well-maintained gardens. The sands of Elbow Beach and Mermaid Beach lie within a 15-minute walk or 5-minute scooter ride. The main building is a former private home dating from 1727. Each two-bedroom cottage has a patio and a fully equipped kitchenette, plus a good-sized tile bathroom with a shower-tub combination. Rooms contain conservatively comfortable furniture. The kitchenettes are more useful than those at Mermaid Beach, but still, better suited to sandwiches and snacks than preparing feasts. There's a medium-sized grocery store across the road.

1 Middle Rd. (P.O. Box PG 294), Paget PG BX, Bermuda. © **800/962-7654** in the U.S. and Canada, or 441/236-6517. Fax 441/236-5528. www.fourwaysinn.com. 6 units, 5 cottages. Apr–Oct $265 double, $365–$585 suite; off season $175 double, $205–$350 suite. Extra person $40. Rates include continental breakfast; MAP (breakfast and dinner) $50 per person. AE, MC, V. Bus: 8. No children under 16 accepted. **Amenities:** Restaurant; bar; heated swimming pool; room service available at dinner; laundry; dry cleaning. *In room:* A/C, TV, kitchenette, minibar, hair dryer, safe.

EXPENSIVE
WARWICK PARISH

Marley Beach Cottages ★ *Value* For two couples traveling together, this may be your best bargain. The pink-walled cottages sit on a steep, beautifully landscaped plot of land. Atop a low cliff on the south shore, near Astwood Park,

---

Your Own Private Villa

Bermuda Rentals (© **416/232-2243;** www.bermudarentals.com) offers more than 40 privately owned cottages, apartments, and villas for rent in Bermuda, at prices beginning at $40 per person per day. Most rentals for two guests range from $90 to $130 daily for a well-equipped and fully furnished unit, with private garden entrances, kitchens, and bathrooms (mainly with shower). Many accommodations also have pools on site as well as easy access to the ocean. The homes are owned by Bermudians for the most part, and are rented when they are not occupied by the owners. If you call her, Fiona T. Campbell (see number above) will answer all your questions.

the resort was used for scenes in *The Deep* and *Chapter Two*. More recently, part of another film, *Bermuda Grace*, was shot there. Three narrow beaches lie at the bottom of the slope that leads to the sea. It's not an ideal place for children, because there's little for them to do other than swimming in the pool or at the beach. Parents who do bring the kids are warned to keep a close eye on them, because of the steep drop-off to the beaches below. We wouldn't recommend this place for anyone who might have a problem with the steps leading down the cliff to the ocean, but reasonably fit guests won't mind.

The spacious cottages have fully equipped bathrooms with shower-tub combinations, kitchens, hibachis, and sea views from the patio. Each cottage has both a suite and a studio apartment, which you can rent as one unit or two. If you're cooking in, you can phone in an order to a local grocery that delivers, or give a list to the staff, who'll phone in your order. There's no delivery charge for orders over $20.

South Shore Rd. (P.O. Box PG 278), Warwick PG BX, Bermuda. ✆ **800/637-4116** in the U.S., or 441/236-1143. Fax 441/236-1984. 13 units. Apr–Oct $203–$290 double; Nov–Mar $125–$170 double. Extra person $37 in summer, $25 off season. AE, M, V. Bus: 7. **Amenities:** Heated freshwater swimming pool; whirlpool. *In room:* A/C, TV, kitchen, fridge, coffeemaker, iron.

Surf Side Beach Club ⭐   With more style than the Mermaid Beach Club, the Surf Side Beach Club occupies a steeply sloping hillside that descends through gardens to a crescent-shaped sweep of private beachfront. (The steps down to the beach may be hard for mobility-impaired guests to manage.) A varied array of flowering trees and panoramic walkways dots the terraced property. From lookout points in the garden, visitors can see grouper and other fish swimming among the distant rocks of the shallow sea.

Accommodations consist of one-bedroom apartments near the terrace pool, and other lodgings in hillside buildings. The self-contained units are simple and sunny, outfitted in bright colors with comfortable accessories. Each has a fully equipped kitchenette (including English china, wineglasses, and even salt and pepper shakers). The small tiled bathrooms are neatly kept and contain showers. A local grocery accepts phone orders and will deliver to your unit, with no delivery charge for orders over $20. The apartments also have private balconies or patios; some have sitting rooms as well.

A small cafe serves breakfast and lunch during the high season. The restaurant and bar, Palms, offers American and international cuisine; the menu changes daily.

South Shore Rd. (P.O. Box WK 101), Warwick WK BX, Bermuda. ✆ **800/553-9990** in the U.S., or 441/236-7100. Fax 441/236-9765. www.surfside.bm. 43 units (10 with shower only). Apr–Oct $250–$350 double, $300–$675 up to 4 people; off season $130–$165 double, $225–$350 up to 4 people. Extra person $50. Off-season extended-stay discounts available. MAP $65 per person. AE, MC, V. Bus: 7. **Amenities:** Restaurant; bar; pool; tennis; mini-spa; hot tub; sauna; salon; laundry, dry cleaning. *In room:* A/C, TV, kitchen, fridge, coffeemaker, hair dryer, safe.

MODERATE
SOUTHAMPTON PARISH

Grape Bay Cottages   This "resort" consists of two well-maintained cottages, each directly beside the sea, and each of which is reserved sometimes 6 months in advance. Each is a cozy saltbox-style cottage, with comfortably unpretentious furniture and lots of reminders of Bermuda's maritime traditions. Each has a nice bathroom containing a shower-tub combination, a fully equipped kitchen, a wide front veranda, and the kind of ambience that's conducive to families taking holidays together and getting to know one another again. Maid service is provided for the bedrooms and living rooms (but not for the kitchens) every Monday to Saturday. The venue is about as *laissez-faire* as you're likely to find anywhere in Bermuda, but it's usually well suited to the many clients who prefer self-catered holidays in a simple cottage by the beach.

Grape Bay Dr. (off Middle Rd.), P.O. Box HM 1851, Hamilton, HM HX Bermuda. ✆ 800/637-4116 in the U.S., or 441/236-1194. Fax 441/236-1662. 2 2-bedroom units. Apr–Oct $315 1–4 persons; Nov–Mar $210 1–4 persons. Extra person $35 in summer, $20 off season. AE, MC, V. Bus: 4. *In room:* A/C, TV, kitchen, coffeemaker, iron.

Munro Beach Cottages   At a secluded seaside resort overlooking a private beach at Whitney Bay, this cottage complex borders the Port Royal Golf Course and its tennis courts. It sits at the western end of the south shore and opens onto Munro Beach, which boasts some of the best bonefishing and snorkeling in Bermuda. Each spacious unit has a fully equipped kitchen, a combination dining, living, and bedroom area, and a separate tiled bathroom equipped with a shower-tub combination. Nonsmoking accommodations are available. All cottages provide homelike comforts, and there is daily maid service. If you don't feel like cooking, several first-class restaurants are within a 10- to 15-minute taxi ride. Snorkeling, sailing, and scuba diving are also close at hand.

2 Port Royal Golf Course Rd., Southampton SN BX, Bermuda. ✆ 800/637-4116 in the U.S., or 441/234-1175. Fax 441/234-3528. www.munrobeach.com. 17 units. Apr–Nov 11 $220 double, $255 triple, $290 quad; off season $125 double, $160 triple, $198 quad. MC, V. Bus: 7 or 8. *In room:* A/C, TV, kitchen, hair dryer, coffeemaker, iron, safe.

WARWICK PARISH

Astwood Cove 🍸   Cameron and Deirdre Hill own this homestead, which was built in 1720 on a dairy farm. (Sisters Maude, Ada, and Mary Astwood stipulated in their will that the house should always carry their name.) The apartment complex occupies a peaceful setting, overlooking lightly wooded meadows and the south shore. The closest large beach, Long Bay, is .5km (¼ mile) away; Astwood Beach and Mermaid Beach are only a 3-minute stroll from the complex.

Each self-contained apartment has a ceiling fan and a terrace or porch. Local phone calls are free. Some units have sitting rooms, and all have kitchens or kitchenettes equipped with English china. Most of the kitchens are generously proportioned units with stoves, microwaves, and enough basic accessories to prepare a real meal. A few smaller units have just microwaves and stovetop burners. Each unit has a small tiled bathroom, with a shower.

There's a mini-mart less than 3km (2 miles) away. A grocery store somewhat farther away delivers orders over $20.

49 South Shore Rd., Warwick WK 07, Bermuda. ✆ 800/637-4116 in the U.S., or 441/236-0984. Fax 441/236-1164. www.astwoodcove.com. 20 units (all with shower only). Apr–Nov 15 $150–$175 double; Nov 16–Mar 31 $110–$150 double; $125–$130 suite. AE, MC, V. Bus: 7. **Amenities:** Pool; sauna; bike rentals; babysitting; laundromat; gas-fired barbecue grills. *In room:* A/C, kitchenette, fridge, coffeemaker, iron.

Sandpiper Apartments *(Kids)*   Built in 1979 and frequently upgraded, this apartment complex is a bargain, attracting self-sufficient families who like the spacious accommodations and who often shop for groceries to prepare some of their own meals—helpful in cutting down on the pricey restaurant bills in Bermuda. Nine units are studios for one or two people, with two double beds, a small tiled bathroom, and a fully equipped kitchenette that's sufficient for simple meals. Five units contain a bedroom (with king-size or twin beds), a kitchen, and a living/dining area with two double pullout sofa beds. Every apartment has a bathroom equipped with a shower-tub combination and balcony. There's daily maid service. The Sandpiper is minutes away from restaurants and the supermarket. The closest beach is 457m (1,500 ft.) away, and the property has gardens for lounging.

South Shore Rd. (P.O. Box HM 685), Hamilton HM CX, Bermuda. ✆ **441/236-7093.** Fax 441/236-3898. www. bermuda.com. 14 units. Apr–Oct $130 double, $170–$200 suite for 3 or 4; off season $105 double, $140–$170 suite for 3 or 4. AE, DC, MC, V. Bus: 7. **Amenities:** Pool; outdoor whirlpool; babysitting; laundromat; barbecue grills. *In room:* A/C, TV, kitchenette, fridge, coffeemaker, hair dryer, iron, safe.

Vienna Guest Apartments   This apartment complex lies on attractively landscaped grounds, with panoramic views of Forest Hills, Gibbs Hill Lighthouse, and Great Sound. It opened in the early 1990s and underwent renovation in 1999. Informality is definitely the theme—you're even welcomed with beer or wine. Five units can accommodate up to four guests each, and one unit holds two people comfortably. Each good-sized apartment has one queen-size bed and one double bed, a combined living and dining room with a ceiling fan, a clock radio, a fully equipped kitchen with a patio, and a small tiled bathroom with a shower and tub combination.

63 Cedar Hill (P.O. Box WK 761), Warwick WK BX, Bermuda. ✆ **441/236-3300.** Fax 441/236-6100. www.netlinkbermuda.com/vienna. 6 units. Apr–Nov $130–$145 double, $20 3rd person, $15 child 4–12; off season $95–$120 double, $20 3rd person, $15 child. AE, MC, V. Bus: 7. **Amenities:** Pool; golf courses and tennis courts nearby; can arrange for watersports; sun deck; coin-op laundry facilities; barbecue facilities. *In room:* A/C, TV, hair dryer, safe.

PAGET PARISH

Paraquet Guest Apartments *(Value)*   If you're looking for a bargain and are happy with rather motel-like accommodations, this is the place for you. This buff-colored collection of Bermudian houses sits in a gentle knoll, a 5-minute walk from Elbow Beach and a 10-minute bus ride from the City of Hamilton. Built in the mid-1970s, the complex is owned by the Portuguese-born Correia family. Nine units have kitchenettes that are attractive and compact but efficient, filled with the basic equipment you'd need to prepare a meal. All the units (which range from small to mid-size) contain functional but comfortable modern furniture, plus a small tiled bathroom with shower. The apartment groupings also operate a decently priced restaurant, Paraquet (reviewed in chapter 5, "Where to Dine"). In addition, a grocery store is a mere 45m (150 ft.) from the hotel.

South Shore Rd. (P.O. Box PG 173), Paget PG BX, Bermuda. ✆ **441/236-5842.** Fax 441/236-1665. www. netlinkbermuda.com/paraquet. 12 units. Apr–Oct $144 double without kitchen, $182 double with kitchen; Nov–Mar $130 double without kitchen, $155 double with kitchen. MC, V. Bus: 7. **Amenities:** Restaurant; laundromat. *In room:* A/C, TV, no phone.

Valley Cottages & Apartments   In a semitropical setting in the center of the island, this is a good choice for self-sufficient types, although we think you get a better deal at the Paraquet Guest Apartments. The complex of typical pink Bermuda buildings lies a short walk from Elbow Beach and a number of food markets and tennis courts. Ferry and bus connections to the rest of Bermuda are easily accessible. These mid-size cottages and studios are in a garden, and contain kitchens, living rooms, and private balconies, along with small tiled bathrooms with shower-tub combinations. The decor is minimalist but comfortable, with good beds.

Valley Rd. (P.O. Box PG 214), Paget PG BX, Bermuda. ✆ **441/236-0628.** Fax 441/236-3895. www.netlink bermuda.com/valley. 9 units. Summer $90–$110 studio double, $150–$180 cottage up to 4 people; off season $70–$90 studio double, $120–$140 cottage up to 4 people. Bus: 8. **Amenities:** Spa pool and sun terrace in a secluded area. *In room:* A/C, TV, kitchen.

PEMBROKE PARISH (CITY OF HAMILTON)

Rosemont ★ *Kids*   Possessing more character and island charm than Valley Cottages or Barnsdale Guest Apartments, Rosemont is a cluster of gray-walled cottages, each with a large veranda, on a flowered hillside near the Hamilton Princess. Two of the cottages are former private homes, built in the 1940s; the rest are more modern structures constructed within the past 2 decades. The harbor is visible from the raised terrace. Business travelers, "subdued" families, and older couples frequent Rosemont; attracted by its peace and tranquillity. There is a policy here to "keep it quiet," so the hotel usually doesn't accept college students or large groups.

Each well-furnished room has a kitchen. We find some units a little on the dark side. As many as three rooms can be joined together to accommodate families. The hotel also has three suites with private entrances and better furnishings. Each accommodation comes with a small but neat private tiled bathroom.

There's no restaurant on the premises; everybody cooks in. A grocery store is close by, downtown City of Hamilton is 10 minutes away, and Elbow Beach is a 15-minute scooter or taxi ride away.

41 Rosemont Ave. (P.O. Box HM 37), Hamilton HM AX, Bermuda. ℂ **800/367-0040** in the U.S., 800/267-0040 in Canada, or 441/292-1055. Fax 441/295-3913. www.rosemont.bm. 48 units. Apr–Nov $164–$270 double; Dec–Mar $150–$230 double. Rates do not include service and taxes. MC, V. **Amenities:** Scooter rentals arranged; babysitting; laundry. *In room:* A/C, TV, dataport, kitchen, fridge, hair dryer.

PEMBROKE PARISH(CITY OF HAMILTON)

Robin's Nest   Consider Robin's nest if you'd like a snug little apartment in a family-managed compound in a residential neighborhood. It consists of three separate buildings, each painted terra cotta, scattered amid a small but well-maintained garden that's supervised by Milt and Renée Robinson. Units are spacious and have a summery-looking decor that includes lots of wicker. Each unit contains a fully equipped kitchen and a bathroom with a shower-tub combination. Hibachis are available in case anyone wants to expand his or her cooking facilities into the Great Outdoors. Two coves, suitable for swimming, lie within a 10-minute walk of the compound.

10 Vale Close, North Shore, Pembroke HM 04 Bermuda. ℂ **800/637-4116** in the U.S., or 441/292-4347. Fax 441/292-4347. rob@bspl.bm. 4 units. Year-round $125 double; $175 triple; $200 quad. Children under 12 $10 each per night. No credit cards. Bus: 4. **Amenities:** Large freshwater swimming pool. *In room:* A/C, TV, kitchen, fridge, coffeemaker, hair dryer, iron, safe.

SANDYS PARISH

Garden House ★ *Finds*   This lovely Bermuda home sits on 1 hectare (3 acres) of landscaped gardens in a secluded location, extending down to Ely's Harbour, where there is a private dock for deep-water swimming. You have a choice of three cottages: a studio, a one-bedroom cottage with a separate living room and kitchen, and, the most luxurious of all, a two-bedroom cottage with an 11m (37-ft.) living room leading to a separate kitchen. Beds are single kings or two twins, although one cottage has a lovely Bermudian antique four-poster bed. Mid-size bathrooms have a full tub and shower combo plus a spacious cupboard faced with a full-length mirror. The living rooms in the units evoke a British country house, accented with Bermudian touches of cedar. The hostess will take you to the grocery store should you need any provisions. All cottages have private patios where you can barbecue on your hibachi.

4 Middle Rd., Somerset Bridge, Sandys Parish, SB 01 Bermuda. ℂ **441/234-1435.** Fax 441/234-3006. 3 units. Summer $120 studio for 2, $135 cottage for 2, $260 2-bedroom cottage for 4; off season $110 studio for 2, $125 cottage for 2, $230 2-bedroom cottage for 4. AE, MC, V. Bus: 7 or 8. Closed Dec–Feb. **Amenities:** Salt-water swimming pool. *In room:* A/C, TV/VCR, kitchen, fridge, coffeemaker, iron.

5 Guesthouses

Bermuda's guesthouses are usually comfortable, old, converted manor houses in garden settings. Some have pools and terraces. The smaller ones are much more casual. They offer fewer facilities than other types of accommodations and are often outfitted with simple, lived-in furniture. Most guesthouses serve breakfast only. Those accommodating fewer than 12 guests are usually private homes. Some have housekeeping units, and others offer shared kitchen facilities for guests to prepare snacks. The vast majority of guesthouse hosts will happily arrange for bicycling, golf, tennis, watersports, or any other activity that you may want to participate in, which the guesthouse does not directly offer.

EXPENSIVE
PEMBROKE PARISH (CITY OF HAMILTON)
Royal Palms Hotel ★ *Kids*   Just a 5-minute walk from the City of Hamilton, the Royal Palms is one of the most sought-after small hotels on the island, thanks to the care and restoration work of brother-and-sister owners Richard Smith and Susan Weare. Built in 1903, it's a fine example of Bermudian architecture, with coral-colored walls, white shutters, a white roof, and a wraparound front porch with rocking chairs and armchairs. Local residents often walk by the garden to admire the marigolds and zinnias. The closest beach is Elbow Beach, a 10-minute taxi or scooter ride or a 30-minute walk away.

The guest rooms were once the living rooms, parlors, and bedrooms of the grand private house. All are spacious, sunny, and comfortably furnished, with rich fabrics throughout. Most units have high ceilings and tall windows, and each comes with a small, well-maintained private bathroom equipped with a shower-tub combination. In the mews next to the hotel are four additional, but less desirable units, which don't include bathrooms. This guesthouse is an excellent choice for budget-minded families traveling together. Family travelers generally request one of the units that come with kitchen facilities.

Cozy public areas include Ascots (reviewed in chapter 5, "Where to Dine"), which serves European and Bermudian cuisine.

24 Rosemont Ave. (P.O. Box HM 499), Hamilton HM CX, Bermuda. (℃) **800/678-0783** in the U.S., 800/799-0824 in Canada, or 441/292-1854. Fax 441/292-1946. www.royalpalms.bm. 25 units. Apr–Nov 15 $160–$240 double; off season $150–$180 double. Extra person $40; children under 16 $25, children under 3 stay free in parent's room. Rates include continental breakfast. AE, MC, V. Bus: 1, 2, 10, or 11. **Amenities:** Restaurant; bar; pool; babysitting; laundry. *In room:* A/C, TV, dataport, some units with kitchens, coffeemaker, hair dryer, iron, safe.

MODERATE
SOUTHAMPTON PARISH
Royal Heights Guest House   At the top of a steep driveway near the summit of Lighthouse Hill, this guesthouse is convenient to the Southampton Princess, with its varied nightlife and dining options. It's a modern, turquoise-trimmed building with two wings that embrace the front entryway. Guests are welcome to gather in the living room of the owners, Russel and Jean Richardson, who are happy to suggest activities. Each tidy but small room has a balcony and comfortable furniture, plus a tiled bathroom with shower. Horseshoe Bay, the closest beach, is a 5-minute taxi or scooter ride or 15-minute walk away. You can watch ships passing by on the Great Sound as you float in the guesthouse's swimming pool.

Lighthouse Hill (P.O. Box SN 144), Southampton SN BX, Bermuda. (℃) **441/238-0043.** Fax 441/238-8445. 7 units. Apr–Nov $145 double, $195 triple; off season $125 double, $175 triple. Rates include continental breakfast. AE, MC, V. Closed Feb. Bus: 7 or 8. **Amenities:** Saltwater pool. *In room:* A/C, TV, fridge, coffeemaker, no phone.

PAGET PARISH

Dawkins Manor   In a quiet residential neighborhood, a 5-minute walk from Elbow Beach, this inn offers simple, unpretentious accommodations. Originally built in the 1930s, it has expanded massively since Jamaica-born Celia Dawkins bought the place in the early 1990s. Off-island lecturers conducting short-term classes at nearby Bermuda College sometimes stay here. Even the simplest rooms contain microwaves and coffeemakers; more elaborate accommodations contain kitchens that are bigger than those in lots of other rental properties, suitable for bona-fide cooking. Each unit comes with a small but tidy tiled bathroom with a shower-tub combination. A grocery store can be found 2 minutes from the Manor.

29 St. Michael's Rd. (P.O. Box PG 34), Paget PG BX, Bermuda. ✆ **441/236-7419.** Fax 441/236-7088. www. bermuda-charm.com. 8 units. Summer $130 double without kitchenette, $150 double with kitchenette, $170 suite for 2 with kitchenette; off season $105 double without kitchenette, $115 double with kitchenette, $125 suite for 2 with kitchenette. No credit cards. Bus: 7. **Amenities:** Pool; bike rentals; babysitting; laundromat. *In room:* A/C, TV, kitchen in some units, fridge, coffeemaker, hair dryer, iron, safe.

PEMBROKE PARISH (CITY OF HAMILTON)

Edgehill Manor   Just outside the city limits and a 15-minute walk from the nearest beach, Edgehill Manor is in a quiet residential area that's convenient to the City of Hamilton's restaurants and shopping. It was built around the time of the American Civil War, exudes an old-fashioned, homey quality, and attracts a rather middle-aged clientele. British-born proprietor Bridget Marshall continues the tradition of serving English tea in the afternoon. Although each unit has its own style, all have small balconies or patios; three have kitchenettes, and all come with small tiled bathrooms with shower units. Ms. Marshall's continental breakfast, she is proud to say, is "all home baked."

Rosemont Ave. (P.O. Box HM 1048), Hamilton HM EX, Bermuda. ✆ **441/295-7124.** Fax 441/295-3850. www. bermuda.com/edgehill. 9 units. Apr–Nov 15 $168 double; off season $140 double. Rates include continental breakfast. Extra person $14; children under 12 in adult's room $20. No credit cards. Bus: 7 or 8. **Amenities:** Freshwater pool; room service available 8–9:30am; babysitting. *In room:* A/C, TV, kitchen in some units, fridge, safe.

Fordham Hall   On a hillside just outside the City of Hamilton, this guesthouse opens onto a panoramic view of Pitts Bay and the harbor beyond. Fordham Hall lies within walking distance of the city's best shops and restaurants, with the ferry practically at its doorstep. Since a change in ownership in 1999, the complex has been vastly improved. The place has a real Bermudian atmosphere, with a breezy lounge. The accommodations are spacious and comfortable, with attractive furnishings, and small tiled bathrooms with shower-tub combinations. You can eat breakfast with a view of the boating activity on Hamilton Harbour. Arrangements can be made for water-skiing, skin-diving, tours, carriages, taxis, and motorbikes.

53 Pitts Bay Rd., Pembroke (P.O. Box HM 692), Hamilton HM CX, Bermuda. ✆ **800/537-4163** in the U.S., or 441/295-1551. Fax 441/295-3906. 12 units. Summer $130 double, $190 suite; off season $120 double, $180 suite. Rates include continental breakfast. MC, V. Bus: 7 or 8. *In room:* A/C, TV, microwave, fridge, hair dryer.

The Oxford House ✪   The Oxford House is one of the best and most centrally located guesthouses in the City of Hamilton, about a 10-minute scooter ride or a 30-minute walk from Elbow Beach. The only property in Bermuda constructed specifically as a guesthouse, it's on a side street that leads to Front Street, near the Bermudiana Hotel.

The guesthouse was built in 1938 by a doctor and his French wife, who requested that some of the architectural features follow French designs. Doric columns, corner mullions, and urn-shaped balustrades flank the white- and cream-colored entrance portico. Inside, a curved stairwell sweeps up to spacious, well-furnished guest rooms, each named after one of Bermuda's parishes. They have high ceilings and dressing areas. Two accommodations are equipped with full bathrooms, the rest contain shower units. There's also a sunny upstairs sitting room. Breakfast might include a fresh fruit salad made with oranges and grapefruit grown in the yard. The gracious host is Welsh-born Ann Smith.

Woodbourne Ave. (P.O. Box HM 374), Hamilton HM BX, Bermuda. © **800/548-7758** in the U.S., 800/272-2306 in Canada, or 441/295-0503. Fax 441/295-0250. www.oxfordhouse.bm. 12 units. Mar 16–Nov $172 double, $220 triple, $248 quad; off season $160 double, $205 triple, $230 quad. Rates include full breakfast. AE, MC, V. Bus: 7 or 8. *In room:* A/C, TV, coffeemaker.

ST. GEORGE PARISH

Aunt Nea's Inn at Hillcrest ✪ *Value* The only true B&B inn in historic St. George, this inviting place is now better than ever following an upgrade and major improvements. The early-18th-century house stands on a hill off Old Maid's Lane. Three beaches with great watersports are within 10 minutes on foot. In 1804, the Irish poet Thomas Moore roomed here for several weeks. He developed a passion for Nea Tucker next door and wrote several romantic verses for her.

Each room is uniquely furnished, with four-poster beds constructed of tropical hardwoods or wrought iron, and complementary armoires and accent pieces. Four rooms have whirlpools, the others come with shower units. Owners Delaey Robinson and Andrea Dismont have given the rooms names such as "Green Turtle" and "Queen Conch," which represent many of the natural treasures of Bermuda. Smoking is not allowed.

1 Nea's Alley (P.O. Box GE 96), St. George GE BX, Bermuda. © **441/297-1630.** Fax 441/297-1908. www.auntneas.com. 20 units. Apr–Oct $160–$250 double, $250–$350 suite. Rates include breakfast. AE, MC, V. Closed Nov–Mar. Bus: 1, 3, 6, 10, or 11. *In room:* A/C, fridge, coffeemaker, hair dryer, iron, safe.

INEXPENSIVE
SOUTHAMPTON PARISH

Greene's Guest House From the outside, this guesthouse overlooking Great Sound is well maintained and unpretentious. A look on the inside reveals pleasant, conservatively furnished rooms that are more impressive than you might have supposed. A pair of lions resting on stone columns flanks the entry. The tables in the dining room, which adjoins the kitchen, are set with full formal dinner service throughout the day. Owners, Walter "Dickie" Greene and his wife, Jane, welcome guests to use the spacious, well-furnished living room and the sun-washed terraces in back. Bedrooms are small to medium in size, each comfortably furnished with a tidily kept compact private bathroom with a shower-tub combination.

There's a swimming pool in the back garden, and Whale Bay Beach lies 3 minutes away by bus or 10 minutes by foot. Dinner is available in the dining room if requested in advance. Facing the sea is a cozy lounge where guests record their drinks on the honor system. The bus to and from the City of Hamilton stops right in front of the house.

71 Middle Rd. (P.O. Box SN 395), Southampton SN BX, Bermuda. © **441/238-0834.** Fax 441/238-8980. 7 units. $140 double. Rates include full breakfast. No credit cards. Bus: 7 or 8. **Amenities:** Pool. *In room:* A/C, TV, fridge, coffeemaker, iron.

PAGET PARISH

Greenbank Guest House This guesthouse stands at the water's edge in Salt Kettle, just across the bay—a 10-minute ferry ride—from the City of Hamilton.

It's an old home (the oldest section dates from the 1700s), hidden under pine and palm trees, with shady lawns and flower gardens. The manager welcomes guests in an antique-filled drawing room. The atmosphere is relaxed, and the service, by the Ashton family, personal.

Greenbank offers accommodations with private entrances and kitchens in waterside and garden-view cottages. Rooms vary in size and shape, but most are small, with small bathrooms as well, each with a shower unit. The furnishings are rather plain but comfortable. The four units in the main house afford less privacy than the cottages. The guesthouse has a private dock for swimming; the charter operation on the property rents motorboats and sailboats. The nearest beach is Elbow Beach, a 15-minute taxi or moped ride away.

17 Salt Kettle Rd. (P.O. Box PG 201), Paget PG BX, Bermuda. ℂ 800/637-4116 in the U.S., or 441/236-3615. Fax 441/236-2427. www.bermudamall.com/greenbank. 11 units. Apr–Nov $150–$165 waterside cottage for 2, $270 waterside apt with 2 bathrooms for 4, $125 garden apt for 2; off season $130–$145 waterside cottage for 2, $250 waterside apt with 2 bathrooms for 4, $105 garden apt for 2. Extra person $25 year-round. AE, MC, V. Ferry from Hamilton. Bus: 7 or 8. In room: A/C, kitchen, fridge, coffeemaker.

Little Pomander Guest House ★ *Finds* This guesthouse is a pink-sided home that once served as the annex to what is now a privately operated tennis club across the street. Little Pomander can trace its history and foundations to the 1630s. The grassy lawn stretches a short distance down to the rocky shoreline, where you can see cruise ships anchored in Hamilton Harbour. The small rooms are tastefully outfitted with floral prints and alpine-style curtains designed by decorator Irene Trott, who owns the inn with her daughters. There are three apartments, each with a full kitchenette. All rooms come with a small bathroom with a combo tub and shower. The closest beach is Elbow Beach; it's a 5-minute scooter ride or 15-minute walk away.

16 Pomander Rd. (P.O. Box HM 384), Hamilton HM BX, Bermuda. ℂ 441/236-7635. Fax 441/236-8332. 5 units. Apr–Oct $130 double; off season $90 double. Rates include continental breakfast. AE, MC, V. Bus: 1, 7, or 8. In room: A/C, TV, kitchenette, fridge, hair dryer.

Salt Kettle House ★★ *Finds* Informal and secluded, this little charmer sits on a narrow peninsula jutting into Hamilton Harbour. You can swim in a cove and watch ships going in and out of the harbor. The core of this guesthouse is a 200-year-old cottage that has been enlarged over the years. In the late 1970s, another cottage was custom built on the lot's only remaining space. Today, the compound is a cheerful architectural hodgepodge that's popular with boaters. Rooms are generally small, but comfortably furnished; they evoke a traditional Bermuda compound, without the glitz of the resort hotels. Four waterside cottages have sitting rooms, shaded patios, and kitchens. The Starboard, the best cottage, can comfortably accommodate four guests. All units have private bathrooms mostly with shower-tub combinations. Guests in the main house also have use of a fully equipped kitchen, and the guest lounge has cable TV. The owner-manager is Mrs. Hazel Lowe.

10 Salt Kettle Rd., Paget PG 01, Bermuda. ℂ 441/236-0407. Fax 441/236-8639. 11 units. Mar–Dec 1 $110 double, $130 cottage for 2; Dec 2–Feb $90 double, $100 cottage for 2. Rates include full breakfast. No credit cards. Hamilton ferry to Salt Kettle 3-min. walk. In room: A/C, kitchen in cottages, iron upon request, safe, no phone.

WARWICK PARISH

Granaway ★ *Finds* A cliché of pink-walled, whitewashed-roofed Bermudian charm, Granaway is a home built in 1734 with guest rooms and a garden cottage. The property opens onto views of Great Sound and its sparsely inhabited islands. This was once prime anchorage for the privateers of the 18th and 19th centuries. Granaway was one of the stately waterfront homes used as a storeroom for the "booty." The old cedar beams of the original house are still maintained, although modern conveniences have been added. The bedrooms are handsomely furnished and comfortable, each with a small private bathroom with shower. Five of the rooms are in the main house, although the most romantic retreat is the separate Granaway Cottage. This former slave quarters has been completely refurbished with a full kitchen, hand-painted Italian floor tiles, and a fireplace. The most scenic way to reach the City of Hamilton is by taking a short walk to Harbour Road where you can board one of the ferryboats. In fair weather, guests are served breakfast in the garden, by a pool surrounded by lush foliage.

Harbour Rd., P.O. Box WK 533, Warwick, Bermuda. (② **441/236-3747.** Fax 441/236-3749. www.granaway. com. 6 units. Summer $130–$160 double, $200–$220 double in cottage; off season $80–$150 double, $150–$220 double in cottage. 3rd person extra $25. Rates include continental breakfast (cottages excluded). AE, MC, V. Bus: 8. **Amenities:** Pool. *In room:* A/C, TV, no phone.

Where to Dine

Wahoo steak, shark hash, mussel pie, fish chowder laced with rum and sherry peppers, Hoppin' John (black-eyed peas and rice), and the succulent spiny Bermuda lobster (called "guinea chick") await you in Bermuda. Of course, you won't find these dishes on all menus, as many resorts and mainstream restaurants specialize in a more Continental or international cuisine. But for a true taste of Bermuda, you might want to search the menu for local grub.

Bermudian food has improved in recent years, but dining out is still not a major reason to visit the island. American and British dishes are common. Truly innovative gourmet fare often isn't—although the prices would make you think you're getting something special. Dining in Bermuda is generally more expensive than it is in the United States and Canada. Because virtually everything except fish must be imported, restaurant prices are closer to those in Europe.

In general, it's not a good idea to order meat very often; it's flown in, and you can't be sure how long it has been in storage. Whenever possible, stick to local food; for a main course, that usually means fish. The seafood, especially Bermuda rockfish, is generally excellent—that is, when local fishers have caught something that day. Sometimes the waters are too rough for fishing. A lot of fish is imported frozen from the United States; you may want to ask before you order. To find the dishes that are truly worthy, you'll have to pick and choose your way carefully through the menu—and that's where we come in.

Most restaurants, at least the better ones, prefer that men wear a jacket and tie after 6pm; women usually wear casual, chic clothing in the evening. Of course, as most of the world dresses more and more casually, Bermuda's dress codes have loosened up a bit—but this is still a more formal destination than many other islands. It's always wise to ask about required dress when you're reserving a table. During the day, no matter what the establishment, be sure to wear a cover-up—don't arrive for lunch sporting a bikini.

Because of the absence of inexpensive transportation, many travelers on a budget eat dinner at their hotels. If you like to dine around and you're concerned about cost, find a hotel that offers a variety of dining options, or stay in or near the City of Hamilton.

BERMUDA'S BEST DINING BETS

You'll find Bermuda's best sushi at the **New Harbourfront Restaurant & Sushi Bar** in the City of Hamilton; the best Chinese and Thai at **Chopsticks Restaurant** in the City of Hamilton; the best sandwiches at **Paradiso Cafe** in the City of Hamilton; the best British pub grub at **Hog Penny** in the City of Hamilton; the best Bermudian cuisine at **M. R. Onions** in the City of Hamilton; the best pasta at **Pasta Pasta** in St. George; the best ice cream at **Bailey's Ice Cream & Food D'Lites Restaurant** in Hamilton Parish; and the best pizza at **Portofino** in the City of Hamilton. Our favorite for brunch is the **Waterlot Inn** in

Southampton Parish. For a wide sampling of Bermuda seafood, go to the **Whaler Inn,** in the Fairmont Southampton Princess. Here you can enjoy the best of the day's catch, preceded, of course, with a bowl of Bermuda fish chowder. For a romantic dinner, head for **Tom Moore's Tavern** in Hamilton Parish, which was built as a private home in 1652. It once housed Thomas Moore, the Irish romantic poet, and the sense of romance still lingers in a refined setting with a classic French and Mediterranean menu.

1 From Rockfish to Island Rum: Dining, Bermuda Style

For years, Bermuda wasn't known for its cuisine; the food was too often bland and lacking in flavor. In recent years, however, there has been a notable change. Bermuda shares the revived interest in fine cuisine that has swept across America. Chefs seem better trained than ever, and many top-notch (albeit expensive) restaurants dot the archipelago. Italian food is in vogue, as is Chinese. (On the other side of the coin, fast food, including KFC, has arrived, too.)

In recent years, some Bermudians have shown an increased interest in their heritage. They've revived many traditional dishes and published the recipes in books devoted to Bermudian cooking (not a bad idea for a souvenir).

Bermuda imports most of its food from the United States. As the population grows, less and less farmland is available on the island. But lots of people still tend their own gardens; at one home, we were amazed at the variety of vegetables grown on a small plot of land, including sorrel, oyster plants, and Jerusalem artichokes.

WHAT'S COOKING?

SEAFOOD Any local fisherman will be happy to tell you that more species of shore and ocean fish—including grunt, angelfish, yellowtail, gray snapper, and the ubiquitous rockfish—are found off Bermuda's coastline than in any other place.

Rockfish, which is similar to Bahamian grouper, appears on nearly every menu. From the ocean, it weighs anywhere from 15 to 135 pounds (or even more). Steamed, broiled, baked, fried, or grilled, rockfish is a challenge for innovation to any chef. There's even a dish known as "rockfish maw," which we understand only the most old-fashioned cooks (there are still a handful on St. David's Island) know how to prepare. It's the maw, or stomach, of a rockfish, stuffed with a dressing of forcemeat (seasoned chopped fish) and simmered slowly on the stove. If you view dining as an adventure, you may want to try it.

The most popular dish on the island is **Bermuda fish chowder,** made with a variety of white fish (often rockfish). Waiters usually pass around a bottle of sherry peppers and some black rum, which you add to your soup; these lend a distinctive Bermudian flavor.

Shark isn't as popular on Bermuda as it used to be, but many traditional dishes, including hash, are made from shark. Some people use shark-liver oil to forecast the weather; it's said to be more reliable than the nightly TV report. The oil is left in the sun in a small bottle. If it lies still, fair weather is ahead; if droplets form on the sides of the bottle, expect foul weather.

The great game fish in Bermuda is **wahoo,** a sweet fish that tastes like albacore. If it's on the menu, go for a wahoo steak. Properly prepared, it's superb.

The **Bermuda lobster** (or "guinea chick," as it's known locally) has been called a first cousin of the Maine lobster. It's in season from September to March. Its high price tag has led to overfishing, forcing the government to issue periodic bans on its harvesting. In those instances, lobster is imported.

You can occasionally get good **conch stew** at a local restaurant. **Sea scallops,** though still available, have become increasingly rare. **Mussels** are cherished in Bermuda; one of the most popular traditional dishes is Bermuda-style mussel pie, with a filling of papaya, onions, potatoes, bacon, curry powder, lemon juice, thyme, and, of course, steamed mussels.

FRUITS & VEGETABLES   In restaurants and homes, **Portuguese red-bean soup**—the culinary contribution of the Portuguese farmers who were brought to the island to till the land—precedes many a meal.

The **Bermuda onion** figures in many recipes, including onion pie. Bermuda-onion soup, an island favorite, is usually flavored with Outerbridge's Original Sherry Peppers.

Bermudians grow more **potatoes** than any other vegetable; the principal varieties are Pontiac red and Kennebec white. The traditional Sunday breakfast of codfish and banana cooked with potatoes is still served in some homes.

"Peas and plenty" is a Bermudian tradition. Black-eyed peas are cooked with onions, salt pork, and sometimes rice. Dumplings or boiled sweet potatoes may also be added to the mix at the last minute. Another peas-and-rice dish, **Hoppin' John,** is eaten as a main dish or as a side dish with meat or poultry.

Both Bermudians and Bahamians share the tradition of **Johnny Bread,** or **Johnnycake,** a simple pan-cooked cornmeal bread. Fishermen would make it at sea over a fire in a box filled with sand to keep the flames from spreading to the boat.

The **cassava** (a starchy root), once an important food on Bermuda, is now used chiefly as an ingredient in the traditional Christmas cassava pie. Another dish with a festive holiday connection is **sweet-potato pudding,** traditionally eaten on Guy Fawkes Day (in early Nov).

Bermuda grows many **fresh fruits,** including strawberries, Surinam cherries, guavas, avocados, and, of course, bananas. Guavas are made into jelly, which in turn often goes into making the famous Bermuda syllabub, traditionally accompanied by Johnnycake.

WHAT TO WASH IT ALL DOWN WITH

For some 300 years, **rum** has been the drink of Bermuda. Especially popular are Bacardi (the company's headquarters are in Bermuda) and Demerara rum (also known as black rum). The rum swizzle (with rum, citrus juices, and club soda) is the most famous cocktail in Bermuda.

Fun Fact **Local Dining Customs**

One of Bermuda's most delightful traditions is the English ritual of **afternoon tea,** which many local homes and hotels maintain.

In hotels, the typical afternoon tea is served daily from 3 to 5pm. Adding a contemporary touch, it's often served around a swimming pool, with guests partaking in their bathing suits—a tolerated lapse from the usual formal social and dress code.

At some places, more formal tea is served at a table laid with silver, crisp white linens, and fine china, often imported from Britain. The usual accompaniments include finger sandwiches made with thinly sliced cucumber or watercress, and scones served with strawberry jam.

(*Tips* **A Note on Reservations**

Nearly all major restaurants prefer that you make a reservation; many popular places require that you do so as far in advance as possible. Weekends in summer can be especially crowded. Some repeat visitors make their reservations for the most popular spots before they leave home.

For decades, the true Bermudian has preferred a drink called **"Dark and Stormy."** Prepared with black rum and ginger beer (pronounced *burr*), it has been called the national drink of the island.

An interesting drink is **loquat liqueur.** It can be made with loquats (a small plumlike local fruit), rock candy, and gin, or more elaborately with brandy instead of gin and the addition of such spices as cinnamon, nutmeg, cloves, and allspice.

You'll find all the usual name-brand alcoholic beverages in Bermuda, but prices on mixed drinks can run high, depending on the brand.

Like the British, Bermudians often enjoy a sociable **pub lunch.** There are several pubs in the City of Hamilton, St. George, and elsewhere on the island. For the visitor, a pub lunch—say, fish and chips or shepherd's pie, a pint or two of ale, and an animated discussion about politics, sports, or the most recent royal visit—is an experience to be cherished as truly Bermudian.

Another favorite meal of the typical Bermudian is **Sunday brunch.** Your hotel is likely to feature a big buffet.

2 Restaurants by Cuisine

AMERICAN
Heritage Court (City of Hamilton, $$, p. 126)
M. R. Onions (City of Hamilton, $$, p. 128)

ASIAN
L'Oriental ✿ (City of Hamilton, $, p. 133)

BARBADIAN
Spring Garden ✿ (City of Hamilton, $, p. 134)

BERMUDIAN
Aqua ✿✿ (Devonshire Parish, $$$, p. 135)
The Beach (City of Hamilton, $, p. 129)
Black Horse Tavern ✿✿ (St. George Parish, $$, p. 137)
Clubhouse Dining Room ✿ (Southampton Parish, $$$, p. 114)

Dennis's Hideaway ✿ (St. George Parish, $$, p. 138)
Heritage Court (City of Hamilton, $$, p. 126)
Hog Penny (City of Hamilton, $, p. 132)
Landfall ✿ (Hamilton Parish, $$$, p. 136)
M. R. Onions (City of Hamilton, $$, p. 128)
North Rock Brewing Company ✿ (Smith's Parish, $$, p. 135)
Paraquet Restaurant (Paget Parish, $, p. 120)
Pawpaws Restaurant & Bar (Warwick Parish, $$, p. 118)
Spring Garden ✿ (City of Hamilton, $, p. 134)
Swizzle Inn (Hamilton Parish, $, p. 137)
Waterloo House ✿ (City of Hamilton, $$$$, p. 120)

Key to abbreviations: $$$$ = Very Expensive; $$$ = Expensive; $$ = Moderate; $ = Inexpensive

White Horse Tavern (St. George Parish, $$, p. 140)

BRITISH
The Beach (City of Hamilton, $, p. 129)
Frog & Onion (Sandys Parish, $, p. 113)
Henry VIII (Southampton Parish, $$, p. 117)
Hog Penny (City of Hamilton, $, p. 132)
Lighthouse Tea Room (Southampton Parish, $, p. 117)
Mrs. Tea's Victorian Tearoom ✪ (Southampton Parish, $, p. 118)
Somerset Country Squire Pub & Restaurant (Sandys Parish, $$, p. 112)
Swizzle Inn (Hamilton Parish, $, p. 137)

CARIBBEAN
Coconuts ✪ (Southampton Parish, $$$, p. 115)
Jamaican Grill (City of Hamilton, $, p. 132)
The Norwood Room ✪✪ (Paget Parish, $$$, p. 120)

CHINESE
Chopsticks Restaurant ✪ (City of Hamilton, $, p. 130)
East Meets West ✪ (City of Hamilton, $$, p. 125)

CONTINENTAL
Bistro J (City of Hamilton, $$, p. 124)
Henry VIII (Southampton Parish, $$, p. 117)
Lighthouse Tea Room (Southampton Parish, $, p. 117)
Little Venice (City of Hamilton, $$, p. 125)
Monte Carlo ✪ (City of Hamilton, $$$, p. 123)
The Norwood Room ✪✪ (Paget Parish, $$$, p. 120)
Pawpaws Restaurant & Bar (Warwick Parish, $$, p. 118)

Tom Moore's Tavern ✪✪ (Hamilton Parish, $$$$, p. 136)
Waterloo House ✪ (City of Hamilton, $$$$, p. 120)

DELI/LIGHT BITES
Bailey's Ice Cream & Food D'Lites Restaurant (Hamilton Parish, $, p. 137)
The Hickory Stick (City of Hamilton, $, p. 131)
Paradiso Cafe (City of Hamilton, $, p. 133)

FRENCH
Ascots ✪ (City of Hamilton, $$$, p. 122)
La Coquille ✪✪ (City of Hamilton, $$$, p. 122)
Le Figaro Bistro & Bar (City of Hamilton, $, p. 133)
Newport Room ✪✪✪ (Southampton Parish, $$$$, p. 114)
Red Carpet Bar & Restaurant (City of Hamilton, $$, p. 129)
Tom Moore's Tavern ✪✪ (Hamilton Parish, $$$$, p. 136)

INDIAN
The Bombay (City of Hamilton, $, p. 130)
East Meets West ✪ (City of Hamilton, $$, p. 125)
House of India ✪ (City of Hamilton, $, p. 132)

INTERNATIONAL
Aqua ✪✪ (Devonshire Parish, $$$, p. 135)
Black Horse Tavern ✪✪ (St. George Parish, $$, p. 137)
Carriage House ✪ (St. George Parish, $$, p. 138)
Clubhouse Dining Room ✪ (Southampton Parish, $$$, p. 114)
Coconut Rock (City of Hamilton, $, p. 131)
Coconuts ✪ (Southampton Parish, $$$, p. 115)
Flanagan's Irish Pub & Restaurant (City of Hamilton, $$, p. 125)

Freddie's Pub on the Square (St. George Parish, $$, p. 138)

Front Street Terrace (City of Hamilton, $, p. 131)

Green Lantern (City of Hamilton, $, p. 131)

The Middleton Room ✿ (Paget Parish, $$$, p. 119)

Monty's (City of Hamilton, $, p. 133)

North Rock Brewing Company ✿ (Smith's Parish, $$, p. 135)

The Pickled Onion ✿ (City of Hamilton, $$$, p. 124)

Pirates Landing (Sandys Parish, $$, p. 112)

The Porch (City of Hamilton, $$, p. 128)

Red Carpet Bar & Restaurant (City of Hamilton, $$, p. 129)

Specialty Inn (Smith's Parish, $, p. 136)

Tamarisk Dining Room ✿✿ (Sandys Parish, $$$, p. 109)

Wickets Brasserie & Cricket Club (Southampton Parish, $, p. 118)

ITALIAN

Aqua ✿✿ (Devonshire Parish, $$$, p. 135)

Ascots ✿ (City of Hamilton, $$$, p. 122)

Il Palio (Sandys Parish, $$, p. 112)

La Trattoria (City of Hamilton, $$, p. 125)

Little Venice (City of Hamilton, $$, p. 125)

Monte Carlo ✿ (City of Hamilton, $$$, p. 123)

New Harbourfront Restaurant & Sushi Bar ✿ (City of Hamilton, $$$, p. 123)

Pasta Basta (City of Hamilton, $, p. 134)

Pasta Pasta (St. George Parish, $, p. 140)

Portofino (City of Hamilton, $, p. 134)

Primavera (City of Hamilton, $$, p. 129)

Red Carpet Bar & Restaurant (City of Hamilton, $$, p. 129)

San Giorgio (St. George Parish, $$, p. 139)

Tio Pepe (Southampton Parish, $$, p. 117)

Tuscany ✿ (City of Hamilton, $$, p. 129)

JAMAICAN

Jamaican Grill (City of Hamilton, $, p. 132)

MEDITERRANEAN

Beethoven's (Sandys Parish, $$, p. 109)

Cafe Lido ✿ (Paget Parish, $$$, p. 119)

East Meets West ✿ (City of Hamilton, $$, p. 125)

Fresco's Restaurant & Wine Bar ✿ (City of Hamilton, $$, p. 125)

Harley's (City of Hamilton, $$, p. 125)

La Coquille ✿✿ (City of Hamilton, $$$, p. 122)

Monte Carlo ✿ (City of Hamilton, $$$, p. 123)

Waterlot Inn ✿✿ (Southampton Parish, $$$$, p. 114)

PACIFIC RIM

The Sea Grape ✿ (Southampton Parish, $$$, p. 115)

SEAFOOD

Barracuda Grill ✿ (City of Hamilton, $$$, p. 122)

Dennis's Hideaway ✿ (St. George Parish, $$, p. 138)

Lobster Pot & Boat House Bar ✿✿ (City of Hamilton, $$, p. 127)

New Harbourfront Restaurant & Sushi Bar ✿ (City of Hamilton, $$$, p. 123)

Somerset Country Squire Pub & Restaurant (Sandys Parish, $$, p. 112)

Whaler Inn ✸ (Southampton
Parish, $$$, p. 116)

SPANISH

Tio Pepe (Southampton Parish, $$,
p. 117)

STEAKS/SEAFOOD

Carriage House ✸ (St. George
Parish, $$, p. 138)
Freeport Seafood Restaurant ✸
(Sandys Parish, $, p. 113)
Greg's Steakhouse ✸ (Southampton Parish, $$, p. 116)
Port O'Call (City of Hamilton, $$,
p. 128)
Rib Room ✸✸ (Southampton
Parish, $$$, p. 115)

SUSHI

Coconut Rock (City of Hamilton,
$, p. 131)
New Harbourfront Restaurant &
Sushi Bar ✸ (City of Hamilton,
$$$, p. 123)

SWISS

Beethoven's (Sandys Parish, $$,
p. 109)

TEX-MEX

Rosa's Cantina (City of Hamilton,
$, p. 134)

THAI

Chopsticks Restaurant ✸ (City of
Hamilton, $, p. 130)

3 Sandys Parish

The following restaurants are all on Somerset Island.

EXPENSIVE

Tamarisk Dining Room ✸✸ INTERNATIONAL   This elegant cottage colony is the top dining spot in the parish for classic cuisine and also for innovative fare. Tamarisk boasts impeccable service. A dress-up place, it makes local eateries such as Pirates Landing and the Frog & Onion look publike.

The formal dining room has a new color decor of salmon and lime green, limed wood, impressive columns, and beamed ceilings, evoking an upscale country club. In warm weather, sliding glass doors extend the dining area onto a rambling, east-facing terrace that overlooks the bay. Princess Margaret no longer dines here; instead you will find groups of lawyers and business leaders, especially at night.

At lunch, you're likely to come across platters of chicken-macadamia salad, a signature pita-bread sandwich (stuffed, California-style, with chicken salad, avocado slices, and bean sprouts), and some of the best cheeseburgers in the parish. The dinner menu changes every night. It nearly always includes snails in garlic butter; chargrilled vegetables fashioned into a spicy terrine; lobster ravioli; saltwater shrimp served with avocado gateaux and a basil with sun-dried tomato sauce; and a rack of lamb with chutney and cardamom sauce.

At Cambridge Beaches Hotel, 30 Kings Point Rd. ✆ 441/234-0331. Reservations required. Jacket required for men dining inside, not for dining on the terrace. Lunch main courses $12–$20; fixed-price 5-course dinner $65. MC, V. Daily 12:30–2:30pm, 7–9pm. Bus: 7 or 8 (each marked "Dockyards").

MODERATE

Beethoven's SWISS/MEDITERRANEAN   A pub-cum-restaurant, this eatery lies within the Clocktower Building at the historic Royal Dockyards. It's owned and operated by two Swiss chefs who feature a formal menu of beautifully presented and well-prepared dishes. There is al fresco dining in the courtyard. The setting is casual and intimate, and the restaurant is a good choice for meals throughout the day and evening. It even serves afternoon tea. A large

Bermuda Dining

ATLANTIC
OCEAN

Ireland Island N.

Ireland Island S.

Mangrove
Bay

Somerset
Village   Watford
               Bridge

Ely's
Harbour   SANDYS

Great
Sound

Somerset
Bridge   Hawkins
               Ferry   Island

Long
Island

For restaurants in Hamilton City, see
"The City of Hamilton Dining" map

Bay Rd.   North Shore R.

PEMBROKE

Hamilton
Front St.

Hamilton
Harbour

Botanical
Gardens

Ports
Island   Hinson
              Island   PAGET

Darrell
Island

Middle Rd.

Little Sound

Harbour Rd.   Middle Rd.

WARWICK

SOUTHAMPTON   South Shore Rd.

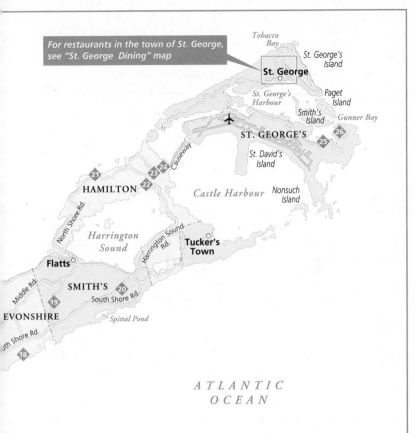

For restaurants in the town of St. George, see "St. George Dining" map

Tobacco Bay

St. George's Island

St. George

St. George's Harbour

Paget Island

Smith's Island

Gunner Bay

ST. GEORGE'S

25

26

St. David's Island

21

23 24

22

HAMILTON

Castle Harbour

Nonsuch Island

Harrington Sound

North Shore Rd.

Harrington Sound Rd.

Tucker's Town

Flatts

Middle Rd.

SMITH'S

20

South Shore Rd.

19

EVONSHIRE

Spittal Pond

South Shore Rd.

18

ATLANTIC OCEAN

✈ Airport

0 ___ 3 mi

0 ___ 3 km

Paraquet Restaurant **14**	Tio Pepe **11**
Pawpaws Restaurant & Bar **13**	Tom Moore's Tavern **22**
Pirates Landing **1**	Waterlot Inn **12**
Rib Room **12**	Whaler Inn **12**
The Sea Grape **8**	Wickets Brasserie & Cricket Club **12**
Somerset Country Squire Pub & Restaurant **4**	
Specialty Inn **19**	
Swizzle Inn **24**	
Tamarisk Dining Room **3**	

lunch menu involves fish chowder, burgers, sandwiches such as Cajun steak, along with daily specials such as fiery jerk chicken, along with about 10 main courses, including the fish of the day or onion quiche with goat cheese and sun-dried tomatoes. At night, the fare is more elaborate, with a fine selection of appetizers, including some especially savory tempura snails with a roasted garlic and teriyaki sauce. Well-crafted main courses that entice are corn-breaded Maryland crab cakes served on mesclun salad with balsamic dressing, and Oriental chicken in an Asian ginger wrap. Other good courses include lemon pepper tuna steak and spicy shrimp with a peanut sauce.

Clocktower Building, Royal Naval Dockyard. (C) **441/234-5009**. Reservations recommended for dinner. Lunch main courses $9–$15; dinner main courses $16–$26. AE, DC, MC, V. May–Oct Sun–Wed 9am–6pm, Thurs–Sat 11am–9pm; Nov–Apr daily 9am–5pm. Bus: 8 or ferry from the City of Hamilton.

Il Palio ITALIAN   Named after the famous horse race in Siena, Italy, and owned and operated by an experienced Siena-born restaurateur named Fosco Nannini, this is one of the most appealing Italian restaurants in Bermuda. Set on the road leading to the Dockyards, within an 80-year-old house crafted from bricks and blocks of Bermuda limestone, it's outfitted inside like what you might have expected within a rustic farmhouse in Tuscany. The cuisine is tried-and-true Italian, with pastas that include fettuccine Alfredo, and main courses that feature veal with lemon-flavored butter sauce; a sinfonia of seafood, wherein a grilled or broiled (your choice) medley of fish and shellfish are artfully arranged on the same platter; tenderloin steak with peppercorns; and T-bone steak *alla fiorentina* are all competently and flavorfully prepared. We also recommend the fresh fish, especially the selection that's sautéed with bits of garlic and paired with pine nuts, capers, and hints of tomato sauce. There's a bar on this place's street level, but you'll have to climb upstairs to reach the dining room.

64 Main Rd. (C) **441/234-1049**. Reservations recommended. Pastas $16; main courses $23–$29. AE, DC, MC, V. Tues–Sun 6–10pm. Bus: 7 or 8.

Pirates Landing INTERNATIONAL   Overlooking the Great Sound, this restaurant offers a diverse menu that pleases diners who aren't too demanding. If you want filling and satisfying food, it's a suitable choice, though it's not quite as fun a spot as Frog & Onion (reviewed below) is. The seating, at pine tables and chairs, is comfortable, and the serving staff (costumed as pirates) is helpful. It's a little hokey, but everyone seems to get into the "pirate-esque" spirit, especially after a rum punch or two. For the most part, the standard lunch fare—soups, burgers, pastas, and grilled specialties—is adequate, but not special. However, the gyros on pita bread are spicy delights, especially the 7-inch gyro pizza made with fresh vegetables, pepperoni, and mozzarella.

At night the kitchen shines brighter, as the chefs look abroad for inspiration. Two of the finest dishes are beef tenderloin with porcini mushrooms and chicken cacciatore. Pastas, made fresh daily, are quite delicious. We are less devoted to the garlic shrimp and fresh fisherman's grill.

Royal Naval Dockyard. (C) **441/234-5151**. Lunch main courses $8–$20; dinner main courses $16–$25, early dinner special (6–7pm) $22. AE, MC, V. Daily 11:30am–4pm, 6–10pm. Closed Jan–Mar. Bus: 7 or 8 or ferry from the City of Hamilton.

Somerset Country Squire Pub & Restaurant BRITISH/SEAFOOD You'll pass through a moon-gate arch to reach the raised terrace of this waterside restaurant in the center of the village. Limestone blocks and hedges ring the terrace; inside, the dining room is located downstairs. Local Bermudian favorites, including curried mussel pie and fresh Bermuda tuna or wahoo, are your best

---

Tips Check, Please! A Note on Service Charges

Although a service charge (typically 10%–15%) is added to most restaurant bills, it's customary to leave something extra if the service has been good. However, it isn't necessary—in fact, many diners find 15% too generous. Be on the lookout for this scam: Some restaurants include the basic 15% service charge in the bill, but leave the service charge line blank. Many diners unknowingly add another 10% to 15%, without realizing they've already paid for service. Scrutinize your bill, and don't be shy about asking if you're not sure what's included.

---

bets here. Look for the specialties of the day. The bill of fare ranges from British pub grub to fresh local fish to traditional roast beef with Yorkshire pudding. You can count on charbroiled and barbecued meats. Most of the food is fairly routine, but the chef is especially proud of his Bermuda fish chowder, a tomato-based soup that some locals consider the best in the West End.

10 Mangrove Bay Rd., Somerset Village. © **441/234-0105.** Lunch main courses $8.50–$9.50; dinner main courses $14–$27. AE, MC, V. Daily 11:30am–1am. Bus: 7 or 8.

INEXPENSIVE

Freeport Seafood Restaurant ★ *Value* STEAKS/SEAFOOD   Come here for the best of locally caught seafood. Somehow this old favorite manages to turn up a fresher catch than its Somerset competitors, and broils it to perfection, a welcome change from the greasy "fish 'n' chips" grub served at the other dockyard spots. There is no great presentation or dramatic flourish to the platters served, but the taste is often delectable, especially the fish platter or one of the broiled Bermuda rockfish dishes, our particular favorite. The menu is less formal—and somewhat less expensive—at lunch than at dinner. During the day, you get the regular chow you'd find almost anywhere, including burgers, salads, pizzas, and steak on the grill. The tasty fish sandwich is usually the star of the lunch menu. In the evening, the fish selection might feature tuna or wahoo. For those who want a good old T-bone, those are on the menu, too. We found the lobster a bit overpriced and overcooked.

At the Royal Naval Dockyard, 1 Freeport Rd. © **441/234-1692.** Lunch main courses $9–$23; dinner main courses $15–$23. AE, MC, V. Daily 11:30am–1am. Bus: 8.

Frog & Onion BRITISH   In the former 18th-century cooperage (barrel-making factory) of the Royal Naval Dockyard, Frog & Onion is the most traditional British pub in Bermuda. It's "named" for the owners, French-born Jean-Paul Magnin (the Frog) and Bermuda-born Carol West (the Onion). You can sit back with a pint of English lager in the shadows of the cooperage's enormous fireplace. Many folks stay to dine: At lunch there are standard sandwiches, salads, lasagna, and some tasty bar pies. We especially like the beef barley pie with Guinness for a real taste of Bermuda, although you might opt for the shepherd's pie. The dinner menu includes all of the lunchtime choices plus some more delicious European dishes. Your best bet for the evening might be the featured local fish plate. Food is not spectacular, but it is well-prepared and rather hearty fare. Since portions are large, no one leaves hungry.

The Cooperage, at the Royal Naval Dockyard. © **441/234-2900.** Lunch sandwiches, salads, and platters $8.50–$16; dinner main courses $10–$24. MC, V. Mon–Sat 11:30am–4pm, 6–9:30pm; Sun noon–4pm, 5:30–9pm. Bar daily noon–midnight. Closed Mon Dec–Feb. Bus: 7 or 8 or ferry from the City of Hamilton.

4 Southampton Parish

VERY EXPENSIVE

Newport Room ★★★ FRENCH   The Newport Room is unequaled in its sumptuous but subtle decor and succulent French cuisine—it's among the best restaurants in Bermuda. The only local establishment that can compete with it is the Waterlot Inn (which is even more famous than the Newport Room). The Newport, however, is much more formal. The dining room, entirely paneled in teak and rosewood with nautical brass touches, suggests the interior of a yacht. A maitre d' stationed beside a ship's compass greets diners at the entrance, and the service is attentive. In the center of the room are exact miniature replicas of two of the former winning sailboats from the Newport-to-Bermuda Race.

Settle into a leather armchair and prepare yourself for what just might be your most memorable meal in Bermuda. The regularly changing menu reads like a textbook of modern gourmet cuisine; it might include duck breast with cinnamon-and-fig sauce, or baby veal chops. The kitchen uses the freshest and best ingredients in its carefully prepared, artfully presented dishes. The wine list includes a wide array of international selections, all served in Irish crystal.

In The Fairmont Southampton Princess, 101 South Shore Rd. © 441/238-8000. Reservations required. Jacket required, tie is optional. Main courses $29–$42. AE, DC, MC, V. Daily 6:30–9:30pm. Usually closed Dec to mid-Jan. Ferry from the City of Hamilton.

Waterlot Inn ★★ MEDITERRANEAN   Less rigidly formal than the Newport, and with a more welcoming staff, this is one of our all-time favorites for a special night out in Bermuda. The service is impeccable, and the culinary repertoire is inventive—doubly impressive given the large number of diners every evening. The restaurant also serves a celebrated Sunday brunch (known here as "buffet breakfast").

About 300 years ago, merchant sailors unloaded their cargo directly into the basement of this historic inn and warehouse. Today, the best way to approach the inn is still by water, and that's precisely what many Bermudians do, mooring their sailing craft in its sheltered cove. Over the years, the inn has attracted such guests as Mark Twain, James Thurber, Eleanor Roosevelt, and Eugene O'Neill.

You can enjoy a drink in an upstairs bar, where a classical pianist entertains. After descending a colonial staircase with a white balustrade, you'll be seated in one of three conservatively nautical dining rooms. Each is filled with captain's or Windsor chairs, oil paintings of old clipper ships, and lots of exposed wood. The bouillabaisse is about as good as it gets on this side of the Riviera, and there are many other temptations, including Bermuda's very best fish chowder. Veal shank served in white corn risotto with caramelized onions and young stuffed vegetables is an especially good choice. Occasionally, we've settled happily for a plate of grilled Mediterranean vegetables, from artichokes to eggplant.

At The Fairmont Southampton Princess, 101 South Shore Rd. © 441/238-8000. Reservations required. Jacket required for men. Main courses $28–$46. AE, MC, V. Daily 6:30–9pm. Closed Jan–Feb. Shuttle from hotel.

EXPENSIVE

Clubhouse Dining Room ★ BERMUDIAN/INTERNATIONAL   This is the main dining room of The Reefs (see chapter 4), and is open to non-guests as well. Against a backdrop of typical Bermudian architecture, including solid limestone walls, a finely honed cuisine is presented. The entire menu changes daily, but many dishes, at least the most popular ones, are regularly repeated. This rather formal restaurant opens onto a private beach. Tantalizing appetizers include five-spice roasted duck breast with a ginger-flavored noodle salad or a selection from the chilled seafood and sushi raw bar. Fresh soups are made daily, not just the standard Bermuda fish chowder, but such savories as roasted pumpkin soup with allspice croutons. For your main course, the chefs fly in fresh steamed Maine lobster or you might opt for the oven-roasted prime rib of beef au jus, truly succulent, and served with buttermilk-mashed potatoes. For dessert, no one can top the blueberry cheesecake with a fruit coulis. You can also order the "world's smallest chocolate mousse parfait."

56 South Shore Rd. (C) **441/238-0222.** Reservations required. Main 4-course fixed-price dinner $52. AE, DC, MC, V. Daily 6:30–8:30pm. Bus: 7.

Coconuts ⚡ (Finds) INTERNATIONAL/CARIBBEAN   When on an island, many diners insist that the view be as good as the cuisine. If view is important to you, we recommend Coconuts, not only for its scenic vista, but also for its cuisine. It lies between high cliff rocks and a sandy pink beach on the south coast. Alfresco dining here is most romantic, although those breezy nights tend to cool your food before you've finished it.

Cozy and personalized, this restaurant is at its best at dinnertime, when a four-course set-price menu is the only dining option for the dozens of diners who make detours to come here. The restaurant is set in an open-sided dining room, richly paneled with varnished cedar, that's positioned within a few steps of the beach. If you prefer a table directly on the sands, the staff can set one up for you, at a net fee of $85 per person with food and wine included, although sand invariably gets into your shoes. Lunch is nothing special—the usual, burgers, salads, sandwiches, and the like. But at night, the chefs strut their stuff, offering a set menu (which changes daily) full of variety, flavor, taste, and scope, and presented with a flair. Freshly grown produce is served with Cajun and West Indian spices, for a "taste of the islands." You're not sure what you're going to get on any given night here, but the scope is wide enough to appeal to most diners unless you have very obscure food tastes—in that case, you'd better call and check.

In the Reefs Hotel, 56 South Shore Rd. (C) **441/238-0222.** Reservations recommended. Lunch main courses $12–$16; set-price 4-course dinner $59 per person. AE, MC, V. Daily noon–3pm, 7–10pm. Bus 7.

Rib Room ⚡⚡ STEAKS/SEAFOOD   This is the only restaurant on the island that compares favorably to one of London's finer chophouses, and its beef dishes are far superior to those served at the more highly touted Henry VIII.

Many of the Rib Room's juicy, tender beef dishes are broiled over charcoal. The broiled lamb chops are classic. Maybe you'll go all out for the roast prime rib of beef with Yorkshire pudding. For those who prefer fish, the chef will prepare the catch of the day, although the aptly named Rib Room is not the best choice for seafood. All dinners come with an extensive salad bar. The Rib Room sits atop the resort's golf pro shop, near the first tee. As you relax in upholstered armchairs, taking in the panoramic view, you might want to start your evening with a "Dark and Stormy," a black rum and ginger beer drink for the adventurous.

In The Fairmont Southampton, 101 South Shore Rd. (C) **441/238-8000.** Reservations recommended. Main courses $24–$44. AE, DC, MC, V. Daily 6:30–9pm. Ferry from the City of Hamilton.

The Sea Grape ⚡ PACIFIC RIM   On an outdoor terrace by the sea, this restaurant prides itself on its Pacific Rim menu. We won't pretend that the cuisine here is great, but we like to go here when the day is hot and we want to dine lightly with a view of the water. It generally includes calorie- and cholesterol-conscious foods with California-, Korean-, and Japanese-inspired sauces on the

---

Moments   Where to Put Together the Perfect Picnic & Where to Enjoy It

The kitchens of many major hotels will prepare a picnic lunch for you, but you need to request it at least a day in advance. On Front Street in the City of Hamilton, you can order sandwiches at a cafe and pick up a bottle of wine or mineral water. If it's a weekday, the best place to buy picnic supplies is **The Hickory Stick** (see review later in this chapter).

If you enjoy picnicking and biking, you can do both in Sandys Parish. Start by crossing Somerset Bridge (heading in the direction of Somerset Village), and continue along Somerset Road to **Fort Scaur Park,** where you'll enjoy a panoramic view of Ely's Harbour.

Another ideal picnic location is **Spanish Point Park** in Pembroke, where you will find a series of little coves and beaches. You don't need to go to the trouble of packing a picnic basket—in warm weather, a lunch wagon rolls around every day at noontime. We also love to picnic at one of the island's best beaches, **Warwick Long Bay.**

---

side. Zesty appetizers range from spiced, poached pineapple with coconut yogurt and candied ginger to grilled shrimp with smoked-bacon guacamole. Main dishes are often grilled and are served with fresh chutneys, salsas, and yakisoba (wheat) noodles. Our favorite main courses are sesame-crusted pork tenderloin and grilled salmon in a roasted chile pepper cream sauce. There's also usually a daily catch, market priced.

In the Sonesta Beach Resort, South Shore Rd. © 441/238-8122. Reservations recommended. Main courses $22–$38; dinner buffet $38. AE, MC, V. Daily noon–3pm, 6:30–9:30pm. Closed Oct–May. Bus: 7.

Whaler Inn ✿ SEAFOOD   This oceanfront restaurant, perched atop a low cliff overlooking rocks and pink sands, is justifiably famous for its seafood. Clusters of sea grapes, Norfolk Island pines, and padded iron armchairs dot its landscaped terraces; and you can watch the sun set over one of the island's most secluded beaches. The panoramic view through the huge windows is the airy restaurant's most prominent feature.

You might begin with baked oysters Rockefeller, Bermuda fish chowder, or something as exotic as roasted pumpkin potato gnocchi served with roasted sunflower seeds. The special main courses are well-seasoned portions of the daily catch—game fish such as yellowfin tuna, barracuda, shark, wahoo, or dolphin fish (mahimahi). All are excellently prepared, either broiled or sautéed in butter. We like to come here for the hearty pasta and seafood combination served in a zesty tomato-basil sauce. The chef can also cook you a savory platter of mussels mariniére that beats out the deep-fried fisherman's platter any day. Locals like the pan-fried local fish, but in our opinion, the almonds and bananas muddle the natural taste of the fresh fish. Desserts are good. Two popular favorites—Key lime cheesecake, and a passion fruit tart—will make you want to come back for a second visit.

In The Fairmont Southampton, 101 South Shore Rd. © 441/238-8000. Reservations recommended. Lunch main courses $12–$17; dinner main courses $22–$38. AE, MC, V. May–Sept daily noon–2:30pm, 6:30–9:30pm; Oct–Apr daily 6:30–9:30pm. Ferry from the City of Hamilton.

MODERATE

Greg's Steakhouse ✿ STEAK/SEAFOOD   This is the island's only real steakhouse, although the chefs prepare other dishes as well, including seafood.

They feature only certified Angus beef, and it's not only aged to perfection but is also well flavored, perfectly cooked, and tender—the best steaks on the island. The chefs also prepare a delectable rack of lamb. Other dishes likely to please you are fresh Bermuda rock fish or else pasta primavera. The prime rib or the T-bone steaks are also excellent, as is a particularly succulent cut of filet mignon. All the dishes come with fresh vegetables and a choice of potatoes.

Port Royal Golf Course, Middle Rd., Port Royal. © 441/234-6092. Reservations recommended Sat–Sun. Main courses $16–$30. AE, DC, MC, V. Mon 11am–5pm; Tues–Fri 11am–11pm; Sat–Sun 7am–11pm.

Henry VIII *Overrated* BRITISH/CONTINENTAL   This restaurant appears here mainly because hundreds of visitors to Southampton patronize it. Sad to report, it used to be good, but has fallen off in recent years. Although, if you like a faux-Tudor place where the waitresses are still called "wenches," it might be your cup of tea. There's nothing wrong with stopping in for a drink at this bustling spot lying below Gibbs Hill Lighthouse. But it's not worth a special trip to dine here. The restaurant is decorated with oak furnishing, brass railings, and period style lighting fixtures, a bit gimmicky and lacking a theme related to the island at all. The English draft beer in the split-level Oak Room is always refreshing, and in summer and on winter weekends, there is often entertainment, usually beginning at 9:45pm. As for the food, proceed carefully—simpler is better. And read the fine print: There's a $20 minimum. Appealing to modern day Henry VIIIs, the menu attempts to entice with beef dishes, but you'll fare better at another "chophouse," the Rib Room (reviewed above).

56 South Shore Rd. (between The Fairmont Southampton and the Sonesta Beach Resort). © 441/238-1977. Reservations required for dinner. Lunch main courses $7.75–$22; dinner main courses $21–$38, early-bird dinner (6–7pm) $30, Sun brunch $25 per person. AE, MC, V. Daily noon–2:30pm and 6–10pm. Bus: 7 or 8.

Tio Pepe ITALIAN/SPANISH   Don't let the Spanish name fool you—the cuisine here is predominantly traditional Italian. The place is more or less in a category of its own, as none of the other restaurants in the parish offers this type of cuisine. A few Spanish dishes do appear on the menu, including roast suckling pig. It's fairly straightforward fare: pizzas, pastas, and classic Italian cuisine in generous portions, all with a bit of Mediterranean pizzazz. The kitchen also prepares local fish, plus salmon and lobster, with subtle Italian flavors. We especially like the huge range of hot Bermuda appetizers; the clams steamed in white wine, garlic, and parsley; and the chef's *penne o solo mio,* which is made with pasta, cauliflower, saffron, raisins, anchovies, capers, garlic, and red pepper in a white wine sauce—truly savory! Seating is on a wide garden-view terrace and in three indoor dining rooms. The restaurant is convenient to the Fairmont Southampton Princess and Horseshoe Bay Beach. In fact, if you're returning from a day at Horseshoe Beach, this place is most convenient. The friendly atmosphere, bountiful food, and prices are right on target.

117 South Shore Rd., Horseshoe Bay. © 441/238-1897. Reservations recommended. Lunch $7.75–$20; pizzas and pastas $20–$28; main courses $22–$29. AE, MC, V. May–Sept daily 11am–10:30pm; off season daily noon–10pm. Bus 7.

INEXPENSIVE

Lighthouse Tea Room *Finds* CONTINENTAL/BRITISH   Step inside this lace-curtained room for a taste of an old-fashioned tearoom. It's a handy place if you're touring in the Southampton area on the south shore. After you've climbed the winding steps to the famous Gibbs Hill Lighthouse, you'll have worked up an appetite. You can enjoy a full English breakfast while taking in a panoramic vista of Great Sound. Afternoon tea includes such delights as Devonshire cream,

Bermuda honey, and homemade tea cakes and scones. If you're lunching, opt for a homemade soup of the day or a freshly made quiche. Salads are also available, along with such English tearoom fare as Cornish-style minced-meat pies, English pork pie, and a ploughman's lunch of cheese and bread.

Gibbs Hill Lighthouse, 68 St. Anne's Rd. © **441/238-8679.** Breakfast $4–$12; lunch $6.75–$13. AE, MC, V. Daily 9am–5pm. Bus: 7 or 8.

Mrs. Tea's Victorian Tearoom ★ *Finds* BRITISH   Opposite Port Royal Golf Course, this much-loved tearoom offers the island's most traditional English tea. The tearoom occupies a small white with black shutters house that was originally conceived as a private home. The authentic and somewhat cluttered Victorian decor is prissy enough that you could even invite the Queen of England here for a cuppa. The dainty china goes perfectly with the floral tablecloths. Locals come here for shepherd's pie at lunch—how British can you get? You can also enjoy stuffed sandwiches such as smoked turkey, or a selection of pastries and scones, with your tea. The tearoom is in a Bermuda National Trust property off the Railway Trail. To reach it, turn off Middle Road by the Esso station.

25 Middle Rd. © **441/234-1374.** Lunch $11; afternoon tea with sandwiches and sweets from $14. No credit cards. Tues–Sun noon–5pm. Bus: 7 or 8.

Wickets Brasserie & Cricket Club *Kids* INTERNATIONAL   Outfitted like a British cricket club, this brasserie and bistro features a health-conscious breakfast buffet with low-sodium and high-fiber offerings, as well as one of the most comprehensive lunch menus on the island. It's good food—nothing more. You'll probably be satisfied with it if your expectations don't run too high. Standard "family fare" includes deli-style sandwiches, soups, chowders, pastas, salads, and platters such as grilled steaks and veal. The most popular fish dish is grilled grouper with citrus-butter sauce, which has more flavor than the routine steaks and chops on the menu.

The restaurant, on the lower lobby level of the Southampton Princess, overlooks the swimming pool and the ocean beyond. Many Bermudians, with kids in tow, come here for a late lunch or a light supper. The informal but traditional restaurant requests only that guests cover their bathing suits with a shirt. A children's menu is available.

In The Fairmont Southampton, 101 South Shore Rd. © **441/238-8000.** Breakfast buffet $14–$19; lunch main courses $9–$15; dinner main courses $16–$25. AE, DC, MC, V. Daily 7–11am, noon–9:30pm. Ferry from the City of Hamilton.

5 Warwick Parish

MODERATE

Pawpaws Restaurant & Bar *Value* CONTINENTAL/BERMUDIAN   This family favorite, located about 5km (3 miles) west of the City of Hamilton, offers a varied and unusual menu at reasonable prices. With the aura and ambience of a European bistro, Pawpaws attracts everybody from couples seeking an upscale dinner to parents with kids. On the walls are murals of papaw (papaya) trees and other scenes, along with trelliswork and paintings by local artists.

The lunch menu features sandwiches, salads, and the restaurant's signature dish, Pawpaw Montespan (made from green papaya, ground beef, and herbs). In the evening, one of the most popular dishes (and deservedly so) is lobster ravioli in basil-cream sauce with strips of smoked salmon. Equally good is the seafood *vol-au-vent* (baked in pastry with a cream sauce). If you're yearning for island cuisine, sample the red snapper in banana sauce. You'll also find more

Some of the upscale restaurants in Bermuda ask that men wear a jacket and tie for dinner; some restaurants require a jacket but not a tie. When making reservations, always ask what the dress code is. "Casual but elegant" dress is preferred at most Sunday buffets.

classic and ordinary dishes, including tender pepper steak in cognac-cream sauce, and leg of lamb steak marinated in herbs.

87 South Shore Rd. © 441/236-7459. Reservations recommended. Lunch main courses $9.75–$20; dinner main courses $15–$26. MC, V. Daily noon–9:30pm. Bar open until 1am. Bus: 7.

6 Paget Parish

EXPENSIVE

Cafe Lido ✯ MEDITERRANEAN   This well-recommended beachfront restaurant consists of an outdoor terrace and an indoor dining room with big windows that fill the room with light. Come here for the location and convenience to Elbow Beach. If you're a serious foodie, you'll find the viands at Horizons and Cottages or at Stonington Beach Hotel tastier. Shades of pale yellow with shades of red predominate, the chairs are comfortable enough to linger in, and the menu is one of the most diverse on the island. We strongly recommend trying cassoulet of calamari with wine-based red sauce, lobster medallions with lime sauce; seafood casserole with Mediterranean-style red sauce and garlic; a very upscale version of surf and turf (filet steak with one-half a Bermuda lobster), Angus rib-eye steak—grilled; and roasted lamb. There is a newly built disco called The Deep. See "Bermuda After Dark," chapter 10.

In the Elbow Beach Hotel Sea Terrace, 60 South Shore Rd. © 441/236-9884. Reservations recommended. Lunch main courses $12–$35; dinner main courses $27–$48. AE, MC, V. May–Nov daily noon–3pm, 6:30–10:30pm; Dec–Apr daily noon–2:30pm, 6:30–9:30pm. Bar open all year until 1am. Bus: 1, 2, or 7.

The Middleton Room ✯ INTERNATIONAL   On a hilltop overlooking 12 hectares (30 acres) of carefully landscaped grounds and a golf course, this popular restaurant lies in a much-expanded building that was originally constructed as a private home in the 17th century. It's a member of the prestigious Relais & Châteaux association of international hotels and restaurants, and it's associated with the clubby and very expensive cottage colony Horizons. The place is more formal and stuffier than the student-operated Norwood Room (see below). The food is better here, but we still like to patronize the Norwood Room for the surprises (usually happy ones).

The eclectic cuisine often encompasses influences from France and the Far East. Menus, served only as fixed-price meals, change daily. They depend on the chef's whim and on whatever fish, produce, and meats are fresh and available that day. Artfully arranged sushi might serve as a foil for the European-style main courses. Examples from past (and memorable) meals include osso buco of ostrich, curried lamb in phyllo pastry, venison in port wine sauce, and filets of marlin, snapper, or tuna. Midsummer diners usually appreciate the medley of chilled soups that is one of the restaurant's trademarks. The cellar has won the *Wine Spectator* international award 8 years in a row.

In Horizons and Cottages, South Shore. © 441/236-0048. Reservations required. Jacket and tie required. Fixed-price menu $60. AE, MC, V. Daily 12:30–3pm, 7–9:30pm. Bus: 7.

The Norwood Room ★★ *Finds* CONTINENTAL/CARIBBEAN   The students are the chefs, but don't be put off by that. They are strictly trained and supervised by chef Fred Ming, a Bermuda legend who has some great insights about the art of Caribbean cookery. Born and raised in Bermuda, Ming learned how to cook as he sat on a stool in the kitchen watching his grandmother, a culinary whiz, whip up dishes. The Norwood Room offers elegant dining in a large, sun-filled room. From the wood-beamed room, a halo of arched windows looks out over the well-maintained lawn and the ocean. The restaurant is part of a state-run hotel training institute (see chapter 4, "Where to Stay"). Although the young staff members are inexperienced, they're thoughtful, courteous, and hard-working. A pianist or harpist provides music in the evening.

The food is generally splendid, and each dish is prepared with care. We always choose the set menu, which is broadly Continental or Caribbean. We once had tenderloin of pork stuffed with dried winter fruit in an exotic chile-plum dressing; another time it was pan-seared duck breast in tart orange sauce, flambéed with Gosling's Black Seal rum. Another memorable meal was grilled filet of mahimahi with tiger shrimp, served over polenta and drizzled with gingered Malaysian sauce. The chef also incorporates a pasta of the day in his frequently changing menu.

In the Stonington Beach Hotel, South Shore Rd. ☎ 441/236-5416. Reservations required. Jacket and tie required in the evening. Fixed-price dinner $65. AE, DC, MC, V. Daily noon–2:30pm, 7–9pm. Bus: 7.

INEXPENSIVE

Paraquet Restaurant *Value* BERMUDIAN   This restaurant doesn't even pretend to offer a cuisine as fine as those restaurants already recommended in the parish, but it's the bargain of the area. In high priced Bermuda, it's a find. Near a major south shore traffic junction, this unpretentious restaurant is at the center of an apartment cluster of the same name. From your table, you can see a circular formal flower garden created by the Portuguese owners. The coffee-shop setting—complete with lime-colored Formica—and the menu of substantial home-style Bermudian fare are straight out of the '50s. You'll find one of the island's largest sandwich menus (both hot and cold), as well as omelets, home-made soups (there's always a fish chowder of the day), and salads. You can order mixed platters, which feature various dishes such as turkey breast and crabmeat; grilled dishes like T-bone steak; fried liver and onions; or a roast half-chicken. A main course platter is a meal in itself.

South Shore Rd. (near the Elbow Beach Hotel). ☎ 441/236-9742. Breakfast special (until 11am) $8.50; sandwiches $2.55–$12; main courses $24–$29. MC, V. Daily 9:30am–1:30am. Closed Feb. Bus: 2 or 7.

7 City of Hamilton (Pembroke Parish)

VERY EXPENSIVE

Waterloo House ★ BERMUDIAN/CONTINENTAL   At the edge of Hamilton Harbour, this former private home—now the most famous inn on Bermuda—is a Relais & Châteaux property. Terraced gardens, which descend to the water, are often the setting for waterside buffets. Guests dine by candlelight on the harbor-front terrace or in the elegantly appointed, English-style dining room, where a fire roars in the fireplace on nippy evenings.

Some reports suggest that the food has declined in quality, but that's not what we found on recent visits. A discriminating reader from Virginia agreed, saying she found the food "absolutely fantastic—though somewhat expensive." Portions at lunch were so large that she skipped dinner. Waterloo has a dramatic

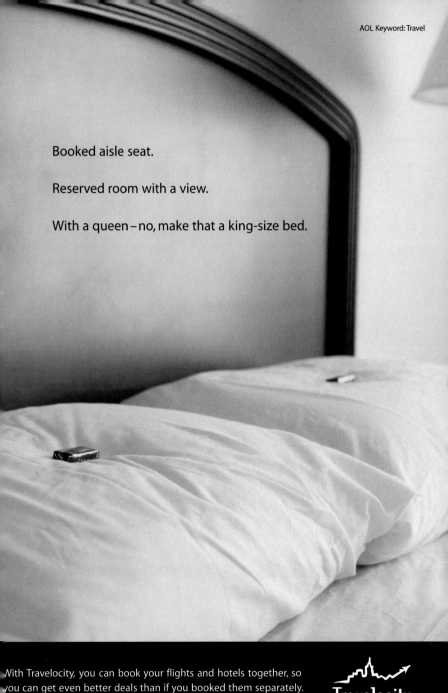

Booked aisle seat.

Reserved room with a view.

With a queen – no, make that a king-size bed.

With Travelocity, you can book your flights and hotels together, so you can get even better deals than if you booked them separately. You'll save time and money without compromising the quality of your trip. Choose your airline seat, search for alternate airports, pick your hotel room type, even choose the neighborhood you'd like to stay in

Travelocity

Visit www.travelocity.com
or call 1 888 TRAVELOCITY

The City of Hamilton Dining

Ascots **1**
Barracuda Grill **21**
The Beach **32**
Bistro J. **25**
The Bombay **36**
Chopsticks Restaurant **34**
Coconut Rock **28**
East Meets West **17**
Flanagan's Irish Pub
   & Restaurant **24**
Fresco's Restaurant
   & Wine Bar **26**
Front Street Terrace **18**
Green Lantern **2**
Harley's **3**
Heritage Court **3**
The Hickory Stick **10**
Hog Penny **21**
House of India **38**
Jamaican Grill **37**
La Coquille **35**
La Trattoria **15**
Le Figaro Bistro & Bar **23**
Little Venice **8**
Lobster Pot &
   Boat House Bar **9**
L'Oriental **8**
M.R. Onions **11**
Monte Carlo **13**
Monty's **5**
New Harbourfront
   Restaurant & Sushi Bar **19**
Paradiso Café **16**

Pasta Basta **12**
The Pickled
   Onion **20**
The Porch **29**
Port O'Call **31**
Portofino **7**
Primavera **6**

Red Carpet
   Bar & Restaurant **27**
Rosa's Cantina **33**
Spot Restaurant **22**
Spring Garden **14**
Tuscany **30**
Waterloo House **4**

Church
Information
Post Office

and elegant setting, although the French and Italian food at Monte Carlo is more cutting edge.

You might begin with seared foie gras or lobster and crab crepe. The best main dishes are grilled filet beef teriyaki, crayfish on a skewer, or house-blackened red snapper.

Pitts Bay Rd. © **441/295-4480**. Reservations required at dinner. Jacket required, tie optional. Lunch main courses $12–$20; dinner main courses $26–$35. AE, MC, V. Daily noon–2:30pm, 7–9:30pm. Bus: 7 or 8.

EXPENSIVE

Ascots ⊛ ITALIAN/FRENCH   This restaurant and its tempting Continental menu are relatively undiscovered—but they deserve to be better known. Ascots is set in a spacious house originally built in 1903, and located in a residential neighborhood at the end of a country lane at the edge of the City of Hamilton. The antique porcelain, Queen Anne armchairs, and Welsh pine evoke a chintz-filled English country house. In the summer, diners sit at candlelit tables on the front porch, and sometimes beneath a tent in the garden.

The menu relies on classic techniques and first-rate ingredients. It includes one of the best selections of hot and cold appetizers in the City of Hamilton, ranging from Mediterranean chicken salad with goat cheese, to fresh homemade ravioli filled with crabmeat and served in smoked-salmon-and-spinach cream sauce. Vegetarian dishes are available. Count on the chef's catch of the day, prepared as you like it, or try blackened mahimahi with tomato, pineapple, and lemon compote. If you prefer more traditional dishes, you might find the grilled sirloin steak with port glaze and roasted thyme polenta more to your taste. For dessert, the crepe Garibaldi (warm crepes filled with bananas and a chocolate-hazelnut sauce, served with fresh berries and crème chantilly) is a good choice. Even more exciting are seasonal berries with Frangelico and chocolate ice cream.

In the Royal Palms Hotel, 24 Rosemont Ave. © **441/295-9644**. Reservations recommended. Lunch main courses $14–$20; dinner main courses $18–$36. AE, MC, V. Mon–Fri noon–2:30pm; Mon–Sat 6:30–10pm. Bus: 1, 2, 10, or 11.

Barracuda Grill ⊛ SEAFOOD   One of Hamilton's more stylish and contemporary-looking restaurants occupies a pair of green, yellow, and olive-toned dining rooms one floor above street level of a building in downtown Hamilton. Established in April of 2002, it boasts an ultra-contemporary lighting design, with dozens of hanging lamps that shed the kind of light that makes virtually everyone look calm and attractive. Amid walls sheathed with unusual modern paintings, you can order a roster of mostly fish-based dishes that change with whatever comes in from local fishermen on the day of your arrival. The best examples include a shrimp "sundae," composed of jumbo prawns arranged in a martini glass and layered with vegetarian chili, Monterey Jack cheese, and olives; tartare of tuna with spicy mango slices; oysters Rockefeller grilled rack of lamb with wild mushroom risotto; and a platter piled high with grilled rockfish and steamed lobster served with braised fennel and beurre blanc or "white butter" sauce.

5 Burnaby Hill. © **441/292-1609**. Reservations recommended. Lunch main courses $11–$24; dinner main courses $21–$38. AE, MC, V. Mon–Fri noon–2:30pm, daily 5:30–10pm. Bus: 1, 2, 10, or 11.

La Coquille ⊛⊛ FRENCH/MEDITERRANEAN   One of the most sophisticated French restaurants in Bermuda sits on the eastern extension of Front Street, within the Bermuda Underwater Exploration Institute. The decor is modern, with clean lines and tones of blue. The staff, among the most polished in Bermuda, hails from France, Germany, Austria, and Italy. The upscale, carefully

---

Tips   A Note on Hotel Dining

In high season (Apr–Nov), many resort hotels require guests to take the Modified American Plan (MAP), or half-board arrangement of breakfast and dinner. To spare guests the routine of eating in the same dining room every night, some hotels offer a "dine around" program. It allows you to dine at other hotels on your own meal plan or at somewhat reduced prices. Ask about dine-around arrangements when booking your room.

---

cultivated cuisine is vaguely Provençal—not typical of Bermuda. The menu is worthy of Paris or New York.

At lunchtime, expect a flavorful, relatively straightforward assortment of artfully presented sandwiches, grilled fish, and steaks. Evening meals are more elaborate. A worthy beginning is pan-fried foie gras with caramelized pears, served *en brioche* in a port wine reduction. Just-picked salad mingles the best of Bermuda with Provence—mesclun, pear tomatoes, local herbs, and kalamata olives. Two dinner dishes of which the chefs are particularly proud are the sautéed breast of duck in blackberry sauce, and the veal T-bone marinated in balsamic vinegar and served with a porcini mushroom fettuccini. Especially succulent is grilled lamb in a rosemary sauce, served with garlic-enriched whipped purple potatoes and sautéed baby artichokes. Monte Carlo still maintains a lead over this place, but few guests leave La Coquille disappointed.

Pembroke Hall, 40 Crow Lane. © 441/292-6122. Reservations recommended. Lunch main courses $9–$21; dinner main courses $27–$34. AE, MC, V. Daily noon–2:30pm; Mon–Sat 6:30–10pm. Bus: 1, 2, 10, or 11.

Monte Carlo   CONTINENTAL/ITALIAN/MEDITERRANEAN   This cheery restaurant celebrates the cuisine of southern France and Italy. Booths and banquettes in the outer dining room sit beneath a local artist's impressions of the countryside around Monaco; seating in the main dining room centers on a brick-sided fireplace. The chefs prepare the best bouillabaisse in the City of Hamilton; using Atlantic seafood, they achieve the savory style that's typical of Marseilles. One of the better dishes is filet of tuna marinated in oil and herbs and grilled over charcoal. The rack of lamb is tender and well seasoned with Provençal herbs. Classic lamb chops appear with the flavoring of the Côte d'Azur, and veal scaloppini is sautéed and served with sun-dried tomatoes and peppers on angel-hair pasta.

9 Victoria St. (behind City Hall). © 441/295-5453. Reservations recommended. Lunch main courses $10–$18; dinner main courses $16–$29. AE, MC, V. Mon–Fri noon–2:30pm, 6–11pm; daily 6–11pm. Bus: 1, 2, 10, or 11.

New Harbourfront Restaurant & Sushi Bar   ITALIAN/SEAFOOD/SUSHI   Front Street was once known only for pubs and fish-and-chips shops, but this restaurant has challenged its neighbors. It offers innovative Continental dishes and the town's best selection of sushi—no longer does fish have to be deep-fried in oil left over from last week. The cuisine fairly bursts with flavors and aromas. Even if some dishes aren't as successful as others, the kitchen should be applauded for trying to wake up the City of Hamilton's sleepy taste buds.

For starters, the inevitable Bermudian fish chowder appears, but miso soup is also available. Of the pasta specialties, our pick is lobster and crab served openfaced with a garlic white wine sauce. Fresh fish appears in a variety of ways, including "fisherman style"—with shrimp, scallops, squid, mussels, and clams in a sun-dried tomato, mushroom, and wine sauce, with angel-hair pasta. You might also try the shrimp and vegetable tower—vegetable ragout surrounded by grilled jumbo shrimp served in champagne-leek sauce. The restaurant also offers poultry and meat, including well-prepared sliced breast of duck served in foie gras tempura. Pastries and cakes are prepared daily, and a wide variety of home-made Italian ice cream is always available.

The spacious restaurant is on the second floor of an old building across from the ferry terminal in the center of town. There's limited seating on the balcony, which juts out over the street and is quite popular in fair weather.

21 Front St. ℭ **441/295-4207.** Reservations recommended. Lunch main courses $17–$32; dinner main courses $18–$32; Monday sushi buffet $24. AE, MC, V. Mon–Sat 11:30am–5:30pm, 6–10pm. Bus: 1, 2, 10, or 11.

The Pickled Onion ★ INTERNATIONAL   In a one-time liquor warehouse overlooking Hamilton Harbour, this is a good, reasonably priced dining choice and after-dark venue. The balcony opens onto Front Street. The menu is satisfying, though not memorable. You might begin with Caribbean seafood salad, loaded with calamari, shrimp, fresh mussels, and other local fish, all in basil vinaigrette. Angus beef, cut and trimmed in-house, is the chef's signature dish; it's tender and cooked to your specifications, accompanied by steak-cut potatoes and zesty peppercorn sauce. Prime rib, sizzling pizza, and some of the island's best fish chowder are regularly featured, as is entertainment.

On Wednesday, the busiest night of the week, the street is closed off and the scene becomes a festive mini-celebration, with street performers and vendors setting the tone.

53 Front St. ℭ **441/295-2263.** Reservations recommended Wed, Fri–Sat. Main courses $13–$26. AE, MC, V. Daily 11am–2am. Bus: 1, 2, 10, or 11.

MODERATE

Bistro J CONTINENTAL   Located in the old-fashioned Chancery Lane, this restaurant is both convenient and good. Decorated in a rustic bistro style, it's a bright addition to the City of Hamilton dining scene. The chef changes the menu every day to take advantage of market-fresh ingredients. For starters, try the chilled shrimp on corn or lemongrass steamed mussels. When we last dropped by, the chef was featuring grilled wahoo with pineapple and rice. The kitchen also does savory pastas, and there is a large wine selection, most of it reasonable in price.

102 Chancery Lane. ℭ **441/296-8546.** Reservations recommended. Main courses $8.50–$20. MC, V. Mon–Sat noon–2:30pm, 6–10pm. Bus: 1, 2, 10, or 11.

Finds **Where The Locals Eat**

Tired of dining with other tourists? If you have a sense of adventure, head for **Spot Restaurant,** on Burnaby Street (ℭ **441/292-6293**), in the City of Hamilton. Nouvelle cuisine here means food served after the turn of the 20th century. The vittles are basic, unadorned, and delicious if you like to fill up on old favorites such as hamburgers, scrambled eggs, bacon, sausages, french fries, pancakes, and the like. Lunch specials are tasty and filling, and prices are aimed to attract local office workers, so nothing is expensive. The only problem is, no one can convince Spot's owners to serve anything more than breakfast or lunch. It shuts down at 7pm.

East Meets West ✶ INDIAN/MEDITERRANEAN/CHINESE   At this restaurant and bistro, the East truly meets the West—the cuisine is globally inspired. Culinary influences range from Asia to California. An appetizer such as cold Mediterranean tuna with potato salad sounds simple but is a well-flavored entry into a meal. From the Bayou country of Louisiana comes a savory jambalaya served atop Cajun rice. The kettle of spicy rice noodles, with a Malaysian accent, is stir-fried. Indian rotis are filled with lamb curry, and chicken breast is well-seasoned and served with fresh broccoli. The chef relies heavily on such ingredients as lime juice, coconut milk, jalapeños, coriander, garlic, and, of course, lemongrass.

27 Bermudiana Arcade. ℂ **441/295-8580.** Reservations recommended. Main courses $6.95–$16. MC, V. Mon–Sat 7:30am–10pm. Bus: 2, 8, 10, or 11.

Flanagan's Irish Pub & Restaurant INTERNATIONAL   Flanagan's occupies a prime position on Front Street, immediately across the street from the spot where cruise ships float at anchor during their Bermuda sojourns. Don't judge the place by what you'll find on the street level, where pool tables and at least seven big-screen TVs will broadcast up to three different international sporting events at a time, as pinball and automated poker games blare away in the corners. Try to get a seat in the upstairs dining room, or on the panoramic veranda. Flanagan's is not known for culinary distinction except in one category: It serves the best fish chowder in Bermuda. Fish chowder is sometimes a bland bowl in other places, tasting like boiled fish in milk, but at Flanagan's, the dish has zest and flavor.

That charbroiled 8-ounce sirloin that appears on your plate tastes even more delectable when served with a zesty peppercorn sauce. The delicious peppercorn sauce also appears with grilled Angus steak. If you're not a meat-eater, opt for the daily changing menu of fresh fish, which will be grilled to perfection for you.

In the Emporium Building, 69 Front St., Hamilton ℂ **441/295-8299.** Main courses $13–$25. AE, MC, V. Daily lunch 11:30am–6pm, dinner 6–9:30pm. Bar daily 11am–1am (happy hour daily 5–7pm). Bus: 7 or 11.

Fresco's Restaurant & Wine Bar ✶ MEDITERRANEAN   Nestled in an early 1900s building with a vaulted ceiling and thick stone walls, this cozy spot feels very much like a European wine cellar. We find dining and drinking wine here to be less boisterous and more satisfying than at the Hog Penny or The Pickled Onion. A trellis-covered courtyard in back holds a handful of tables for alfresco dining. Oenophiles will appreciate the selection of more than 160 different wines from around the world. The dress code is casual and the atmosphere is relaxed. The menu changes monthly. Fresco's most celebrated dish—once voted best pork dish in a Caribbean competition—is pork filet mignon, rolled in ginger, with eggplant and star fruit julienne, accompanied by raisin and pineapple polenta, waffle potatoes, and Caribbean salsa. Another delectable option is sea scallops framed with potato and basil dumplings. Whenever possible, local flavors such as papaya, cassava, and loquats are used. One of the best desserts on Bermuda is Fresco's chocolate mousse cake, freshly baked and served warm with vanilla ice cream and fresh-mint custard sauce.

Chancery Lane (between Reid and Front sts.). ℂ **441/295-5058.** Reservations recommended. Lunch main courses $15–$21; dinner main courses $26–$29. AE, MC, V. Mon–Fri noon–2:30pm; Mon–Sat 6:30–10:30pm. Bus: 1, 2, 10, or 11.

Harley's MEDITERRANEAN   The food at this popular place used to be merely safe and predictable, but now it exhibits some flair, making this restaurant a worthwhile choice even if you aren't a Hamilton Princess hotel guest. In warm weather, outdoor tables sit near the swimming pool, creating the effect of a flowering terrace on the Italian Riviera.

People who are shopping in the City of Hamilton for the day often drop by for lunch, when there's a large selection of salads. Our favorite is the classic Caesar with grilled *goujons* (slices) of grouper. The catch of the day is available grilled, and there are burgers galore, including one served "topless." Pizzas are also featured, and one part of the menu is designed just for kids. The dinner menu is significantly better, with a choice of pastas—the best is grilled salmon filets on linguine. We also recommend the prime rib, mahimahi, grouper, salmon and kingfish. Many of the main dishes conjure up thoughts of sunny Italy. Beef tenderloin with shrimp and chicken supreme is served with a trio of sauces; and tender breasts of chicken come with sun-dried tomatoes, olives, red onions, mushrooms, and fresh herbs.

In The Fairmont Hamilton Princess, 76 Pitts Bay Rd. ℂ 441/295-3000. Reservations recommended at dinner. Lunch main courses $12–$20; dinner main courses $20–$40. AE, MC, V. Tues–Sun noon–2:30pm, 6–10pm. Bus: 7 or 8.

Heritage Court AMERICAN/BERMUDIAN   Inside the Fairmount Hamilton Resort, this is a good choice for anything from a late breakfast to a light lunch, perhaps afternoon tea or a rib-sticking dinner. It gets rather festive in the evening, when live piano music is a feature, and the bartender is skilled at making rum punches. There is also an excellent selection of single malt whiskies along with both wine and champagne sold by the glass. Mainly people go here for the food, which includes such specialties as charbroiled filet of beef with a sweet butter and chipotle glaze with arugula-stuffed potatoes. Perhaps you'll opt for the chef's daily pasta special, or else pan-roasted salmon with a tomato mushroom ragout with a brandy lobster and brandy reduction. Appetizers are tangy and tasty, especially the Bloody Mary prawn cocktail or the sweet chile and garlic-flavored pork ribs. Every day a different special is featured at lunch, perhaps tandoori rockfish with saffron Basmati rice and banana chutney. At lunch you can also enjoy Bermuda fish chowder, delicious club sandwiches, and even spiny lobster burgers.

76 Pitts Bay Rd. ℂ 441/295-3000. Breakfast $15. Salads and sandwiches $10–$21. Afternoon teas $5.50. Dinner main courses $18–$28. AE, DC, MC, V. Daily 10am–midnight. Bus: 7 or 8.

La Trattoria ITALIAN   This family-oriented restaurant is tucked away in a narrow alley 2 blocks north of the City of Hamilton's harbor front. There's not a single cutting-edge or glamorous thing about it, and that's just what the loyal regulars like. The decor is straight out of old Naples, with a wood-burning pizza oven (the only one in Hamilton) and hanging Chianti bottles. The attentive, if somewhat harried, wait staff serves generous portions of rather standard, well-flavored Italian food. You'll find 14 kinds of pizza, and the kitchen is happy to create variations for you. Pastas include lasagna, spaghetti pescatore, and angel hair with shrimp, pesto, and sun-dried tomatoes. Veal can be ordered parmigiana style or as *scaloppini al limone,* and there's a revolving array of fresh fish. If you're very demanding of your Italian cuisine, you'll fare better at Little Venice (see below).

Washington Lane (in the middle of the block bordered by Reid, Church, Burnaby, and Queen Sts.). ℂ 441/295-1877. Reservations recommended. Pizzas $12–$15; lunch $7–$20; main courses $15–$25. AE, MC, V. Mon–Sat 11:30am–3:30pm; daily 5:30–10:30pm. Bus: 1, 2, 10, or 11.

Little Venice ITALIAN/CONTINENTAL   This is one of the most prominent Italian restaurants on Bermuda, a staple that has been here as long as anyone can remember. The owner, Emilio Barberrio (originally from Capri), is

---

Kids Family-Friendly Restaurants

Bailey's Ice Cream & Food D'Lites Restaurant (p. 137)   Bailey's is a great place to take the kids for some all-natural ice cream on a hot, sunny day. They also serve sandwiches if you're looking for more than just a snack.

M. R. Onions (p. 128)   M. R. Onions is one of the best family restaurants in the City of Hamilton. Everybody loves the barbecued chicken, ribs, and steak, and the array of burgers won't fail to please even the fussiest kids.

Rosa's Cantina (p. 134)   This house of chili, burritos, fajitas, nachos, tacos, and enchiladas in the City of Hamilton has no equal on the island. The kids get balloons, as well as paper and crayons to keep them busy once they're seated.

Wickets Brasserie & Cricket Club (p. 118)   The children's menu at this popular spot in the Southampton Princess Hotel makes this a great place to take the kids. If you arrive before 6:30pm, kids can order dinner from the lower-priced lunch menu.

---

justly proud of his specialties. One star is a savory *casseruola di pesce dello chef,* which consists of a medley of local seafood—including lobster, shrimp, mussels, clams, and several kinds of fish—cooked together with white wine, herbs, and tomatoes. Other choices include flavorful fish chowder, spaghetti with seafood, several veal dishes, and an array of pastas, including superb homemade ravioli stuffed with tomatoes and ricotta. Italian wines are featured, in bottles and (less expensively) in carafes. An abbreviated menu is offered at lunchtime. The downside? Service here leaves much to be desired.

Bermudiana Rd. (between Par-la-Ville Rd. and Woodbourne Ave.). ✆ 441/295-3503. Reservations recommended. Lunch main courses $7–$25; dinner main courses $18–$34. AE, DC, MC, V. Mon–Fri noon–2:15pm; daily 6–10pm. Bus: 1, 2, 10, or 11.

Lobster Pot & Boat House Bar ★★ SEAFOOD   For standard island dishes, this traditional favorite one-ups its neighbors M. R. Onions and Hog Penny. Near the Hamilton Princess Hotel, within a 5-minute drive of the heart of the City of Hamilton, this is one of the most consistently popular restaurants on the island—a fixture since 1973. The Lobster Pot's cedar plank walls sport brass and bamboo trim, and such underwater touches as fishing nets, branches of coral, and sea fans. There's a bar near the entrance if you want a before-dinner drink, and a dining room behind it. Menu items include both Maine and spiny Caribbean lobster, each prepared four different ways. Fish sandwiches and platters of hogfish, wahoo, tuna, and rockfish are prepared any way you want; we prefer them grilled with amandine, banana, or lemon-butter sauce. The best starter is a cup or bowl of steaming Bermuda fish chowder. It's savory brown and enhanced with sherry peppers and shots of black rum. If you like it, you won't be alone—visitors haul quarts of the stuff (frozen) back to North America.

6 Bermudiana Rd. ✆ 441/292-6898. Reservations recommended. Lunch main courses $17–$25; dinner main courses $20–$45; lobster $27–$55. AE, MC, V. Mon–Fri 11:30am–3pm; daily 5:30–11pm. Bus: 1, 2, 10, or 11.

M. R. Onions *Kids* AMERICAN/BERMUDIAN   The name of this popular restaurant and bar, a chicken-and-ribs kind of place, is a colloquialism: Bermudians are known as onions, and "M. R." stands for "'em are," or "they are." The restaurant resembles an Edwardian-era bar, with potted palms, leaf-green walls, and brass and oak trim. Caricatures of many Bermudians hang on the walls. If you go early, plan to have a drink at the large, rectangular bar that fills most of the front room. During happy hour (daily 5–7pm), it's a favorite rendezvous for local office workers. There is a cybercafe in the bar, where you can surf the Web or check e-mail while enjoying a drink. The charge is $10 for the first hour and $5 for each additional hour.

Both the bar and the dining room serve well-prepared meals that are favorites with locals and visitors alike (especially families). Specialties include the house onion soup, and fresh fish—including tuna, wahoo, rockfish, and mahimahi—which can be charbroiled, pan-fried, or served with slivered almonds or spicy Cajun seasoning. Tasty barbecued chicken, ribs, burgers, and steak (no-fuss meals popular with kids), are also available. Maybe you'll even have enough room left for mud pie, cheesecake, or another creation from the dessert trolley. Meals here are generally satisfying but hardly memorable. There's a nonsmoking dining room, much appreciated by families because smoking is allowed in many of Bermuda's restaurants.

11 Par-la-Ville Rd. ① 441/292-5012. Lunch $8–$22. Main courses $15–$25; 3-course early-bird dinner (5–6:15pm) $21. AE, DC, MC, V. Daily lunch noon–5pm and dinner 5–10pm. Bar daily 11:30am–1am (happy hour daily 5–7pm). Bus: 1, 2, 10, or 11.

The Porch INTERNATIONAL   Lined with bricks and aged paneling, this warmly decorated restaurant occupies a century-old building. As the restaurant's name implies, it boasts a porch with a sweeping view over the City of Hamilton's harbor, plus a wide outdoor terrace for dining in nice weather. There's also an English-style pub. Food is available throughout, even in the pub-style areas.

The menu offers routine fare, with an emphasis on meat, including prime sirloin steak (10 oz.); prime roast rib of beef with Yorkshire pudding; and steak with shrimp. Lunch features sandwiches, salads, fresh fish, crab cakes, burgers, and oysters. It's all quite competently prepared and straightforward. This is a nice place to just drop by for a drink and soak up the atmosphere, but don't expect too much. Navigate the stairs carefully as you climb up from Front Street, and be even more careful as you come down after having a drink or two.

93 Front St. (between Burnaby and Parliament Sts.). ① 441/292-4737. Reservations recommended. Lunch main courses $11–$16; dinner main courses $19–$26. AE, MC, V. Mon–Sat 11:30am–3pm, 5–10pm. Bus: 1, 2, 10, or 11.

Port O'Call STEAKS/SEAFOOD   Housed in a cedar- and brass-trimmed room reminiscent of an old-fashioned yacht, this restaurant specializes in fresh local fish, four different preparations of lobster, and steaks. If you're fond of lobster, consider the curried version. Other seafood choices include grilled shrimp and blackened scallops, and Bermuda yellowfin tuna with salsa. New menu items include rack of lamb and a seafood casserole covered with mashed potatoes. Desserts are suitably caloric and include a choice of parfaits. During the off season, if business is slow, the place might close early, so call ahead to check if you're dining late. Port O'Call is more intimate and cozy than Primavera and Red Carpet (see below), and we prefer it for that reason. The food is also slightly better.

87 Front St. ① 441/295-5373. Reservations recommended at dinner. Lunch main courses $11–$20; dinner main courses $16–$28. AE, MC, V. Mon–Fri noon–2:30pm; daily 6–11pm. Bus: 1, 2, 10, or 11.

Primavera ITALIAN   Tired of the traditional steak and seafood served at most City of Hamilton restaurants? Long a staple on the dining scene, Primavera offers the zesty flavors of Italy, from regions ranging from Rome to Sicily, and even some Sardinian dishes. We won't say that this is the overall best Italian food in the City of Hamilton, because many diners prefer Little Venice or Tuscany. But what you get here is retro fare that would have suited the Rat Pack. You might begin with cold or hot antipasto (for example, cold seafood salad or hot baked clams in marinara sauce) and follow with soup (perhaps minestrone) or a salad (probably Caesar). The pasta dishes include tortellini Primavera and black ravioli with lobster. Other options are good chicken cacciatore, and sautéed veal with fresh vegetables. Top off your meal with an espresso or a frothy cappuccino. The service is impeccable.

In Hamilton West, 69 Pitts Bay Rd. (between Front St. and The Fairmont Hamilton Princess). © **441/ 295-2167.** Reservations recommended. Lunch main courses $13–$26; dinner main courses $17–$32. AE, MC, V. Mon–Fri 11:45am–2:30pm; daily 6:30–10:15pm. Bus: 7 or 8.

Red Carpet Bar & Restaurant ITALIAN/FRENCH/INTERNATIONAL In a 150-year-old building, Red Carpet serves up Italian dishes despite its English pub-style ambience. This place does a thriving lunch business, thanks to the many offices nearby. After work, the dimly lit bar is a popular place for people to relax with a beer. Lunch offerings include sandwiches, cold platters, and a few hot dishes such as pan-fried fish (including Bermuda tuna and wahoo). Dinners feature a wider array—veal scaloppine, veal Marsala, chicken cacciatore, filet mignon, New York strip sirloin, and a variety of pasta dishes. Primavera, Little Venice, and especially Tuscany serve better Italian food, but at slightly higher prices. What you get here is quite good, familiar fare.

In the Armoury Building, 37 Reid St. © **441/292-6195.** Reservations recommended. Lunch main courses $17–$24; dinner main courses $18–$34. AE, MC, V. Mon–Sat 11:30am–2:45pm, 6:30–9:45pm. Bar open until 1am. Bus: 1, 2, 10, or 11.

Tuscany ★ ITALIAN   When local chefs have a night off, they often dine at this popular local eatery, which serves the best pizzas and the best Italian food of any eatery in the City of Hamilton, including Little Venice (see above). The decor is upscale with an air of sophistication. If the weather's right, there's seating on the balcony, with panoramic views of the main street of the City of Hamilton and its harbor. The friendly waiters always seem willing to advise about what's good that evening. Try the Portobello mushroom with tiger prawns, asparagus wrapped in prosciutto, or veal roulade topped with eggplant and mozzarella cheese. One good choice of pizza is the four stagioni (artichoke hearts, asparagus, mozzarella, and tomato). Other specialties are pan-fried rockfish in a zesty lemon-butter and herb sauce and local rockfish baked in phyllo pastry with baby shrimp. Veal is imported frozen and available almost any way you like it; other tempting selections include the fresh fish of the day and succulent homemade pastas.

95 Front St. © **441/292-4507.** Reservations recommended. Lunch main courses $13–$20; dinner main courses $16–$29. AE, MC, V. Mon–Fri 11:45am–2pm; Mon–Sat 6:30–10:30pm. Bus: 1, 2, or 10.

INEXPENSIVE

The Beach BRITISH/BERMUDIAN   To escape the routine of dining aboard ship, an international crowd of visitors flocks to this eatery across from the cruise-ship docks. It's one of the most casual and laid-back places in the City of Hamilton. Sports fans watch the giant TV, others enjoy the gaming machines, and others dine at picnic tables. From Monday to Thursday, there is happy hour

---

Moments Afternoon Tea, Island Style

Bermuda observes the British tradition of afternoon tea. Many visitors prefer to have tea at their hotels, which provides a good opportunity to meet fellow guests. Others like to visit a variety of hotels for afternoon tea; all of the big resort hotels (including Elbow Beach, The Fairmont Hamilton Princess, Sonesta Beach Resort, and The Fairmont Southampton Princess) offer tea to guests and nonguests. Our favorites are the traditional spreads at the Hamilton Princess and Elbow Beach.

Tea is usually served daily from 3 to 5pm indoors or out, depending on the weather. Dress is more casual than in London; men can wear Bermuda shorts and a shirt with sleeves, and women can wear a simple cotton dress (swimwear, however, is frowned upon unless tea is served right at the pool). It's always a good idea to call ahead and reserve a table (see chapter 4, "Where to Stay," for contact information).

Among restaurants and cafes, the one offering the best traditional afternoon tea is **Paradiso Cafe** (reviewed later in this section).

(4–8pm). Pub fare is the order of the day, and most patrons seem to order big, juicy hamburgers. Local fish is available seared in a pan or deep-fried. Sandwiches and tacos round out the bill of fare. At the bar you can sample Bermuda's famous "Dark and Stormy" (black rum and ginger beer). It's a food pit stop—nothing special—but, because of its location, it attracts a lot of attention.

103 Front St. © **441/292-0219**. Main courses $8–$17. MC, V. Daily 10am–3am. Bus: 1 or 2.

The Bombay INDIAN Can't face another meal of grilled fish or steak? The best Indian cuisine on the island might be just the thing to break up Bermuda's routine offerings. This third-floor hideaway serves expertly prepared authentic dishes in a relaxed atmosphere. Visitors from London or New York may be used to better Indian fare; but still, it's a nice change of pace. For lunch, the daily Bombay buffet includes a variety of dishes, from mulligatawny soup to chicken, beef, lamb, and seafood served with a choice of sauces, in spicy curry, or roasted in the tandoori oven. The Indian chefs will prepare your dishes with the mild, delicate tastes of coastal India if you prefer, but there are more fiery dishes for the brave. There are lots of vegetarian options, of course, and even a handful of Continental selections.

In the Rego Furniture Building, 75 Reid St. © **441/292-0048**. Reservations required. Fixed-price lunch $12; fixed-price dinner $20, $28, and $37. AE, MC, V. Mon–Sat noon–2:30pm; 6–11pm. Bus: 1, 2, 10, or 11.

Chopsticks Restaurant ⭐ CHINESE/THAI Sooner or later, that craving for Chinese food rears its head. Although off the beaten track at the eastern end of the City of Hamilton, Chopsticks offers Bermuda's best Chinese and Thai food, including spicy soup, tangy pork ribs, and seafood. The chef specializes in Szechuan, Hunan, Thai, and Cantonese dishes, with an emphasis on fresh vegetables and delicate sauces. We love the excellent jade chicken, with spears of broccoli, mushrooms, and water chestnuts in a mild Peking wine sauce. Peking duck (served only for two) must be ordered 48 hours in advance. The best Thai dish is green curry chicken (chicken breast strips simmered with onions and bamboo shoots and served with fresh basil, coconut milk, and green-curry paste); it can be prepared mild, spicy, or hot. Most of the dishes are the standard ones you'd find in any North American Chinese restaurant, including sweet-and-sour chicken, beef in oyster sauce, and shrimp in lobster sauce. Some dishes, including the duck in red curry, have real flair. Vegetarians will find a haven here.

88 Reid St. ✆ **441/292-0791.** Reservations recommended. Lunch main courses $5:50–$13; dinner main courses $13–$25. AE, MC, V. Mon–Fri noon–2:30pm; daily 5–11pm. Bus: 1, 2, 10, or 11.

Coconut Rock INTERNATIONAL/SUSHI   This lively, informal eatery in the center of the City of Hamilton is both a drinking and a dining destination. German-born Christian Herzog presides over a main restaurant and two popular bars where music videos play. The place is a bit of a discovery and not likely to be overrun. Your best bet for dinner is the fish of the day, most often pan-seared and served in lemon-butter sauce with potatoes and vegetables. Spicy linguine, and tiger shrimp in spicy tomato sauce are two of our favorites. Chicken quesadillas are a fast-moving item, as are Buffalo chicken wings in honey and hot sauce. Drinks are discounted during the daily happy hour (5–7pm).

The restaurant recently added a sushi bar, Yashi, with one of the widest and best selections in Bermuda, including such exotica as flying fish egg and wahoo.

20 Reid St. ✆ **441/292-1043.** Reservations recommended Sat–Sun. Lunch main courses $7.95–$18; dinner main courses $9.95–$19. AE, MC, V. Mon–Sat 11:30am–2:30pm, daily 6–10:30pm. Bus: 1, 2, 10, or 11.

Front Street Terrace INTERNATIONAL   On the ground floor of one of the City of Hamilton's largest department stores, this independently managed waterfront bistro opens onto an outdoor patio. It attracts midday shoppers who enjoy healthy salads, sandwiches, soups, and platters. If you're caught in the rain, you can duck onto the cedar-trimmed veranda.

The light cuisine reflects international influences, always with an emphasis on healthy ingredients. Everything, including the rough-textured, six-grain bread, is organic and locally grown. Look for offerings like tuna sandwiches with fresh pineapple-avocado mayonnaise; Thai chicken in a light curry sauce enhanced with Asian greens; and charcoal-grilled vegetable lasagna served with fresh local goat cheese. A popular salad includes grilled chicken, fresh greens, roasted red peppers, and olives in a zesty vinaigrette.

In the A. S. Cooper & Sons, Ltd. building, 59 Front St. ✆ **441/296-5265.** Soups, salads, and platters $6.75–$14. MC, V. Mon–Sat 9am–5pm. Bus: 1, 2, 10, or 11.

Green Lantern *Value* INTERNATIONAL   This unpretentious restaurant is like an upscale diner. A great value in the often-expensive City of Hamilton, this is a good place to fill up, but not a prime spot for collecting recipes for *Gourmet* magazine. The limited menu changes every day, but you'll always find fresh fish, roasted chicken, and roast beef. The menu might also feature meatloaf and pork chops; lamb chops and stewed oxtail; or curried chicken and steak. No liquor is served, but you can bring your own bottle. The setting is a century-old house about a mile west of the city limits of Hamilton; the outside is painted—guess what—a pale shade of green.

Serpentine Rd. (at Pitts Bay Rd.). ✆ **441/295-6995.** Main courses $9–$16. MC, V. Mon–Tues and Thurs–Sat 9am–9pm; Wed 9am–3pm. Closed first 2 weeks in Mar. Bus: 1, 2, 10, or 11.

The Hickory Stick DELI/LIGHT BITES   Near the Hamilton Princess, The Hickory Stick is the most popular delicatessen and takeout restaurant in the city. It serves 1,000 customers a day, including lots of office workers. Although one section seems like a coffee shop (with scones, doughnuts, and morning coffee), most customers come here for overstuffed sandwiches and takeout meals. Offerings include steaming portions of chicken Parmesan and fish cakes. Even more popular are the salads, sandwiches, and hot dogs, all of which can be wrapped up for a picnic—the staff provides paper napkins and plastic cutlery on request. The restaurant has added a sushi bar. Advance telephone orders are accepted— a good idea if you don't want to wait.

2 Church St. (at Bermudiana Rd.). ✆ **441/292-1781.** Salads $3.25–$5.50; sandwiches and platters $3.50–$8. No credit cards. Mon–Fri 6:30am–4pm. Bus: 1, 2, 10, or 11.

Hog Penny BRITISH/BERMUDIAN   A bit tired these days, Hog Penny remains Bermuda's most famous and enduring pub, serving draft beer and ale to each new generation of mainlanders who head here, probably on the advice of their grandparents. The dark paneled rooms are decorated in the British style, with old fishing and farm tools, bentwood chairs, and antique mirrors. At lunch you can order pub specials (including shepherd's pie) or tuna salad and the like. The kitchen prepares a number of passable curries, including chicken and lamb. Fish and chips, and steak-and-kidney pie are the perennial favorites, and they are comparable to what you'd find in a London pub. Dinner is more elaborate; the menu might include a whole lobster, a fresh fish of the day (per-haps Bermuda yellowfin tuna), and excellent Angus beef. The food is better upstairs at the Fisherman's Reef. There's nightly entertainment from 9:30pm to 1am; dress is casual.

5 Burnaby Hill. ✆ **441/292-2534.** Reservations recommended. Lunch main courses $10–$16; dinner main courses $16–$26, early-bird dinner (5:30–7pm) $25. AE, MC, V. Oct–Mar daily noon–3pm, 5:30–10pm; Apr–Sept daily 11:30am–3pm, 5:30–10:30pm. Bus: 1, 2, 10, or 11.

House of India ★ *Finds* INDIAN   This is one of only two Indian restaurants in Bermuda, and the only one in the City of Hamilton itself. As such, it's viewed as something of a dining oddity. Within a dining room that's decorated with Indian paintings and woodcarvings, on the northern edge of the City of Hamil-ton, you'll enjoy a menu that specializes in the slow-cooked, often-spicy cuisine of Northern India. There are a wide variety of vegetarian, beef, lamb, and chicken dishes, prepared to whatever degree of spiciness you request. Our favorite dishes on the menu are lamb maas (lamb simmered in an array of spices) and beef rogan josh (Indian curry with a variety of spices, plus yogurt and toma-toes). A buffet lunch is served weekdays, including a wide selection of vegetar-ian dishes. The chefs point out that all dishes are gluten and wheat free except for breads and pastries.

Park View Plaza, 57 North St. ✆ **441/295-6450.** Main courses $9.50–$18. AE, DC, MC, V. Mon–Fri 11:30am–2:30pm; daily 5:30–9:45pm. Bus: 7 or 8.

Jamaican Grill JAMAICAN/CARIBBEAN   This casual, family-run eatery specializes in the spicy cookery of Jamaica and also serves other West Indian spe-cialties. It's geared mostly to the takeout crowd who place their orders down-stairs. You can also sit at tables upstairs. No alcohol is offered but customers consume natural juices or else ice tea at their meals. Many of the juices are of the health bar variety, including mango, carrot, or a ginger-flavored pineapple concoction. The Jamaican national dish, ackee and salt fish, is served here with rice 'n peas. You can also order such classics as jerk chicken, curried goat, or oxtail stew. We are especially fond of the pineapple-glazed chicken, and there are also such old favorites as macaroni and cheese or else roast beef in a mushroom sauce. Unless you order lobster, most main dishes are priced at the lower end of the scale (see below).

32 Court St. ✆ **441/296-6577.** Reservations recommended on Sat–Sun. Main courses $8–$30. AE, DC, MC, V. Mon–Thurs 7am–10pm; Fri–Sat 7am–11pm; Sun 3–9pm. Bus: 7 or 8.

Le Figaro Bistro & Bar FRENCH   With its oversize posters and two little dining areas, this bistro attracts visitors and locals in almost equal numbers. The chef comes from Bordeaux, and he brings the flavors of southern France to his kitchen. The setting is intimate, and the wines are some of the best in the City of Hamilton (the restaurant runs its own wine shop, called Bacchus). Dig into hearty cassoulet; rockfish (local grouper) with a coconut crust and a hint of tarragon; or baked oysters with red pepper pesto. Young duck is stewed in a savory almond and red-wine sauce, and old favorites such as coq au vin (chicken cooked in wine) and a rib-eye steak with *pommes frites* (french fries) are always on the menu. Save room for the delectable chocolate crème brûlée. Even though Monte Carlo and La Coquille have a better cuisine, this remains a favorite of ours because of its snug setting and friendly service.

63 Reid St. ✆ **441/296-4991.** Reservations required. Lunch main courses $8–$13; dinner main courses $19–$26. AE, MC, V. Mon–Fri noon–2:30pm; Sat–Sun 6–10:30pm. Bus: 1, 2, 10, or 11.

L'Oriental ⚓ ASIAN   Located in the same building as Little Venice, L'Oriental is a pan-Asian restaurant with a penchant for gracefully mixing cuisines as diverse as those of Malaysia, Thailand, Japan, and China. The restaurant is situated in a mahogany-and stone-lined room with bridges, a pagoda, and lots of Oriental art. Within the efficiently organized space, you'll find an oyster, salmon, sushi, and caviar bar; and a teppanyaki table where a team of Japan-trained chefs prepares food on a super-hot grill right in front of you. Since the place prides itself on the variety of its all-Asian cuisine, no one will mind if you "fuse" together a meal from the far corners of the world's biggest continent. One of the most appealing nights here is Tuesday, when an all-Chinese "sampler" menu, with tastings from most of the selections on the menu, is available for $27 per person. The cuisine is reliable and good, without ever rising to the ranks of sublime. L'Oriental is a good choice for the vegetarian and the health conscious.
   Most dishes are at the lower end of the price scale listed below.

32 Bermudiana Rd. (above Little Venice restaurant). ✆ **441/295-9627.** Reservations recommended. Lunch main courses $5–$25; dinner main courses $18–$37. AE, MC, V. Mon–Fri noon–2pm, 6–10pm; Sat–Sun 6–11pm. Bus: 7 or 11.

Monty's INTERNATIONAL   On the western waterfront road leading to the most congested part of the City of Hamilton, this family-style choice is a simple, friendly place to sit down for a meal. The atmosphere is bright, airy, and casual; many guests of the nearby Hamilton Princess head here.
   Monty's serves a variety of dishes, with an emphasis on English and classic Bermudian fare. Hot dishes include bangers and mash; Angus beef with mashed potatoes; and curried chicken; plus more exotic choices like smoked salmon with mango sauce and pumpernickel bread. There's a selection of hot and cold sandwiches and burgers. This is a great choice for breakfast if you're in the mood to venture out. Stop by on Sunday morning for a traditional Bermudian breakfast of codfish and potatoes. The food—solid, reliable fare—rises above mediocre without ever becoming superlative.

75 Pitts Bay Rd. ✆ **441/295-5759.** Reservations recommended Fri–Sat. Sandwiches and burgers $8.50; lunch $7–$15; main courses $17–$26. AE, MC, V. Mon–Fri 7:30–2:30pm; Sat 7:30am–1pm; Mon–Sat 6–10pm. Bus: 7 or 8.

Paradiso Cafe DELI/LIGHT BITES/PASTRIES   One of the City of Hamilton's most consistently crowded lunch spots, the Paradiso Cafe serves hundreds of office workers every day. The most popular choices are pastries, sandwiches, and endless cups of tea and coffee, and the platters of the day are full meals in themselves. Depending on what's available at the market, daily specials might include lasagna with a side salad; savory breast of chicken with greens; or a platter of "deep-fried rice" with minced beef or pork.

In the Washington Mall, Reid St. (at Queen St.). © **441/295-3263**. Reservations not accepted. Tea or coffee $1.50; sandwiches $6–$8.50; daily specials $7.50. AE, DC, MC, V (for purchases of $25 or more). Mon–Fri 7am–5pm; Sat 8am–5pm. Bus: 1, 2, 10, or 11.

Pasta Basta ITALIAN   This is the larger of the two Bermuda restaurants that serve the same cafeteria-style pasta-and-salad combination. (The other, Pasta Pasta, is in St. George; the slight difference in spelling has caused a lot of discussion.) Pasta Basta's Italian cuisine ranks far below those restaurants already recommended, but its prices are very low.

In a summery setting, customers are offered two kinds of salad (tossed and Caesar) and about a dozen varieties of pasta. Served in full or half portions, they include two kinds of lasagna (one is meatless), plus a frequently changing array of pastas topped with a choice of meat, seafood, and vegetarian sauces. The daily special is likely to be shells with sausage and onions, in a pink sauce. This restaurant is a great place to fill up on decent food at a reasonable price. *Note:* No wine, beer, or alcohol is served, and local licensing laws do not permit you to bring your own drinks.

1 Elliott St. © **441/295-9785**. Reservations not accepted. Pastas $6 (half portion) or $10 (full portion). No credit cards. Mon–Sat 11:45am–11pm; Sun 5–11pm. Bus: 1, 2, 10, or 11.

Portofino NORTHERN ITALIAN   The warm and inviting decor of this trattoria, complete with hanging lamps, evokes northern Italy. We think Tuscany, La Trattoria, and Little Venice will feed you better, but this place has its devotees.

You'll find well-prepared, reasonably priced specialties, including classic minestrone; three kinds of spaghetti; freshly made pastas, including lasagna, ravioli, and cannelloni; and 18 varieties of 9-inch pizzas. There are also familiar Italian dishes such as Venetian-style liver, veal parmigiana, chicken cacciatore, and beefsteak pizzaiola. Your best bet is one of the freshly made daily specials. There's a limited selection of Italian wines.

Bermudiana Rd. © **441/292-2375**. Reservations recommended. Main courses $13–$36; pizzas $13–$16. AE, MC, V. Mon–Fri 11:30am–4pm; daily 6pm–midnight. Bus: 1, 2, 10, or 11.

Rosa's Cantina *Kids* TEX-MEX   Head here for your Tex-Mex fix, especially if you're a traveling frugal family who likes South-of-the-Border food. You can fill up here on beef and chicken fajitas, zesty chili, nachos, tacos, enchiladas, and burritos (the largest on the island), accompanied by frozen margaritas to put the fire out. While mariachi music plays in the background, you might begin with hearty black-bean soup, then move on to *carne asado* (mesquite-grilled rib-eye steak)—a chef's specialty. The prices are reasonable, and the best place to sit is on the balcony.

121 Front St. © **441/295-1912**. Reservations required Fri–Sat. Lunch main courses from $4.95–$15; dinner main courses $12–$24. AE, MC, V. Daily noon–1am. Bus: 1, 2, 10, or 11.

Spring Garden ★ *Finds* BARBADIAN/BERMUDIAN   Battered, convivial, and cheerful, this restaurant duplicates the cuisine of Barbados and the ambience of the southern West Indies. Diners enjoy Spring Garden's palm-shaded courtyard, and 40-seat dining room lined with oil paintings by Barbados-based artists. Victor Alleyne, your host, presides over a bar where the activity continues long after the last dinner is served. Beneath a cedar ceiling, or under the open sky, depending on where you sit, you'll enjoy fried flavor-filled dishes that have real Bajan or West Indian flavor. Naturally, peas and rice accompany most dishes. The rotis here are as good as the authentic ones of Trinidad, and salads are made fresh daily, along with well-stuffed sandwiches if you visit for lunch. That specialty of Barbados, pan-fried flying fish, is served here with tartar sauce, and you can order a savory lamb curry.

You can also choose from a selection of Bermudian staples such as fish chowder, fish cakes, and tasty oxtail soup; a great choice for a chilly day.

19 Washington Lane. ℂ 441/295-7416. Reservations recommended. Lunch main courses $6–$15; dinner main courses $10–$24. AE, MC, V. Mon–Sat 11:30am–3pm; daily 6–10:30pm. Bus: 7 or 11.

8 Devonshire Parish
EXPENSIVE

Aqua ★★ BERMUDIAN/INTERNATIONAL/ITALIAN   With a maritime theme, this is a rather exciting new dining choice in the Ariel Sands Hotel. Sometimes, one of the resort's owners, actor Michael Douglas, might drop in with one of his vacationing pals such as Jack Nicholson. You're in for even more of a treat if it's his wife, Catherine Zeta-Jones, star of the hit film, *Chicago.* Try for a table overlooking the sea, an al fresco setting popular with those who like moonlight dining. This is one of the few restaurants in Bermuda that offers a dining experience literally steps from the water.

Our party recently dropped in for lunch, feasting on such dishes as a Cajun styled mahimahi, jerk snapper, and a ceviche of mixed seafood, all quite tasty. At night the chefs get more elaborate, tempting you with their tandoori spiced lamb rack, or their loin of fresh tuna with chile mole on beer-battered eggplant. A Mexican loin of veal is filled with black beans and spring onions and served with a cucumber salsa. The appetizers are full of flavor, especially the honey-brushed duck breast with a red curry dressing and green mango salad. The perfect accompaniment is the side of kumquat jam. Or else you might opt for the roast quail on an eggplant "pickle," with fresh spinach and a spicy shi-itake sauce.

34 Shore Rd. ℂ 441/236-1010. Reservations required. Lunch $13–$25. Main courses $24–$35. AE, DC, DISC, MC, V. Daily 8–10am, 12:30–2:30pm, 6:30–9:30pm.

9 Smith's Parish
MODERATE

North Rock Brewing Company ★ *Finds* INTERNATIONAL/BERMU-DIAN   Although beer is brewed by other enterprises in Bermuda, this is the only brewery on the island that serves most, if not all, of its product on the premises. The setting is a smoky, and sometimes rowdy, replica of an English pub, complete with ceiling beams and paneling; plus a tony and casually upscale dining room outfitted in tones of burgundy and forest green. Most patrons tend to gravitate to the dining room, but died-in-the-wool locals sometimes opt to spend their entire time, meal and all, in the pub section, where views of copper-sided fermentation vats are visible through plate-glass windows.

If you come here to drink the local brew, that's fine, but we suggest you stick around for the cuisine too. This is not the typical pub grub dished up at one of those Front Street drinking emporiums in the City of Hamilton. Dishes here have flair, like the Brewmaster's duck-breast-and-goat-cheese salad, with arugula, and a raspberry vinaigrette. You can also order pub classics such as steak-and-ale pie or perhaps beef and mushrooms simmered in porter ale. The fish and chips aren't bad either, and we like the luscious pork tenderloin and the codfish cakes. Unless you order expensive shellfish, most dishes are inexpensively priced.

10 South Rd. ℂ 441/236-6633. www.bermudashorts.bm/northrock. Lunch main courses $11–$22; dinner main courses $18–$28. AE, MC, V. Lunch daily 11:30am–4:30pm; dinner daily 6pm–9:30pm. Bus: 1.

INEXPENSIVE

Specialty Inn INTERNATIONAL   This south-shore restaurant's international menu revolves around Bermudian cuisine with Italian zest. Seating 35 to 40 (mostly locals, not visitors), the inn is known for its good value, generous portions, and fine cooking. Red bean soup, an ideal starter, reflects the island's Portuguese influence; and the Bermuda fish chowder is particularly good. The fresh catch of the day is usually delectable. Pasta dishes, including lasagna, are homemade. Poultry and meat, though frozen, are generally excellent—the roast lamb and barbecued chicken are especially tasty.

Many other dishes display influences that run from Chinese and Indian to Mexican, Spanish, and Portuguese.

Collectors Hill. ℂ **441/236-3133.** Lunch main courses $9.50–$12; dinner main courses $14–$19. MC, V. Mon–Sat 6am–10pm. Bus: 1.

10 Hamilton Parish

VERY EXPENSIVE

Tom Moore's Tavern ⭐⭐ FRENCH/CONTINENTAL   Bermuda's oldest restaurant, built in 1652 as a private home, is on Walsingham Bay, near the Crystal Caves. The Irish romantic poet Thomas Moore visited in 1804 and wrote some of his verses here; he referred to a calabash tree that still stands some 200 yards from the tavern. The most famous dining room in Bermuda has gone through many incarnations. When Bologna-born Bruno Fiocca and his Venetian partner, Franco Bortoli, opened the present tavern in 1985, it quickly became one of the island's most popular upscale restaurants. With its four fireplaces and darkened cedar walls, this landmark establishment serves classic French and Italian cuisine.

Seafood is a specialty. During the summer, there's usually a tank of Bermuda lobsters outside. Local fish selections are likely to include rockfish and yellowtail, which may be your best bet. One reader wrote that he found the place "very expensive, but worth the price, as the service and atmosphere are both top-notch." He also noted that: "The cuisine is not light, however. Extremely well-prepared meals contain very rich sauces." He's right. But if you're in the mood for a rich dinner, we recommend the chef's specialty: quail filled with goose liver, morels, and truffles, then baked in puff pastry. Two other recommendations are sautéed sweetbreads in creamy basil sauce and Latino-style jambalaya. The setting, English silver, German crystal, Luxembourg china, and general ambience contribute to a memorable visit.

Walsingham Lane, Walsingham Bay. ℂ **441/293-8020.** Reservations required. Jacket required. Main dishes $19–$39. AE, V. Daily 7–10pm. Closed Jan 5–Feb 1. Bus: 1 or 3.

EXPENSIVE

Landfall ⭐ BERMUDIAN   Landfall has thrived in the district near the airport for almost as long as anyone can remember. It's set within a white-sided antique home that's at least 200 years old, with a view that some locals claim is the best in Bermuda. Though far from the sea, the view encompasses large stretches of seacoast, as well as faraway St. David's Island. One of the island's best-known chefs, Sean Ming, has taken over here. An expert on Bermuda's cuisine, Ming brings many island specialties to the new menu, incorporating fresh local foodstuffs whenever he can. Try his rockfish in orange sauce, Bermuda lobster, fish chowder, pumpkin soup, and cassava cake.

At Clearview Suites and Villas, Sandy Lane, ℭ 441/293-1322. Lunch main courses $10–$13; dinner main courses $20–$32. AE, DC, MC, V. Daily 7:30am–2:30pm; dinner seatings daily 6:30–9:30pm. Bus: 10 or 11.

INEXPENSIVE

Bailey's Ice Cream & Food D'Lites Restaurant *Kids* DELI/LIGHT BITES/ICE CREAM   This ice-cream parlor occupies a small cottage across from the Swizzle Inn (see below). For all-natural, homemade ice cream, there's no comparable spot in Bermuda—the staff concocts 30 flavors in the shop's 40-quart ice-cream maker. You can enjoy Bermuda banana; coconut; white-chocolate cherries and chips; or other exotic flavors at one of the outdoor tables. The popular sandwiches are served on fresh-baked bread. Also featured are fresh fruit ices, frozen yogurt, and bottled juices—perfect on a hot, sunny day.

At Wilkinson Ave. and Blue Hole Hill, Bailey's Bay. ℭ 441/293-8605. Sandwiches $4–$6; ice cream $2.35 per scoop. No credit cards. Daily 11am–6pm. Closed Dec–Feb. Bus: 1, 3, 10, or 11.

Swizzle Inn BERMUDIAN/BRITISH   The oldest pub in Bermuda—some 300 years old—is also the home of the famous Bermuda rum swizzle drink (made with sugar and citrus juice). The pub lies west of the airport, near the Crystal Caves. Thousands of business cards and reams of graffiti cover the walls. The meaty Swizzleburger was voted best in Bermuda; other freshly prepared pub favorites include fish and chips, conch fritters, and shepherd's pie. These dishes are at least a notch above typical Bermudian pub grub. At lunch, the Bailey's Bay fish sandwich and onion rings are popular with both locals and visitors. The larger, more varied dinner menu appeals to many tastes and diets. Pub grub is available for dinner, as is a seafood medley (rockfish, mussels, and shrimp in marinara sauce), catch of the day, and some tasty Asian curries. Seating is available inside and on the upper and lower patios; upstairs there's also a non-smoking room and a gift shop.

3 Blue Hole Hill, Bailey's Bay. ℭ 441/293-1854. Reservations accepted only for parties of 8 or more. Lunch main courses $10–$17; dinner main courses $15–$30. AE, MC, V. June–Sept daily 11am–1am; off season daily 11am–midnight. Closed first 2 weeks of Jan. Bus: 3 or 11.

11 St. George Parish

MODERATE

Black Horse Tavern ★★ INTERNATIONAL/BERMUDIAN   If you should land here, in a section of the island that Bermudians call "the country," you'll dine with the locals, many of whom maintain (with some justification) that this is the best place for "an authentic taste of Bermuda." Black House Tavern looks like a private home—dusty rose with green shutters and a glassed-in porch in the rear that looks over Smith's Sound. Over the years, the tavern has attracted many celebrities; some diners arrive in yachts.

You can begin your meal with curried conch stew, shark hash (made with minced puppy shark), fish chowder, or curried mussels. Other choices include sandwiches, burgers, and platters of fish and chips, or chicken and chips. The chef also prepares good sirloin steak. If your luck holds, the only Bermuda Triangle you'll encounter is Black Horse's delicious drink—pineapple juice, orange juice, black rum, and Bermuda gold liqueur. This place is more of a conventional restaurant than the equally famous Dennis's Hideaway (see below).

101 St. David's Rd., St. David's Island. ℭ **441/297-1991.** Reservations recommended for parties of 4 or more. Main courses $18–$33. AE, MC, V. Tues–Sat 11am–1am; Sun noon–1am. Bus: 6.

Carriage House ❧ STEAKS/SEAFOOD/INTERNATIONAL In an old waterfront storehouse, the restored Carriage House specializes in beef and seafood. It retains an 18th-century warehouse look with two rows of bare brick arches, spruced up with hanging baskets of greenery. You can dine on the terrace outdoors by the harbor side. The chef specializes in prime rib (priced according to size), which is cut to order and served British style, with creamed horseradish. Other specialties include English lamb chops with rosemary, and—our favorite—tasty versions of Bermuda rockfish, black grouper, and snapper. Especially well-prepared dishes are oven-roasted Barbary duck breast and pan-fried steak Diane flambéed at your table with cognac. Ingredients are imported, but chefs somehow manage to conceal that fact. A different soup is offered every day. At lunch, there's a large selection of hamburgers, as well as sandwich platters, Bermuda fish chowder, pastas, soups, and oysters. The dessert choices are always excellent.

Most prices are at the lower end of the price scale below, except for high-priced Bermudian lobster.

22 Water St., Somers Wharf. ℭ **441/297-1730.** Reservations recommended. Lunch main courses $8–$25; dinner main courses $17–$35; 4-course early-bird special (5:30–6:45pm) $24; Sunday buffet $33 per person. AE, DC, MC, V. Daily 11:30am–2:30pm, 5:30–9:30pm; Sunday brunch noon–2pm. Bus: 3, 10, or 11.

Dennis's Hideaway ❧ *Moments* BERMUDIAN/SEAFOOD Dennis Lamb, a burly St. David's islander, is one of the treasures of Bermuda. So is his quaint little restaurant, in the island's easternmost parish. As you approach (by land or sea), you're likely to see Dennis working in his garden in front—he grows cabbage for coleslaw and beets for pickling, among other things. He'll show you into his fisher's cottage, situated by one of the island's little coves. Inside, you might feel as if you've left Bermuda and are visiting a pocket-size country with its own distinctive personality.

Descended from whalers and pilots ("wooden ships and iron men"), Dennis is now retired. His son, "Seaegg," will offer you dishes that have virtually disappeared from Bermuda's restaurants and are normally available only in private homes. For $34, you get "the works": an array of dishes, including conch stew, mahimahi, herb-flavored shark hash, shrimp, conch fritters—you name it (but please don't order the turtle, an endangered species). If you don't want to eat so much, ask for the $17 fish dinner.

We recommend Dennis's Hideaway only to the adventurous. The offbeat, informal ambience isn't for everyone. Some readers give it high marks and say they've made at least 20 pilgrimages here; others feel that we shouldn't send diners to "this grubby place." You may bring your own wine. Don't dress up.

Cashew City Rd., St. David's Island. ℭ **441/297-0044.** Reservations required. Fixed-price dinners $17–$34; platters $23. No credit cards. Daily 10am–10pm. Bus: 3.

Freddie's Pub on the Square INTERNATIONAL In a restored 18th-century building with a balcony overlooking King's Square, this popular local hangout suits diners on a variety of budgets. You can come here for sandwiches and English pub fare, such as fish and chips or shepherd's pie. The more formal areas serve some very expensive fish dishes, mostly based on the catch of the day. Linen tablecloths and subdued lighting at night enhance the elegant

St. George

Hamilton

Carriage House **3**
Freddie's Pub
on the Square **5**
Pasta Pasta **2**
San Giorgio **1**
White Horse Tavern **4**

atmosphere. Red snapper is grilled and served with passion-fruit sauce. Wahoo often appears in a coconut curry, and pan-seared tuna has a tangerine flavor. Portions are very large, judging from our Angus beef and rack of lamb. The salads, including Greek, avocado, Caesar, Chef's, Mexican, and seafood, are among the best in St. George.

3 King's Sq. 🕻 441/297-1717. Reservations recommended. Sandwiches $8–$16; vegetarian dishes $9–$16; meat dishes $19–$38; seafood $20–$36. MC, V. Daily 11am–3am. Bus: 7.

San Giorgio ITALIAN   This little restaurant is your best bet for Italian dining in the East End, though not as good as competitors in the City of Hamilton. The building housing the restaurant originated as a sea captain's house 200 years ago, and has been hugely expanded since then. It has the most appealing and panoramic terrace in St. George, with a view of the harbor and of St. David's Island. This is not the most sophisticated Italian cuisine we've ever sampled, but it is reliable, tastes good, and is made with quality products. The antipasto is a bit routine, but there are several savory pastas, including tortellini and creamy lasagna (only if you've already lost the battle of the bulge). The chicken breast was enjoyable, but the bacon wrap won't appeal to certain modern tastes. The freshly made salmon salad looked tempting but lost to freshly broiled wahoo served with a lemon-butter sauce.

Water St. (opposite the Post Office). *©* **441/297-1307.** Reservations recommended. Lunch main courses $9.50–$16; dinner main courses $10–$27. Daily 11:30am–2:30pm, 6:30–10pm. MC, V. Bus: 3, 10, or 11.

White Horse Tavern BERMUDIAN   The oldest tavern in St. George is the most popular in Bermuda; it's always jammed with visitors. Under new management, this white building with green shutters has a restaurant and cedar bar with a terrace jutting into St. George's Harbour. New rooms like a mini casino and a cyber cafe have been added. In nice weather, guests usually sit on the terrace. The most popular item on the menu is fish and chips, cooked in beer (St. David's Island style) and often overdone. Bermuda fish chowder is good, as are pork chops and grilled wahoo (the local catch). At lunch, there are burgers, fresh salads, and open-faced sandwiches. The food is passable, but not special. Another horsy tavern, the Black Horse Tavern (see above), serves a more authentic Bermudian cuisine.

Finish off with fresh strudel if you have room. Dress is casual, and there's often enjoyable entertainment.

King's Sq. *©* **441/297-1838.** Reservations accepted only for groups. Lunch main courses $10–$22; dinner main courses $15–$28. MC, V. Daily noon–4pm, 5:30–10pm. Bar daily 11:30am–1am. Bus: 3, 10, or 11.

INEXPENSIVE

Pasta Pasta, York St., St. George (*©* **441/297-2927**), is the smaller sibling of Pasta Basta (reviewed earlier in this chapter). The menu, prices, and hours are the same at both restaurants. Bus: 8, 10, or 11.

Fun in the Surf & Sun

Although people visit Bermuda mainly to relax on its spectacular pink sand beaches, the island also offers a wealth of activities, both onshore and off. In fact, Bermuda's sports facilities are better than those on most Caribbean and Bahamian islands.

The most popular outdoor pursuits in Bermuda are tennis and golf, but sailing ranks high, too. You'll find a fair number of tennis courts and renowned golf courses around the island. If you hesitate to pick up a racket or golf club because you've neglected your game, fear not: Your Bermudian partner, on the court or on the links, would deem it quite improper to remark that your play was anything but superb. If a word of friendly criticism is ever offered, be assured that it will be as gentle as the island's ocean breezes.

Bermuda's waters are the clearest in the western Atlantic. Reefs, shipwrecks (many in such shallow water that they're even accessible to snorkelers), a variety of marine life and coral formations, and underwater grottoes make Bermuda ideal for scuba diving and snorkeling.

1 Beaches

Bermuda is one of the world's leading beach resorts. It boasts kilometers of pink shoreline, broken only now and then by cliffs that form sheltered coves. Many stretches have shallow, sandy bottoms for some distance out, making them safe for children and nonswimmers. Some beaches (usually the larger ones) have lifeguards; others do not. The Parks Division of the Department for Agriculture and Fisheries supervises public facilities. Hotels and private clubs often have their own beaches and facilities. Even if you're not registered at a hotel or resort, you can often use their beach and facilities if you become a customer by having lunch there.

You'll find dozens of spots for sunbathing, swimming, and beachcombing; here's a list of the island's most famous sands, arranged clockwise beginning with the southshore beaches closest to the City of Hamilton.

ELBOW BEACH

One of the most consistently popular beaches in Bermuda, Paget Parish's Elbow Beach incorporates almost 1.5km (1 mile) of (occasionally interrupted) pale pink sand. Private homes and resort hotels dot the edges. Because protective coral reefs surround it, Elbow Beach is one of the safest beaches on the island—and it's the family favorite. This is also the beach of choice for college students on spring break.

Bermuda's government provides lifeguards as a public service. The **Elbow Beach Hotel** (*C* 441/236-3535) offers a variety of facilities and amenities free to hotel guests, but off-limits to others. Amenities and facilities include sun chairs, cabanas, changing rooms, showers, restrooms, and beach towels distributed three times a day by beach attendants who are trained in water safety and lifeguard techniques. The hotel also rents paddleboats, sea kayaks (around $20 per hr. for one kayak, $25 per hr. for two), and snorkeling equipment ($10 per hr.) to anyone on the beach. Take bus no. 2 or 7 from the City of Hamilton.

ASTWOOD COVE

This Warwick Parish public beach has no problem with overcrowding during most of the year—it's in a remote location, at the bottom of a steep, winding road that intersects with South Shore Road. Many single travelers and couples head here to escape the families that tend to overrun beaches like Elbow Beach in the high season. We like this beach for many reasons, one of them being that its cliffs are home to longtail bird nests. Astwood Beach has public restrooms but not many other facilities. An added advantage is nearby Astwood Park, a favorite picnic and hiking area. If you like your beaches small and secluded, head here. Take bus no. 2 or 7 from Southampton.

WARWICK LONG BAY

Like Astwood Cove, this is one of the best places for people who want to escape the family crowds and find solitude. Unlike the sheltered coves of nearby Chaplin and Horseshoe bays (see below), this popular beach features a 1km (½-mile) stretch of sand, the longest on the island. This expanse is conducive to social interaction, but also offers plenty of space to stretch out solo—it all depends on what you prefer. Against a backdrop of scrubland and low grasses, the beach lies on the southern side of South Shore Park, in Warwick Parish. Despite the frequent winds, the waves are surprisingly small thanks to an offshore reef. Jutting above the water less than 60m (200 ft.) from the shore is a jagged coral island that, because of its contoured shape, appears to be floating above the water's foam. There are restrooms at the beach's western end, plus lots of parking, but no other facilities. There are no lifeguards because the undertow is not very strong. Take bus 7.

JOBSON'S COVE

This Warwick Parish beach has the feel of a secret hideaway, thanks to pink sands, gentle waves, and calm waters. Where the horseshoe-shaped bay opens to the ocean, it's only 9m (30 ft.) wide. Adjacent to the much larger and more popular Warwick Long Bay, it's excellent for snorkeling—the water is about 2m (6 ft.) deep for a long way out into the bay. There are no buildings along the water, adding to the feeling of seclusion and peace. There are no facilities here, but it's close enough to Warwick Long Bay to walk over and use their restrooms if necessary. Take bus 7.

STONEHOLE BAY

Near Jobson's Cove in Warwick Parish, Stonehole Bay is more open and less sheltered than Jobson's, with a sandy shoreline that's studded with big rocks. It's almost never crowded, and wading is safe even though strong waves sometimes make the waters cloudy (so they're less than ideal for snorkeling). There are no facilities at Stonehole Bay. Take bus 7.

CHAPLIN BAY

Straddling the boundary between Warwick and Southampton parishes, this small but secluded beach disappears almost completely during storms and exceptionally high tides. Geologists come here to admire the open-air coral barrier that partially separates one half of the beach from the other. Chaplin Bay, like its more famous neighbor, Horseshoe Bay (see below), lies at the southern extremity of South Shore Park. From Chaplin, you can walk over to use the facilities and equipment at Horseshoe, but you'll enjoy more solitude here than at the more active Horseshoe Bay. Take bus no. 7 from the City of Hamilton.

HORSESHOE BAY BEACH

With its long, curved strip of pink sand, Horseshoe Bay, on South Shore Road in Southampton Parish, is one of Bermuda's most famous beaches. That means it's likely to be crowded, especially if cruise ships are in port. Although families flock here, Horseshoe Bay isn't the safest beach on Bermuda. Don't be fooled by the seemingly smooth surface; there can be dangerous undercurrents. If you're using the beach after a storm, be especially careful that you don't encounter a Portuguese man-of-war—they often wash up here in greater numbers than elsewhere on Bermuda.

One advantage this beach has over others is the **Horseshoe Bay Beach Cafe** (*©* **441/238-2651**), which offers changing rooms, toilets, beach-gear rentals, and showers. It also serves snacks and sandwiches from 9am to 5pm daily. A lifeguard is on duty from May to September. *Insider's tip:* When you tire of the crowds at Horseshoe Bay, take one of the little trails that wind through the park nearby; they'll lead you to secluded cove beaches that afford more privacy. Our favorites are Port Royal Cove to the west, and Peel Rock Cove and Wafer Rocks Beach to the east. You might also sneak over to Chaplin Bay to the east (see above). Take bus no. 7 from the City of Hamilton.

CHURCH BAY

This beach off West Side Road lies along Bermuda's southwestern edge, at the point in Southampton Parish where the island hooks off to the northeast. The waves pound much of the shore mercilessly, but rows of offshore reefs shelter Church Bay. Marine life abounds in the relatively calm waters, much to the delight of snorkelers. If you're just planning to lounge in the sun, this is a great place: The beach offers unusually deep pink sands. There are toilets at the top of the hill near the parking area, but don't expect much in the way of facilities (unless a concession has opened by the time you visit). Rent your snorkeling equipment before you get here. Take bus no. 2 or 7 from the City of Hamilton.

SOMERSET LONG BAY

When offshore storms stir up the waters northwest of Bermuda, the water here is unsafe for swimming. Because its bottom isn't always sandy or of a consistent depth, many people find Somerset Long Bay better suited to beachcombing or long walks than to swimming. Nevertheless, many single travelers favor this beach when they're looking for seclusion. The undeveloped parkland of Sandys Parish shelters it from the rest of the island, and the beach's crescent shape and length—about .5km (¼ mile)—make it unusual by Bermudian standards. It has restrooms and changing facilities. We think this is one of the best places on Bermuda to watch the sunset. A plus is the beach's proximity to the Bermuda Audubon Society Nature Reserve, where you can go for long walks and enjoy moments of solitude—except on weekends, when family picnics abound. Take bus no. 7 from the City of Hamilton, or take Cambridge Road in Sandys Parish.

SHELLY BAY

This beach of abundant pink sand is suitable for both families and those seeking solitude. Because it's not well known, it's unlikely to be crowded, and its calm, shallow basin makes it safe for swimming. Off North Shore Road in Hamilton Parish, Shelly Bay lies in a cove whose encircling peninsula partially shelters it from mid-Atlantic waves. There are trees to sit under when the beach gets too hot, and the beach house rents snorkeling equipment, lounge chairs, beach towels, and other items; there are also public restrooms. Buses from the City of Hamilton heading east along the north shore, primarily number 11, stop here.

ST. GEORGE'S ISLAND

This island makes up St. George Parish, the easternmost parish on Bermuda. It's the site of the island's oldest community and the airport, plus lots of low-lying, sun-blasted scrublands. A single bridge (the St. George Causeway) connects this island to the other, more congested islands of the archipelago. St. George's Island's beaches include Achilles Bay, Tobacco Bay, and St. Catherine's Beach (formerly known as the Club Med beach), all of which are sandy, with clean bottoms. The water on the south shore is a bit rougher than the north shore's.

   Natural Arches Beach, one of the loveliest beaches on St. George's Island, is unfortunately open only to members of the private Mid-Ocean Golf Club. At this beach, near Tucker Town, wave and wind erosion have worn away the limestone to a weird series of jagged rocks. Swimmers sunbathe near striking rock formations, a few of which have formed arches.

TOBACCO BAY

Lovely **Tobacco Bay** is an East End family favorite. It's the most popular beach on St. George's Island, especially among those who come for the day to visit the historic town of St. George. With its broad sands, Tobacco Bay resembles a southshore beach. Its pale pink sand lies within a sheltering coral-sided cove just a short walk west of Fort St. Catherine and St. Catherine's Beach. The major disadvantage here is that the beach is likely to be overrun with cruise-ship passengers; when they're in port, you may want to seek more secluded beaches such as St. Catherine's. You can sunbathe here and even go for a swim, but don't venture out too far; the currents are dangerously strong.

Look for the **Tobacco Bay Beach House,** Naval Tanks Hill, St. George, which has toilets, changing rooms, showers, and a snack bar. At beachfront kiosks, you can rent flotation devices and snorkeling gear by the hour from May to September. Stands also sell cold sodas and sandwiches (tuna, grilled cheese, hamburgers, hot dogs, french fries, and the like). Take bus no. 10 or 11 from the City of Hamilton.

JOHN SMITH'S BAY

This is the only public beach in Smith's Parish. It's more popular with residents of Bermuda's eastern end than with visitors, who often don't know about it. It's ideal for those seeking solitude. Long, flat, wide, and rich with pale pink sand, this beach has a lifeguard from May to September. Some shallow areas are perfect for snorkeling. There are toilet and changing facilities. Take bus no. 1 from the City of Hamilton.

2 Snorkeling

Bermuda is known for the gin-clear purity of its waters and for its vast array of coral reefs. If you're ready to explore, all you need is a snorkel, mask, and fins—if you can swim, you can snorkel. A handful of companies can help you; otherwise, you can hit the water on your own.

The best places to go snorkeling are public beaches (see "Beaches," above). Many hotels that are right on the beach will lend or rent you fins, masks, and snorkels, and will advise you of the best sites in your area. You almost never have to travel far.

Die-hard snorkelers, some of whom visit Bermuda every year, prefer **Church Bay** above all other snorkeling spots on Bermuda. It lies on the south shore, west of the Fairmont Southampton Princess Golf Club and Gibbs Hill Lighthouse. The little cove, which seems to be waiting for a movie camera, is carved out of coral cliffs. It's well protected and filled with snug little nooks. Another advantage is that the reefs are fairly close to land. However, the seas can be rough (as is true anywhere in Bermuda), so we always advise caution.

At the eastern end of the south shore, **John Smith's Bay,** east of Spittal Pond Nature Reserve and Watch Hill Park, is another top spot, especially if your hotel is nearby. Even more convenient, especially for snorkelers staying at St. George or at a hotel near the airport, is **Tobacco Bay,** north of St. George's Golf Club. Another good small snorkeling spot is **West Whale Bay;** it lies along the south shore at the west end of Southampton, west of the Port Royal Golf Course.

Although snorkeling is a year-round pursuit, it's best from May to October. Snorkelers usually wear wet suits in winter, when the water temperature dips into the 60s. The waters of the Atlantic, which can be tempestuous at any time of the year, can be especially rough in winter. Winter snorkelers should head for the more sheltered waters of **Castle Harbour** and **Harrington Sound,** both on the East End, where you'll find bizarre coral formations, underwater caves, grottoes, and schools of brilliantly hued fish.

Some of the best snorkeling sites are accessible only by boat. If you want to head out on your own, and you have a knowledge of Bermuda's waters, we suggest renting a small boat (see "Sailing," under "More Fun in the Water," later in this chapter), some of which have glass bottoms. If you rent a boat, the rental company will advise you on where to go and not to go. Countless wrecked boats lie on the many reefs that surround Bermuda. If you're not familiar with Bermuda's waters, you should stay in the sounds, harbors, and bays, especially in

Moments A Look Under Bermuda's Waters

The Ocean Discovery Centre at the Bermuda Underwater Exploration Institute, East Broadway (℃ **441/292-7219**), hopes to give visitors an underwater adventure. The highlight of a visit is a simulated dive 3,600m (12,000 ft.) to the bottom of the Atlantic. Author Peter Bench-ley's videotaped commentary adds to the fun of exploring Bermuda's reefs. You'll learn about newly discovered ocean animals that live in the murky depths. Displays include large murals of sea creatures, arti-facts rescued from long-sunken vessels off the coast, and even a scale model of a ship that wrecked centuries ago. On-site facilities include gift shops, a theater showing films, and La Coquille, a French bistro that specializes, of course, in seafood. Admission is $11 for adults, $5.50 for children; hours are daily from 10:50am to 5:50pm.

Castle Harbour and Harrington Sound. If you want to visit the reefs, it's better and easier to take one of the snorkeling cruises recommended below than to cap-tain your own boat. The use of snorkeling equipment is included in the prices listed.

Also see "Scuba Diving," below.

Bermuda Water Sports   Friendly captains offer glass-bottom snorkel cruises aboard an 18m (60-ft.) motorized catamaran. The design allows the boat to anchor in very shallow waters, which is ideal for novices or unsure swimmers. The cost—around $45 for a 3½-hour cruise—includes free use of snorkeling equipment and the expertise of a crew that really knows the marine life of Bermuda's offshore reefs. There's a cash bar and a shower on board.

36 Market Wharf, St. George. ℃ 441/293-2640. Booking mid-Apr to Oct daily 9am–9pm. Bus: 10 or 11.

Bermuda Water Tours Ltd.   Bermuda Water Tour's Captain Butch offers two options: The shorter cruise, 2 hours on a glass-bottom boat, costs $35 and departs daily at 10am. The 3-hour glass-bottom-boat cruise includes time for snorkeling; it costs $50 and departs daily at 1:15pm.

Tours leave from the docks near the City of Hamilton's Ferry Terminal. ℃ 441/236-1500. Booking 24 hr. Bus: 1, 2, 10, or 11.

Salt Kettle Yacht Charters   Salt Kettle offers private sailing/snorkeling char-ters on a 17m (55-ft.) sloop, the luxury yacht *Bright Star.* The outfitter also books charters on its 11m (35-ft.) motorized *Magic Carpet* for sightseeing or snorkeling among the wrecks and reefs. Charters for 8 to 18 people cost $425 for 3 hours, $535 for 4 hours, and $750 for 6 hours.

Salt Kettle, Paget Parish. ℃ 441/236-4863. Booking 24 hr. Ferry from the City of Hamilton every 30 min.

3 Scuba Diving

Bermuda is a world-class dive site, known for its evocative and often eerie ship-wrecks, teeming with marine life. All scuba diving outfitters go to all sites. It's a matter to be worked out between the diver and the dive master as to what each diver would like to see, including any or all of the various wrecks which are accessible off the coast and not viewed as dangerous.

THE DIVING SITES

The Constellation   When Peter Benchley was writing *The Deep* (later made into a film), he came here to study the wreck of *The Constellation* for inspiration. Lying in 9m (30 ft.) of water, this wreck is 13km (8 miles) northwest of the Royal Naval Dockyard. Built in 1918, *The Constellation* is a four-masted, wooden-hulled schooner. During World War II, it was the last wooden cargo vessel to leave New York harbor. She wrecked off the coast of Bermuda on July 31, 1943, and all the crew survived. Today her hull, broken apart, can be seen on a coral and sand bottom. You can see the 80,000 pounds of cement she was carrying, and morphine ampoules are still found at this site. Large populations of parrot fish, trumpet fish, barracuda, grouper, speckled eels, and octopus inhabit the wreck today.

The *Cristóbal Colón*   Bermuda's largest shipwreck is the *Cristóbal Colón,* a Spanish luxury liner that went down on October 25, 1936 between North Rock and North Breaker. A transatlantic liner, it weighed in excess of 10,000 tons. She was traveling to Mexico to load arms for the Spanish Civil War, when she crashed into a coral reef at a speed of 15 knots. During World War II, the U.S. Air Force used the ship as target practice before it eventually settled beneath the waves. Its wreckage is scattered over a wide area on both sides of the reef. It is recommended that you take 2 dives to see this wreck. Most of the wreck is in 9m to 17m (30 ft.–55 ft.) of water, but the range is actually from 4.5m (15 ft.) at the bow to 24m (55 ft.) at the stern. Some artillery shells from WWII remain unexploded, so don't have a blast, please.

The *Hermes*   This 1984 American freighter rests in some 24m (80 ft.) of water about 1.5km (1 mile) off Warwick Long Bay on the south shore. The 825-ton, 50m (165-ft.) freighter is popular with divers because its U.S. Coast Guard buoy tender is almost intact. The crew abandoned this vessel (they hadn't been paid in 6 months), and the Bermuda government claimed it for $1, letting the dive association deliberately sink it to make a colorful wreck. The visibility at the wreck is generally the finest in Bermuda, and you can see her galley, cargo hold, propeller, and engines.

L'Herminie   This 1838 French frigate lies in 6m to 9m (20 ft.–30 ft.) of water off the west side of the island, with 25 of its cannons still visible. A large wooden keel remains, but the wreck has rotted badly. The marine life here is among the most spectacular of any shipwreck off the coast of Bermuda: brittle starfish, spiny lobster, crabs, grouper, banded coral shrimp, queen angels, and tons of sponges.

Marie Celeste   This is one of the most historic wrecks in the Atlantic, a 207-ton paddle-wheeled steamer from the Confederacy. The steamer was a blockade runner during the Civil War. In exchange for guns, this vessel would return to Bermuda with cotton and cash. Evading capture for most of the war, she was wrecked off the cost of Bermuda on September 25, 1864. The ship sank in 17m (55 ft.) of water, where its ruins lie like a skeleton today. The location is off the coast from the Sonesta Hotel. This is not a great dive site for observing marine life, bit the wreck is evocative and offers many caves and tunnels to explore.

North Carolina   This iron-hulled English Barque lies in 7.5m to 12m (25 ft.– 40 ft.) of water off the western sector of the island. It went down on New Year's Day in 1879 when it struck the reefs, while en route to England. The bow and stern remain fairly intact. There is often poor visibility here, making the wreck appear almost like a ghost ship. Hog fish, often reaching huge sizes, inhabit the site, along with schools of porgies and snapper.

Rita Zorvetta   This Italian cargo steamer was built in 1919 in Glasgow and went aground off St. David's Island in 1924. The ship lies in 6m to 21m (20 ft.–70 ft.) of water just off St. David's Head. The wreck measures 120m (400 ft.) long, and its stern is relatively intact. Divers go through the shaft housings to see the large boilers. Stunning schools of rainbow-hued fish inhabit the site.

Tauton   This Norwegian coastal steamer ran afoul on Bermuda's treacherous reefs on November 24, 1920. The 68m (228-ft.) steeled-hull vessel sank in 3m to 12m (10 ft.–40 ft.) of water off the northern end of the island. Her boilers and steam engines are still visible. This is a favorite dive for beginners, as the wreck lies in shallow water. Because of its breathtaking varieties of fish, it is a favorite site for photographers.

South West Breaker   Some 2.5km (1½ miles) off Church Bay, this was the location chosen for the famous Jacqueline Bisset scene in Peter Benchley's movie, *The Deep.* The breaker was supposed to be a hideout for a man-eating squid. In reality, the breaker was actually created from fossilized prehistoric worms (believe it or not). It has an average depth of 8.5m (28 ft.), and on most days a visibility of 30m (100 ft.). New divers prefer this site, as it is not considered dangerous and has a large variety of hard and soft coral. It is also a good place for snorkelers. A large tunnel split through the center of the breaker provides a protective cover for green moray eels and spiny lobsters. Schools of barracuda are also encountered here.

Moments   **Walking Underwater**

Helmet diving enjoys great popularity in Bermuda. Underwater walkers—clad in helmets equipped with air hoses connected to the surface—stroll along the sandy sea floor in water to depths of 3m to 4m (10 ft.–12 ft.).

Anybody can take part in this adventure, which has been featured in *LIFE* magazine. Undersea walks among the coral reefs are safe for anyone from age 8 to 85, even nonswimmers. You can walk underwater wearing your contact lenses or glasses, and you won't even get your hair wet. A guide places a helmet on your shoulders as you climb down the ladder of the boat to begin your walk. An experienced guide conducts the tours, and it's as simple as walking through a garden. On your helmet dive, you can feed dozens of rainbow-hued fish, which take food right from your hands. You can also see sponges breathing and coral feeding.

You can arrange your walk with Bermuda's original helmet-diving company by contacting **Bermuda Bell Diving,** 5 North Shore Rd. (P.O. Box FL 281), Flatts FL BX, Bermuda (© **441/292-4434**). A 12m (40-ft.) boat, *Cameron,* leaves Flatts Village daily at 10am and 2pm. The underwater wonderland walk costs $60 per person (adults and children). Children under 8 aren't allowed. Take bus no. 10 or 11. For more information visit www.belldive.bm.

Tarpon Hole   This series of large breakers lies directly off the western extremity of the South Shore's Elbow beach. The site is named Tarpon Hole because of the large schools of tarpon that often cluster here, some in excess of 2m (7 ft.) long. It is a sea world of lush fans and soft corals, made all the more intriguing with its tunnels, caves, and overhangs.

DIVING SCHOOLS AND OUTFITTERS

Diving in Bermuda is great for novices, who can learn the fundamentals and go diving in 6m to 7.5m (20 ft.–25 ft.) of water on the same day as their first lesson. In general, Bermuda's reefs are still healthy, despite talk about dwindling fish and dying coral formations. On occasion, in addition to the rainbow-hued schools of fish, you may even find yourself swimming with a barracuda.

Although scuba fanatics dive all year, the best diving months are May to October. The sea is the most tranquil at that time, and the water temperature is moderate—it averages 62°F (17°C) in the spring and fall, 83°F (28°C) in the summer.

Weather permitting, scuba schools function daily. Fully licensed scuba instructors oversee all dives. Most dives are conducted from a 12m (40-ft.) boat, and outfitters cover a wide range of dive sites. Night dives and certifications are also available.

All dive shops display a map of wreck sites that you can visit—there are nearly 40 in all, the oldest of which dates to the 17th century. Although locals believe there may be some 300 wrecks, the mapped sites are the best known and in the best condition. Dive depths at these sites run 7.5m to 26m (25 ft.–85 ft.). Inexperienced divers may want to stick to the wreck sites off the western coast, which tend to be in shallower waters—about 9.5m (32 ft.) or less. These shallow wreck sites are popular with snorkelers as well.

Many hotels have their own watersports equipment. If yours doesn't, the outfitters below rent equipment.

Note: Spearfishing is not allowed within 1.5km (1 mile) of any shore, and spear guns are not permitted in Bermuda.

Blue Water Divers & Watersports Ltd.   Bermuda's oldest and largest full-service scuba-diving operation offers introductory lessons and half-day dives for $99. Daily one- and two-tank dive trips cost $55 and $75, respectively. Snorkeling trips are $40 per half-day. Full certification courses are available through PADI, NAUI, and SSI. All equipment is provided, and reservations are required. In 2002, the outfitter added something new in the form of underwater scooters called DPVs or "diver propulsion vehicles." This exciting new vehicle takes adventurers through underwater caves and canyons. Who knows? You may even discover a shipwreck from long ago.

Robinson's Marina, Southampton. ℂ **441/234-1034.** Daily 9am–5pm. Bus: 6 or 7.

Fantasea Diving   This outfitter is known for its daily two-tank wreck and reef dives, costing $75, although you can also go out on a one-tank dive for $55. A resort course lesson plus dive is $95. It's also possible to go along just to snorkel off the boat, costing $40. A one-tank night dive, increasing in popularity, costs $75. A resort course lesson plus dive is $95 and includes all of the equipment. The company has two fully equipped, custom-built fiberglass dive boats with the latest approved safety gear. A new Nitrox system can effectively lengthen time spent underwater at certain depths by increasing the safety margin. Air tanks are filled with more pure oxygen, decreasing the amount of nitrogen, which adds to the safety factor. Reducing the amount of nitrogen also decreases the chance of getting the "bends" and can help divers grow less fatigued. Nitrox diver certification (for certified divers), tank fills from 32% to 80%, oxygen servicing and tank rentals are also available through this operator. This is a NAUI- and PADI-affiliated dive center. Prices do not include equipment rentals, which are $20 for snorkel gear, $20 for tank, $10 for mask and fins, and $10 for a wet suit.

At the Sonesta Beach Resort, South Shore Rd., Southampton. ☎ 441/238-1833. Call a day in advance. Daily 8:30am–5pm. Closed 2 weeks in Jan or Feb. Mar. Bus: 7.

Nautilus Diving Ltd.   This is one of the island's leading dive operators. It offers a popular "Discover Scuba" resort course ($120 for 3 hr.) that begins daily at 10:15am and 1:15pm. Course participants get to complete a shallow-water scuba dive by the end of the day. All dives are from a 12m (40-ft.) boat. The one-tank dive ($70) goes to reef or wreck sites. A two-tank dive, including a view of a shipwreck and the exploration of a reef in 7.5m to 9m (25 ft.–30 ft.) of water, costs $90 (equipment not included). This is a PADI, five-star center.

At The Fairmont Southampton Princess, 101 South Shore Rd., Southampton Parish; and The Fairmont Hamilton Princess, 76 Pitts Bay Rd., Pembroke Parish. ☎ 441/238-2332 or 441/295-9485. Daily 8am–6pm.

4 More Fun in the Water
FISHING
Bermuda is one of the world's finest destinations for anglers, especially in light-tackle fishing. Blue marlin catches have increased dramatically in recent years, and Bermuda can add bill fishing (for marlin, swordfish, and sailfish) to its already enviable reputation. Fishing is a year-round sport, but it's best from May to November. No license is required.

You can obtain fishing information from the International Game Fish Association's representatives for Bermuda: **Keith Winter** at ☎ **441/292-7131** or **John Barnes** at ☎ **441/234-2070.** They can only be reached at home in the evening.

DEEP-SEA FISHING
Wahoo, amberjack, blue marlin, white marlin, dolphin, tuna, and many other varieties of fish call Bermuda's warm waters home. A number of island outfitters offer the equipment to help you fish for them; this is our favorite:

Bermuda Sportsfishing   The De Silva family runs Bermuda Sportsfishing, which has been in business for many years. They charge $700 for a half-day of fishing and $1,000 to $1,300 for a full day, depending on the size of the boat. Boats range from 11m to 14m (35 ft.–46 ft.), and all equipment is provided.

Creek View House, 8 Tulo Lane, Pembroke Parish HM 02, Bermuda. ☎ 441/295-2370. Daily 7am–10pm. Bus: 1, 2, 10, or 11.

REEF FISHING
Three major reef banks lie off Bermuda, and they're likely to yield such catches as greater amberjack, almaco jack, great barracuda, little tunny, Bermuda chub, gray snapper, yellowtail snapper, and assorted bottom fish. The closest one begins about 1km (½ mile) offshore and stretches for nearly 8km (5 miles). The Challenger Bank is about 23km (14 miles) offshore, and Argus Bank is about 50km (30 miles) distant. The farther out you go, the more likely you are to turn up larger fish.

Several companies offer half- or full-day charters. Arrangements can also be made through Bermuda Sportsfishing (see "Deep-Sea Fishing," above).

Tips **Anglers Aweigh: How to Make Your Big Catch a Winning One**

The **Bermuda Game Fishing Tournament** is open to any angler who takes the time and trouble to fill out the tournament application when he or she catches a really big fish. No special license is required, but your catch must be weighed and three witnesses must sign an affidavit attesting to its weight. Special prizes are awarded each year for top catches of 17 species of game fish. For more information on registering the ones that didn't get away, contact the **Bermuda Department of Tourism,** Global House, 43 Church St., Hamilton HM 12, Bermuda (✆ **441/292-0023**). Open daily 9am–5pm.

SHORE FISHING

Shore fishing turns up such catches as bonefish, palometa (pompano), gray snapper, and great barracuda. Locals and most visitors prefer shore fishing at Spring Benny's Bay or West Whale Bay; Great Sound and St. George's Harbour are other promising grounds. The activities director at your hotel can help make fishing arrangements for you. **Windjammer Watersports,** with an outlet at Royal Naval Dockyard and another at Cambridge beaches (✆ **441/234-0250**), rents fishing rods ($15) and tackle and bait ($5) for the day.

PARASAILING

Bermuda Island Parasail Company This outfitter features harness-style parasail rides that last 7 to 8 minutes. Adults pay $50; children under 12, $35. Tandem rides go for $84. Dry takeoff and landing are on the *Nordic 28;* you'll parasail above Hamilton Harbour.

Ordnance Island, St. George. ✆ **441/232-2871**. Apr–Oct daily 9am–5pm (7pm in summer).

St. George's Parasail Water Sports Ltd. Parasailers soar above St. George's Harbour after taking off from the deck of K-2. Rides are single or tandem and cost $50 per person for adults, $35 for children under 12. Rides last approximately 8 to 10 minutes.

Somers Wharf, St. George. ✆ **441/297-1542**. Apr–Oct Mon–Fri 9am–6pm; Sat 11am–5pm.

Skyrider Bermuda Ltd. Skyrider takes a maximum of eight passengers into the Great Sound and north-shore area for two-person chair parasail rides. The 8- to 10-minute ride costs $50 for adults, $35 for children under 12. Boat passengers who do not parasail pay $15.

Royal Naval Dockyard, Sandys Parish. ✆ **441/234-3019**. Apr–Oct Tues–Sun 10am–5pm.

SAILING

Bermuda is one of the world's sailing capitals. Sail-yourself boats are available to rent for 2, 4 (half-day), and 8 (full-day) hours. A number of places charter yachts with licensed skippers.

Bermuda Caribbean Yacht Charter The owner of the 11m (35-ft.) ketch *Selina King,* Hal White operates guided tours from April to November and offers keen insight on the islands. He charges $400 for a half-day (10am–1pm or 1:30–4:30pm) or $650 for a full-day for six passengers. Each extra person pays $20.

2A Light House Rd., Southampton Parish. ✆ **441/238-8578**. Daily 9am–5pm. Bus: 7 or 8.

Blue Hole Water Sports   This outfitter rents sail-yourself Windsurfers or Sunfish for $25 for the first hour, $10 for each additional hour. A wide range of other equipment is on hand, including single and double kayaks. Kayaks are $20 per hour, $10 for each additional hour.

Grotto Bay Beach Hotel, 11 Blue Hole Hill, Hamilton Parish. ℂ **441/293-2915.** Daily 8:30am–5:30pm. Bus: 1, 3, 10, or 11.

Pompano Beach Club Watersports Centre   This is one of the island's best outfitters, mainly because of its variety of modern boats. Windsurfers, which hold one novice or experienced passenger, rent for $15 per hour. One or two people can rent a Sunfish sailboat or a Dolphin paddleboat. Single-person kayaks go for $20 for 1 hour. Two-person Sun Cats, which travel 9.5kmph (6 mph) and look like motorized lawn chairs, go for $35 per hour or $25 per half-hour.

36 Pompano Beach Rd., Southampton Parish. ℂ **441/234-0222.** May to mid-Oct daily 10am–6pm.

Somerset Bridge Watersports   Somerset Bridge is the best outlet for renting Boston whalers for island-hopping on your own. A 4m (13-ft.) Boston whaler (25 or 30 hp) carries four and costs $65 for 2 hours, $105 for 4 hours, and $165 for 8 hours. Somerset provides lots of extras, such as canopies, special maps, a ladder, a viewing box, and a fish and coral ID card. "Jet Ski Adventures" cost $90 for one, $115 for two, and $135 for three people. The jet ski reaches speeds of up to 81kmph (50 mph). There may be a fee for gas ($10–$20).

Somerset Bridge, Ely's Harbour, Sandys Parish. ℂ **441/234-0914.** Daily 8am–sunset.

WATER-SKIING

You can water-ski in the protected waters of Hamilton Harbour, Great Sound, Castle Harbour, Mangrove Bay, Spanish Point, Ferry Reach, Ely's Harbour, Riddells Bay, and Harrington Sound. May to September, when the waters are usually calm, is the best time for water-skiing. Bermuda law requires that a licensed skipper take water-skiers out. Only a few boat operators handle this sport, and charges fluctuate with fuel costs. Rates include the boat, skis, safety belts, and usually an instructor. Hotels and guesthouses can assist with arrangements.

Bermuda Waterski Centre   Up to five people can water-ski at the same time from a specially designed Ski Nautique. Lessons are also available. The charge for a party of any size (not per person) is $40 for a 15-minute session, $70 for a 30-minute session, and $120 for a 60-minute session. The driver is included in the price.

Robinson's Marina, Somerset Bridge, Sandys Parish. ℂ **441/234-3354.** May–Sept daily 8am–7:30pm. Bus: 6 or 7.

5 Where to Play Some of the World's Best Golf

Since the island's first course was laid out in 1922, golf has been one of Bermuda's most popular sports. You can play year-round, but spring, fall, and early winter offer the best seaside conditions. You must arrange tee times at any of the island's eight courses in advance through your guesthouse or hotel. Women's and men's clubs (right- and left-handed) are available at each course, and most leading stores in Bermuda sell golf balls. Generally speaking, children are not welcome on golf courses; definitely check in advance if you have any underage duffers in your party.

Bermuda's Best Golf Courses

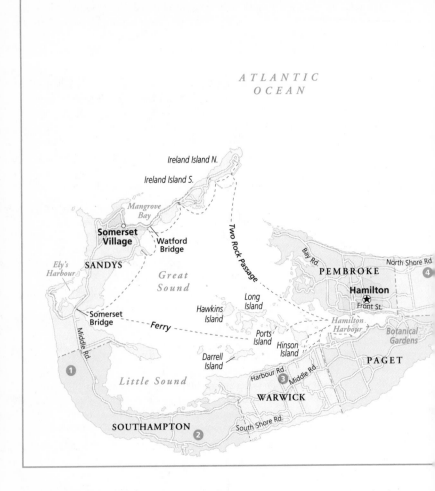

The **Tucker's Point Club** is one of the most scenic courses on the island (though it is a private club), while the **Port Royal** course, designed by Robert Trent Jones, is a challenge. Two famous courses—the **Mid Ocean Club** at Tucker's Town and the **Riddells Bay Golf and Country Club**—are private, and require introduction by a member before you can play. Certain luxury hotels can sometimes secure playing privileges at the Riddells Bay course. One of the most photographed courses on Bermuda is the **Southampton Princess Golf Club,** where a landscape of rolling hills and flowering shrubs add to the players' enjoyment.

The golf courses listed below that are part of hotel complexes permit nonguests to use their facilities. All of these golf courses have pros and offer lessons.

Top players participate in tournaments throughout the year. For information, contact the **Bermuda Golf Association,** P.O. Box HM 433, Hamilton HM BX, Bermuda (℃ **441/238-1367**).

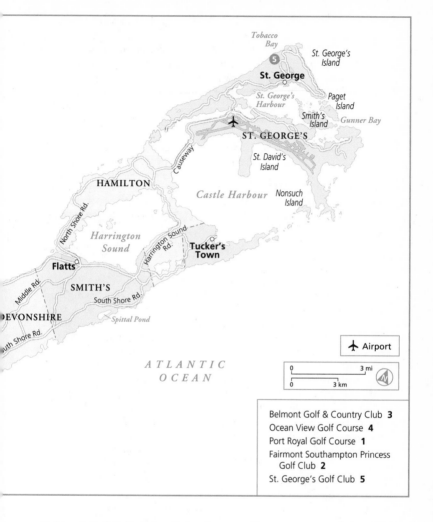

Belmont Golf & Country Club **★★** Airport

Belmont Golf & Country Club 3
Ocean View Golf Course 4
Port Royal Golf Course 1
Fairmont Southampton Princess
  Golf Club 2
St. George's Golf Club 5

Belmont Golf & Country Club Scotsman Emmett Devereux designed this course in 1923, and its layout has long been a challenge to golfers. The resort closed in 2003 for a restoration but may be open by the time of your visit—call first. The golfing magazines write of its par-5 11th hole, with a severe dogleg left and blind tee shot. It's sometimes difficult to finish uphill at number 18. Crystal caves under the turf sometimes cause the ball to roll unpredictably. In spite of these disadvantages, golf pros recommend the Belmont for beginners; the first hole is said to be "confidence building." It's estimated that with a 9 or 10 handicap, golfers will shoot in the 70s at Belmont—but there are no guarantees. Most of the course is inland, so unlike many golf courses in Bermuda, this one provides few views of the Atlantic.

Greens fees (which include golf carts) are $90 Monday to Friday, $95 weekends. A full set of clubs rents for $25. The dress code requires shirts with collars.

Between Harbour Rd. and Middle Rd., Warwick Parish. ✆ **441/236-6400.** Mon–Fri 7am–5pm; Sat–Sun 7am–5pm. Holes: 18. Par: 70. Length: 5,199m (17,331 ft.). Ferry from the City of Hamilton.

Fairmont Southampton Golf Club   On the grounds of one of the most luxurious hotels on Bermuda, this course occupies not only the loftiest but also one of the most scenic settings on the island. Elevated tees, strategically placed bunkers, and plenty of water hazards make it a challenge, and golfers have been known to use every club in their bags when the wind blows in from the Atlantic. Against the backdrop of the Gibbs Hill Lighthouse, the 16th hole sits in a cup ringed by flowering bushes. The vertical drop on the 1st and 2nd holes is almost 60m (200 ft.). Even experienced golfers like to "break in" on this course before taking on some of Bermuda's more challenging ones. This well-irrigated course is often green when some other courses suffer a summer brownout.

Greens fees and cart are $66; 18 holes for both hotel guests and visitors. There are also "Sunset Rates" if you begin playing in the afternoon. You will need to contact the course to get the "Sunset Rates" times (usually 2:30 or 3:30 pm). Adults can walk the course for $25 or add a cart for an additional $20. There are no caddies, and club rental is $25. Dress code: shirts with collars; no bathing suits or cutoffs.

101 South Shore Rd., Southampton Parish. ✆ **441/239-6952.** Daily 7am–sunset. Holes: 18. Par: 54. Length: 2,454m (8,052 ft.). Bus: 7 or 8.

Ocean View Golf Course   In the 1950s, this was a club for African Bermudians. Later, as other clubs started to admit black players, the course was neglected and fell into disrepair. Ocean View's reputation for spotty maintenance lives on despite a $2 million renovation that vastly improved the course. However, the course is nicer than many people think it is. In the center of Bermuda, in Devonshire Parish, the course offers panoramic views of the ocean from many of its elevated tees. Many golfers consider the terrain unpredictable; that, combined with rambling hills, makes the course more challenging than it appears. A few holes have as many as six tees. Winds from the Great Sound can have a greater effect on your score than you might think. The green on the 162m (531-ft.), par-3 5th hole has been cut into the coral hillside. Because the hole is draped with semitropical vines, golfers sometimes have the eerie feeling that they're hitting the ball into a cave.

On weekdays, this course tends to be the least crowded on Bermuda. Greens fees are $54 weekdays, rising to $56 on weekends, with carts costing $12 and clubs costing $24. Golf shoes are mandatory and can be rented for $8. Dress code: shirts with collars; no jeans or "short shorts."

2 Barkers Hill Rd., Devonshire Parish. ✆ **441/295-9092.** Daily 7:30am–6:30pm. Holes: 9. Par: 35. Length: 2,940 yd. Bus: 2,10,11.

Port Royal Golf Course   Famed golf architect Robert Trent Jones designed this government-owned and -operated course, which lies along the ocean. Jack Nicklaus might be found at the famous 16th hole, a favorite for photo layouts in golf magazines. The 15th and 16th holes ring the craggy cliffs around Whale Bay; sometimes winds from the Atlantic taunt the golf balls hit from these tees. The 7th and 8th holes are a dogleg par-5 and a windy par-3, respectively.

Port Royal is so popular that some avid golfers reserve starting times a year in advance. Greens fees for 18 holes are $95. There are no caddies. A full set of clubs rents for $28, and handcarts rent for $11. Gas-powered carts go for $25. The clubhouse, which overlooks the ocean and the 9th and 18th greens, contains a bar and a restaurant, The Putter's Green, which serves breakfast, lunch, and dinner. Dress code: shirts with collars.

Middle Rd., Southampton Parish. ✆ **441/234-0974.** Daily 7:30am–6:30pm. Holes: 18. Par: 71. Length: 6,003m (19,695 ft.). Bus: 7 or 8.

St. George's Golf Club   Redesigned by Robert Trent Jones, this is the newest of the Bermuda government's courses. On a headland at the northeastern tip of the island, it's within walking distance of St. George. Links run along the hillsides, providing panoramic vistas of the ocean. The winds off the water will significantly affect your game. On some par-3s, players need everything from a 9 iron to a driver to reach the green. The greens are the smallest on the island; some no more than 7m (24 ft.) across. The abundant salt air makes them slick.

This course isn't usually crowded at midweek. Greens fees for 18 holes are $57. There are no caddies. A full set of clubs rents for $24; gas golf carts go for $12 per person, handcarts for $8. Dress code: Bermuda-length shorts or slacks with a collared shirt; no jeans.

1 Park Rd., St. George Parish. ✆ 441/297-8067. Apr–Oct Mon–Fri 7:45am–6pm; off season Mon–Fri 7:45am–5:30pm. Holes: 18. Par: 62. Length: 3,697m (12,129 ft.). Bus: 6, 8, 10, or 11.

6 Other Outdoor Pursuits: Biking, Horseback Riding & Tennis

BIKING
With a year-round average temperature of 70°F, Bermuda is often ideal for bicycling. Not only is biking a great way to have fun and stay in shape, but it allows you to take a hands-on approach to your sightseeing. Although many tourism brochures extol the glories of bicycling on Bermuda, the roads are unfortunately not suitable for beginners. Think carefully and ask around when you're deciding where you or your children can ride safely and comfortably.

Most roadways are well paved and maintained. Although the island's speed limit is 32kmph (20 mph) for all vehicles, exercise caution when riding a bike or scooter. The roads are narrow and winding, and car traffic, especially during the day, tends to be heavy. Most drivers are considerate of cyclists, but a car may approach without warning, because the government discourages unnecessary horn honking. Fellow cyclists might even overtake you—bicycle racing is one of the most popular local sports.

Much of the island's terrain consists of flat stretches, although the hills provide what the locals call "challenges." Some climbs are steep, especially on roads that run north and south. South Shore Road, through Southampton and Warwick parishes, often leaves bikers huffing and puffing.

RENTING A BIKE
Push bikes (or pedal bikes), the terms Bermudians use to distinguish bicycles from mopeds, are a popular form of transportation. You can rent a bicycle by the hour, by the day, or for your entire stay. For information about bicycle and scooter rentals, see "Getting Around," in chapter 3, "Getting to Know Bermuda." All of the recommended shops rent bicycles. Many hotels have bicycles for guests' use, with or without a fee. Rentals generally cost $20 for the first day, plus $5 for each additional day. Three- and ten-speed bikes are usually available. It's always a good idea to call as far in advance as possible, because demand is great, especially from April to October.

WHERE TO BIKE ON BERMUDA
Only the hardiest cyclists set out to traverse the 34km (21-mile) length of Bermuda in 1 day. For most people, it's far better to focus on smaller sections at different times. So, decide what interests you parish by parish, and proceed from there. To save time, you can take your bike aboard various ferries (they're free), and then begin cycling.

A good choice for beginning riders is the **Bermuda Railway Trail** (see below). Some of the most interesting cycling trails are in **Devonshire and Smith's parishes.** The hills throughout these areas guarantee that you'll get your exercise for the day, and the beautiful landscapes make your effort worthwhile. **Spittal Pond,** a wildlife sanctuary with bike paths running along seaside cliffs, is one of the most rewarding destinations. Stop by a cycle shop for a trail map and some advice. Nearly all bike shop owners know Bermuda intimately and will mark up a map for you or give you any special guidance you need.

If you're a real demon on a bike, you can go farther west for the challenge of pumping up to **Gibbs Hill Lighthouse,** the oldest cast-iron lighthouse in the world. The panoramic view from the foot of the lighthouse is well worth the effort.

If you'd like to combine a picnic with your bicycle outing, head for **Sandys Parish.** First cross Somerset Bridge, the smallest drawbridge in the world, then pedal along Somerset Road to Fort Scaur Park. There you can relax and admire the view of Ely's Harbour while enjoying your picnic.

THE BERMUDA RAILWAY TRAIL   An interesting bicycle option is the **Bermuda Railway Trail** (see the box "Rattle & Shake: The Bermuda Railway Trail" in chapter 8, "Island Strolls," for more information), which is restricted to bicyclists and pedestrians. The Railway Trail consists of seven sections, each with its own character. You can decide how much of the trail you'd like to cover in 1 day, and which sections to focus on. Pick up a copy of the *Bermuda Railway Trail Guide,* available at the Bermuda Department of Tourism in the City of Hamilton or the Visitors Service Bureaus in the City of Hamilton and St. George, to help you plan your route.

HORSEBACK RIDING

Spicelands Riding Centre   This stable offers trail rides for $60 per person hourly. The regularly scheduled 1-hour jaunts begin at 7am, 8:00am, and 10:30am daily, year-round. On spring, summer, and fall weekends, there are also rides at 3 and 5pm. Book at least 1 day ahead, calling between 6am and 7pm.

Middle Rd., Warwick Parish. ℰ **441/238-8212.** Bus: 8.

TENNIS

Nearly all the big hotels, and many of the smaller ones, have courts, most of which can be lit for night play. Pack your tennis clothing and sneakers, because a tennis outfit (which no longer needs to be white) may be required.

Each of the facilities listed below has a tennis pro on duty, and lessons can be arranged. All rent racquets and sell balls.

Elbow Beach Hotel   The Elbow Beach Hotel has five LayKold courts (one for lessons only). Lessons cost $35 for 30 minutes, $70 for 1 hour. Racquets can be rented for $5, and balls are $6 per can of three.

60 South Shore Rd., Paget Parish. ℰ **441/236-3535.** Call for bookings daily 9am–5pm. Bus: 1, 2, or 7.

The Fairmont Southampton   This resort has Bermuda's largest tennis court layout, with 11 Plexipave courts, three of which are lit for night play. The price for guests is $12 per hour; non-guests $14. Evening rates for guests are $16; non-guests $18. Racquets rent for $6 per hour, balls cost $6 per can. Lessons are $75 for 1 hour.

101 South Shore Rd., Southampton Parish. ℰ **441/238-8000.** Daily 8am–7pm (until 6pm in winter). Bus: 7 or 8.

Finds Exploring Bermuda's Natural Wonderlands

The National Trust in Bermuda has wisely protected the island's nature reserves. If you play by the rules—that is, don't disturb animal life or take plant life as a souvenir—you can explore many of these natural wonderlands. If you enjoy nature trails, they're one of the most rewarding reasons to visit Bermuda.

The best and largest sanctuary is **Spittal Pond Nature Reserve** in Smith's Parish. Birders visit the reserve—especially from September to April—to see herons, ducks, flamingos, terns, and many migratory fowl (which can't be seen after Mar). This 24 hectare (60-acre) untamed seaside park is always open to the public with no admission charge. **The Department of Parks (© 441/236-4201)** offers free guided tours. Tours are offered primarily from November to May; call for schedules and additional information.

The island abounds with other places of natural wonder. Craggy formations shaped over the centuries out of limestone and coral dot the beaches along the southern coast, with towering cliffs forming a backdrop. The best place to view these formations is **Natural Arches,** one of the most photographed sights in Bermuda. Two limestone arches, which took nature centuries to carve, rise 11m (35 ft.) above the beach. Natural Arches is signposted almost at the end of South Shore Road, directing you to Castle Harbour Beach (which houses the arches).

Government Tennis Stadium   There are three clay and five Plexicushion courts here. Charges to play are $8 per adult, $4 per junior. Playing at night on one of the three lit courts costs $8 extra. Tennis attire is mandatory. Racquets rent for $5 per day; balls cost $6 per can.

Cedar Ave., Pembroke Parish. © 441/292-0105 to reserve a court or arrange lessons. Mon–Fri 8am–10pm, Sat–Sun 8am–7pm. Bus: 1, 2, 10, or 11.

Grotto Bay Beach Club   This resort across from the airport has some of the best tennis courts on the island. The 8.5 hectare (21-acre) property offers four courts, two of which are well lit for night games. Both hotel guests and nonguests pay $10 for daytime play, and $15 for night play. The hotel also rents rackets ($4) and tennis balls ($6) at the on-site pro shop.

11 Blue Hole Hill, Hamilton. © 441/293-8333. Daily 24 hr. Bus: 1, 3, 10, or 11.

7 Spectator Sports

In this tradition-bound British colony, the most popular spectator sports are cricket, soccer, field hockey, and the not-terribly-genteel game of rugby. As you might expect, boating, yachting, and sailing are also popular. The Bermuda Department of Tourism can provide dates and venues for upcoming events; see "Visitor Information," in chapter 2, "Planning Your Trip to Bermuda," for contact information before you go, and "Orienting Yourself: The Lay of the Land," in chapter 3, "Getting to Know Bermuda," for information once you've arrived. Also see the "Bermuda Calendar of Events," in chapter 2, "Planning Your Trip to Bermuda."

CRICKET

Far more Bermudians than you might suspect have memorized this terribly British sport's arcane rules. If you arrive in midsummer (the game's high season), you'll probably see several regional teams practicing on cricket fields throughout the island. Each match includes enough pageantry to remind participants of the game's imperial antecedents and enough conviviality (picnics, socializing, and chitchat among the spectators) to give you a real feel for Bermuda.

The **Cup Match Cricket Festival** is Bermuda's most passionately watched cricket event, with hundreds of viewers turning out to cheer on family members and friends. Conducted during late July or early August, it pairs Bermuda-based teams against one another. The event usually occurs at the headquarters of 2 of the island's approximately 30 cricket teams, either the **St. George's Cricket Club,** Willington Slip Road (© 441/297-0374), or the **Somerset Cricket Club,** Broome Street off Somerset Road (© 441/234-0327). Buy your tickets at the gate on the day of each event, and expect to pay between $12 and $15 per ticket for entrance to this long-standing Bermuda tradition. For more information, contact the **Bermuda Tourist Office** (© 441/292-0023).

GOLF TOURNAMENTS

Bermuda offers some of the finest golfing terrain in the world, partly due to the climate, which supports lush driving ranges and putting greens. In addition, the ever-present golfers play at surprisingly high levels. Golf tournaments are held throughout the year, culminating in the annual, much-publicized **Bermuda Open** at the Port Royal Golf Course in early October. Amateurs and professionals are welcome to vie for one of the most sought-after golfing prizes in the world. For information or an application, contact the secretary of the Bermuda Golf Association (© 441/238-1367; fax 441/238-0983).

HORSE RACING & EQUESTRIAN COMPETITIONS

Contact the **National Equestrian Centre,** Vesey Street, Devonshire Parish (© 441/291-7223), for information about upcoming events. From September to Easter, harness races take place about twice a month.

A major equestrian event is in October: the FEI/Samsung Dressage Competition and Show-Jumping. Details are available from the **Bermuda Equestrian Federation,** P.O. Box DV 583, Devonshire DV BX, Bermuda (© 441/234-0485; fax 441/234-3010; www.bef.bm). If you can't reach the federation on the phone (which is quite likely), ask for information at the tourist office, or check the local newspaper.

SOCCER

Bermudians view soccer as an important part of elementary education and actively encourage children and teenagers to participate. In early April, teams from countries around the Atlantic and Caribbean compete in three age divisions for the Diadora Youth Soccer Cup. Games are held on various fields throughout the island. More accessible to spectators at other times are the many high school games held regularly throughout the year. Contact the tourist office for a schedule.

YACHTING

Bermuda capitalizes on its geographical position in the mid-Atlantic to lure the yachting crowd. The racing season runs from March to November, with most races scheduled on weekends in the relatively calm waters of Bermuda's Great Sound. The best land vantage points include Spanish Point, the islands northeast of Somerset, and Hamilton Harbour. Shifting sightlines can make it confusing to watch races from land. Better views are available from the decks of privately owned boats that anchor near the edge of the racecourse, so it's good to befriend a private boat owner. Although the carefully choreographed regattas might be confusing to newcomers, the sight of a fleet of racing craft with spinnakers and pennants aloft is always exciting.

Bermuda is the final destination in two of the most important annual yacht races: the **Annapolis-Bermuda Race** and the even more prestigious **Newport-Bermuda Race,** both held in late June. Both provide enough visual distraction and maritime pageantry to keep you enthralled. Participating yachts range from 9m to 30m (30 ft.–100 ft.) in length, and their skippers are said to be among the most dedicated in the world.

Around Halloween, the autumn winds propel dozens of less exotic racing craft through the waters of the Great Sound. They compete in a series of one-on-one playoffs for the **King Edward VII Gold Cup International Match Racing Tournament.**

The island's yachting events are by no means limited to international competitions. Bermuda's sheltered bays and windswept open seas provide year-round enticement for anyone who has ever wanted to experience the thrill of a snapping jib and taut mainsail. See "Sailing," under "More Fun in the Water," earlier in this chapter, for details on yacht charters.

7

Seeing the Sights

Even though a large number of people live on this small island, you should never feel crowded. There are no billboards or neon signs, and relatively few cars to spoil the rolling countryside. Most houses seem to fit quite naturally into the landscape.

Bermuda consists of nine parishes (or counties). From west to east, they are Sandys (pronounced *sands*), Southampton, Warwick, Paget (which has the greatest concentration of hotels), Pembroke (home to the City of Hamilton), Devonshire, Smith's, Hamilton (not to be confused with the City of Hamilton), and St. George, which includes the U.S. naval air base and the little island of St. David's. Pembroke, which encloses the capital city of Hamilton, is the largest parish in population; St. George has the largest land area.

Because of Bermuda's small size, it's easy to get to know the island parish by parish. There's much to see, whether you travel by bike, ferry, bus, or taxi. You'll need plenty of time, though, because the pace is slow. Cars and other motorized vehicles, such as mopeds, must observe the maximum speed of 24kmph (15 mph) in the City of Hamilton and St. George, and 32kmph (20 mph) in the countryside. The speed limits are rigidly

enforced, and there are severe penalties for violations.

If you're visiting for the first time, you may want to follow the traditional tourist route, basically the equivalent of visiting New York and seeing the Statue of Liberty and the Empire State Building. The Aquarium, Devil's Hole, and cruise-boat outings are all popular for first-time visitors. For travelers on a second, third, or fourth visit to Bermuda, a different experience unfolds. Once you've done all the "must-sees," you'll want to walk around and make discoveries on your own. The best parishes for walking are Somerset, St. George, and the City of Hamilton.

But don't fill your days with too much structured sightseeing. You'll also want time to lounge on the beach, play in the water or hit the links, and to enjoy moments like sitting by the harbor in the late afternoon, enjoying the views as the yachts glide by. Absorbing Bermuda's beauty at your own pace and stopping to chat with the occasional islander will give you a real taste of Bermuda.

In this chapter, we'll go on a do-it-yourself tour, taking in Bermuda, parish by parish. Also consider taking one or more of the walking tours that we describe in chapter 8, "Island Strolls."

1 What to See If You Don't Have Much Time: The Island's Highlights

THE TOP ATTRACTIONS

Although Bermuda is small, you really can't see much of it in a day or 2. If you have more time, you may want to explore it methodically, parish by parish. That's what we'll do in this chapter—visit each parish's attractions in detail,

---

Tips **The Fun of Getting Lost**

Many guidebooks contend that you can't get lost in Bermuda. Don't believe them! As you travel along the narrow, winding roads, originally designed for the horse and carriage, you may go astray—several times—especially if you're looking for an obscure guesthouse on some long-forgotten lane. But don't worry, because you won't stay lost for long. Bermuda is so narrow that if you keep going east or west, you'll eventually come to a main road. At its broadest point, Bermuda is only about 3km (2 miles) wide. The principal arteries are North Shore Road, Middle Road, and South Shore Road, so you'll usually have at least some sense of what part of the island you're in.

---

from west to east. If your time is limited, however, you may want to consider heading straight for the following highlights. For details, see the appropriate parish section in this chapter.

- A walking tour of historic St. Georgetown (see chapter 8, "Island Strolls").
- A walking tour of the City of Hamilton, Bermuda's largest city and the seat of its government. (See chapter 8, "Island Strolls"; if you want to combine shopping and sightseeing; also check out chapter 9, "Shopping.")
- A fascinating ode to Bermuda's nautical heritage housed in a 19th-century fortress: the Bermuda Maritime Museum, at the Royal Naval Dockyard on Ireland Island in Sandys Parish.
- The Bermuda Aquarium, Natural History Museum & Zoo, a wonderful complex along North Shore Road across Flatts Bridge in Hamilton Parish.
- A guided tour of spectacular Crystal Caves, including crystal-clear Cahow Lake, in Hamilton Parish.
- The 18th-century mansion known as Verdmont in Smith's Parish. It stands on property once owned by the man who left Bermuda to found South Carolina.
- Fort Hamilton, a massive Victorian fortification overlooking the City of Hamilton and its harbor. (See "Walking Tour 1: The City of Hamilton," in chapter 8, "Island Strolls.")
- The Botanical Gardens, a Shangri-La in the mid-Atlantic, on South Shore Road in Paget Parish.
- Gibbs Hill Lighthouse in Southampton Parish, the oldest cast-iron lighthouse in the world.
- Southampton Parish's Horseshoe Bay Beach, the most photographed of the island's pink sandy beaches. (See "Horseshoe Bay Beach" in chapter 6, "Fun in the Surf & Sun.")
- Paget Parish's Elbow Beach, Bermuda's top stretch of sand for fun in the surf and sun. (See "Elbow Beach" in chapter 6, "Fun in the Surf & Sun.")

HIGHLIGHTS FOR ARCHITECTURE LOVERS

All of Bermuda interests architecture aficionados. Mark Twain wrote of the color of Bermuda houses and roofs: "It is exactly the white of the icing of a cake, and has the same emphasized and scarcely perceptible polish. The white of marble is modest and retiring compared with it . . . clean-cut fanciful chimneys—too pure and white for this world—that will charm one's gaze by the hour." For more details and lore, see the appendix, in addition to the rest of this chapter.

THE TOWN OF ST. GEORGE

The oldest and most historic settlement on the island is likely to hold the greatest fascination for architecture buffs. Also see chapter 8, "Island Strolls," for a walking tour.

The **Old State House,** constructed in 1620, is the oldest stone house on Bermuda. The governor at the time, Nathaniel Butler, believed he was building the house in an Italianate style. He ordered the workmen to use a combination of turtle oil and lime as mortar, a convention seen in many other buildings in Bermuda. You can view the inside of the house on Wednesdays only, from 10am to 4pm. Admission is free.

Many architects have wanted to finish the **Unfinished Cathedral,** which you can reach using Blockade Alley. Construction began in 1874, but a schism developed in the church, and there was no money to continue the project. To this day, true to its name, it remains unfinished.

The **Old Rectory,** now a private residence, was built by a former pirate in 1705. Located on Broad Alley, it's distinguished by its Dutch doors, chimneys, shutters, and what's called a "welcoming arms" staircase, which widens in an "embrace" toward the ground level. The rectory is open for visitors November to March only, daily from noon to 5pm. Admission is free.

From an architectural point of view, one of the most intriguing structures in St. George is **St. Peter's Church,** on Duke of York Street. This is the oldest Anglican Church in the Western Hemisphere, dating from 1620. It was constructed to replace an even older structure (from 1612) that had been poorly built from posts and palmetto leaves. A storm destroyed the 1620 church in 1712. The present St. Peter's was rebuilt and enlarged in 1713. In 1833, the church gained galleries on each side. The section around the triple-tiered pulpit is believed to be the oldest part of the structure, dating from the 1600s. The first governor of the island, Richard Moore, ordered construction of the dark red Bermuda cedar altar in 1615. It's the oldest surviving piece of woodwork from Bermuda's colonial period.

Tucker House, on Water Street, was built of native limestone. The house is furnished in an interesting manner, mostly with pieces from the mid-1700s and early 1800s. It's open Monday to Saturday from 10am to 4pm. Admission is $3 adults, $2 children.

SMITH'S PARISH

Another notable architectural structure is **Verdmont,** a mansion on Verdmont Lane. Dating from around 1710, it was owned by a wealthy ship owner, and also by the founder of the colony of South Carolina. Other owners included an American Loyalist, John Green, who fled from Philadelphia to Bermuda at the end of the Revolutionary War. Built to resemble an English manor house, Verdmont has a striking double roof and a quartet of large chimneys. Each room has a fireplace. The style of the sash windows was once fashionable in English manor houses.

2 Organized Tours

It's relatively easy to explore Bermuda on your own. But, if you prefer help from island-born and -bred residents, it's available.

OFFSHORE TOURS

Bermuda Island Cruises This outfitter offers the best sojourns at sea. You can book over the phone or through various hotel tour desks.

Moments **Frommer's Favorite Bermuda Experiences**

Strolling Bermuda's Pink Sands. The pink sand beaches are reason enough to come to Bermuda. Find your favorite cove (perhaps Whale Bay, Astwood Cove, or Jobson's Cove) and stroll aimlessly at dawn, at twilight, or whenever your fancy dictates. See the map "Bermuda's Best Public Beaches & Snorkeling Sites" in chapter 6, "Fun in the Surf & Sun."

Cycling. On a rented bicycle, or maybe a moped built for two, explore Bermuda from end to end. Start in St. George in the East End and go all the way to the Royal Naval Dockyard in the West End, or vice versa. You can do this in 1 day or stretch it out. See "Other Outdoor Pursuits: Biking, Horseback Riding & Tennis" in chapter 6, "Fun in the Surf & Sun."

Following the Bermuda Railway Trail. As you follow this intermittent trail from one end of the island to the other, you'll take in panoramic seascapes, see exotic flora and fauna, hear the soothing sounds of the island's bird life, and often have long stretches of trail completely to yourself. See "Rattle & Shake: The Bermuda Railway Trail" in chapter 8, "Island Strolls."

Touring by Horse & Buggy. No one has ever improved on this old-fashioned method of sightseeing and shopping along the City of Hamilton's Front Street. Better yet, go on a 2-hour shopping tour of Somerset Village in the West End. See "By Horse-Drawn Carriage" under "Getting Around" in chapter 3, "Getting to Know Bermuda."

Viewing Bermuda from Gibbs Hill Lighthouse. Climb the 185 steps of the oldest cast-iron lighthouse in the world for one of the greatest views of the Atlantic Ocean. Springtime visitors may be lucky enough to see migrating whales beyond the shore reefs. See p. 173.

Two-hour glass-bottom-boat tours will take you to Bermuda's famous reefs and shipwrecks. The cruises, which include commentary by a knowledgeable guide, leave Monday to Friday at 10am and 1:30pm, and Saturday at 1:30pm, only from Hamilton Harbour. The cost is $35 for adults, $18 for children 6 to 12.

The "Don't Stop the Carnival" evening cruise at Hawkins Island includes a barbecue dinner, music from a "Tropical Heat" band, a "Hot Spice Limbo" show, and an open bar. The cost is $79 per adult, $45 for children 7 to 17, free for children under 7. A parent must accompany children under 18. The cruise runs from 7 to 10:30pm on Tuesday, Wednesday, Friday, and Saturday.

The Island Band Cruise leaves the City of Hamilton at 2pm and returns at 5pm. It includes complimentary swizzles and costs $52 per person.

East Broadway Marina, Pembroke Parish. ✆ 441/292-8652.

Bermuda Water Tours Ltd.   This company offers 2- and 3½-hour trips for $35 and $50, respectively. Most tours include a visit to the sea gardens, where you can see the wonders of coral reefs and fish through the boat's glass bottom. Other water trips, including snorkeling expeditions, are also available.

P.O. Box 1572, Hamilton. ✆ 441/236-1500.

Attractions Around the Island

ATLANTIC OCEAN

Ireland Island N. 1
3 2
Ireland Island S.

Bermuda Arts Centre at Royal Dockyard

Mangrove Bay

Somerset Village
4
Watford Bridge
SANDYS

Ely's Harbour
5 6
7

Great Sound

Long Island

8
9
Ferry

Hawkins Island

Ports Island

Darrell Island

Hinson Island

Middle Rd.

Little Sound

18

Bay Rd.
19 20
North Shore R
PEMBROKE

Hamilton
14 Front St.

Hamilton Harbour
15
16 17
13
PAGET

Harbour Rd. Middle Rd.
12
WARWICK
South Shore Rd.

SOUTHAMPTON
10
11

Two Rock Passage

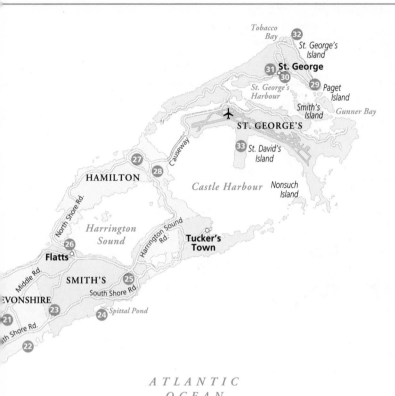

Tobacco Bay

32

St. George's Island

31 **St. George**

30

St. George's Harbour

29 *Paget Island*

Smith's Island *Gunner Bay*

✈

ST. GEORGE'S

33 *St. David's Island*

27

28

Causeway

HAMILTON

Castle Harbour *Nonsuch Island*

North Shore Rd.

Harrington Sound

Harrington Sound Rd.

Tucker's Town

26

Flatts

Middle Rd.

SMITH'S

25

South Shore Rd.

EVONSHIRE

23

24 *Spittal Pond*

21

th Shore Rd.

22

ATLANTIC OCEAN

✈ Airport

| 0 | | 3 mi |
| 0 | | 3 km |

ENVIRONMENTAL TOURS

The nonprofit **Bermuda Biological Station for Research** has collected the world's most comprehensive data on the oceanographic absorption of human-released carbon dioxide. It has tracked carbon dioxide levels for more than 40 years over a 21km (13-mile) area southeast of Bermuda. The National Science Foundation awarded the station a $500,000 grant to study climate change, the greenhouse effect, and the carbon cycle. The station has also compiled an extensive record on acid rain in the North American atmosphere.

You can learn firsthand what the station's scientists are studying by taking a free 90-minute guided tour of the grounds and laboratory in St. George. Guides explain what scientific studies are being conducted in Bermuda and how they relate to the overall world environment. They also discuss the island's natural areas, including the coral reefs, which are protected by strict conservation laws, and how humans have produced changes in the fragile ecological environment.

Trained volunteers and scientists who are carrying out studies conduct the special educational tours, offered at 10am on Wednesday. Visitors should assemble before 10am in the Biological Station's Hanson Hall. For more information, contact the **Bermuda Biological Station for Research,** 17 Biological Lane, Ferry Reach, St. George (© **441/297-1880**).

3 Sandys Parish

Sandys Parish is one of the island's real beauty spots. If you're looking for a place to just wander about and get lost on a summer day, this lovely parish is well worth your time. Fort Scaur and the Royal Naval Dockyard on Ireland Island are the major attractions. If you're pressed for time, skip the Gilbert Nature Reserve and St. James' Anglican Church.

To explore this tip of the fishhook that is Bermuda, it's best to take a ferry (the fare is $4). The trip from the City of Hamilton to Watford Bridge takes 45 minutes, and you can take your bike on board free (there's a $4 charge for scooters and mopeds). In addition to the above-mentioned stop on Watkins Island, ferries originating in Hamilton also stop at Cavello Bay, Somerset Bridge, Boaz Island, and the Royal Naval Dockyard. The **Visitors Service Bureau** is at the Royal Naval Dockyard (© **441/234-3824**), across from the ferry terminal. From May to October, hours are Monday to Friday and Sunday from 9am to 5pm (closed Sat); off-season hours are Monday to Friday from 9:30am to 2pm and Sunday from 11am to 3pm.

Gilbert Nature Reserve (aka National Trust)   In the center of the island lies the Gilbert Nature Reserve, 2 hectares (5 acres) of unspoiled woodland. It bears the name of the family that owned the property from the early 18th century until 1973, when the Bermuda National Trust acquired it (in conjunction with the Bermuda Audubon Society).

Somerset Rd. © 441/236-6483. Free admission. Organized tours are available. Daily sunrise–sunset. Bus: 7 or 8 from the City of Hamilton.

Fun Fact   **Just Where Is Bermuda?**

Bermuda is definitely not a Caribbean island. Many visitors learn with surprise that it lies closer to Nova Scotia than to any island in the Caribbean.

(Kids) Especially for Kids

Bermuda is a great destination for the entire family. Most resorts offer children's activities and special family packages. Most of the larger properties also give Mom and Dad an opportunity to spend some time alone by offering babysitting services for minimal fees.

Even more important, Bermuda offers many activities that will keep kids interested all day long. Kid-friendly activities include sailing, water-skiing, snorkeling, and glass-bottom-boat trips from April to October, plus tennis, visits to museums and caves, and a wide array of walking tours. Here are some of Bermuda's top sights and activities for kids:

Bermuda Aquarium, Natural History Museum & Zoo   This complex offers kids a wonderful introduction to the undersea world. Hand-held cassette tapes let you listen to a history of marine life as you visit live exhibits of Bermuda's native fish. See p. 180.

Bermuda Maritime Museum   Everyone in the family takes equal delight in seeing the exhibits of Bermuda's nautical history in this authentic Victorian fortress museum. See p. 170.

Bermuda Railway Trail   This nature walk, with strolls overlooking the seashore and along quiet tree-lined alleyways, is suitable for the entire family. You can pick up the 34km (21-mile) trail at many points and explore as many sections as you like, according to your stamina and interests. See "Rattle & Shake: The Bermuda Railway Trail" in chapter 8, "Island Strolls," and p. 158 in chapter 6.

Crystal Caves   Two boys chasing a runaway ball in 1907 discovered an enormous cavern surrounded by an underground lake. Easily naviga-ble walkways, and good guides, take parents and kids down into the caverns in Hamilton Parish. See p. 181.

Devil's Hole Aquarium   This aquarium near Harrington Sound, founded in 1834, was the first established attraction on Bermuda. Kids toss baited lines (without hooks) to feed fish and turtles in this natu-ral marine environment. See p. 181.

Bermuda Bell Diving   Kids can explore the ocean floor on their own—all they need is an underwater helmet and a little guidance. Following a pre-dive educational lecture aboard the ship, the kids can walk along the ocean floor for face-to-face encounters with friendly sea creatures. For children 8 years and older only. See "Walking Underwater" in chapter 6, "Fun in the Surf & Sun."

Scaur Hill Fort Park ✪   On the highest hill in Somerset, Fort Scaur was part of a ring of fortifications constructed in the 19th century, during a period of troubled relations between Britain and the United States. Intended as a last-ditch defense for the Royal Naval Dockyard, the fort was skillfully constructed, taking advantage of the land contours to camouflage its presence from detection at sea. The fort has subterranean passages and a dry moat that stretches across the land from Ely's Harbour to Great Sound.

Open to visitors since 1957, Fort Scaur has become one of Somerset's most popular tourist attractions. The fort has panoramic views of Ely's Harbour and Great Sound; using the free telescope, you'll see such faraway points as St. David's Lighthouse and Fort St. Catherine. The fort sits on 9 hectares (22 acres) of parkland filled with interesting trails, picnic areas, a rocky shoreline for fishing, and a public dock. Picnic tables, benches, and restrooms are available.

Ely's Harbour, Somerset Rd. © 441/236-5902. Free admission. Daily 9am–6pm. Closed Dec 25, Jan 15. Bus: 7 or 8 from the City of Hamilton.

St. James' Anglican Church   This is one of the most beautiful churches on Bermuda. It was constructed on the site of a structure that was destroyed by a hurricane in 1780. The present church was built 9 years later. A unique feature is the altar, which faces west instead of the customary east. The north and south aisles were added in 1836, the entrance gate in 1872, and the spire and chancel in 1880. The church was struck by lightning in 1939 and restored shortly thereafter.

90 Somerset Rd. © 441/234-0834. Free admission. Daily 8am–5pm. Bus: 7 or 8 from the City of Hamilton.

IRELAND ISLAND & THE ROYAL NAVAL DOCKYARD

Bermuda Arts Centre   Works by local artists are the focus in this gallery, with exhibits changing about every 6 weeks. An eclectic range of original art and prints is for sale. Local artists in residence include a cedar sculptor, and jewelry maker. On the premises you'll see four artists laboring over their respective art forms: woodsculpting, jewelry making, oil painting, and weaving. There's a small gift shop on-site, displaying and selling the wares of these and other artists.

4 Freeport Rd. © 441/234-2809. Free admission. Daily 10am–5pm. See travel information under the Royal Naval Dockyard listing.

Bermuda Craft Market   This is the prime place to watch local artists at work and to buy their wares, which make ideal souvenirs. Established in 1987, it offers items made from Bermuda cedar, candles, clothing, dolls, fabrics, hand-painted goods, jewelry, metal and gem sculpture, needlework, quilts, shell art, glass panels, and woven-cane goods, among other things.

In the Cooperage Building, 4 Freeport Rd. © 441/234-3208. Free admission. Hours are 10am–5pm when crew ship is docked, 9:30am–6pm if not; Sun 10am–6pm. See travel information under the Royal Naval Dockyard listing.

Bermuda Maritime Museum ★★ *Kids*   Housed in a 19th-century fortress built by convict labor, this museum exhibits artifacts, models, and maps pertaining to Bermuda's nautical heritage. The fortress's massive buildings of fitted stone, with their vaulted ceilings of English brick, are worth a visit on their own. So are the 9m (30-ft.) defensive ramparts; the underground tunnels, gun ports, and magazines; and the water gate and pond designed for boats entering from the sea. Exhibits in six large halls illustrate the island's long, intimate connection with the sea—from Spanish exploration to 20th-century ocean liners; from racing dinghies to practical fishing boats; from shipbuilding and privateering to naval exploits.

(*Fun Fact*   The World's Smallest Drawbridge

After leaving Fort Scaur, you can continue over the much-photographed 17th-century **Somerset Bridge,** the world's smallest drawbridge. When it's open for marine traffic, the space between the spans is a mere 22 inches at road level—just large enough for the mast of a sailboat to pass through.

Finds **A Park of Your Own**

Just when you thought that everything in "Paradise" (as locals call Bermuda) had been discovered, you happen upon 15 hectare (38-acre) **Hog Bay Park.** In spite of its unattractive name, this is one of the beauty spots of Bermuda, and one of its least visited attractions. To reach the park from the City of Hamilton, take a ferry across Great Sound, getting off at the Somerset Bridge ferry stop. Cross the Somerset drawbridge and follow the trail of the old Bermuda Railway. Cross Middle Road into the park. Once at the park you'll pass ruins of lime kilns once used for making lime to paint the famous whitewashed roofs of island homes. As you meander, you'll come across old abandoned cottages, finally reaching Sugar Loaf Hill with its Look Out Point. From here you'll be rewarded with one of the greatest panoramic views on Bermuda. As Barbra Streisand might put it: "On a clear day you can see forever."

Tony Fernandes, founder of Rock Ramblers, an eco-heritage Bermudian group, organizes a 2-hour walking tour of the park Friday at 10am. For more information, call ✆ **441/238-3438.**

The museum's most famous exhibit is in the 1837 Shifting House, which opened in 1979. You can see such artifacts as gold bars, pottery, jewelry, silver coins, and other items recovered from 16th- and 17th-century shipwrecks. The collection includes some earthenware and pewter that belonged to the English settlers on their way to Jamestown aboard the *Sea Venture,* which was wrecked in 1609. Most visitors come here to gaze at the Tucker Treasure. A well-known local diver, Teddy Tucker, made a significant find in 1955 when he discovered the wreck of the *San Antonio,* a Spanish vessel that had gone down off the coast of Bermuda in a violent storm in 1621. One of the great treasures of this find, the Pectoral Cross, was stolen in 1975 just before Queen Elizabeth II officially opened the museum. The priceless original cross was replaced by a fake. To this day, the original cross has not been recovered, and its mysterious disappearance is still the subject of much discussion.

As you enter the Parade Ground at the entrance to the museum, you'll notice a 3m- (10-ft.-) high figure of King Neptune. This has been duplicated in Indiana limestone from a figure that was recovered from HMS *Irresistible,* when the ship was broken up in 1891. The Queen's Exhibition Hall houses general maritime exhibits, including displays on navigation, whaling, and cable and wireless communications. A "Bermuda in Five Hours" exhibit focuses on Pan American's early "flying boats." The building itself was constructed in 1850 for the purpose of storing 4,860 barrels of gunpowder.

The Forster Cooper Building (1852) illustrates the history of the Royal Navy in Bermuda, and includes the Bromby Bottle Collection, boasting more than 2,000 rare and antique bottles that have washed up on Bermuda's shores. Princess Margaret opened the exhibit in 1984. The Boatloft houses part of the museum's boat collections, including the century-old fitted dinghy *Victory,* the 5m (17-ft.) *Spirit of Bermuda,* and the *Rambler,* the only surviving Bermuda pilot gig (a commanding officer's light boat kept on a large ship). On the upper floor, the original dockyard clock, which is still working, chimes on the hours and the quarter-hours. In 2000, one of the Dockyard's most impressive colonial-era buildings, **The Commissioner's House,** was restored and opened to the public. The ground floor of its stately looking interior is devoted to exhibits showing the contribution of Bermudians to the First World War; the second floor is devoted to exhibitions about the history of marine traffic and sailing in Bermuda, and the third floor contains some of the many water colors that ladies of distinction used to paint, usually of the Dockyards, during the 19th and early 20th century. Admission to the Commissioner's House, like everything else in the Dockyards, is included in the entrance price.

Royal Naval Dockyard. ✆ 441/234-1418. Admission $7.50 adults, $6 seniors and students, $3 children 17 and under, family (2 adults and up to 5 children) $15; free for children 4 and under. Daily 9:30am–4:30pm. Closed Dec 25. See travel information under the Royal Naval Dockyard listing.

The Royal Naval Dockyard ★★ The Dockyard, with its Bermuda Maritime Museum, is the number-one tourist attraction on Bermuda. Even if you plan to spend all your precious Bermuda time on the pink sandy beaches, try to schedule at least a half-day to check it out.

The Royal Naval Dockyard has been transformed into a park, with Victorian street lighting and a Terrace Pavilion and bandstand for concerts. When the Bermudian government bought this dockyard, which had been on British Admiralty land, in 1953, it marked the end of British naval might in the western Atlantic. A multimillion-dollar cruise-ship dock has been built and a tourist village has emerged; today, vendors push carts filled with food, dry goods, and local crafts. There's a full-service marina with floating docks, a clubhouse, and showers. The area also houses the Bermuda Maritime Museum, the Neptune Theatre, the Crafts Market, and the Bermuda Arts Centre, which are all described below. Closed Good Friday and Christmas Day. Call the Visitors Service Bureau for more information (✆ **441/234-3824**).

Ferries from the City of Hamilton stop at Ireland Island, at the western end of Bermuda, once each hour 7am–6pm. The fare is $4 each way. Buses (no. 7 or 8) leave the City of Hamilton for the Royal Naval Dockyard Mon–Sat every 15 min. from 6:45am–11:45pm. The trip takes 1 hr. and costs $4 for adults, $1 for children 5–15; free for children under 5. **Note:** Drivers accept this bus fare in coins only.

Moments **Stepping Back into the Ice Age**

Bermuda has one of the highest concentrations of limestone caves in the world. Most began forming during the Pleistocene Ice Age. As early as 1623, the adventurer Capt. John Smith wrote that he had encountered "vary strange, darke, cumbersome caves."

In Bermuda, nature's patient, relentless underground sculpting has left behind a dream world for even the casual spelunker. Deep in the majestic silence of the earth's interior, you can roam in caverns full of great stalactites and stalagmites of Gothic grandeur, delicacy, and beauty. This awesome underground has been the inspiration for creative achievements as diverse as Shakespeare's *The Tempest* and Henson Associates' *Fraggle Rock*.

You can visit Crystal Caves on guided tours; the cave complex is along Harrington Sound Road in Hamilton Parish (p. 181).

4 Southampton Parish

Most visitors pass through Southampton for the beaches, if for no other reason. Even if you're not staying here, it's worth a journey to see the view from Gibbs Hill Lighthouse—there's no finer panorama in all of Bermuda.

Gibbs Hill Lighthouse ★ Southampton's main attraction is this lighthouse, built in 1846. It's the oldest cast-iron lighthouse in the world. Although there's a 185-step climb to the top, the panoramic view of Bermuda and its shoreline from the balcony make the exertion worthwhile. You can also view the same panorama that Queen Elizabeth II gazed on in 1953; just find the commemoration plaque by the entrance to the lighthouse. The lighthouse keeper will explain the workings of the machinery. If you visit in the spring, you may spot migrating whales beyond the south shore reefs.

Gibbs Hill, Lighthouse Rd. (between South Shore Rd. and Middle Rd.). © **441/238-0524**. Admission $2.50; free for children under 5. Daily 9am–4:30pm. Closed Feb. Bus: 7 or 8 from the City of Hamilton.

5 Warwick Parish

This parish has few sightseeing attractions, but it is a place of natural beauty. Visitors come here mostly for the sandy beach, **Warwick Long Bay,** on South Shore Road—it's one of the finest on Bermuda (see "Beaches," in chapter 6, "Fun in the Surf & Sun," for details). Nearby, you can visit **Christ Church,** across from the Belmont Hotel on Middle Road. Built in 1719, it's one of the oldest Scottish Presbyterian churches in the New World.

Warwick is also the site of some of the best golf and horseback riding in Bermuda. See chapter 6, "Fun in the Surf & Sun," for specifics on these activities.

6 Paget Parish

On every visit to Bermuda, we schedule a long stopover at the Botanical Gardens. They are worth the trip, even if you're staying in the East End. Once you're here, Waterville, one of the oldest houses in Bermuda, merits a look. You could cap your visit with a walk through unspoiled Paget Marsh, although you might skip it if you've already seen Spittal Pond (see "Smith's Parish," later in this chapter).

The Birdsey Studio Jo Birdsey Lindberg, daughter of the island's best-known artist, Alfred Birdsey (1912–96), sells original artwork, watercolors, and oils. An experienced painter, she continues a family tradition by producing and showing her work here, in a garden setting. Her Impressionistic style appears in compositions ranging from landscapes of Bermuda to architectural and nautical themes. Prices range from $50 to $350 for watercolors, $700 to $1,000 for oils. Also available are notecards reproduced from paintings by Alfred Birdsey. Studio hours are Monday to Friday from 10:30am to 1pm March to July, and September to November, and by appointment.

5 Stowe Hill. © **441/236-6658**, or 441/236-5845 in the evening. Free admission. Bus: 8 from the City of Hamilton.

Botanical Gardens ★ This 14-hectare (36-acre) landscaped park, maintained by the Department of Natural Resources, is one of Bermuda's major attractions. Hundreds of clearly identified flowers, shrubs, and trees line the pathways. Attractions include collections of hibiscus and subtropical fruit, an aviary, banyan trees, and even a garden for the blind. It's best to take one of the 90-minute walking tours, which depart at 10:30am on Tuesday, Wednesday, and

Friday from the visitor center. The cafe sells sandwiches and salads (soup and chili in winter). **Masterworks Foundation** has built a growing art exhibit in the gardens. Displaying various types of oil paintings and watercolor paintings.

Point Finger Rd. (at South Shore Rd.). ℂ 441/236-5291. Free admission. Daily sunrise–sunset. Bus: 1, 2, 7, or 8. By bike or moped, turn left off Middle Rd. onto Tee St.; at Berry Hill Rd., go right; about 1km (½ mile) farther on the left is the signposted turnoff to the gardens; take a right fork to the parking lot on the left.

Paget Marsh   This nature reserve comprises 10 hectares (25 acres) of unspoiled native woods and marshland, with vegetation and bird life of ecological interest. Because it's a fully protected area with few trails, prospective visitors should call first and make special arrangements, and obtain a map from the Bermuda National Trust. A boardwalk installed in 1999 allows you to view the marsh better.

Middle Rd. ℂ 441/236-6483. Free admission. Mon–Fri 9am–5pm by special arrangement. Bus: 8 from the City of Hamilton.

Waterville   Built before 1735, Waterville is one of the oldest houses on Bermuda. It was home to seven generations of the prominent Trimingham family. From the house's cellar storage rooms in 1842, James Harvey Trimingham started the business that was to become Trimingham Brothers—now one of Bermuda's finest Front Street department stores. Major renovations were undertaken in 1811, and the house has been restored in that period's style. The two main rooms hold period furnishings, mainly Trimingham family heirlooms specifically bequeathed for use in the house. Waterville is the headquarters of the Bermuda National Trust, and houses its offices and reception rooms. It's just west of the Trimingham roundabout, near the City of Hamilton.

5 The Lane (Harbour Rd.), at Pomander Rd. ℂ 441/236-6483. Free admission. Mon–Fri 9am–5pm. Bus: 7 or 8 from the City of Hamilton.

7 Pembroke Parish & the City of Hamilton

The ideal way to see the City of Hamilton and its parish, Pembroke, for the first time, is to sail in through Hamilton Harbour, past the offshore cays.

In 1852, the cornerstone was laid for the Hamilton Hotel, Bermuda's first hotel, completed in 1863. It survived until a fire destroyed it in 1955. When the Hamilton Princess opened in 1887, it overshadowed the Hamilton Hotel and became the island's hotel of choice. Hamilton Hotel's colorful history includes being taken over by Allied agents during World War II.

If Queen Victoria's daughter Princess Louise were to visit Bermuda today, she would probably stay at **Government House,** on North Shore Road and Langton Hill. Because this is the residence of the governor of the island, it's not open to the public. This Victorian home has housed many notable guests, including Queen Elizabeth II and Prince Philip, Prince Charles, Sir Winston Churchill, and Pres. John F. Kennedy. In 1973, Gov. Sir Richard Sharples, his aide, Capt. Hugh Sayers, and the governor's dog were assassinated while they were walking on the grounds. The tragedy led to a state of emergency in Bermuda.

While touring Pembroke Parish, visitors often stop at **Black Watch Well,** at the junction of North Shore Road and Black Watch Pass. Excavated by a detachment of the Black Watch Regiment, the well was dug in 1894, when Bermudians were suffering through a long drought.

Another choice spot to visit is **Admiralty House Park,** off North Shore Road at Spanish Point Road. In 1816, a house was erected here to offer accommodations for the commanding British admiralty, who worked at the naval base at the dockyard. Over the years, the house was rebuilt several times. In the 1850s, it gained a series of subterranean tunnels, plus a number of galleries and caves carved into the cliffs above the sea. By 1951, the Royal Navy withdrew, and most of the house was torn down—except for a ballroom, which survives. Today, you can explore the parklike grounds. The sheltered beach at Clarence Cove is good for swimming.

THE CITY OF HAMILTON ★★★

The capital of Bermuda was once known as the "show window of the British Empire." Both Mark Twain and Eugene O'Neill, who lived in lodgings that opened onto Hamilton Harbour, cited its beauty.

Named for former governor Henry Hamilton, the City of Hamilton was incorporated as a town in 1793. Because of its central location and its large, protected harbor, it replaced St. George as the island's capital in 1815. The City of Hamilton encompasses only 73 hectares (182 acres) of land, so most visitors explore it on foot.

Long before it became known as "the showcase of the Atlantic," the City of Hamilton was a modest outlet for the export of Bermuda cedar and fresh vegetables. Today, it's the hub of the island's economy.

The City of Hamilton is more popular for its shops and restaurants than for its attractions. The City of Hamilton boasts the largest number of restaurants and bars on Bermuda, especially on and near Front Street. The restaurants run a wide range of prices, and there are many English-style watering holes if you'd like to go for a traditional pub crawl. And religion isn't neglected—there are 12 churches within the city limits, one or two of which merit a visit.

If you'd like to go sightseeing, take our walking tour (see chapter 8, "Island Strolls") for a comprehensive view of the City of Hamilton. The only sights that are worth in-depth visits are Fort Hamilton (seen on the walking tour), the Bermuda Historical Society Museum, and the Bermuda National Gallery. You can safely skip the rest if you're pressed for time.

A stroll along **Front Street** ★ will take you by some of the City of Hamilton's most elegant stores, but you'll also want to branch off into the little alleyways to check out the shops and boutiques. If you get tired of walking or shopping (or both), you can go down to the docks and take one of the boats or catamarans waiting to show you the treasures of Little Sound and Great Sound.

Ferries back to Paget, Warwick, and Sandys parishes leave daily between 6:50am and 11:20pm. On Saturday and Sunday, there are fewer departures.

On certain days you may be able to see locals buying fresh fish—the part of the catch that isn't earmarked for restaurants—right from the fishers at the

---

Tips **From the Land & from the Sea**

The City of Hamilton should be seen not only from land, but also from the water. Try to make time for a boat tour of the harbor and its coral reefs. If you're visiting from another parish, the ferry will let you off at the west end of Front Street, which is ideal if you'd like to drop by the Visitors Service Bureau, which is right near the Ferry Terminal, and pick up a map. The staff also provides information and helpful brochures; hours are 9am to 4:45pm Monday to Saturday.

African Diaspora Heritage Trail

To celebrate the role African slaves played in the formation of Bermuda, The African Diaspora Heritage Trail has been launched. Free brochures are available from tourist offices to take you along this self-guided tour which highlights peak points in the black cultural history of the island. A special commemorative plaque marks each site.

Thirteen sites have been identified including the site of the slave ship Enterprise incident which like the similar, better-known *Amistad* affair, involved the rescuing of slaves seeking refuge and freedom; the historic Slave Graveyard at St. Peter's Church (ca. 1612), both located in St. George's (UNESCO's newest World Heritage Site); the Crow Lane site of the execution of Sally Bassett, slave revolt leader; sites associated with Mary Prince, the Bermudian slave who wrote the first account of slavery actually authored by a slave, which played a key role in the struggle to abolish slavery; and Cobb's Hill Wesleyan Methodist Church, built by slaves by moonlight.

Front Street docks. Rockfish is the most abundant, and you'll also see snapper, grouper, and many other species.

Opposite the Visitors Service Bureau stands the much-photographed **"Birdcage,"** where you used to be able to see a Bermuda shorts-clad police officer directing traffic on a pedestal likened to a birdcage. Such a sight is rare now. Visitors often wondered if the traffic director was for real or placed there for tourist photographs.

Nearby is Albouy's Point, site of the Royal Bermuda Yacht Club, founded in 1844. The point, named after a 17th-century professor of "physick," is a public park overlooking Hamilton Harbour.

To reach the sights listed below, take bus number 1, 2, 10, or 11.

Bermuda Historical Society Museum   After leaving the harbor, proceed up Queen Street to the public library and the Bermuda Historical Society Museum. The museum has a collection of old cedar furniture, antique silver, early Bermuda coins (hog money), and ceramics imported by early sea captains. You'll see the sea chest and navigating lodestone of Sir George Somers, whose flagship, the *Sea Venture,* became stranded on Bermuda's reefs in 1609, resulting in Bermuda's first European settlers. You'll also find portraits of Sir George and Lady Somers, and models of *Patience, Deliverance,* and the ill-fated *Sea Venture.*

The museum is in Par-la-Ville Park on Queen Street. It was designed by William Bennett Perot, the City of Hamilton's first postmaster (from 1818–62), who was a somewhat eccentric fellow; as he delivered mail around town, he is said to have placed letters in the crown of his top hat in order to preserve his dignity.

13 Queen St., Par-la-Ville Park. (*) **441/295-2487**. Free admission. Mon–Sat 9:30am–3:30pm.

Bermuda National Gallery   Located in the east wing of City Hall, the Bermuda National Gallery is the home of the Masterworks Foundation Bermudiana Collection, with works by such artists as Georgia O'Keeffe, Winslow Homer, Charles Demuth, Albert Gleizes, Ogden Pleissner, and Jack Bush. The

Masterworks Foundation was established in 1987 to return to the island works of art that depict Bermuda, and to exhibit them. The gallery is also home to the Hereward T. Watlington Collection, which includes 15th- to 19th-century paintings by such masters as Reynolds, Gainsborough, and de Hooch. The gallery also displays smaller paintings and watercolors collected by the Bermuda Archives and National Trust.

Bermuda's humid climate and damaging sunlight make proper climate control and lighting essential. To create an appropriate gallery, the Bermuda Fine Art Trust was developed and incorporated by an Act of Parliament in 1982. In 1988, the Hon. Hereward T. Watlington bequeathed his collection of European paintings to the people of Bermuda on the condition that they be housed in a European-standard climate-controlled environment. The Corporation of Hamilton offered the use of the East Exhibition Room of City Hall and made a financial contribution toward the construction of a proper facility.

City Hall, 17 Church St. ℂ **441/295-9428**. Free admission. Mon–Sat 10am–4pm. Tours Mon, Tues, Thurs, and Fri at 1pm.

Cathedral of the Most Holy Trinity (Bermuda Cathedral)   This is the mother church of the Anglican diocese in Bermuda. It became a cathedral in 1894 and was formally consecrated in 1911. The building features a reredos (ornamental partition), stained-glass windows, and ornate carvings. If you have the stamina, climb the 157 steps to the top of the tower for a panoramic view of the City of Hamilton and the harbor. The roof of the cathedral has been fully restored where visitors can see from the tower as well as the City of Hamilton and the harbor.

Church St. ℂ **441/292-4033**. Free admission to cathedral; admission to the cathedral tower $3 adults, $2 seniors and children. Cathedral daily 8am–5pm and for Sunday services; tower Mon–Fri 10am–3pm.

Hamilton City Hall & Arts Centre   The City Hall, also home of the Bermuda Society of Arts, is an imposing white structure with a giant weather vane and wind clock to tell maritime-minded Bermudians which way the wind is blowing. Completed in 1960, the building is the seat of the City of Hamilton's municipal government. The theater on the first floor books stage, music, and dance productions throughout the year, and is the main site of the Bermuda Festival. The Bermuda National Gallery (see above) is also here.

Since 1956, the Bermuda Society of Arts has encouraged and provided a forum for contemporary artists, sculptors, and photographers. Its gallery, with ever-changing exhibitions, displays the work of local and visiting artists. This society is a separate entity from the newer Bermuda National Gallery. Expect the steepest admission price in Bermuda.

17 Church St. ℂ **441/292-1234** or 441/292-3824. $25 to $35 per show. City Hall: Mon–Fri 9am–5pm. Bermuda Society of Arts: Mon–Sat 10am–4pm.

Perot Post Office   Bermuda's first stamp was printed in this landmark building. Beloved by collectors from all over the world, the stamps—signed by William Bennett Perot, Bermuda's first postmaster—are priceless. It's said that Perot and his friend Heyl, who ran an apothecary, conceived the first postage stamp to protect the post office from cheaters. People used to stop off at the post office and leave letters, but not enough pennies to send them. The postage stamps were printed in black or carmine.

Philatelists can purchase contemporary Bermuda stamps here. For its 375th anniversary, Bermuda issued a series of stamps honoring its discovery in 1609.

One stamp portrays the admiral of the fleet, Sir George Somers, along with Sir Thomas Gates, the captain of the *Sea Venture*. Another depicts the settlement of Jamestown, Virginia, which was on the verge of extinction when Sir George and the survivors of the Bermuda shipwreck finally arrived with supplies late in 1610. A third shows the *Sea Venture* stranded on the coral reefs of Bermuda. Yet another shows the entire fleet, originally bound for Jamestown, leaving Plymouth, England, on June 2, 1609.

Queen St., at the entrance to Par-la-Ville Park. © 441/292-9052 or 441/295-5151. Free admission. Mon–Fri 9am–5pm.

Sessions House   This Italian Renaissance–style structure was originally built in 1819. Its clock tower, added in 1887, commemorates the Golden Jubilee of Queen Victoria. The House of Assembly meets on the second floor from November to May, and visitors are permitted in the gallery. Call ahead to learn when meetings are scheduled. On the lower level, the chief justice presides over the Supreme Court.

21 Parliament St. © 441/292-7408. Free admission. Mon–Thurs 9am–12:30pm, 2–5pm; Fri 10am to closing (times vary with sessions).

8 Devonshire Parish

If you're passing through Devonshire, consider a stop at the following attractions.

Old Devonshire Parish Church   The Old Devonshire Parish Church is believed to have been built on this site in 1624, although the present foundation dates from 1716. An explosion virtually destroyed the church on Easter in 1970, but it was reconstructed. Today, the tiny structure looks more like a vicarage than a church. Some of the church's contents survived the blast, including silver dating from 1590, which may be the oldest on the island. The Old Devonshire Parish Church stands northwest of the "new" Devonshire Parish Church, which dates from 1846.

Middle Rd. © 441/236-3671. Free admission. Daily 9am–5:30pm. Bus: 2.

Palm Grove   This private estate, 4km (2½ miles) east of the City of Hamilton, is one of the delights of Devonshire Parish. It's famous for its pond, which features a relief map of Bermuda in the middle. On the map, each parish is an immaculately manicured grassy division. The site, which has well-landscaped flower gardens, opens onto a view of the sea.

38 South Shore Rd. No phone. Free admission. Mon–Thurs 8:30am–5pm. Bus: 1.

Finds An Explorer—Not Just a Tourist

A series of new tours and programs has been announced by the **Bermuda Explorers Program,** including an art and architecture walk through the capital city of Hamilton, with visits to local galleries. The Gumba Trail is a "cultural nature walk" that describes the background of Caribbean Junkanoo dancers and their link to the "Goombeys" of Bermuda, along with a commentary on the island's plant life. To learn more, call © 800/ **BERMUDA** or visit one of the local tourist offices when you arrive on Bermuda.

Wildlife Reserve Opens to Public

Visitors to Bermuda can now explore the island's most treasured wildlife reserve—**Nonsuch Island**. This unique habitat is a representation of the prehistoric "native" environment of Bermuda. For the first time in history, visitors can explore this unique living museum on weekly excursions offered by the Bermuda Biological Station for Research (BBSR) in conjunction with conservationist Dr. David Wingate.

The half-day tour, which operates on Thursday morning, is an educational experience that is restricted to 25 hikers a week. Participants will learn first-hand from Dr. Wingate about his lifetime's work recreating the island as a living example of Bermuda's "native" environment, and the reintroduction of the indigenous Cahow bird. The trails and observation sites have all been carefully planned so as to give access to all the main features without causing disturbances to island life.

The tour costs $75, which includes the guided tour of the island, onboard learning about Bermuda's marine life, and lunch. The tour leaves from the BBSR dock at 9:15am and returns by 1:30pm. There is a second collection point at 9:30am from St. George's. For further information or to reserve a space, call ✆ **441/297-1880** or visit www.bbsr.edu.

9 Smith's Parish

Even if you're staying in remote Sandys Parish, the 18th-century mansion of Verdmont is worth a detour, as the good folks at Michelin say. If you're in the area, Spittal Pond Nature Reserve also merits some attention.

Spittal Pond Nature Reserve   Follow steep Knapton Hill Road west to South Shore Road, turning at the sign for Spittal Pond, Bermuda's largest wildlife sanctuary. The most important of the National Trust's open spaces, it occupies 24 hectares (60 acres) and attracts about 25 species of waterfowl, from November to May. Visitors are asked to stay on the scenic trails and footpaths provided. Bird-watchers especially like to visit in January, when as many as 500 species can be observed wintering on or near the pond.

South Shore Rd. ✆ **441/236-6483**. Free admission. Daily sunrise–sunset. Bus: 1 or 3.

Verdmont ✪   This 18th-century mansion is of special significance to Americans who are interested in colonial and Revolutionary War history. It stands on property that was owned in the 17th century by William Sayle, who left Bermuda to found South Carolina and become its first governor. The house was built before 1710 by John Dickinson, a prosperous ship owner who was also speaker of the House of Assembly in Bermuda from 1707 to 1710. Verdmont passed to Mr. Dickinson's granddaughter, Elizabeth, who married the Hon. Thomas Smith, collector of Customs. Their oldest daughter, Mary, married Judge John Green, a Loyalist who came to Bermuda in 1765 from Philadelphia. During and after the American Revolution, Green was judge of the Vice-Admiralty Court and had the final say on prizes brought in by privateers. Many American ship owners lost their vessels because of his decisions. The

---

⟨Moments⟩ The Sounds of Silence (& Gregorian Chant)

In crowded Bermuda, the search for solitude and tranquillity grows harder and harder. But one of our staff recently stumbled upon the 17.5 hectares (43-acre) **Heydon Trust,** Heydon Dr. (② **441/234-1831**), in Sandys Parish, open daily dawn to dusk. This setting, which is also a sanctuary for migratory birds, is Bermuda the way it used to be. The grounds are filled with flower gardens, citrus orchards, walkways, and even a tiny chapel dating from 1620, where Monday to Saturday services are held at 7am and 3pm in Gregorian chant. Park benches are found throughout the preserve where you can sit and contemplate nature or your navel.

---

house, which the National Trust now administers, contains many antiques, china, and portraits, along with the finest cedar stair balustrade on Bermuda.

6 Verdmont Lane, Collectors Hill. ② **441/236-7369**. Admission $3 adults, $2 children 6–18; free for children under 6. Tues–Sat 10am–4pm. Bus: 1 from the City of Hamilton or St. George.

10 Hamilton Parish

Even if you have limited sightseeing time, try to budget at least a half-day for Hamilton Parish. It has some of the most intriguing attractions on the island, notably the Bermuda Aquarium, Natural History Museum & Zoo, and Crystal Caves and Leamington Caves. If you have time for only one set of caves, we recommend Crystal Caves. However, if you've seen some of the great caves of America or Europe (or beyond), you may find Bermuda's caves less thrilling. While you're in the neighborhood, and if you have time, you might also want to check out the Bermuda Perfumery.

Bermuda Aquarium, Natural History Museum & Zoo ★ *Kids*   This complex is home to a large collection of tropical marine fish, turtles, harbor seals, and other forms of sea life. In the museum, you'll see exhibits ranging from the geological development of Bermuda, to deep-sea exploration, to humpback whales. The zoo is home to alligators, monkeys, and Galapagos tortoises, along with a collection of birds, including parrots and flamingos.

The North Rock Exhibit, in a 140,000-gallon tank, allows visitors to experience a coral reef washed by ocean surge. The tank houses a living coral reef, as well as reef and pelagic fish species. It's the first living coral exhibit on this scale in the world, made possible by the Bermuda Aquarium, Natural History Museum & Zoo's success in the science of coral husbandry.

There's parking for cycles and cars across the street from the aquarium.

North Shore Rd., Flatts Village. ② **441/293-2727**. Admission $10 adults, $5 seniors and children 5–12; free for children under 5. Daily 9am–4pm. Closed Dec 25. Bus: 10 or 11 from the City of Hamilton or St. George. From the City of Hamilton, follow Middle Rd. or North Shore Rd. east to Flatts Village; from St. George, cross the causeway and follow North Shore Rd. or Harrington Sound Rd. west to Flatts Village.

Bermuda Perfumery   The perfumery makes Lili Perfumes. On guided tours, visitors can see the perfume-making process, including the old method of extracting scents from native flowers. Among the fragrances produced are passionflower, Bermuda Easter lily, and oleander jasmine. A small botanical garden with a seating area and walkways provides an attractive resting place. You can also visit the orchid house, which contains more than 500 varieties of orchids. The nature trail passes through a large area planted with tropical flowers, shrubs, and trees. The perfumery also has a gift shop.

212 North Shore Rd., Bailey's Bay. ⓒ **441/293-0627.** Free admission. Apr–Oct Mon–Sat 9:15am–5pm, Sun 10am–4pm; Nov–Mar Mon–Sat 9am–5pm. Closed all holidays and Sun in winter. Bus: 1 or 3.

Crystal Caves 🌟 *Kids*   This network of subterranean lakes, caves, and caverns houses translucent formations of stalagmites and stalactites, and includes the crystal clear Cahow Lake. A sloping path and a few steps lead to Crystal Caves, which was discovered in 1907; at the bottom, about 36m (120 ft.) below the surface, is a floating causeway. It follows the winding cavern, where hidden lights illuminate the interior. In 2002, a second cave was opened to visitors. All tours through Crystal Caves are guided. Using the lighting system, the guides make shadow puppets and are fond of pointing out the similarity to the skyline of Manhattan. If you suffer from claustrophobia, you might find this space too tight. Recent improvements have included a small cafe and a gift shop.

8 Crystal Caves Rd., off Wilkinson Ave., Bailey's Bay. ⓒ **441/293-0640.** Admission $12 adults, $7 children 5–11; free for children under 5. To visit 2 caves, $16 adults, $9 children. Daily 9:30am–4:30pm. Bus: 1 or 3.

Devil's Hole Aquarium *Kids*   The sea feeds a pool created by a collapsed cave, through 1km (½ mile) of subterranean passages. A natural aquarium open to the public since 1834, the pool is stocked with some 400 individual fish, including moray eels, sharks, giant groupers, and massive green turtles. Visitors can tempt the pond's inhabitants with baited (but hookless) lines.

92 Harrington Sound Rd. ⓒ **441/293-2072.** Admission $10, seniors $5, free for children 11 and under. Daily 9:30am–4:30pm. Bus: 1 or 3.

11 St. George Parish

A great way to explore this historic town is by following the "Historic St. George Town" walking tour in chapter 8, "Island Strolls."

Fun Fact **That'll Teach You!**

Right on King's Square you'll see a pillory and stock. Honeymooners like to be photographed in them today, but in earlier times they were used in deadly earnest. Victims were placed in the pillory for a certain number of hours—sometimes with one ear nailed to the post! Criminals were burned on the hand or branded, fined in tobacco, nailed to the post, or declared "infamous." Often, they had their ears cut off or were forced to "stand in a sheet on the church porch."

The list of offenses for which Bermudians were punished in the early 1600s offers a glimpse into the life of the time. Along with such "usual" crimes as treason, robbery, arson, murder, and "scandal," punishable offenses included concealing finds of ambergris, exporting cedarwood, railing against the governor's authority, hiding tobacco, being "notorious cursers and swearers," leading an "uncivil life and calling her neighbor an old Bawd and the like," neglecting to receive Holy Communion, acting in a stage play of any kind, and playing at unlawful games such as dice, cards, and ninepins.

Moments **Special Places Where You Can Be Alone**

Bermuda is both popular and small—but that doesn't mean that you can't escape the crowds and find peace and serenity in a lovely spot, hopefully with someone you love.

Sandys Parish Visitors don't seem to spend a lot of time here, but for wandering about, getting lost, and finding enchanting little vistas, Sandys is without equal on Bermuda. Where Daniel's Head Road meets Cambridge Road, paths will take you to Somerset Long Bay Park, where you can swim. After that, take one of the unmarked trails to the Bermuda Audubon Society Nature Reserve, a gem of nature. The place is often deserted on weekdays. When the white-eyed vireos and the bluebirds call to you from fiddlewood trees, you'll really feel close to nature.

Southampton Parish In this windswept, tourist-trodden parish, you'd think there was no place to find solitude. Not so! Signposted from Middle Road, a trail goes 1km (½ mile) down to the entrance to Seymour's Pond Nature Reserve. Under the management of the Bermuda Audubon Society, this 1-hectare (2½-acre) site attracts the occasional birder as well as romantic couples looking for a little privacy. Just past the pond, you'll spot pepper trees and old cedars that escaped the blight; you might encounter bluebirds and an egret or two as well. After traversing Cross Church Road, you'll come upon the old Bermuda Railway Trail, where in summer you can see fennel growing wild. In the distance are panoramic views of shipwreck-clogged Black Bay and Five Star Island.

Warwick Parish With its beautiful pink sand beaches, seaside parklands, natural attractions, and winding country lanes, this is one of the most charming parishes for exploring and escaping the crowds. Even many longtime local residents haven't seen some of Warwick's beauty spots. The place to head is Warwick Pond, a sanctuary for several rare

---

THE TOWN OF ST. GEORGE ★★★

King's Square, also called Market Square and King's Parade, is the center of life in St. George. It holds the colorful **White Horse Tavern,** where you may want to stop for a drink after your tour of the town.

The street names in St. George evoke its history. Petticoat Lane (sometimes called Silk Alley) reputedly got its name when two newly emancipated slaves paraded up and down the lane rustling their colorful new silk petticoats. Barber's Lane is also named for a former slave. It honors Joseph Hayne Rainey, a freedman from the Carolinas who fled to Bermuda during the Civil War aboard a blockade-runner and became a barber. After the war, he returned to the United States and was elected to Congress, becoming the first black member of the House of Representatives during Reconstruction.

The St. George branch of the **Visitors Service Bureau** is on King's Square (© **441/297-1642**); it's open Monday to Saturday from 9am to 5pm. Here you species of birds. Administered by the Bermuda National Trust, it's open daily from sunrise to sunset. You can reach it by following the Bermuda Railway Trail until you come to Tribe Road No. 3; climb this road for a few hundred yards before it dips down a hill to the pond. You might spot the occasional birder in search of a kiskadee blue heron or a cardinal. The pond, fed by a subterranean channel from the sea, reminds us of Thoreau's Walden Pond.

St. David's Island   Part of St. George Parish, St. David's is Bermuda "the way it was." Virtually unknown to the average visitor, it awaits your discovery. This is real down-home Bermuda—it's said that some St. David's islanders have never even visited "mainland" Bermuda. You can begin your walk at Great Head Park in the eastern part of St. David's, southeast of the cricket fields. At the end of the parking lot, follow the trail into a wooded area filled with cherry trees and palmettos. After about 250 yards, bear right at the fork. Eventually you'll spot St. David's Lighthouse, an octagonal red-and-white tower in the distance to the southwest. The trail forks left until you come to a ruined garrison with a panoramic sea view. It's one of the remotest, loveliest spots on the island—and, chances are, you'll have it all to yourself.

Devonshire Parish   This parish is off the beaten track but home to some lovely spots—if you're adventurous enough to seek them out. Old Devonshire Church on Middle Road is a landmark; almost directly across the road lies Devonshire Marsh, a natural water basin still in an untamed state. You'll also find two nature reserves, Firefly and Freer Cox Memorial, on some 4 hectares (10 acres) of marshland. The Bermuda Audubon Society has set aside this protected area as a bird sanctuary for many endangered wild species. You can also see some of the most unusual Bermudian plants, including orchids. The marsh is always open to the public.

can get a map and other information before setting out to explore. The bureau is opposite the Town Hall.

If you're really pressed for time, don't worry that you're missing out if you skip interior visits to the sights listed below. The entire town of St. George, with its quaint streets and old buildings, is the attraction, not just one particular monument. If you have time to visit only one attraction's interior, make it St. Peter's Church. Otherwise, just wander around, do a little shopping, and soak in the atmosphere.

To reach these attractions, take bus number 1, 3, 8, 10, or 11 from the City of Hamilton.

The Bermuda National Trust Museum   This was once the Globe Hotel, headquarters of Major Norman Walker, the Confederate representative in Bermuda. Today, it houses relics from the island's involvement in the American Civil War—from a Bermudian perspective. St. George was the port from which ships carrying arms and munitions ran the Union blockade. A replica of the Great Seal of the Confederacy is fitted to a Victorian press so that visitors can emboss copies as souvenirs. There's also a video presentation, *Bermuda: Centre of the Atlantic*, tracing the island's early history.

At the Globe Hotel, King's Sq. ℂ **441/297-1423**. Admission $4 adults, $2 children 6–18, free for children under 6. Mon–Sat 10am–4pm. Closed Dec 25.

Bridge House Gallery   This long-established gallery displays antiques and collectibles, old Bermudian items, original paintings, and Bermuda-made crafts. It contains a studio belonging to Jill Amos Raine, a well-known Bermuda water-color artist. The house, constructed in the 1690s, was home to several of the colony's governors. Its most colorful owner was Bridger Goodrich, a Loyalist from Virginia, whose privateers once blockaded Chesapeake Bay. So devoted was he to the king that he sabotaged Bahamian vessels trading with the American colonies.

1 Bridge St. ℂ **441/297-8211**. Free admission. Wed and Sat 10am–6pm.

Carter House (St. David's Island Historical Site)   Low-slung and historic, and set on a hillside about 1.5km (1 mile) east of Swing Bridge, Carter House is believed to be the oldest dwelling place in St. David's parish, at least 3½ centuries old. Reopened in September 2001, after a 3-year renovation, it's now a museum dedicated to the life and values of the people of St. David's, one of the most rugged and hardy districts of Bermuda. The museum houses exhibitions on the history of whaling, piloting, fishing, and farming. Various artifacts of Bermudian life are displayed here, including a 4m (14-ft.) Bermuda sailing dinghy, dolls and children's toys crafted from palmetto leaves, and artifacts and paneling crafted from the original, now-extinct, Bermuda cedar.

South Side Ave., St. David's. ℂ **441/297-1642**. Free admission (donations accepted). Apr–Oct Tues–Thurs and Sat 10am–4pm; Nov–Mar Sat only 10am–4pm.

Deliverance   Across from St. George's town square and over a bridge is Ordnance Island, where visitors can see a full-scale replica of *Deliverance*. The ship-wrecked survivors of the *Sea Venture* built the pinnace (small sailing ship) in 1610 to carry them on to Virginia. A tape recording guides visitors through the ship. Alongside *Deliverance* is a ducking stool, a replica of the horrible contraption

---

⌒ Fun Fact   St. George: A World Heritage Site

Historic St. George and its related fortifications are now a World Heritage Site designated by UNESCO. The architecturally rich, 400-year-old town joins such select sites as the Great Wall of China, Statue of Liberty, Taj Mahal, and the historic center of Florence.

As the oldest continuously inhabited town of English origin in the Western Hemisphere, the town and its surrounding buildings, monuments, and structures illustrate the residents' lifestyles through the 17th, 18th, and 19th centuries. Historic St. George remains in authentic condition, featuring unique and diverse examples of Bermudian architecture spanning the past 4 centuries. The various forts of St. George are like a textbook illustrating British artillery and the changing styles of fort architecture from 1612 to 1956.

used in 17th-century witch trials; it's demonstrated on Wednesday and Thursday at noon.

Adventure Enterprises owns *Deliverance* and also runs sightseeing and snorkeling adventures aboard its boat *ARGO*. Bermuda's only high-speed tour boat, *ARGO* (which fits neatly into small harbors), takes passengers along the barrier reef, the southshore beaches, the historic forts, and the billionaires' mansions at Tucker's Town. Call for details, which change seasonally.

Ordnance Island. ℂ **441/297-1459**. Admission $3 adults, $1 children under 12. Apr–Oct daily 9am–5pm; Nov–Mar call for hours.

Old Rectory   Built by a reformed pirate in 1705, this charming old cottage was later home to Parson Richardson, who was nicknamed "the Little Bishop." Now a private home, it's administered by the Bermuda National Trust.

At the head of Broad Alley, behind St. Peter's Church. ℂ **441/236-6483**. Free admission (donations appreciated). Nov–Mar Wed noon–5pm.

Old State House   Behind the Town Hall is Bermuda's oldest stone building, constructed with turtle oil and lime mortar in 1620. Unless there's a special event, the landmark building doesn't offer much to see—you might settle for a look at the exterior, then continue on with your sightseeing. The Old State House, where meetings of the legislative council once took place, was eventually turned over to the Freemasons of St. George's. The government asked the annual rent of one peppercorn and insisted on the right to hold meetings here upon demand. The Masonic Lodge members, in a ceremony filled with pageantry, still turn over one peppercorn in rent to the Bermuda government every April.

For those who have never witnessed the 45-minute spectacle of the annual **Peppercorn Ceremony,** it takes place in early to mid-April. The ceremony begins around 11am with the gathering of the Bermuda Regiment on King's Square. Then the premier, mayor, and other dignitaries arrive, amid the bellowing introductions of the town crier. As soon as all the principals have taken their places, a 17-gun salute is fired as the governor and his wife make a grand entrance in their open horse-drawn landau. His Excellency inspects a military guard of honor while the Bermuda Regiment Band plays. The stage is now set for the presentation of the peppercorn, which sits on a silver plate atop a velvet cushion. Payment is made in a grand and formal manner, after which the Old State House is immediately used for a meeting of Her Majesty's Council.

Princess St. ℂ **441/297-1206**. For information on the Peppercorn Ceremony, call ℂ **800/223-6106**. Free admission. Wed 10am–4pm or by appointment.

St. George's Historical Society Museum   In a home built around 1700, this museum contains an original 18th-century Bermuda kitchen, complete with utensils from that period. Other exhibits include a 300-year-old Bible, a letter from George Washington, and Native American ax heads. Some early settlers on St. David's Island were Native Americans, mainly Pequot.

Duke of Kent St., St. George's. ℂ **441/297-0423**. Admission $5 adults, $2 children under 12. Mon–Fri 10am–4pm.

St. Peter's Church ★   From King's Square, head east to Duke of York Street, where you'll find St. Peter's Church, believed to be the oldest Anglican place of worship in the Western Hemisphere. Colonists built the original church in 1612 almost entirely of cedar, with a palmetto-leaf thatched roof. A hurricane in 1712 destroyed it almost completely. Some of the interior, including the original altar from 1615 (still used daily), was salvaged, and the church was rebuilt in 1713.

It has been restored many times since, providing excellent examples of the architectural styles of the 17th to the 20th centuries. The tower was added in 1814. Before the Old State House was built, the colony held public meetings in the church. The first assize (legislative assembly) convened here in 1616, and the first meeting of Parliament was held in 1620. The church holds Sunday and weekday services.

Some of the tombstones in the Graveyard of St. Peter's (entrance opposite Broad Alley) are more than 3 centuries old; many tombs mark the graves of slaves. Here you'll find the grave of Midshipman Richard Dale, an American who was the last victim of the War of 1812. The churchyard also holds the tombs of Gov. Sir Richard Sharples and his aide, Capt. Hugh Sayers, who were assassinated while strolling on the grounds of Government House in 1973.

Duke of York St. ✆ 441/297-8359. Free admission (donations appreciated). Daily 10am–4:30pm; Sun services 11am; guide available Mon–Sat.

Somers Garden   The heart of Sir George Somers was buried here in 1610; a stone column perpetuates the memory of Bermuda's founder. The garden was opened in 1920 by the Prince of Wales (later King Edward VIII, and then the Duke of Windsor). They have built a large beautiful fountain in the middle of the garden to enhance the beauty, where visitors may also take pictures, using the foundation for a background.

Duke of York St. ✆ **441/297-1532.** Free admission. Apr–Nov daily 7:30am–8pm; off season daily 7:30am–5pm.

Town Hall   Officers of the Corporation of St. George's, headed by a mayor, meet in the Town Hall, located near the Visitors Service Bureau. There are three aldermen and five common councilors. The Town Hall holds a collection of Bermuda cedar furnishings, along with photographs of previous mayors.

7 King's Sq. ✆ 441/297-1532. Free admission. Mon–Sat 10am–4pm.

Tucker House Museum   This was the home of the well-known Tucker family of England, Bermuda, and Virginia. It displays a notable collection of Bermudian furniture, portraits, and silver. Also in the Tucker House is the Joseph Rainey Memorial Room, where the African-American refugee (mentioned above in the section about King's Square) of the Civil War practiced barbering. A new exhibit on the ground floor traces the archaeological history of the site. They have restored the kitchen and have made it an exhibit for visitors to see.

5 Water St. ✆ 441/297-0545. Admission $3 adults, $2 children 6–18, free for children under 6. Mon–Sat 10am–4pm.

Unfinished Cathedral   After leaving Somers Garden, head up the steps to the North Gate, which opens onto Blockade Alley. The structure here is known as the "folly of St. George's." The cathedral, begun in 1874, was intended to replace St. Peter's. But the planners ran into money problems, and a schism within the church developed. As if that weren't enough, a storm swept over the island, causing considerable damage to the structure. Result: the Unfinished Cathedral.

Blockade Alley.

HISTORIC FORTS THAT NEVER SAW MUCH ACTION
From its earliest days, St. George has been fortified. Although it never saw much military action, reminders of that history are interesting to explore. Take Circular Drive to reach the forts, on the outskirts of town. As forts go, these two are

of relatively minor interest (unless, of course, you're a fort buff—in that case, be our guest). If you have time for only one fort on Bermuda, Fort Hamilton on Happy Valley Road is the most intriguing. See Walking Tour 1, "The City of Hamilton," in chapter 8, "Island Strolls," for details.

Along the coast is Building Bay, where the shipwrecked victims of the *Sea Venture* built their vessel, the *Deliverance,* in 1610.

Fort St. Catherine ★   Towering above the beach where the shipwrecked crew of the *Sea Venture* came ashore in 1609 is Fort St. Catherine, completed in 1614 and named for the patron saint of wheelwrights and carpenters. The fortifications have been upgraded over the years. The last major reconstruction took place from 1865 to 1878, so the fort's appearance today is largely the result of work done in the 19th century.

In the museum, visitors first see a series of dioramas, "Highlights in Bermuda's History." Figures depict various activities that took place in the magazine of the fort, restored and refurnished as it was in the 1880s. In the keep, which served as living quarters, you can see information on local and overseas regiments that served in Bermuda. Also here are a fine small-arms exhibit, a cooking area display, and an exhibit of replicas of England's crown jewels. There's a short audiovisual show on St. George's defense systems and the forts of St. George.

15 Coot Pond Rd. ① **441/297-1920.** Admission $5 adults, $2 children under 12. Daily 9:30am–4:30pm. Closed Dec 25.

Gates Fort   Gates Fort was built in 1609 by Sir Thomas Gates, one of the original band of settlers from the *Sea Venture.* Gates was governor-designate for the colony of Virginia.

Cut Rd. No phone. Free admission. Daily 10am–4:30pm.

Island Strolls

You can cover much of Bermuda, especially the harbor city of Hamilton and the historic town of St. George, on foot. Indeed, if you had the time, you could walk or bike through all of the parishes and visit the major attractions. Some visitors would rather devote their vacation time to less taxing pursuits, such as relaxing on the beach or playing a leisurely game of golf. If you're interested in seeing the island's sights, however, do consider taking at least one walking tour.

WALKING TOUR 1 · THE CITY OF HAMILTON

Start:	The Visitors Service Bureau/Ferry Terminal.
Finish:	Fort Hamilton.
Time:	2½ hours.
Best Time:	Any sunny day.
Worst Time:	When cruise ships are anchored in Hamilton Harbour.

Begin your tour along the harbor front at the:

❶ Visitors Service Bureau/Ferry Terminal

Pick up some free maps and brochures of the island here.

From the bureau, you'll emerge onto Front Street, the City of Hamilton's main street and principal shopping area. Before 1946, there were no cars here. Today, the busy traffic includes small automobiles (driven only by Bermuda residents), buses, mopeds, and bicycles. You'll also see horse-drawn carriages, which are the most romantic (and, alas, the most expensive) way to see the City of Hamilton.

At the docks behind the Ferry Terminal, you can find the ferries to Warwick and Paget parishes; for details on their attractions, see chapter 7, "Seeing the Sights." You can also take a ferry across Great Sound to the West End and Somerset.

Walk south from the Ferry Terminal toward the water, taking a short side street between the Visitors Service Bureau and the large Bank of Bermuda. You'll come to:

❷ Albouy's Point

This is a small, grassy park with benches and trees, which opens onto a panoramic vista of the boat- and ship-filled harbor. Nearby is the Royal

Tips **Planning Pointer**

It's enlightening to take a ferry ride around the inner harbor before or after your City of Hamilton walking tour. You can get an overview of the City of Hamilton before concentrating on specific landmarks or monuments, or gain a new perspective on what you've just seen.

Walking Tour: The City of Hamilton

Legend/Key:

- Church
- (i) Information
- "Take a Break"

1 Visitors Service Bureau/Ferry Terminal
2 Albouy's Point
3 Bank of Bermuda
4 "Birdcage"
5 Par-la-Ville Park
6 Bermuda Historical Society Museum
7 Perot Post Office
8 Hamilton City Hall
9 Victoria Park
10 St. Theresa's
11 Bermuda Cathedral
12 Sessions House (Parliament Building)
13 Cabinet Building
14 Cenotaph
15 Fort Hamilton

Bermuda Yacht Club, which has been an elite rendezvous for the Bermudian and American yachting set—including the rich and famous—since the 1930s. To use the word *royal* in its name, the club obtained special permission from Prince Albert, Queen Victoria's consort. The club sponsors the widely televised Newport-Bermuda Race.

After taking in the view, walk directly north, crossing Point Pleasant Road, to the:

❸ Bank of Bermuda

You can visit the bank Monday to Friday from 9:30am to 3pm. On its mezzanine is Bermuda's most extensive coin collection—there's at least one sample of every coin minted in the United Kingdom since the reign of King James I in the early 17th century. Many Spanish coins used in colonial days are on display. You'll also see the most famous Bermudian currency, the first coins minted on the island, called "hog money." In use since the early 1600s, the hog coin is stamped on one side with the ill-fated *Sea Venture* and on the other side with a wild hog, the main source of food (barring fish) for the early settlers. Look for an 1887 £5 piece depicting Queen Victoria; its appearance led to a protest throughout the British Empire, when critics claimed that the queen's small crown made her look foolish.

Upon leaving the bank, head east along Front Street to the intersection with Queen Street. This is the site of the:

❹ "Birdcage"

This is the most photographed sight in Bermuda. Here you can sometimes find a police officer directing traffic. If the "bobby" is a man, he's likely to be wearing regulation Bermuda shorts. The traffic box was named after its designer, Michael "Dickey" Bird. It stands at Heyl's Corner, which was named for an American southerner, J. B. Heyl, who operated a nearby apothecary in the 1800s.

Continue north along Queen Street until you reach:

❺ Par-la-Ville Park

This was once a private garden attached to the town house of William B. Perot, Bermuda's first postmaster. Perot, who designed the gardens in the 19th century, collected rare and exotic plants from all over the globe, including an Indian rubber tree, which was seeded in 1847. Mark Twain wrote that he found the tree "disappointing" in that it didn't bear rubber overshoes and hot-water bottles.

Also opening onto Queen Street at the entrance to the park is the:

❻ Bermuda Historical Society Museum

This museum, at 13 Queen St., is also the Bermuda Library. It's filled with curiosities, including cedar furniture, collections of antique silver and china, hog money, Confederate money, a 1775 letter from George Washington, and other artifacts. The library has many rare books, including a 1624 edition of John Smith's *General Historie of Virginia, New England and the Somers Isles,* which you can ask to view. If you'd like to rest and catch up on your reading, you'll also find a selection of current local and British newspapers and periodicals here.

Across the street is the:

❼ Perot Post Office

William Perot ran this post office from 1818 to 1862. It's said that he'd collect the mail from the clipper ships, then put it under his top hat in order to maintain his dignity. As he proceeded through town, he'd greet his friends and acquaintances by tipping his hat, thereby delivering their mail at the same time. He started printing stamps in 1848. A Perot stamp is extremely valuable today—only 11 are known to exist, and Queen Elizabeth II owns several. The last time a Perot stamp came on the market, in 1986, it fetched $135,000.

Continue to the top of Queen Street, then turn right onto Church Street to reach:

⑧ Hamilton City Hall

Located at 17 Church St., the city hall dates from 1960 and is crowned by a white tower. The bronze weather vane on top is a replica of the *Sea Venture*. Portraits of the queen and paintings of former island leaders adorn the main lobby. The Bermuda Society of Arts holds frequent exhibitions in this hall. The Benbow family's collection of rare stamps is also on display.

> **TAKE A BREAK**
> The **Paradiso Cafe**, on the ground floor of the Washington Mall, a shopping and office complex on Reid Street, which is parallel to Church Street to the South (© 441/295-3263), serves the most irresistible pastries in town. You can also order ice cream, tartlets, quiches, croissant sandwiches, espresso, and cappuccino. (For a review, see chapter 5, "Where to Dine.")

In back of Hamilton City Hall, opening onto Victoria Street, lies:

⑨ Victoria Park

Office workers frequent this cool, refreshing oasis on their lunch breaks. It features a sunken garden, ornamental shrubbery, and a Victorian bandstand. The 1.6 hectare (4-acre) park was laid out in honor of Queen Victoria's Golden Jubilee in 1887. Outdoor concerts are held here in summer. Contact the tourist office for dates.

Cedar Avenue is the eastern boundary of Victoria Park. If you follow it north for 2 blocks, you'll reach:

⑩ St. Theresa's

This Roman Catholic cathedral is open daily from 8am to 7pm and for Sunday services. Its architecture was inspired by the Spanish Mission style. Dating from 1927, it's one of a half-dozen Roman Catholic churches in Bermuda; its treasure is a gold-and-silver chalice—a gift from Pope Paul VI when he visited the island in 1968.

After seeing the cathedral, retrace your steps south along Cedar Avenue until you reach Victoria Street. Cedar Avenue now becomes Burnaby Street; continue south to Church Street and turn left. A short walk along this street (on your left) will bring you to the:

⑪ Bermuda Cathedral

Also known as the Cathedral of the Most Holy Trinity, this is the seat of the Anglican Church of Bermuda, and it towers over the city skyline. Its style is neo-Gothic, characterized by stained-glass windows and soaring arches. The lectern and pulpit duplicate those of St. Giles in Edinburgh, Scotland.

Leave the cathedral and continue east along Church Street to the:

⑫ Sessions House (Parliament Building)

Located on Parliament Street, between Reid and Church streets, the Sessions House is open to the public Monday to Friday from 9am to 12:30pm and 2 to 5pm. The speaker wears a full wig and a flowing black robe. The Parliament of Bermuda is the third oldest in the world, after Iceland's and England's.

Continue south along Parliament Street to Front Street, and turn left toward the:

⑬ Cabinet Building

The official opening of Parliament takes place here in late October or early November. Wearing a plumed hat and full regalia, the governor makes his "Throne Speech." If you visit on a Wednesday, you can see the Bermuda Senate in action. The building is located between Court and Parliament streets, and is open Monday to Friday from 9am to 5pm.

In front of the Cabinet Building is the:

⑭ Cenotaph

The Cenotaph is a memorial to Bermuda's dead from World War I

(1914–18) and World War II (1939–45). In 1920, the Prince of Wales laid the cornerstone. (In 1936, as King Edward VIII, he abdicated to marry an American divorcée, Wallis Simpson, and during World War II, as the Duke of Windsor, he served as governor of the Bahamas.) The landmark is a replica of the Cenotaph in London.

Continue east along Front Street until you reach King Street, then turn left and head north until you come to Happy Valley Road. Go right on this road until you see the entrance (on your right) to:

⓯ Fort Hamilton

This imposing old fortress lies on the eastern outskirts of town. The Duke of Wellington ordered its construction to protect Hamilton Harbour. Filled with underground passageways and complete with a moat and 18-ton guns, the fort was outdated before it was even completed, and it never fired a shot. It does, however, offer panoramic views of the city and the harbor, and it's worth a trip just for the view. In summer, try to be here at noon, when the kilted Bermuda Isles Pipe Band performs a skirling ceremony on the green, accompanied by dancers and drummers.

WINDING DOWN
Enjoy old-fashioned tea at the **Fort Hamilton Tea Shoppe** (no phone), where you can also order light refreshments.

WALKING TOUR 2 | **HISTORIC ST. GEORGE TOWN**

Start:	King's Square.
Finish:	Somers Wharf.
Time:	2 hours, not counting the time you spend inside the buildings.
Best Time:	Any sunny day except Sunday, when many destinations are closed.
Worst Time:	When a cruise ship is anchored in the harbor.

At the eastern end of Bermuda, St. George was the second English town established in the New World (after Jamestown, Virginia). For the history buff, it holds more interest than the City of Hamilton.

We'll begin the tour at:

❶ King's Square

Also known as Market Square and King's Parade, the square is the very center of St. George. Only about 200 years old, it's not as historic as St. George itself. This was formerly a marshy part of the harbor—at least when the shipwrecked passengers and crew of the *Sea Venture* first saw it. At the water's edge stands a branch of the Visitors Service Bureau, where you can pick up additional information on the area. On the square you'll notice a replica of a pillory and stocks. The devices were used to punish criminals—and, in many cases, the innocent. You could be severely punished here for such "crimes" as casting a spell over your neighbor's turkeys.

From the square, head south across the small bridge to:

❷ Ordnance Island

The British army once stored gunpowder and cannons on this island, which juts into St. George's Harbour. Today, the island houses the *Deliverance,* a replica of the vessel that carried the shipwrecked *Sea Venture* passengers on to Virginia. Alongside the vessel is a ducking stool, a contraption used in 17th-century witch trials.

1 King's Square
2 Ordnance Island
3 White Horse Tavern
4 Town Hall
5 Bridge House
6 Old State House
7 Somers Gardens
8 Unfinished Cathedral
9 St. George's Historical Society Museum
10 Featherbed Alley Printery
11 Old Rectory
12 St. Peter's Church
13 Bermuda National Trust Museum
14 Barber's Alley & Petticoat Lane
15 Tucker House
16 Somers Wharf

Retrace your steps across the bridge to King's Square. On the waterside stands the:

❸ White Horse Tavern

This restaurant juts out into St. George's Harbour. Consider the tavern as a possible spot for lunch later (for a review, see chapter 5, "Where to Dine"). For now, we'll focus on its history: It was once the home of John Davenport, who came to Bermuda in 1815 to open a dry goods store. Davenport was a bit of a miser; upon his death, some £75,000 in gold and silver was discovered stashed away in his cellar.

Across the square stands the:

❹ Town Hall

Located near the Visitors Service Bureau, this is the meeting place of the corporation governing St. George. It has antique cedar furnishings and a collection of photographs of previous lord mayors. *Bermuda Journey,* a multimedia audiovisual presentation, is shown here several times a day.

From King's Square, head east along King Street, cutting north (left) on Bridge Street. You'll come to the:

❺ Bridge House

Constructed in the 1690s, this was once the home of several governors of Bermuda. Located at 1 Bridge St., it's furnished with 18th- and 19th-century antiques and houses an art gallery and souvenir shop.

Return to King Street and continue east to the:

❻ Old State House

The State House opens onto Princess Street, at the top of King Street. This is the oldest stone building in Bermuda, dating from 1620, and was once the home of the Bermuda Parliament. It's the site of the Peppercorn Ceremony, in which the Old State House pays the government a "rent" of one peppercorn annually. See chapter 7, "Seeing the Sights," for details on this grand ceremony.

Continue your stroll down Princess Street until you come to Duke of York Street and the entrance to:

❼ Somers Garden

The heart of Sir George Somers, the admiral of the *Sea Venture,* is buried here. The gardens, opened in 1920 by the Prince of Wales, contain palms and other tropical plants.

Walk through Somers Gardens and up the steps to the North Gate onto Blockade Alley. Climb the hill to the structure known as "the folly of St. George's," the:

❽ Unfinished Cathedral

This cathedral was intended to replace St. Peter's Church (see stop number 12 on this tour). Work began on the church in 1874, but ended when the church was beset by financial difficulties and a schism in the Anglican congregation.

After viewing the cathedral, turn left onto Duke of Kent Street, which leads down to the:

❾ St. George's Historical Society Museum

Located at Featherbed Alley and Duke of Kent Street, the museum building is an example of the rather plain 18th-century Bermudian architecture. It contains a collection of Bermudian historical artifacts and cedar furniture.

Around the corner on Featherbed Alley is the:

❿ Featherbed Alley Printery

Here you can see a working replica of the type of printing press invented by Johannes Gutenberg in Germany in the 1450s.

Go up Featherbed Alley and straight onto Church Street. At the junction with Broad Lane, look to your right to see the:

⓫ Old Rectory

The Old Rectory is located at the head of Broad Alley, behind St. Peter's Church. Now a private home administered by the National Trust, it was built in 1705 by a reformed pirate. You can go inside only on Wednesdays from noon to 5pm.

Rattle & Shake: The Bermuda Railway Trail

One of the most unusual sightseeing adventures in Bermuda is following the Bermuda Railway Trail (or parts thereof), which stretches for 34km (21 miles) along the old railroad way, across three of the interconnected islands that make up Bermuda. Construction of this rail line may have been one of the most costly ever on a per-kilometer basis. Opened in 1931, the Bermuda Railway ceased operations in 1948. Once the island's main mode of transportation, the train eventually gave way to the popularity of the automobile.

Before setting out on this trek, arm yourself with a copy of the *Bermuda Railway Trail Guide*, which is available at the Bermuda Department of Tourism in the City of Hamilton and the Visitors Service Bureaus in Hamilton and St. George. You're now ready to hit the trail of the old train system that was affectionately called "Rattle and Shake." You can explore the trail on horseback, bicycle, or foot.

Although the line covered 34km (21 miles), from St. George in the east to Somerset in the west, a 5km (3-mile) stretch has been lost to roads in and around the capital city of Hamilton. For the most part, however, the trail winds along an automobile-free route.

In the West End, the trail begins near the Watford Bridge, but there are many convenient access points. In the East End, it's most convenient to pick up the trail on North Shore Road.

Along the way, you'll see some rare Bermuda cedar, which nearly vanished as a result of the blight that struck the island in the early 1940s. There's also much greenery and semitropical vegetation, such as the poinsettia, oleander, and hibiscus. You can see and visit Fort Scaur, the 1870s fortress, in Sandys Parish. The tour of Sandys Parish, below, follows the detailed section of the route that includes Fort Scaur.

If you only have time to see a small part of the trail, we recommend you take in something of the 2-hectare (5-acre) Gilbert Nature Reserve. The most scenic view begins at Somerset Bridge; head west from there.

After seeing the Old Rectory, go through the church's back yard, opposite Broad Alley, to reach:

⑫ St. Peter's Church

The church's main entrance is on Duke of York Street. St. Peter's is believed to be the oldest Anglican place of worship in the Western Hemisphere. In the churchyard, you'll see many headstones, some 300 years old. The assassinated governor, Sir Richard Sharples, was buried here. The present church was built in 1713, with a tower added in 1814.

Across the street is the:

⑬ Bermuda National Trust Museum

When it was the Globe Hotel, this was the headquarters of Major Norman Walker, the Confederate representative in Bermuda. It was once a hotbed of blockade running (artillery smuggling during the Civil War).

Go west along Duke of York Street to

⑭ Barber's Alley & Petticoat Lane

Barber's Alley honors Joseph Hayne Rainey. A former slave from South

Carolina, Rainey fled to Bermuda with his French wife at the outbreak of the Civil War. He became a barber in St. George and eventually returned to South Carolina, where in 1870 he was elected to the U.S. House of Representatives—the first African American to serve in Congress.

Nearby is Petticoat Lane, also known as Silk Alley. The name dates from the 1834 emancipation, when two former slave women who'd always wanted silk petticoats like their former mistresses finally purchased some—and paraded up and down the lane to show off their new finery.

Continue west until you reach:

⓯ Tucker House

Opening onto Water Street, this was the former home of a prominent Bermudian family, whose members included an island governor, a treasurer of the United States, and a captain in the Confederate Navy. The

building houses an excellent collection of antiques, including silver, portraits, and cedar furniture. One room is devoted to memorabilia of Joseph Hayne Rainey.

TAKE A BREAK
Diagonally across from the Tucker House is the **Carriage House,** 22 Water St., Somers Wharf (℟ **441/297-1730**), a former waterfront storehouse and an excellent place for lunch. You can sample famous Bermuda fish chowder here. Sandwich platters, soups, salads, and juicy burgers are also available. (For a review, see chapter 5, "Where to Dine.")

End your tour across the street at:

⓰ Somers Wharf

This multimillion-dollar waterfront restoration project contains shops, restaurants, and taverns.

WALKING TOUR 3	SANDYS PARISH

Start:	Somerset Bridge.
Finish:	Somerset Long Bay Park.
Time:	7 hours.
Best Time:	Any sunny day.
Worst Time:	When the weather's bad.

Sandys (pronounced *sands*), the far western parish of Bermuda, consists of Somerset Island (the largest and southernmost island), and Watford, Boaz, and Ireland islands. When Bermudians cross into Somerset on Somerset Bridge, they say they are "up the country."

Craggy coastlines, beaches, nature reserves, fisher's coves, old fortifications, winding lanes, and sleepy villages characterize this area. All of Sandys' major attractions lie along the main road from Somerset Bridge to the Royal Naval Dockyard, which is at the end of Ireland Island.

Although we describe this as a walking tour, you may want to rent a bicycle or moped to help you cover the longer stretches.

From the center of the City of Hamilton, you can take a ferry to Somerset. Check the schedule: Some boats take only 30 minutes, others up to an hour. The longer trip affords a more leisurely opportunity to enjoy the waters of Great Sound. You can bring your cycle or moped aboard the ferry. You can also see the West End by bus (for details, see "Getting Around," in chapter 3, "Getting to Know Bermuda").

1 Somerset Bridge
2 Railway Trail
3 Fort Scaur
4 Sound View Road
5 Cavello Bay
6 Royal Naval Dockyard
7 Bermuda Arts Centre
8 Lagoon Park
9 Somerset Village
10 Somerset Long Bay Park

Royal Naval Dockyard

Ireland Island North

Pender Rd.

Cut Bridge

Cockrange Rd.

Graddock Rd.

Ireland Island South

Lagoon Rd.

Grey's Bridge

Malabar Rd.

Boaz Island

Kitchener Rd.

Watford Island

Watford Bridge

Mangrove Bay Wharf

Mangrove Bay

SOMERSET VILLAGE

East Shore Rd.

Cavello Bay

Scott's Hill Rd.

Sound View Rd.

SOMERSET ISLAND

Fort Scaur (Scaur Hill)

Cambridge Rd.

finish here

Somerset Long Bay

Greenfield Lane

West Side Rd.

Somerset Rd.

start here

Somerset Bridge

Daniel's Head

Daniel's Island

Skeeter's Corner

Great Sound

Pearl Island

Alpha Island

N

0   0.5 mi
0   0.5 km

--- Ferry
Railway
"Take a Break" stop

Hamilton

Sandys Parish

To begin the tour, take the ferry from the City of Hamilton to:

❶ Somerset Bridge

This bridge links Somerset Island with the rest of Bermuda. It was among the first three bridges constructed on Bermuda in the 1600s, and it's said to be the smallest drawbridge in the world—its opening is just wide enough to accommodate a sailboat mast. Near the bridge you can see the old Somerset Post Office and an 18th-century cottage known as Crossways.

Next, walk up Somerset Road about 69m (225 ft.) to the entrance to the:

❷ Railway Trail

Open only to pedestrians and bikers, the trail follows the path of old "Rattle and Shake," the Bermuda Railway line that once ran the length of the island. This section of the trail—between Somerset Bridge and Sound View Road—is one of the most attractive segments (good to know if you don't want to walk the whole trail—although some hearty visitors do just that). Parts of the trail open onto the coast, affording panoramic vistas of the Great Sound. See "Rattle & Shake: The Bermuda Railway Trail," above, for more information.

TAKE A BREAK
The trail goes across the parkland of Fort Scaur (see below), with its large moat. If you're here around noontime, you might want to consider this as a picnic spot (get your picnic fixings in the City of Hamilton). If you can spend all day in Somerset (which we highly recommend), you might also want to take time out for a swim before returning to your walking or cycling.

Follow the signposts to:

❸ Fort Scaur

In the 1870s, the British feared an attack from the United States, so they built this fort on the highest hill in Somerset to protect Her Majesty's Royal Naval Dockyard. It sits on 9 hectares (22 acres) of land and opens onto Somerset Road; the huge dry moat cuts right across Somerset Island. You can wander at leisure around this fort, which proved unnecessary because the invasion never materialized. If you stand on the ramparts, you'll be rewarded with a marvelous view of Great Sound. Through a telescope, you can see such distant sights as St. David's Lighthouse and Fort St. Catherine in the East End of Bermuda. If you follow the eastern moat all the way down to the Great Sound shore, you'll find ideal places for swimming and fishing.

After exploring the surrounding Scaur Hill Fort Park, resume your walk along the railway track and continue north for more than 1.5km (1 mile), then turn right onto:

❹ Sound View Road

Take a stroll along this sleepy residential street, which has some of the finest cottages in Bermuda.

Continue around a wide arc, passing Tranquillity Hill and Gwelly and Saltsea lanes. When you come to Scott's Hill Road, take a right and go about 78m (255 ft.) to East Shore Road. At the first junction, take a little road, Cavello Lane, which branches off to the right; it will take you to:

❺ Cavello Bay

The sheltered cove is a stopping point for the City of Hamilton ferry.

Wait for the next ferry and take it (with your cycle or moped) to Watford Bridge or directly to the:

❻ Royal Naval Dockyard

There's so much to see here, you could spend an entire afternoon exploring the area. The dockyard is a sprawling complex encompassing 2½ hectares (6 acres) of Ireland Island. The major attraction is the **Bermuda Maritime Museum** (see chapter 7), opened by Queen Elizabeth II in 1975. There's an exhibit of Bermuda's old boats, documenting the island's rich maritime history. You can cross a moat to explore the keep and the 9m- (30-ft.-) high defensive ramparts.

Across the street from the Bermuda Maritime Museum is the Old Cooperage Building, site of the Neptune Cinema. Adjacent to the cinema is the Craft Market, which sells interesting items. Next door is the:

7 Bermuda Arts Centre

Princess Margaret opened the Centre in 1984. Showcasing the visual arts and crafts of the island, this nonprofit organization has a volunteer staff.

From the dockyard, it's a long walk to Somerset Village, but many people who have walked or cycled the distance considered it one of the highlights of their Bermuda trip. You'll find some of the best beaches here, so if you get tired along the way, take time out for a refreshing dip in the ocean.

Leave through the dockyard's south entrance and walk down Pender Road about 1km (½ mile). Cross Cockburn's Cut Bridge and go straight along Cockrange Road, which will take you to:

8 Lagoon Park

Enter the park as you cross over the Cut Bridge onto Ireland Island South. Walking trails crisscross the park, which has a lagoon populated with ducks and other wild fowl. There are places for picnicking in the park, which is free and open to the public.

To continue, cross Grey's Bridge to Boaz Island, and walk or cycle along Malabar Road. On your right you'll see the calm waters of Mangrove Bay. You'll eventually arrive at:

9 Somerset Village

Somerset is one of the most charming villages on Bermuda. Only one road goes through the village. Most of the stores are branches of larger stores in the City of Hamilton.

TAKE A BREAK
Somerset Country Squire Pub & Restaurant, 10 Mangrove Bay Rd. (☎ 441/234-0105), is an English-style pub that serves sandwiches, burgers, and such pub grub as steak-and-kidney pie, and bangers and mash (sausages and mashed potatoes). The kitchen is also noted for its desserts. (For a review, see chapter 5, "Where to Dine.")

Follow Cambridge Road west to:

10 Somerset Long Bay Park

Families like this park because of its good beach and shallow waters, which open onto Long Bay. You can picnic here. The Bermuda Audubon Society operates the nature reserve, and the pond attracts migrating birds, including the Louisiana heron, the snowy egret, and the purple gallinule, in both spring and autumn.

9

Shopping

Retailers on less prosperous islands attribute Bermuda's continuing reputation as a shopping mecca not only to the superb climate, but also to many years of skillful marketing. Indeed, no one has ever accused Bermudians of not knowing how to sell their island—or their rich inventories of goods.

Bermuda, once widely hailed as a "showcase of the British Empire," is still that, at least in its variety of goods. The retail scene draws upon its British antecedents: Shopkeepers are generally both polite and discreet, and merchandise is unusual and well made. In addition, most retailers take full advantage of location. Shops usually occupy charming cottages or historically important buildings, making shopping even more fun. Even visitors who intend to do no more than window shop are likely to break down and make a purchase or two.

In most cases, shopping on Bermuda is about quality, not bargains. The low prices of yesterday are gone with the wind. Shops face huge import tariffs, plus employee-related taxes. Costs have had a ripple effect in the retail industry, leading to what some view as outrageously high prices. Once you're on Bermuda, it rarely pays to comparison shop. Prices are rather uniform: The price of a watch in a branch store in St. George is likely to be exactly the same as it is in the main shop in the City of Hamilton.

BERMUDA'S BEST BUYS

Most of Bermuda's best shops are along Front Street in the City of Hamilton, where shopping is relaxed and casual. Among the choicest items are imports from Great Britain and Ireland, such as Shetland and cashmere sweaters, Harris tweed jackets, Scottish woolen goods and tartan kilts, and even fine china and crystal. Many items cost appreciably less than in their country of origin.

Because of a special "colonylike" arrangement with Great Britain, certain British goods are cheaper in Bermuda than in the United States, thanks to lower import tariffs. Some frequent visitors stock up on porcelain, crystal, silverware, jewelry, timepieces, and perfume, perhaps anticipating a wedding gift several months in advance. The island abounds with merchandisers of fine tableware, including Royal Copenhagen, Wedgwood, and Royal Crown Derby. Crystal is also plentiful, with many of the finest manufacturers in Europe and North America providing wide selections of merchandise. For a fee, items can be shipped, usually in well-wrapped packages that minimize chances of breakage.

Liquor is also a good buy in Bermuda. U.S. citizens are allowed to bring back only 1 liter duty-free, but even adding U.S. tax and duty, you can save 35% to 50% on liquor purchases, depending on the brand. Liqueurs offer the largest savings.

The island's wealth of antiques and collectibles is extraordinary. Antique lovers appreciate Bermuda's fusion of British aesthetic and mid-Atlantic charm.

The island has a wealth of antique engravings and 19th-century furniture. Its modern artwork and handmade pottery and crafts are elegant souvenirs. And anyone interested in carrying home a piece of Bermuda's nautical heritage is likely to find oversize ship's propellers, captain's bells, brass nameplates, scale models of sailing ships, or maybe even an old-fashioned ship's steering wheel from a salvaged shipwreck.

Other good buys are "Bermudiana"—products made on Bermuda or manufactured elsewhere exclusively for local stores. They include cedarwood gifts, carriage bells, coins commemorating the 375th anniversary of the island's settlement, flower plates by Spode, pewter tankards, handcrafted gold jewelry, traditional-line handbags with cedar or mahogany handles, miniature cottages in ceramic or limestone, shark's teeth polished and mounted in 14-karat gold, decorative kitchen items, Bermuda shorts (of course), silk scarves, and watches with a map of Bermuda on their faces.

Although some items might be less expensive than they are stateside, be aware that this isn't always the case. In fact, many, many items are overpriced. You should be familiar with the prices of comparable goods back home before committing yourself to serious purchases.

1 The Shopping Scene

WHERE TO GO
THE CITY OF HAMILTON
The best and widest range of shopping choices is in the City of Hamilton (see "In the City of Hamilton," below). Most shops are on Front Street, but you should explore the back streets as well, especially if you're an adventurous shopper.

The Emporium on Front Street, a restored building constructed around an atrium, houses a number of shops, including jewelry stores. Windsor Place on Queen Street is another Bermuda-style shopping mall.

HISTORIC ST. GEORGE
The "second city" of St. George also has many shops, stores, and boutiques, including branches of the City of Hamilton's famous Front Street stores. King's Square, the center of St. George, is home to many shops. The other major centers are Somers Wharf and Water Street.

In recent years, this historic port has emerged as a big-time shopping competitor to the City of Hamilton. It's easier to walk around St. George than the City of Hamilton, and St. George is more architecturally interesting than the City of Hamilton, so more and more customers are choosing to do their shopping here. Of course, St. George doesn't have as vast an array of merchandise as the City of Hamilton, so the serious shopper might want to explore both cities.

Tips **The Eternal Search for Bargains**

To find the real bargains, you must shop harder and longer than before; you'll usually find them in the off season (autumn and winter), when, with no uniformity, stores often reduce prices to make way for goods for the new season. But sales come and go year-round—there's no particular season. Keep an eye out for "sale" signs no matter when you're in Bermuda.

SANDYS PARISH

Don't overlook the shopping possibilities of the West End. Somerset Village in Sandys Parish has many shops (though quite a few are branches of the City of Hamilton stores). Of even greater interest may be the Royal Naval Dockyard area on Ireland Island. You can visit the Craft Market, Island Pottery, and the Bermuda Arts Centre at Dockyard, where you'll see local artisans at work.

WHAT YOU SHOULD KNOW

STORE HOURS

Stores in the City of Hamilton, St. George, and Somerset are generally open Monday to Saturday from 9am to 5:30pm. When large liners are in port, stores sometimes stay open later, and are sometimes open on Sundays.

FINDING AN ADDRESS

Some Front Street stores post numbers on their buildings; others don't. Sometimes the number posted or used is the "historic" number of the building, which has nothing to do with the modern number. You can always ask for directions, and most Bermudians are willing to help. Outside the City of Hamilton, don't expect to find numbers on buildings at all—or even street names in some cases.

SALES TAX & DUTY

There's no sales tax in Bermuda, but it's not a duty-free island. Depending on which country you're returning to, you may have to pay duty. See "Entry Requirements & Customs," in chapter 2, "Planning Your Trip to Bermuda," for details.

   Note: Like various other countries and territories, including several in the Caribbean, Bermuda is covered by the U.S. law regarding "Generalized System of Preferences" status. That means that if at least 35% of an item has been crafted in Bermuda, you can bring it back duty-free, regardless of how much you spent. If you've gone beyond your $800 allotment, make a separate list of goods made in Bermuda. This will make it easier for the customs officials and, ultimately, for you.

2 In the City of Hamilton

DEPARTMENT STORES

H. A. & E. Smith, Ltd.   This store has been selling top-quality merchandise since 1889, at substantial savings over U.S. prices. Smith's comprehensive stock includes sweaters for men and women (in cotton, cashmere, lamb's wool, and Shetland), British cosmetics, and a collection of top French perfumes. Smith's is noted for its selection of handbags, gloves, a very limited array of Liberty fabrics by the yard, and children's clothing. It also carries such merchandise as Burberry's rainwear from London and Rosenthal china. A subsidiary, "The Treasure Chest," located across the street from the main store, carries a full line of French perfumes and gifts, plus souvenirs. 35 Front St. (441/295-2288.

Marks & Spencer   This branch of the famous British chain (sometimes oddly called "St. Michael") carries the same reliable merchandise as its sibling stores in the British Isles. You'll find men's, women's, and children's fashions in everything from resort wear to sleepwear, including lingerie. There are also well-tailored dresses and suits, dress shirts, blazers, and British-tailored trousers, as well as swimwear, toiletries, and English sweets and biscuits. 7 Reid St. (441/295-0031.

Shopping in the City of Hamilton

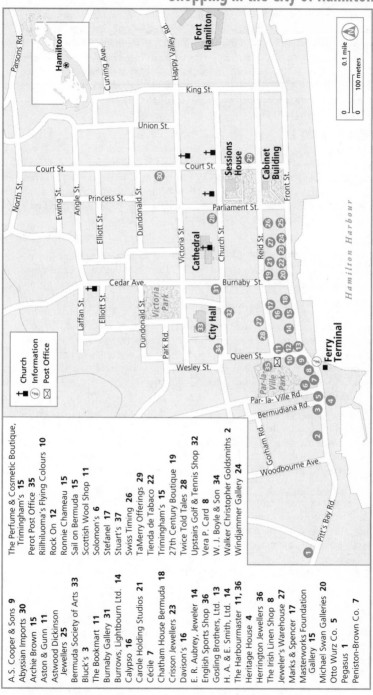

A.S. Cooper & Sons **9**
Abyssian Imports **30**
Archie Brown **15**
Aston & Gunn **11**
Astwood Dickinson Jewellers **25**
Bermuda Society of Arts **33**
Bluck's **3**
The Bookmart **11**
Burnaby Gallery **31**
Burrows, Lightbourn Ltd. **14**
Calypso **16**
Carole Holding Studios **21**
Cécile **7**
Chatham House Bermuda **18**
Crisson Jewellers **23**
Davison's **16**
E. R. Aubrey, Jeweler **14**
English Sports Shop **36**
Gosling Brothers, Ltd. **13**
H. A. & E. Smith, Ltd. **14**
The Harbourmaster **11, 36**
Heritage House **4**
Herrington Jewellers **36**
The Irish Linen Shop **8**
Jeweler's Warehouse **27**
Marks & Spencer **17**
Masterworks Foundation Gallery **15**
Michael Swan Galleries **20**
Otto Wurz Co. **5**
Pegasus **1**
Peniston-Brown Co. **7**

The Perfume & Cosmetic Boutique, Trimingham's **15**
Perot Post Office **35**
Riilhiluoma's Flying Colours **10**
Rock On **12**
Ronnie Chameau **15**
Sail on Bermuda **15**
Scottish Wool Shop **11**
Solomon's **6**
Stefanel **17**
Stuart's **37**
Swiss Timing **26**
TaMerry Offerings **29**
Tienda de Tabaco **22**
Trimingham's **15**
27th Century Boutique **19**
Twice Told Tales **28**
Upstairs Golf & Tennis Shop **32**
Vera P. Card **8**
W. J. Boyle & Son **34**
Walker Christopher Goldsmiths **2**
Windjammer Gallery **24**

203

Trimingham's Since 1842, Trimingham's has been Bermuda's largest department store, offering a full range of fine merchandise and featuring the largest selection of duty-free items on the island. You'll find Bermuda's best selection of cosmetics and perfumes, including exclusives from Estée Lauder and Clinique. Waterford, Lenox, Portmeirion, and other fine china and crystal are for sale at up to 30% off U.S. prices. Fine jewelry is often a good buy here. The store also stocks a wide range of Bermuda shorts, cashmere sweaters, and polo shirts. 37 Front St. ℂ **441/295-1183.**

GOODS A TO Z
ANTIQUES
Heritage House This outlet sells nautical prints, English antiques, old maps, modern porcelain, and the largest collection of Bermudian fine art on the island. Many new gift items have been recently added, including one of the best collections of costume jewelry in town. Look for the large collection of "Halcyon Days" pillboxes. 26 Church St. W. ℂ **441/295-2615.**

ART
Bermuda Society of Arts Loosely associated with the Bermudian government, this store is devoted to the exhibition of works by Bermuda-based artists and is one of the focal points of the island's arts scene. The West Wing of Hamilton's City Hall (the island's Fine Arts Museum occupies the East Wing), is the permanent home of the oldest arts society on Bermuda. The site contains two separate exhibition areas, where the artwork changes every 2 to 3 weeks. Themes range from the moderately avant-garde to the conservative, and every show includes dozens of examples of Bermudian landscapes, seascapes, or architectural renderings, any of which would make worthwhile souvenirs of your stay on the island. All merchandise can be packed for airplane transport. W. Wing of City Hall, 17 Church St. ℂ **441/292-3824.**

Burnaby Gallery In the heart of the City of Hamilton, this new yet prestigious gallery is dedicated to showcasing the best of Bermuda's artists. Deborah Harper runs the gallery with the aid of a panel of local art experts who help select the pieces that are exhibited here. Every 4 to 6 weeks a new exhibition opens. The LOM Building, corner of Burnaby and Reid sts. ℂ **441/292-8641.**

Carole Holding Studios Carole Holding is well known and well respected for her skill in what might be Bermuda's most-loved art form: watercolor painting. Many of Ms. Holding's works depict the peace and serenity of Bermuda's homes and gardens. Individuals commission a few of her works; more frequently, however, the subjects of her paintings come from her own imagination. Although other gift shops around the island carry Ms. Holding's works, most of them are in one of her shops. Her main store is now in the City of Hamilton (the St. George shop has been closed). She has another store at the Royal Naval Dockyard on Ireland Island. 81 Front St. ℂ **441/296-3431.**

Masterworks Foundation Gallery Established in 1987 by a group of international philanthropists, this foundation showcases paintings by renowned European, Bermudian, and North American artists. It serves to some extent as the island's most visible arts center. The foundation sponsors frequent art exhibitions, which have included works by Georgia O'Keeffe (who painted in Bermuda during the early 1930s), seascapes by Winslow Homer, and watercolors by Ogden Pleissner. The foundation also arranges guided art and architectural tours around the island and coordinates other artistic endeavors and exhibitions throughout the year. Bermuda House Lane, 97 Front St. ℭ 441/295-5580.

Michael Swan Galleries   For about 3 decades, Michael Swan has been one of the best-known Bermudian artists, using the medium of the airbrush and acrylic paints. In a style often called "ethereal," he often paints in soft pastels, which he views as the "true colors of nature," and focuses on light and shadow. His work is valued by collectors for its unique portrayal of island life. He also has a small outlet at the Royal Naval Dockyard. Butterfield Place, Front St. ℭ 441/296-5650.

Windjammer Gallery   In a coral cottage, this gallery exhibits paintings and bronze sculptures by local and international artists. It also carries an extensive selection of cards, prints, and limited editions. Adjacent to the gallery is the last private garden in the city, used for the display of sculpture and exhibitions. Reid and King sts. ℭ 441/292-7861.

ARTS & CRAFTS

Ronnie Chameau   Noted local artist Ronnie Chameau, known throughout the island for her charming handmade dolls, crafts doll-shaped ornaments from such natural objects as banana leaves, hazelnuts, and grapefruit leaves, gathered from her own and her friends' gardens. Each ornament has a unique personality and comes individually boxed and gift-wrapped. The small dolls are reasonably priced. Ms. Chameau also creates dolls wearing authentic 19th-century costumes, as well as wooden doorstops designed to look like Bermuda cottages. At Trimingham's, 37 Front St. ℭ 441/295-1183.

BEACHWEAR & SUNGLASSES

Calypso   Calypso carries casual, fun fashions (including unusual garments from around the world) and the most comprehensive selection of swimwear on Bermuda. The shop also features Italian leather goods, espadrilles, hats, bags, pareos, Italian ceramics, and whimsical gift items. It's the exclusive island retailer of Louis Vuitton luggage and accessories. There are branches at The Fairmont Southampton Princess, The Fairmont Hamilton Princess, the Sonesta Beach Hotel, the Coral Beach Club, and the dockyard. 23–24 Front St. ℭ 441/295-2112.

Sail on Bermuda   The locals shop at this store, which carries a unique collection of casual wear, bathing suits, and gifts. A recent poll of shoppers named Sail on Bermuda's T-shirts the best on Bermuda. A small addition, called "Shades of Bermuda," has the finest collection of sunglasses on the island. They also sell sailing suits. Old Cellar, Front St. ℭ 441/295-0808.

BOOKS

The Bookmart   This is the biggest bookstore on Bermuda. It specializes in bestsellers—mainly from the U.S. market—and carries works by British authors as well. One section is devoted to books about the island. There's also a well-stocked section for the kiddies. Phoenix Centre, 3 Reid St. ℭ 441/295-3838, ext. 412.

CHINA & GLASSWARE

Also see Trimingham's under "Department Stores," above.

A. S. Cooper & Sons   Bermuda's oldest and largest china and glassware store—family-owned since 1897—offers a broad range of fine bone china, earthenware, glassware, and jewelry. Among the famous names represented are

Minton, Royal Doulton, Belleek, Aynsley, Wedgwood, and Royal Copenhagen. The Crystal Room displays Orrefors, Waterford, Royal Brierley, and Kosta Boda, among others. The Collector's Gallery is known for its limited editions of Bing & Gröndahl, Royal Doulton, and Lladró. The perfume department offers selections from the world's greatest perfumeries. 59 Front St. ✆ 441/295-3961.

Bluck's   Established in 1844, Bluck's is well known for carrying some of the finest names in china, including Royal Worcester, Spode, Aynsley, Royal Doulton, and Herend porcelain from Hungary. The choice in crystal is equally impressive: Kosta Boda, Waterford, Baccarat, Daum, and Lalique (exclusive with Bluck's). Upstairs is the Antiques Room, filled with fine English furniture, antique Bermuda maps, and an array of old English silver. Bluck's has branch shops on Water Street in St. George and in The Fairmont Southampton Princess. 4 Front St. ✆ 441/295-5367.

FASHION

Also see "Shoes," "Sportswear," and "Woolens," below.

Aston & Gunn   This shop sells career-oriented clothing for men (imported from Germany and Holland). In addition to the usual collection of shirts, ties, jackets, and suits, Aston & Gunn is the exclusive island distributor of Hugo Boss. 2 Reid St. ✆ 441/295-4866.

Cécile   Well-stocked Cécile is the center for high fashion on Bermuda. Management boasts that visiting one of Cécile's shops (the others are in England) is like calling upon the fashion capitals of the world—you'll find everything from German high fashion to Gottex swimwear. Its sweater and accessory boutique is also outstanding. 15 Front St. W. (near the Visitors Service Bureau and the Ferry Terminal). ✆ 441/295-1311.

Stefanel   This is the island's only outlet for the clothing of Carlo Stefanel, a well-known Italian designer. Stocking merchandise for women, the store sells handmade skirts (some of them knit) with contrasting jackets. There's a stylish array of accessories and a line of clothing for infants and children. 12 Reid St. ✆ 441/295-5698.

27th Century Boutique   Long known as a stylish, trendsetting shop, this high fashion boutique carries designer clothing, silver costume jewelry, and accessories. The European clothing is styled for women ages 13 and up—on our recent visit, a 16-year-old and a grandmother bought the same shirt. The clothing is rather conservative and in good taste. The store also has a nice collection of shoes, for both men and women, from Canada and London. 4 Burnaby St. (between Front and Church sts.). ✆ 441/292-2628.

GIFTS

Riihiluoma's Flying Colours   This is everybody's favorite catchall emporium for inexpensive, impulse-purchase souvenirs and T-shirts with perky slogans. You'll also find paperweights; beach cover-ups; sarongs like actress Dorothy Lamour used to wear; key chains shaped like Bermuda; and arts and crafts. The establishment's hard-to-spell name comes from the Finnish-born family that established it in 1937 and still manages it today. 5 Queen St. ✆ 441/295-0890.

Vera P. Card   Vera P. Card is known for its "gifts from around the world," including the island's largest collection of Lladró and Hummel figurines. Famous-name watches include Nivada, Borel, and Rodania. The dinnerware collection features such brands as Rosenthal, and the crystal department offers a wide assortment of Czech and Bohemian crystal, giftware, and chandeliers. Look for the "Bermuda Collection" of 14-karat gold jewelry. Other branches are at 7 Water St. in St. George and at the Sonesta Beach Resort. 11 Front St. ☎ 441/ 295-1729.

JEWELRY

Astwood Dickinson Jewellers   Here you'll find a treasure trove of famous-name watches, including Patek Philippe, Cartier, Tiffany, Tag Heuer, Tissot, and Omega, plus designer jewelry, all at prices generally below U.S. retail. From the original Bermuda collection, you can select an 18-karat gold memento of the island (jeweled representations of local flora, fauna, and landmarks). There is a branch in the Walker Arcade. 83–85 Front St. ☎ 441/292-5805.

Crisson Jewellers   Crisson is the exclusive Bermuda agent for Rolex, Ebel, Seiko, Cyma, and Gucci watches, and for other well-known makers. It also car-ries an extensive selection of fine jewelry and gems. Branches are on Queen Street and in several of the major hotels, including the Elbow Beach Hotel, the Sonesta Beach Resort, and the Fairmont Princess hotels. 55 and 71 Front St. ☎ 441/ 295-2351.

E. R. Aubrey, Jeweler   This shop carries an extensive collection of gold chains, rings with precious and semiprecious stones, and charms, including one of the Bermuda longtail bird. 19 Front St. W. (opposite the Ferry Terminal). ☎ 441/295-3826.

Herrington Jewellers   This leading jewelry store offers a good selection of gold and silver items. It's the authorized dealer for Citizen watches, sells Timex watches, and carries a vast selection of 14-karat gold chains and rings set with precious and semiprecious stones. 1 Washington Mall. ☎ 441/292-6527.

Solomon's   Some aficionados of the shopping scene consider Solomon's one of the most appealing jewelry stores. Don't expect a supermarket-style empo-rium with vast inventories: Solomon's is small, select, and ever so polite, with a range of valuable stones mostly set in 18-karat gold (and, to a lesser degree, in platinum). 17 Front St. (opposite the cruise-ship terminal). ☎ 441/292-4742.

Finds Counterculture Shopping

If you view yourself as part of the counterculture, and Bermuda is a bit prim for you, we have a few unusual stores to suggest: Try dropping in at **Twice Told Tales,** 34 Parliament St. (☎ 441/296-1995), in the City of Hamilton, where kindred spirits gather at one of the few tables for coffee and conversation. We can't think of a better name for this store, which is a secondhand bookshop.

Here's a chance to meet the locals—**Rock On,** 67 Front St. (☎ 441/ 295-3468), in the City of Hamilton, provides a full range of herb teas, nutritional supplements, and books and magazines devoted to health issues.

Ethiopia provides the stock to fill **Abyssin Imports,** 79 Court St. (☎ 441/292-3208), in the City of Hamilton. African garments, incense, silver, leather bags, oils, and carvings from the continent's west coast are sold.

> **Tips** Shoppers Beware
>
> Many of our readers carry only the Discover Card. But be warned in advance that the popular U.S. card isn't accepted in Bermuda. One reader, John Fisher, writes that, because Discover is not accepted: "Many of the items we had looked forward to purchasing in Bermuda we had to pass up." MasterCard and Visa are accepted by most stores.

Swiss Timing All the best names in Swiss watchmaking are found here, including Maurice Lacroix, Michel Herbelin, and Versace, along with a selection of semi-precious jewelry, gold chains, and bracelets. 95 Front St. © 441/295-1376.

Walker Christopher Goldsmiths For the last decade or so, the *Bermudian* magazine has cited this goldsmith for selling the finest jewelry on the island. The shop showcases everything from classic diamond bands to strands of South Sea pearls to modern hand-hammered chokers. The store also carries a collection of rare coins—gold doubloons and silver "pieces of eight" salvaged from sunken galleons, as well as Greek and Roman coins which can be mounted and worn as pendants, earrings, and cufflinks. Even Egyptian artifacts have been transformed into wearable art. Customers who have their own design in mind can work with a master jeweler to craft a one-of-a-kind piece. The on-site workshop also produces Bermuda-inspired gold jewelry and sterling silver Christmas ornaments. 9 Front St. © 441/295-1466.

LEATHER GOODS
The Harbourmaster This is your best bet for luggage and leather goods. These good value items are from Colombia, and are often sold at prices 30% lower than in the United States. There are more expensive leather goods from Italy (such as handbags), plus an extensive collection of wallets, and nylon and canvas tote bags. The shop also stocks travel accessories, including luggage carts. The branch at the corner of Reid and Queen streets (© **441/295-4210**) carries essentially the same merchandise. Washington Mall. © 441/295-5333.

LINENS
The Irish Linen Shop At Heyl's Corner, near the "Birdcage" police officer post, this shop stocks pure linen tablecloths from Ireland and a large variety of other merchandise from Europe—everything from quilted place mats to men's shirts in French cotton from Souleiado of Provence. The shop also carries a large selection of Le Jacquard Francais table linens. They are the biggest distributors of luxury bed linens. The owners go to Europe twice a year and bring back exceptional items such as Madeira hand embroidery and Belgian lace. You can often save as much as 50% over American prices. 31 Front St. (at Queen St.). © 441/295-4089.

LIQUOR & LIQUEURS
Burrows, Lightbourn Ltd. Be aware that the maximum amount of spirits you can take from Bermuda is 1 liter. Orders must be placed 24 hours before your departure, except on Sunday, when a 48-hour advance purchase is required. The store will deliver your packages to the airport or to your ship. There are two locations in the City of Hamilton and one each in St. George, Flatts Village, Paget, Somerset, and the Royal Naval Dockyard. 57 Front St. © 441/295-0176.

Gosling Brothers, Ltd.   This large competitor of Burrows, Lightbourn has also been selling liquor on Bermuda since 1806. You can buy Gosling's Black Seal dark rum—perhaps one bottle to sample on the island and another as an "in-bond" purchase to take home. "In-bond" items cannot be consumed on the island; they can only be exported. The bottle you drink on the island is likely to cost 50% more than the "in-bond" bottle. If you want to buy liquor to take home under your duty-free allowance, you can arrange to have it sent to the airport. There's another location, the Black Seal Shop (under the same ownership despite having a different name), at 17 Dundonald St. Front and Queen sts. ℂ 441/ 295-1123.

PERFUMES

Peniston-Brown Co.   This shop carries almost all of the world's most popular perfumes. Its "fragrance specialists" will be happy to teach you something about the art of choosing and wearing perfume. There is another location at 6 Water St. in St. George. 23 Front St. W. (opposite the Ferry Terminal). ℂ 441/295-0570.

The Perfume and Cosmetic Boutique, Trimingham's   On the ground floor of Bermuda's largest department store is the island's most comprehensive emporium of prestigious fragrance and cosmetics lines—available duty-free. The beauty-care exclusives include Estée Lauder, Elizabeth Arden, Chanel, and Christian Dior. Famous-name fragrance exclusives include Boucheron, Tiffany, Clinique, Iman and Issey Miyake. There is also another location of this store at the Dockyard called "Uncommon Scents." 37 Front St. ℂ 441/295-1183.

PHOTOGRAPHIC EQUIPMENT

Stuart's   This is Bermuda's leading outlet for photographic and electronic equipment. They are the official reps of Minolta, Canon, Sony, Nikon, Pentax, and other big names. The store also carries top-of-the-line picture frames and camera bags. Also sold are tapes, film, tape recorders, and other supplies. 5 Reid St. ℂ 441/295-5496.

SHOES

W. J. Boyle & Son   In business since 1884, this shop offers footwear for men, women, and children. With the best collection in town, it specializes in brand-name footwear from England, Spain, Brazil, and the United States (including Clarks of England, Cole Haan and Enzo Angiolini). Queen St. ℂ 441/295-1887.

SILVER

Otto Wurz Co.   Otto Wurz is at the western end of Front Street, past the Ferry Terminal and the Bank of Bermuda. It specializes in articles made of silver, including jewelry, charms, and bracelets. One section of the store is devoted to gift items, such as pewter ware, cute wooden signs, and glassware, which the store can engrave for you. 2 Vallis Building, 3–5 Front St. (between Par-la-Ville Rd. and Bermudiana Rd.). ℂ 441/295-1247.

Branching Out

You'll often find branches of City of Hamilton's stores at major resorts. The prices—even when there's a sale—are the same as those charged by the parent stores in the City of Hamilton. Although the selection is more limited, resort boutiques remain open on Sunday when most stores in the City of Hamilton are shuttered.

SPORTSWEAR

Davison's   Sportswear with a Bermudian flair is the specialty at this emporium. Along with virtually anything you'd need to wear for almost any sport on Bermuda—or to the country club at home—it carries accessories and sporting equipment. The store features bags by Vera Bradley. Also available are culinary gift packages including such items as Bermuda fish or clam chowder, fish-based sauces, and island herbs. Other locations are at the Clocktower in the Royal Naval Dockyard, on Water Street in St. George, and at The Fairmont Southampton Princess. 27 and 73 Front St. ℂ 441/292-1556.

Upstairs Golf & Tennis Shop   Everything you'll need for the tennis courts or the golf links is available in this amply stocked store. For golfers, there's merchandise by Ping, Callaway, Titleist, and Adams. Tennis enthusiasts will recognize products by Dunlop, Slazenger, and many others. There is also men's and women's rainwear from Scotland, which is suitable for Bermuda's wet winters. 26 Church St. ℂ 441/295-5161.

STAMPS

Perot Post Office   Philatelists from all over the world visit this office to buy postage stamps from Bermuda. Highly prized by collectors, they often feature historic figures and the island's flora and fauna. A stamp showing the *Sea Venture* stranded on coral reefs is one of the most coveted stamps. Open Monday to Friday from 9am to 5pm. Queen St., at the entrance to Par-la-Ville Park. ℂ 441/292-9052 or 441/295-5151, ext. 1192.

TOBACCO

Many Americans come to Bermuda to enjoy Cuban cigars, which can't be brought back into the United States, but must be smoked while abroad. This increasingly fashionable (but not very healthy) indulgence can be enjoyed at the following outlets:

Chatham House Bermuda   This shop seems as if it's been around since Columbus discovered Taíno Indians smoking the leaves of a plant called *cohiba* in 1942. Chatham House is a historic retailer of Cuban cigars. Bermuda used to harvest its own tobacco, but Castro blessed those on sale here—well, almost. Corner of Front and Burnaby sts. ℂ 441/292-8422.

WOOLENS

Archie Brown   In business for more than half a century, this shop features sweaters for men and women in cashmere, cotton, lamb's wool, and Shetland; it also carries matching kilts for ladies and children. Men's kilts can be special ordered. Colors range from neutral to vibrant. 55 Front St. ℂ 441/295-2928.

English Sports Shop   This shop, established in 1918, is one of the island's leading retailers of quality classic and British woolen goods for men, women, and children. This store features brands like Pringles and Marks and Spencer. 49 Front St. ℂ 441/295-2672.

3 Around the Island

As you leave the City of Hamilton and tour the island, you may want to continue looking for typical Bermudian items at the shops listed below.

For other shopping suggestions, consider the **Bermuda Craft Market** (see "Sandys Parish," in chapter 7, "Seeing the Sights") and the **Birdsey Studio** in Paget Parish (see "Paget Parish," in chapter 7, "Seeing the Sights").

Finds **Searching for That Little Treasure**

In Southampton Parish, **Deja-Vu Flea Market,** 40 Middle Rd. (📞 **441/238-8525**), has recently started to attract a lot of attention from shoppers looking for offbeat and secondhand items. You never know what's been resting in those Bermudian attics all these years. On this island of sea-going men, many unusual finds were brought back from around the world. As you rummage around, you could find anything from Tibetan rubbings to a complete dinner set used by the Carringtons on the TV soap *Dynasty.*

SANDYS PARISH
IRELAND ISLAND
Bermuda Arts Centre at Dockyard   In one of the stone-sided warehouses originally built by the British during their military tenure in Bermuda, this art gallery specializes in paintings, sculptures, and crafts, mostly by Bermudian artisans. New artists are featured every 6 weeks. Not to be confused with the nearby Bermuda Crafts Centre, with which it is not associated, it's sponsored by a local foundation and strives for more than a purely commercial approach to art. Canvases range in price from $175 to around $5,000; less expensive craft items are also for sale. Some of the staff members are well versed in the nuances of the art. Museum Row, 4 Freeport Rd., Royal Naval Dockyard. 📞 **441/234-2809.**

SOUTHAMPTON PARISH
Desmond Fountain Gallery   Bermuda's most prominent sculptor, Desmond Fountain, has created some of the island's most visible public art. In recent years much of his work has been commissioned for upscale private homes and gardens around the world. The gallery also features original works by local artists. On the ground floor of the Imporium, 69 Front St. 📞 **441/296-3518.**

Rising Sun Shop   This eclectic outlet, the only real "country store" left on Bermuda, lies 1km (½ mile) west of the Waterlot Inn. The owner, Anne Powell, has assembled a little bit of everything. We always like to stop in just in case we see something we can't live without. In addition to one of Bermuda's warmest welcomes, it offers a frequently changing inventory. You'll find everything from weather vanes to old hobbyhorses, saddlery to wine coolers. 159 Middle Rd. 📞 **441/238-2154.**

Sharon Wilson Gallery   Only minutes by foot from Horseshoe Beach, local artist Sharon Wilson is known for going beyond the picture-postcard view of island life in an attempt to portray Bermuda's spirit in more depth. She explores the scope of Bermudian life and its people through limited and open edition lithographs and notecards. The gallery is also home to her picture-book illustrations, the most well known being the award-winning *The Day Gogo Went to Vote.* 2 Turtle Place. 📞 **441/238-2583.**

HAMILTON PARISH
Bermuda Glass-Blowing Studio and Showroom   Bermuda's only glass-blowing studio employs both locally trained Bermudians and Europeans. Although some of the studio's glass pieces have been commissioned, most are inspired by cutting-edge developments in the art-glass world. Pieces on display

cost $5 to $850. The minimum commission accepted is usually more than $500. The studio offers a workshop where customers can create a dish or paper-weight of their own design for $150 per hour. The custom pieces are then taken home by the customer. There are also demonstrations held by experts from Monday to Friday 10am to 5 pm. 16 Blue Hole Hill. ✆ **441/293-2234.**

ST. GEORGE PARISH

The Book Cellar Built in the 18th century, this small but choice bookshop lies below Tucker House, a National Trust property. It caters to both visitors and locals, including a lot of "yachties" who stop by to pick up reading material for their time at sea. A lot of people come here for the Cellar's line of books on Bermuda. There's also a wide array of fiction and nonfiction by British and American writers. Parents might be interested in picking up one of the children's books published in Britain—many are quite different from similar editions in America. Water St. ✆ **441/297-0448.**

Bridge House Gallery In one of the parish's oldest buildings—a two-story 18th-century building that was home to two of the island's governors and is now maintained by Bermuda's National Trust—this may be the best-stocked empo-rium on the island's East End. It carries a wide selection of antique and modern Bermudiana, including old lace, Christmas ornaments, imported English porce-lain, antique maps, old bottles, postcards, and unique mementos of Bermuda's unusual geography and history. One corner of the building is the studio and sales outlet of local watercolor artist Jill Amos Raine (see chapter 7, "Seeing the Sights"). 1 Bridge St. ✆ **441/297-8211.**

Cow Polly Named after a rather unpleasant-looking fish that abounds in Bermuda's waters, this upscale gift shop prides itself on its collection of unusual objects imported from virtually everywhere. The theme is aquatic designs, often inspired by fish and underwater mythology. Items for sale include hand-painted shirts and jackets, costume jewelry, and unusual neckties. 16 Water St., Somers Wharf. ✆ **441/297-1514.**

Frangipani This is a world of fun, colorful "dressy casual" fashion for women. You'll find a large selection of comfortable cottons, bright silks, and soft rayons. The store is known for its unusual merchandise, including exclusive island designs. There's also a fine collection of swimwear and unusual acces-sories. 16 Water St., Somers Wharf. ✆ **441/297-1357.**

Taylors Go here for the finest selection of kilts, skirts, and other tartans from Scotland, even if you can't play the pipes. 30 Water St. ✆ **441/297-1626.**

Tips Last-Minute Purchases

The international airport in Bermuda has recently launched duty-free shops for those last-minute purchases. One shop is found in the interna-tional departures lounge, and the other lies near the U.S. departures lounge. U.S. citizens clear customs before flying back to the States. For that specialty purchase, you should still shop around the island. But now you can buy routine duty-free purchases such as perfume, cigarettes, and liquor right before getting on the plane. That sure beats the old system of buying such goods a day or so in advance and having them delivered to the airport.

Tips Comparison Shopping at Somers Wharf

The best place to begin shopping is at the new **Somers Wharf & Branch Stores** along Water Street, a coterie of shops that includes all the big names from the City of Hamilton such as A.S. Coopers, Trimingham's, and the Crown Colony Shop. Of course, the parent stores in the City of Hamilton are better stocked, but Somers Wharf makes shopping a pleasure because all the island's "name" shops are clustered together, making comparison shopping much easier.

10

Bermuda After Dark

As we mentioned already, nightlife is not one of the compelling reasons to go to Bermuda, although there is some after-dark action, mainly in the summer. If you visit during the winter, we trust you'll be content to nurse a drink in a pub.

In the summer, activity seems to float from hotel to hotel, which makes it hard to predict which pub or nightspot will have the best steel-drum or calypso band at any given time. Many pubs feature singalongs at the piano, a popular form of entertainment in Bermuda. Most of the big hotels offer shows after dinner, with combos filling in between shows for couples who like to dance.

The island's visitor centers and most hotels distribute free copies of such publications as *Preview Bermuda, Bermuda Weekly,* and *This Week in Bermuda,* which list the latest scheduled activities and events. There's also a calendar of events in the *Bermudian,* sold at most newsstands.

You can also tune in to the local TV station, which constantly broadcasts information for visitors, including details on cultural events and nightlife offerings around the island. Radio station 1160 AM (VSB) broadcasts news of Bermuda's cultural and entertainment events from 7am to noon daily.

1 The Club & Music Scene

DEVONSHIRE PARISH

Clay House Inn   Although calypso and steel-band music originated on islands south of Bermuda, this nightclub offers up those musical forms with panache. You're likely to see a folkloric celebration of island dances, with vocal and instrumental music; it's a carefully contrived package of Caribbean-style nostalgia. Shows are Wednesday and Thursday year-round; doors open at 9:45pm, and the entertainment lasts until right after midnight. Friday and Saturday, the club features reggae music from 11pm to 3am. 77 North Shore Rd. © **441/292-3193** for reservations. Cover $25 per person (includes 2 drinks). Bus: 10 or 11.

PAGET PARISH

After Hours   The idea of an after-hours spot in sleepy Bermuda, where many guests turn in at 9pm, seems incongruous—but there is such a place. Local night owls flock here for good burgers and good times, downing food and drink until they're turned away. The cafe is very popular with the locals, especially those who don't have to get up at 7am to report to work. The kitchen also turns out well-stuffed sandwiches and Indian curries for those late-night munchies. Open Monday to Saturday 7pm to 4am. 117 South Rd. (past the intersection with Middle Rd.). © **441/236-8563.** Bus: 7.

Café Lido/"The Deep"   At the first-class Elbow Beach Hotel, this is Bermuda's latest hot spot. The club alone can seat 250 "dancing fools." This new state-of-the-art nightclub is a sports bar as well as a venue for dancing and entertainment. There are marble floors and mirrors everywhere, with a mezzanine upstairs overlooking the main dance floor. The club is open Monday to Saturday from 10am to 3am (very, very late for early-to-bed Bermuda). 60 South Shore Rd. ✆ 441/234-9884. Cover $20. Bus: 1,2, or 7.

PEMBROKE PARISH (CITY OF HAMILTON)

Club 40   This upscale spot features music from the '70s and '80s, along with Latin and Top-40 selections. Live music is also presented. The dress code forbids jeans or sneakers—smart casual is the way to go. Open Tuesday through Saturday 10pm to 3am. 119 Front St. ✆ 441/292-9340. Cover $10 after 11pm. Bus: 1, 2, 10, or 11.

Coconut Rock   With a name more evocative of the Caribbean than of Bermuda, this restaurant has two of the most active bars in town. It draws locals and visitors (in equal numbers) with background music and videos of the hottest acts in the U.K. and America. On slow nights, only one bar is open; on Friday, the second, the Bourbon Lounge, becomes a venue for jazz. Happy hour is Monday to Friday from 5 to 7pm. Open daily 11:30am to 1am. Williams House, 20 Reid St. ✆ 441/292-1043. Bus: 7 or 8.

The Ozone Nightclub & the Lucky Strike Casino   One of Bermuda's leading clubs, the Ozone is on the third floor of a stylish commercial building in the center of the City of Hamilton. It has been renovated into a modern, trendy club, and there's lots of special-effects lighting. The extensive music repertoire includes the top hits climbing the charts. After the Ozone, visit the small Lucky Strike Casino to try your luck at the slots. Drink prices range from $4 to $7. Open daily 9:30pm to 3am. In the Emporium Building, 69 Front St. ✆ 441/292-4978. Cover $20 daily high season; $10 off season Fri–Sat only. Bus: 3, 7, or 11.

The Spinny Wheel   If you'd like to escape from the tourist hordes and enjoy a pint with the locals, head to this longtime favorite, a virtual institution since opening in 1970. Named for the Fifth Dimension (remember them?) song, it's a relaxing place that has an outdoor pool area with a bar. There's live music downstairs. An upstairs section for disco dancing draws a young crowd. Happy hour is 6 to 8pm Monday to Friday. Open daily noon to 3am. 33 Court St. ✆ 441/292-7799. Cover $10 Fri–Sun. Bus: 7 or 8.

SOUTHAMPTON PARISH

Henry VIII   This restaurant (see chapter 5, "Where to Dine," for a review) is also a good bet for music and comedy. Piano music and singing is often featured, as are comedians. Performances begin at 9:45pm and last until the restaurant closes at 1am. The stage is visible from the pub and from one of the restaurant's three dining areas. South Shore Rd. ✆ 441/238-1977. Bus: 7 or 8.

2 The Bar Scene

HAMILTON PARISH

Swizzle Inn   The home of the Bermuda rum swizzle, this bar and restaurant lies west of the airport, near the Crystal Caves and the Bermuda Perfumery. You can order a Swizzleburger and fish and chips throughout the day (see chapter 5, "Where to Dine," for a restaurant review). There is live entertainment every night except Mondays and Wednesdays. In the old days, you might've run into Ted Kennedy here; now his wife steers him to more sedate places. The tradition is to tack your business card to anyplace you can find a spot, even the ceiling.

The jukebox plays both soft and hard rock. Happy hour is Monday to Friday 6pm to 7pm. Open daily 11am to 1am. 3 Blue Hole Hill, Bailey's Bay. ℂ **441/293-1854.** Bus: 3 or 11.

PEMBROKE PARISH (CITY OF HAMILTON)

Blue Juice   This is the latest hangout joint in town, and it has quickly become one of the most popular watering holes. You can party in the courtyard under the stars, enjoying great tunes. This place is still going strong at 3am (or until you say so) when much of the rest of Bermuda is asleep. You can watch the latest music videos on a large outdoor screen while sipping your favorite drink. There's also a light menu if you get the munchies. The bar is found on a little piazza evocative of a European setting. Open daily 11am to 3am. Bermuda House Lane. ℂ **441/292-4507.** Bus: 1 or 2.

Casey's   There's nothing flashy about this long, narrow room, which seems to be a favorite with locals. The owner, Wesley Robinson, knows many of his patrons and is an expert at mixing the house specialty, a "Dark and Stormy" (Black Seal Rum with splashes of ginger beer). Look for yellowed photographs of old Bermuda and a carefully preserved, wall-mounted marlin caught by the owner in 1982. Friday nights here are the most popular on the island, and the joint overflows. Monday is karaoke night and on Wednesdays and Saturdays, they have a DJ. Go here if you like to wander far off the beaten tourist trail and want to hang out with local Bermudians. Open Monday to Saturday 10am to 10pm. 25 Queen St. (between Reid and Church sts.). ℂ **441/292-9994.** Bus: 1, 2, 10, or 11.

Docksider   This sports bar on the City of Hamilton's main drag is lively into the early morning hours. At a long cedar bar, you'll find some of the most avid sports fans on Bermuda. There are 15 TVs. One section is a wine bar, which is more intimate; another section is a pool bar. You can order pub grub, such as fish and chips or shepherd's pie. On Friday, there is a live DJ. Happy hour is daily from 5 to 7pm. Open daily 11am to 1am (until 2am Fri–Sat). 121 Front St. ℂ **441/296-3333.** Bus: 1, 2, 10, or 11.

Flanagan's   On the second floor of a landmark building, this restaurant-pub is the domain of Irishman Thomas Gallagher, who extends a *cead mile failte,* or "100,000 welcomes." This club has some of the town's best music—reggae, rock, soca, and what is often called "party music." There are two bars that feature exotic drinks. Happy hour is daily from 5 to 7pm. In the sports bar, you can watch European soccer matches or others sports; there are eight 27-inch screens. Open daily 11am to 1am. Emporium Building, 69 Front St. ℂ **441/295-8299.** Bus: 7 or 8.

The Pickled Onion   For years, Ye Old Cock & Feather was one of Bermuda's landmark pubs. In 1997, it glaringly changed its image (as well as its name), and the once fairly staid pub became a stop on the after-dark circuit. Funky fabrics cover the booths and tables where patrons listen to music that ranges from blues to oldies of the past 50 years. Live music starts at 8pm. Happy hour is Monday to Friday from 5 to 7pm. Open daily 11:30am to around 1am (until 3am Sat–Sun). 53 Front St. ℂ **441/295-2263.** Bus: 7 or 8.

Robin Hood Pub & Restaurant   The merry women and men of Bermuda flock here for a variety of entertainment options. Robin Hood serves fine pub fare, including some of Bermuda's best pizzas. It's also the island's number-one sports bar, with video coverage of various U.S. and British league competitions.

The pub has recently been renovated. On other nights you can enjoy everything from live entertainment to casual trivia quizzes with other patrons. Friday and Saturday are jukebox nights devoted to reggae or rock. Sometimes prizes are awarded to the patron who can drink a pint of ale the fastest. Open Monday to Saturday 11am to 1am, Sunday noon to 1am. 25 Richmond Rd. ℂ **441/295-3314.** Bus: 1 or 2.

SANDYS PARISH

Frog & Onion   Converted from an 18th-century cooperage, or barrel-making factory, this British-style pub is in the Royal Naval Dockyard (see chapter 5, "Where to Dine," for a restaurant review). It serves bar snacks throughout the afternoon and evening. Operated by a "frog" (a Frenchman) and an "onion" (a Bermudian), the pub is open daily 11:30am to 1am. The Cooperage, Royal Naval Dockyard, Ireland Island. ℂ **441/234-2900.** Bus: 7 or 8.

SMITH'S PARISH

North Rock Brewing Company   If you want to find us in Bermuda, chances are we'll be at this watering hole, Bermuda's first brewpub. The draft beer is brewed on the premises right before your eyes. Pub seating envelops the glass-enclosed brewery where Old Colony Bitters and Somers Ale are brewed. You may be surprised to find that some of the mugs are 22 ounces. These brews are only for local consumption and not sold elsewhere. You'll find a selection of fresh ales on any given day, including "Whale of a Wheat" and "North Rock Porter." The outdoor roadside patio adds a British flavor. See the restaurant recommendation in chapter 5, "Where to Dine," for more details. The pub is open daily from 11am to 11pm. 10 South Rd. ℂ **441/236-6633.** Bus: 1.

SOUTHAMPTON PARISH

Longtail Lounge & Café   Set in the lobby of the Sonesta Beach Resort (see review in chapter 4, "Where to Stay"), this place functions as a simple garden-style restaurant during the lunch hour, and as a pulsating bar and lounge every evening after sundown. From one of its deep-cushioned armchairs, you'll have a sweeping view of the beach through big windows. Live entertainment, usually a pianist or calypso trio, is provided every night from 9:30am to 11pm. The house specialty drink, priced at $8.20, is the aforementioned "Dark and Stormy," made from local Black Seal Rum mixed with ginger beer. Food is served daily from noon to 10pm, with platters costing $11 to $16. Bar and snack service is daily from 11:30am to 1am. In the Sonesta Beach Resort South Shore Rd. ℂ **441/239-3119.** Bus: 7.

ST. GEORGE PARISH

The little port of St. George and adjoining St. David's Island is a pubber's haven. Our favorite is **Black Horse Tavern** (p. 137), a perfect spot for a congenial evening in good company. It lies on St. David's Island immediately adjoining St. George and is worth the trek over. If you get hungry, you can always order a plate of shark hash to go with your beer. Back in St. George itself, **Freddie's Pub on the Square** (p. 138) is always a lot of fun. Its selection of draft beers is among the best on the island. The oldest pub in St. George, **White Horse Tavern** (p. 140), remains an enduring favorite. It's jammed most evenings with a mixture of locals and visitors. We especially like the location of this one, as it stands at water's edge overlooking the harbor. Don't expect speedy service in any of these joints.

3 The Performing Arts

You can order tickets for Bermuda's major cultural events through the box office at the **Visitors Service Bureau** in the City of Hamilton (✆ **441/292-8572**) with your MasterCard, Visa, or American Express card. Students and senior citizens are sometimes eligible for discounts to various entertainment events.

BALLET

The Bermuda Civic Ballet presents classical ballets at various venues. On occasion, a major European or American guest artist appears with the troupe. The National Dance Theater of Bermuda also stages performances, both classical and modern, around the island. Ask at the tourist office or call the box office at the Visitors Service Bureau (see above) to check the troupe's schedules during your visit; prices vary with the performance.

CLASSICAL MUSIC

The **Bermuda Philharmonic Society,** conducted by Graham Garton, presents four regular concerts during the season. Special outdoor **"Classical Pops" concerts** are presented on the first weekend in June in St. George and at the Royal Naval Dockyard. Concerts usually feature the Bermuda Philharmonic orchestra, the choir, and guest soloists. You can get tickets and concert schedules from the **Harbourmaster,** Washington Mall (✆ **441/295-5333**). Tickets generally cost $18 to $20; seniors and students are often granted discounts, depending on the performance.

GOMBEY DANCING

Ask at the tourist office or call the box office at the Visitors Service Bureau (see above) to see whether the gombey dancers will be performing during your stay. This is the island's single most important cultural expression of African heritage. Once part of slave culture, the tradition dates from the mid-1700s. The local dance troupe of talented men and women often performs at one of the big hotels in winter (and on occasion, aboard cruise ships for passengers). On holidays, you'll see the gombeys dancing through the streets of the City of Hamilton in their colorful costumes.

MUSICAL THEATER

An all-volunteer organization based in the City of Hamilton, the **Gilbert & Sullivan Society of Bermuda,** P.O. Box HM 3098, Hamilton HM NX

The Big Event: The Bermuda Festival

Bermuda's major cultural event is the Bermuda Festival, staged every January and February. Outstanding international classical, jazz, and pop artists perform, and major theatrical and dance companies from around the globe stage productions. During the festival, performances take place every night except Sunday. Ticket prices start at $35. Some festival tickets are reserved until 48 hours before curtain time for visitors. Tickets can also be ordered online at www.bermudafestival.com. Most performances are at **City Hall Theatre,** City Hall, Church Street, the City of Hamilton. For more information and reservations, contact the **Bermuda Festival,** P.O. Box HM 297, Hamilton HM AX, Bermuda (✆ **441/295-1291**; fax 441/295-7403).

(© 441/295-3218), is known for producing at least one large-scale musical per year. These days, only about 20% of the repertoire is based on the works of Gilbert and Sullivan; it now includes such musicals as *Evita, Chicago,* and Sondheim's *A Little Night Music,* among others. The society performs at the City of Hamilton's City Hall, on Church Street. Be warned that this is a volunteer organization; the sole production runs for 2 weeks at most, usually in October. Tickets cost $30. Society members sometimes contribute their talents to the Bermuda Festival (see the box above).

Bermuda is the only place outside of Cambridge where Harvard University's **Hasty Pudding Theatricals** are staged. Performances have been presented in Bermuda during College Weeks (in Mar and Apr) since the 1960s. They're staged at the City Hall Theatre on Church Street in the City of Hamilton; call the box office at the Visitors Service Bureau (see above) for tickets, which cost about $25 each.

Appendix:
Bermuda in Depth

Welcome to an island of no pollution, no billboards, no graffiti, no litter, no rental cars, no unemployment (well, almost), no tolerance for drugs, no illiteracy (well, almost), and no nude or topless beaches. In a changing world, Bermuda remains . . . well, Bermuda.

If there's a sore point among Bermudians today, it's their extreme desire to separate themselves from the islands of the Caribbean, particularly from The Bahamas, in the eyes of the world. They often send angry letters to publishers of maps, reference sources and travel guides, insisting that Bermuda is not in the Caribbean. As one irate Bermudian put it, "You don't claim that Washington, D.C., is part of Dallas, Texas. They're the same distance apart that Bermuda is from the Caribbean."

Bermuda prides itself on its lack of economic, socioeconomic, and racial problems, many of which plague the Caribbean islands. Bermuda does not tolerate unsavory businesses. What the island would really like to be known for is its stellar performance in banking and multinational business.

During these first years of the millennium, international business is positioning itself to overtake tourism as Bermuda's primary source of revenue. With China's takeover of Hong Kong, Bermuda persuaded some of the biggest names in world business to create official domiciles on the island. The trend began in the 1970s, when some Hong Kong businesspeople formed low-profile shipping, trading, and investment companies in Bermuda—companies that became, in essence, corporate cash cows. That trend continues to positively affect Bermuda's economy.

When Britain surrendered Hong Kong to China in 1997, Bermuda became the largest British colony. A local businessman watched the televised ceremonies in which Britain handed over control, and gleefully remarked, "All we can say is: Thank you very much, Hong Kong, because here come the insurance companies and pension funds." By the end of the 20th century, nearly half of the companies listed on the Hong Kong Stock Exchange—and even some of the Chinese government's own holding companies—had established a legal presence in Bermuda, because Bermuda provided such hefty tax breaks. Amazingly, tiny Bermuda has emerged as the biggest and most prosperous of all of Britain's colonies, the bulk of which are now in the Caribbean.

In the early years of the 21st century, Bermuda continued to attract a growing number of American companies who are incorporating in Bermuda to lower their taxes without ever giving up the benefits of doing business in the United States. Insurance companies have led the way, but now manufacturers and other kinds of companies are following. It's been heralded in the press as "profits over patriotism." Becoming a Bermuda company is a paper transaction that can save millions annually.

And as aggressively as Bermuda is pursuing business, it's also more aware than ever of its fragile environment. There aren't too many Al Gores on the scene, but attention is being paid. Bermuda's population density is the third highest in the world, after Hong Kong and Monaco. Because the number of annual visitors is 10 times higher than the population, Bermuda has had to take strong initiatives to protect its environment and natural resources. Environmental protection takes the form of stiff anti-litter laws, annual garbage clean-up campaigns, automobile restrictions, cedar replanting (a blight in the '40s and '50s wiped out the native trees), lead-free gasoline, a strict fishing policy, and other measures.

Along the shaky road to self-government, Bermuda had some ugly racial conflicts. Riots in 1968 built up to the assassination of the British governor in 1973. But that was a long time ago; today, Bermuda has the most harmonious race relations in this part of the world, far better than those in the United States, the Caribbean, or The Bahamas. There's still a long way to go, but Bermudians of African descent have assumed important political, administrative, and managerial posts in every aspect of the local economy. Bermuda hasn't quite reached the point where the color of your skin is unimportant, but it has made more significant advancement toward that goal than its neighbors to the south.

In the early 21st century, Bermuda's average household income rose to a healthy $68,500—contrast that to some of the less fortunate islands in the south, many of which don't even have the budgets to compile such statistics. Compared to Puerto Rico, Jamaica, and certainly Haiti, no one is really poor in Bermuda. On the downside, home prices in Bermuda are at least three times the median cost of a house in the United States or Canada.

As a tourist destination, Bermuda has impeccable credentials. It was a resort long before Florida, Hawaii, Mexico, and many other places. Over the years, it has successfully exploited its position in the northwest Atlantic between North America and Europe. It is even working to throw off its image as a staid resort, hoping to project a lively, more "with-it" atmosphere (although it has a long way to go in that department). The United States remains its largest market—about 86% of visitors are Americans—but in recent years more and more visitors from Europe, the Far East, and the Near East have been seen dining, drinking, and shopping in the City of Hamilton.

1 The Natural World: An Environmental Guide to Bermuda

Lying 918km (570 miles) east-southeast of Cape Hatteras, North Carolina, Bermuda is actually a group of some 300 islands, islets, and coral rocks clustered in a fishhook-shaped chain about 35km (22 miles) long and 3km (2 miles) wide at its broadest point. The archipelago, formally known as "The Bermudas," forms a landmass of about 54 sq. km (21 sq. miles).

Only 20 or so of the islands are inhabited. The largest one, called the "mainland," is Great Bermuda; about 23km (14 miles) long, it's linked to nearby major islands by a series of bridges and causeways. Bermuda's capital, the City of Hamilton, is on Great Bermuda.

The other main inhabited islands include Somerset, Watford, Boaz, and Ireland in the west, and St. George's and St. David's in the east. This chain of major islands encloses the archipelago's major bodies of water, which include Castle Harbour, St. George's Harbour, Harrington Sound, and Great Sound. Most of the other smaller islands, or islets, lie within these bodies of water.

Bermuda is far north of the Tropic of Cancer, which cuts through the Bahamian archipelago. Bermuda's archipelago is based on the upper parts of an extinct volcano, which may date from 100 million years ago. Through the millennia, wind and water brought limestone deposits and formed these islands far from any continental landmass. Today, the closest continental landmass is the coast of the Carolinas. Bermuda is about 1,250km (775 miles) southeast of New York City, some 1,660km (1,030 miles) northeast of Miami, and nearly 5,555km (3,450 miles) from London. It has a balmy climate year-round, with sunshine prevailing almost every day. The chief source of Bermuda's mild weather is the Gulf Stream, a broad belt of warm water formed by equatorial currents. The stream's northern reaches separate the Bermuda islands from North America and, with the prevailing northeast winds, temper the wintry blasts that sweep across the Atlantic from west and north. The islands of Bermuda are divided, for administrative purposes, into parishes. (See "Orienting Yourself: The Lay of the Land," in chapter 3, "Getting to Know Bermuda.")

MORE THAN ONIONS: THE ISLAND'S FLORA

Bermuda's temperate climate, abundant sunshine, fertile soil, and adequate moisture account for the exceptionally verdant gardens that you'll find on the archipelago. Some of the best gardens, such as the Botanical Gardens in Paget Parish, are open to the public. Bermudian gardeners pride themselves on their mixtures of temperate-zone and subtropical plants, both of which thrive on the island, despite the salty air.

Bermuda is blessed with copious and varied flora. Examples include the indigenous sea grape, which flourishes along the island's sandy coasts (it prefers sand and saltwater to more arable soil), and the cassava plant, whose roots resemble the tubers of sweet potatoes. When ground into flour and soaked to remove a mild poison, the cassava root is the main ingredient for Bermuda's traditional Christmas pies. Also growing wild and abundant are prickly pears, aromatic fennel, yucca, and the Spanish bayonet, a spiked-leaf plant that bears a single white flower in season.

Bermuda's only native palm, the palmetto, proved particularly useful to the early settlers. Its leaves were used to thatch roofs, and when crushed and fermented, the palm fronds produced a strong alcoholic drink called bibby, whose effects the early Puritans condemned. Palmetto leaves were also fashioned into women's hats during a brief period in the 1600s, when they represented the height of fashion in London.

The banana, one of Bermuda's most dependable sources of fresh fruit, was introduced to the island in the early 1600s. It is believed that Bermudian bananas were the first to be brought back to London from the New World. They created an immediate sensation, leading to the cultivation of bananas in many other British colonies.

The plant that contributed most to Bermuda's renown was the Bermuda onion *(Allium cepa)*. Imported from England in 1616, it was grown from seeds brought from the Spanish and Portuguese islands of Tenerife and Madeira. The Bermuda onion became so famous along the East Coast of the United States that Bermudians themselves became known as "Onions." During the 1930s, Bermuda's flourishing export trade in onions declined due to high tariffs, increased competition from similar species grown in Texas and elsewhere, and the limited arable land on the island.

Today, you'll see oleander, hibiscus, royal poinciana, poinsettia, bougainvillea, and dozens of other flowering shrubs and vines decorating Bermuda's gently rolling land. Of the island's dozen or so species of morning glory, three are indigenous; they tend to grow rampant and overwhelm everything else in a garden.

CLOSE ENCOUNTERS WITH THE LOCAL FAUNA
AMPHIBIANS

Because of the almost total lack of natural freshwater ponds and lakes, Bermuda's amphibians have adapted to seawater or slightly brackish water. Amphibians include the tree frog *(Eleutherodactylus johnstonei* and *Eleuthero-dactylus gossei),* whose nighttime chirping newcomers sometimes mistake for the song of birds. Small and camouflaged by the leafy matter of the forest floor, the tree frog appears between April and November.

More visible are Bermuda's giant toads, or road toads *(Bufo marinus),* which sometimes reach the size of an adult human's palm. Imported from Guyana in the 1870s in hopes of controlling the island's cockroach population, giant toads search out the nighttime warmth of the asphalt roads—and are often crushed by cars in the process. They are especially prevalent after a soaking rain. The road toads are not venomous and, contrary to legend, do not cause warts.

Island reptiles include colonies of harmless lizards, often seen sunning themselves on rocks until approaching humans or predators scare them away. The best-known species is the Bermuda rock lizard *(Eumeces longirostris),* also known as a skink. It's said to have been the only non-marine, non-flying vertebrate on Bermuda before the arrival of European colonists. Imported reptiles include the Somerset lizard *(Anolis roquet),* whose black eye patches give it the look of a bashful bandit, and the Jamaican anole *(Anolis grahami),* a kind of chameleon.

BIRD LIFE

Partly because of its ample food sources, Bermuda has a large bird population; many species nest on the island during their annual migrations. Most of the birds arrive during the cooler winter months, usually between Christmas and Easter. Birders have recorded almost 40 different species of eastern warblers, which peacefully coexist with species of martins, doves, egrets, South American terns, herons, fork-tailed flycatchers, and even some species from as far away as the Arctic Circle.

Two of the most visible imported species are the cardinal, introduced during the 1700s, and the kiskadee. Imported from Trinidad in 1957 to control lizards and flies, the kiskadee has instead wreaked havoc on the island's commercial fruit crops.

The once prevalent eastern bluebird has been greatly reduced in number since its preferred habitat, cedar trees, were depleted by blight. Another bird native to Bermuda is the gray-and-white petrel, known locally as a cahow, which burrows for most of the year in the sands of the isolated eastern islands. During the rest of the year, the cahow feeds at sea, floating for hours in the warm waters of the Gulf Stream. One of the most elusive birds in the world—it was once thought to be extinct—the petrel is now protected by the Bermudian government.

Also native to Bermuda is the cliff-dwelling tropic bird, which you can identify by the elongated plumage of its white tail. The bird resembles a swallow and is the island's harbinger of spring, appearing annually in March.

Although the gardens and golf courses of many of the island's hotels attract dozens of birds, some of the finest bird-watching sites are maintained by the Bermuda Audubon Society or the National Trust. Isolated sites known for sheltering thousands of native and migrati ng birds include Paget Marsh, just south of the City of Hamilton, the Walsingham Trust in Hamilton Parish, and Spittal Pond in Smith's Parish.

SEA LIFE

In the deep waters off the shores of Bermuda, some of the finest game fish in the world, including blackfin tuna, marlin, swordfish, wahoo, dolphin, sailfish, and barracuda, fin their way through the sea. Also prevalent are bonefish and pompano, both of which prefer sun-flooded shallow waters closer to shore. Any beachcomber is likely to come across hundreds of oval-shaped chitons *(Chiton tuberculatus)*, a mollusk that adheres tenaciously to rocks in tidal flats; locally, it is known as "suck-rock."

Beware of the Portuguese man-of-war *(Physalia physalis)*, a floating colony of jellyfish whose stinging tentacles sometimes reach 15m (50 ft.) in length. Give this dangerous and venomous marine creature a wide berth: Severe stings may require hospitalization. Avoid the creature when it washes up on Bermuda beaches, usually between March and July—the man-of-war can sting even when it appears to be dead.

The most prevalent marine animal in Bermuda is responsible for the formation of the island's greatest tourist attraction—its kilometers of pale pink sand. Much of the sand consists of broken shells, pieces of coral, and the calcium carbonate remains of other marine invertebrates. The pinkest pieces are shards of crushed shell from a single-celled animal called foraminifer. Its vivid pink skeleton is pierced with holes, through which the animal extends its rootlike feet *(pseudopodia)*, which cling to the underside of the island's reefs during the animal's brief life, before its skeleton is washed ashore.

2 Life in the Onion Patch

GETTING TO KNOW THE "ONIONS"

Even though Bermuda isn't in the onion business the way it used to be, a born and bred islander is still called an "Onion." The term dates from the early 20th century, when the export of Bermuda onions and Easter lilies to the U.S. mainland were the island's major sources of income.

The "Onions"—a term that still carries a badge of pride—have their own lifestyle and even their own vocabulary. For example, "Aunt Haggie's children" are frustrating, stupid people; "married by 10 parsons" is a reference to a woman with huge breasts; "backin' up" means gay. You don't vomit in Bermuda, you

---

Fun Fact **Bermuda Shorts: Not Too Far Above the Knee**

Most Bermudians consider the winter months too cold for Bermuda shorts; but by May, just about every businessman along Front Street has traded in his trousers for a pair. Bermuda shorts weren't initially Bermudian; they originated when the British army was sent to India. Later, when British troops were stationed in Bermuda, they were issued the shorts as part of the military's tropical kit gear.

By the 1920s and 1930s, the shorts had become quite fashionable, although they were not considered acceptable at dinner parties or at church. Now suitable attire for businessmen, the shorts are worn with a blazer, collared shirt, tie, and knee socks. They shouldn't be more than 3 inches above the knee, and they must have a 3-inch hem.

"Go Europe." "Cockroach killers" (a term you may also hear in the American Southwest) are pointy-toed shoes. Although you'll rarely see it on local menus, the bream fish is called a "shit-bubbler."

Residents of more troubled islands to the south often look with envy upon the "Onions," who have a much higher standard of living than Caribbean islanders do; they also pay no personal income tax and suffer from only a 7% unemployment rate. The literacy rate is high: An estimated 99% of females age 15 and older can read and write, as can 98% of all Bermudian males.

Today's 61,000 residents are mostly of African, British, and Portuguese descent. Bermuda's population density, one of the highest in the world, is about 3,210 per 2.5 sq. km (1 sq. mile). The population is about 61% black, 39% white. Many ethnic minority groups are represented, the largest and most established being the Portuguese; the majority of inhabitants, however, are islanders from the Caribbean or The Bahamas. Some Bermudians can even trace their ancestry back to the island's first settlers, and some to successful privateers and freed slaves.

Britain's influence in Bermuda is obvious in the predominantly English accents, police who wear helmets like those of London bobbies, and cars that drive on the left. Schools are run along the lines of the British system and provide a high standard of preparatory education. Children 5 to 16 years of age must attend school. The Bermuda College, which offers academic and technical studies, boasts a renowned hotel and catering program.

WHO'S MINDING THE STORE?

In essence, Bermuda is a self-governing dependency of Britain, which protects its security and stability. The governor, appointed by the Queen, represents Her Majesty in the areas of external affairs, defense, and internal security.

By choosing to remain a British dependency, Bermuda rejected the trail that many former colonies in the Caribbean (including Antigua) blazed by declaring their independence. Although they remain under the protection of the British, Bermudians manage their own day-to-day affairs. And ever since the people of Bermuda were granted the right to govern themselves in 1968, they have done so admirably well.

Bermuda has a 12-member cabinet headed by a premier. The elected legislature, referred to as the Legislative Council, consists of a 40-member House of Assembly and an 11-member Senate. Bermuda's oldest political party is the Progressive Labour Party, formed in 1963. In 1964, the United Bermuda Party was established; it stayed in power until it was toppled by the Progressive Labour Party in 1998.

Bermuda's legal system is founded on common law. Judicial responsibility falls to the Supreme Court, headed by a chief justice in a powdered wig and a robe. English law is the fundamental guide, and in court, English customs prevail.

The island consists of nine parishes, each managed by an advisory council. The capital, the City of Hamilton, is in Pembroke Parish. (For details on the individual parishes, see "Orienting Yourself: The Lay of the Land," in chapter 3, "Getting to Know Bermuda.")

TOURIST DOLLARS & NO INCOME TAX

Bermuda's political stability has proved beneficial to the economy, which relies heavily on tourism and foreign investment.

For much of the island's early history, the major industry was shipbuilding, made possible by the abundant cedar forests. In the second half of the 19th century, when wooden ships gave way to steel ones, the island turned to tourism. Today, tourism is the country's leading industry, with annual revenues estimated at $450 million. Approximately 550,000 visitors come to Bermuda each year; an estimated 86% arrive from the United States, 4% from Britain, and 7% from Canada. Bermuda enjoys a 42% repeat-visitor rate.

Because Bermuda has enacted favorable economic measures, more than 6,000 international companies are registered there. The companies engage mostly in investment holding, insurance, commercial trading, consulting services, and shipping—but fewer than 275 companies are actually on the island. The reason for this curious situation? Bermuda has no corporate or income tax, so companies register their businesses on Bermuda, and then live in their home countries, thereby avoiding taxes that their home country would otherwise deduct.

The island's leading exports are pharmaceuticals, concentrates (primarily black rum and sherry peppers), essences, and beverages. Leading imports include foodstuffs, alcoholic beverages, clothing, furniture, fuel, electrical appliances, and motor vehicles. Bermuda's major trading partners are the United States, Great Britain, Canada, the Netherlands, and the Caribbean states.

3 History 101

THE EARLY YEARS

The discovery of The Bermudas is attributed to the Spanish—probably the navigator Juan Bermúdez—sometime before 1511, because in that year a map published in the *Legatio Babylonica* included "La Bermuda" among the Atlantic islands. A little over a century later, the English staked a claim to Bermuda and began colonization.

In 1609, the flagship of Admiral Sir George Somers, the **Sea Venture,** was wrecked on Bermuda's reefs while en route to the colony at Jamestown, Virginia. The dauntless crew built two *pinnaces* (small sailing ships) and headed on to the American colony, but three sailors hid out and remained on the island. They were Bermuda's first European settlers. Just 3 years later, the Bermuda islands were included in the charter of the Virginia Company, and 60 colonists were sent there from England. St. George Town was founded soon after.

Bermuda's status as a colony dates from 1620, when the first parliament convened. Bermuda's is the oldest parliament in continuous existence in

Dateline

- **ca. 1503** Juan Bermúdez discovers Bermuda while sailing aboard the Spanish ship *La Garza.*
- **1609** The British ship *Sea Venture* is wrecked on the reefs of Bermuda; all on board make it to shore safely and the settlement of Bermuda begins.
- **1612** The Virginia Company dispatches the *Plough* to Bermuda with 60 colonists on board. Richard Moore is appointed governor of Bermuda.
- **1620** The first Bermuda parliament session is held in St. Peter's Church, St. George.
- **1684** The British Crown takes over the Bermuda Company's charter. Sir Robert Robinson is appointed the Crown's first governor of Bermuda.
- **1775** Gunpowder is stolen in St. George and shipped to the American colonies for use against the British.
- **1861** Bermuda becomes involved in the American Civil War when it runs supplies to the South to undermine the Union's blockade.
- **1919–33** Bermudians profit from Prohibition in the United States by engaging in rumrunning.
- **1940–45** Bermuda plays an important role in World War II counterespionage for the Allies.

the British Commonwealth. In 1684, Bermuda became a British Crown Colony under King Charles II and Sir Robert Robinson was appointed the colony's first governor.

Slavery became a part of life in Bermuda shortly after the official settlement. Although the majority of slaves came from Africa, a few were Native Americans. Later, Scots imprisoned for fighting against Cromwell were sent to the islands, followed in 1651 by Irish slaves. This servitude, however, was not as lengthy as that of plantation slaves in America and the West Indies. The British Emancipation Act of 1834 freed all slaves.

RELATIONS WITH AMERICA

Early on, Bermuda established close links with the American colonies. The islanders set up a thriving mercantile trade on the Eastern Seaboard, especially with southern ports. The major commodity sold by Bermuda's merchant ships was salt from Turks Island.

During the American Revolution, the rebellious colonies cut off trade with Loyalist Bermuda, despite the network of family connections and close friendships that bound them. The cutoff in trade proved a great hardship for the islanders, who, having chosen seafaring over farming, depended heavily on America for their

- 1946 The automobile is introduced on Bermuda.
- 1957 Great Britain withdraws militarily after 2 centuries of rule.
- 1963 Voter registration is open to all citizens.
- 1968 Bermudians are granted a new constitution that, while protecting them under the umbrella of the British Commonwealth, allows them to govern themselves.
- 1973 The governor, Sir Richard Sharples, and an aide are assassinated.
- 1979 Bermudians celebrate as their own Gina Swainson wins the Miss World contest.
- 1987 Hurricane Emily causes millions of dollars' worth of damage; some 70 people are injured.
- 1990 Prime Minister Margaret Thatcher confers with President George Bush in Bermuda.
- 1991 Prime Minister John Major meets with President Bush in Bermuda.
- 1995 Bermudians vote to maintain traditional ties with Britain.
- 1997 Pamela Gordon, 41, becomes the island's first female prime minister.
- 1998 The Labour Party sweeps into power with another female prime minister.
- 2000 It's announced that 75% of U.S. Fortune 500 companies make Bermuda their home port.
- 2003 Bermuda launches its quincentennial celebrations.

food. Many of them, now deprived of profitable trade routes, turned to privateering, piracy, and "wrecking" (salvaging goods from wrecked or foundered ships).

Britain's loss of its important American colonial ports led to a naval buildup in Bermuda. Ships and troops sailed from Bermuda in 1814 to burn Washington, D.C. and the White House during the War of 1812.

Bermuda got a new lease on economic life during the American Civil War. The island was sympathetic to the Confederacy. With the approval of the British government, Bermuda ran the blockade that the Union had placed on exports, especially of cotton, by the Southern states. St. George's Harbour was a principal Atlantic base for the lucrative business of smuggling manufactured goods into Confederate ports and bringing out cargoes of cotton and turpentine.

When the Confederacy fell, so did Bermuda's economy. Seeing no immediate source of income from trading with the Eastern states, the islanders turned their attention to agriculture and found that the colony's fertile soil and salubrious climate produced excellent vegetables. Portuguese immigrants arrived to farm the land, and soon celery, potatoes, tomatoes, and especially onions were being shipped to the New York market. So brisk was the onion trade that the City of Hamilton became known as "Onion Town."

During Prohibition, Bermudians again profited from the situation in the United States—they engaged in the lucrative business of rumrunning (smuggling alcohol to the States). The distance from the island to the East Coast was too great for quick crossings in small booze-laden boats, which worked well from The Bahamas and Cuba. Nevertheless, Bermuda accounted for a good part of the alcoholic beverages transported illegally to the United States before the repeal of Prohibition in 1933.

A HOTBED OF ESPIONAGE

Bermuda played a key role in World War II counterespionage for the Allies. The story of the "secret war" with Nazi Germany is told dramatically in William Stevenson's *A Man Called Intrepid.*

Beneath the Hamilton Princess Hotel, a carefully trained staff worked to decode radio signals to and from German submarines and other vessels operating in the Atlantic, close to the United States and the islands offshore. Unknown to the Germans, the British, early in the war, had broken the Nazi code using a captured German coding machine called "Enigma." The British also intercepted and examined mail between Europe and the United States.

Bermuda served as a refueling stop for airplanes flying between the two continents. While pilots were being entertained at the Yacht Club, the mail would be taken off the carriers and examined by experts. An innocent-looking series of letters from Lisbon, for example, contained messages written in invisible ink. The letters were part of a vast German spy network. The British became skilled at opening sealed envelopes, examining their written contents, and carefully resealing them.

The surreptitious letter-readers were called "trappers." Many of them were young women without any previous experience in counterespionage work, yet a number of them performed very well. As Stevenson wrote, it was soon discovered that "by some quirk in the law of averages, the girls who shone in this work had well-turned ankles." A medical officer involved with the project reported it as "fairly certain that a girl with unshapely legs would make a bad trapper." So, amazingly, the word went out that women seeking recruitment as trappers would have to display their gams.

During the course of their work, the trappers discovered one of the methods by which the Germans were transmitting secret messages: They would shrink a whole page of regularly typed text to the size of a tiny dot, then conceal the dot under an innocuous-looking punctuation mark! The staff likened these messages, with their secret-bearing dots, to the English dessert plum duff, for these "punctuation dots [were] scattered through a letter like raisins in the suet puddings." The term "duff method" came to be applied to the method that the Germans used to send military and other messages through the mail.

When the United States entered the war, FBI agents joined the British in their intelligence operations in Bermuda.

BERMUDA COMES INTO ITS OWN

In 1953, British prime minister Winston Churchill chose Bermuda, which he had visited during the war, as the site for a conference with U.S. Pres. Dwight D. Eisenhower and the French premier. Several such high-level gatherings have followed in the decades since; the most recent one, between former British prime minister John Major and former U.S. Pres. George Bush, took place in 1991.

Bermuda's increasing prominence led to changes in its relations with Great Britain and the United States, as well as significant developments on the island itself. In 1957, after nearly 2 centuries of occupation, Britain withdrew its military forces, and decided to grant self-government to its oldest colony. Under the Lend-Lease Agreement signed in 1941, the United States continues to maintain a naval air station at Kindley Field, in St. George Parish. The agreement is due to expire in 2040.

As Bermudians assumed greater control over their own affairs, they began to adopt significant social changes, but at a pace that did not satisfy some critics. Although racial segregation in hotels and restaurants ceased in 1959, schools were not integrated until 1971. Women received the right to vote in 1944, but the law still restricted suffrage to property holders only. That restriction was rescinded in 1963, when voter registration was opened to all citizens.

On the rocky road to self-government, Bermuda was not without its share of problems. Serious rioting broke out in 1968, and British troops were called back to restore order. Then, in 1973, Sir Richard Sharples, then governor, was assassinated; in 1977, those believed to have been the assassins were executed.

These events, which occurred at a time when several of the islands in the region and in the Caribbean were experiencing domestic difficulties, proved to be the exception rather than the rule. In the years since, the social and political climate in Bermuda has been markedly calm—all the better for the island's economic well-being, because it encourages the industries on which Bermuda depends, including tourism.

In 1972, the Bermuda dollar gained its independence from the pound sterling; it's now pegged through gold to the U.S. dollar on an equal dollar-for-dollar basis.

During the 1990s, the political status of the island again became a hot topic among Bermudians. Some people felt it would be advantageous to achieve complete independence from Britain, whereas others believed it was in Bermuda's best interest to maintain its ties to the Crown. In 1995, the majority of voters in an independent referendum rejected a proposal to sever ties with Great Britain, preferring to maintain their status with Great Britain.

In 1997, the governing party of Bermuda, the United Bermuda Party, chose the daughter of a well-known civil rights leader as its prime minister. Pamela Gordon, former environment minister, was named to the post at the age of 41, the youngest leader in the island nation's 400-year history and the first woman to be prime minister. David Saul, the reigning prime minister, resigned in favor of this younger and more popular leader. In her first months in office, Ms. Gordon, a relative political newcomer, pledged to bridge differences between Bermuda's majority black population and its white business elite.

In that stated goal, at least based on election returns, she did not succeed. In November 1998, the Progressive Labour Party, supported by many of Bermuda's blacks, ended 30 years of conservative rule by sweeping its first victory in general elections. Although Ms. Gordon is black, as was most of her cabinet, many locals saw her party as "part of the white establishment."

The Labour Party's leader, Jennifer Smith, became the new prime minister, claiming Bermuda's residents had met their "date with destiny." The Labour

Party has moved more from the left to the center in recent years, and Ms. Smith has sought to reassure the island's white-led business community that it will be "business as usual" with her in power. The Labour Party made the economy an issue in the campaign, promising higher wages and better benefits to workers, even though Bermuda residents enjoy one of the highest standards of living in the world.

In the 21st century, Bermuda faces many problems, including what many see as a declining quality of life. There are environmental concerns—notably over-fishing and damage to precious reefs. Traffic jams are now common in spite of the ban against visitors renting automobiles. Affordable housing becomes scarcer year by year. Nonetheless, the more unfortunate islands to the south still envy Bermuda's standard of living.

As more and more cruise lines launch megaliners, Bermuda is also concerned that its tight harbors will not be able to handle the traffic.

Although Bermuda and tourism seemed linked like a horse and carriage, the Bermuda-shorts-wearers' businesses dominated the focus at the turn of the new century when it was announced that 75% of U.S. Fortune 500 companies had made Bermuda their home base.

In 2003, Bermuda honored its past as the island nation commemorated the 500th anniversary of Bermuda's first sighting by Spanish explorer Juan Bermúdez in 1503.

4 Bermuda Style at Its Best—Island Architecture

Today, Bermuda's unique style is best represented by its architecture: primarily, those darling little pink cottages that grace postcards. The architecture of the island—a mélange of idiosyncratic building techniques dictated by climate and the types of building materials available—is the archipelago's only truly indigenous art form.

Bermuda's early settlers quickly recognized the virtues of the island's most visible building material, coral stone. A conglomerate of primeval sand packed with crushed bits of coral and shells, this stone has been quarried for generations on Bermuda. Cut into oblong building blocks, it is strong yet porous. However, it would be unusable in any area where the climate has cycles of freezing and thawing, because it would crack. Mortared together with imported cement, the blocks provide solid and durable foundations and walls.

Bermuda's colonial architects ingeniously found a way to deal with a serious problem on the island: the lack of an abundant supply of fresh water. During the construction of a house or any other sort of building, workers excavated a water tank, or cistern, first. The cistern was created either as a separate underground cavity away from the house or as a foundation for the building. These cisterns served to collect rainwater funneled from rooftops via specially designed channels and gutters. The design of these roof-to-cellar water conduits led to the development of what is Bermuda's most distinct architectural feature, the gleaming rooftops of its houses. Gently sloping, and invariably painted a dazzling white, they are constructed of quarried limestone slabs sawed into "slates" about an inch thick and between 12 and 18 inches square. Roofs are installed over a framework of cedarwood beams (or, more recently, pitch pine or pressure-treated wood beams), which are interconnected with a series of cedar laths. The slates are joined together with cement-based mortar in overlapping rows, then covered with a cement wash and one or several coats of whitewash or synthetic paint. This process corrects the porosity of the coral limestone slates, rendering them watertight. The result is a layered effect, since each panel of limestone appears in high relief atop its neighbor. The angular, step-shaped geometry of Bermudian roofs has inspired watercolorists and painters to emphasize the rhythmically graceful shadows that trace the path of the sun across the rooflines.

Unlike those in the Caribbean, Bermudian houses are designed without amply proportioned hanging eaves. Large eaves may be desirable because of the shade they afford, but smaller ones have proved to be structurally sounder during tropical storms. The interiors of Bermudian houses are usually graced with large windows and doors, and, in the older buildings, floors and moldings crafted from copper-colored planks of the almost extinct Bermuda cedar. Also common is a feature found in colonial buildings in the Caribbean and other western Atlantic islands as well: tray ceilings, so named because of their resemblance to an inverted serving tray. This shape allows ceilings to follow the lines of the inside roof construction into what would otherwise be unused space. The effect of these ceilings, whether sheathed in plaster or planking, gives Bermudian interiors unusual height and airiness.

Despite the distinctively individualistic nature of Bermuda's architecture, decor remains faithfully—some say rigidly—British, and somewhat more formal than you might expect. Interior designs seem to be a felicitous cross between what you'd expect in a New England seaside cottage, and how a nautically minded society hostess would accent her drawing room in London. Bermuda homes usually have lots of Chippendale or Queen Anne furniture (sometimes authentic, sometimes reproduction). Decorators love to include, whenever possible, any piece of antique furniture crafted from almost-extinct copper-colored Bermuda cedar. Combine these features with the open windows, gentle climate, and carefully tended gardens of the fertile, mid-Atlantic setting, and the result is some very charming and soothing interiors.

No discussion of Bermudian architecture should neglect to mention a garden feature that many visitors consider unique to Bermuda: the moon gate. A rounded span of coral blocks arranged in a circular arch above a wooden gate, the moon gate was introduced to Bermuda around 1920 by the Duke of Westminster's landscape architect, who got his inspiration from such gates in China and Japan.

5 The Rhythms of Bermuda

Modern Bermudian music, which you hear today mainly in hotel lounges, is a blend of traditional Bermudian music with sounds from Jamaica, Trinidad, and Puerto Rico, as well as the United States and Britain. However, these aren't the sounds you'll predominantly hear: As elsewhere, American and British rock, modified by local rhythms, has proved the strongest and most lasting influence.

Visitors are often pleased to discover that the island's best-known singers and musicians, many of whom are discussed below, can be heard at many of the hotels and nightclubs. Inquire as to which local artist is performing during the cocktail hour at your hotel; chances are it may be one of the most popular.

GOMBEY DANCING

Despite new pop forms, Bermuda is proud of its original musical idioms. Gombey dancing is the island's premier folk art. Gombey combines West Africa's tribal heritage with the Native American and British colonial influences of the New World. Gombey dancers are almost always male; in accordance with tradition, men pass on the rhythms and dance techniques from generation to generation in their family. Dancers outfit themselves in masquerade costumes, whose outlandish lines and glittering colors evoke the brilliant plumage of tropical birds.

Gombey (spelled goombay in some other places, such as The Bahamas) signifies a specific type of African drum, as well as the Bantu word for "rhythm." These rhythms escalate into an ever faster and more hypnotic beat as the movements of the dancers become increasingly uninhibited, and the response of the spectators grows ever more fervent. The most strenuous dances are usually performed during the Christmas season.

Although gombey dancing, with its local rituals and ceremonies, can be seen as one of Bermuda's major cultural contributions, it's not unique to the island. Variations are found elsewhere in the western Atlantic, as well as in the Caribbean. Indeed, during its development, Bermuda's gombey dancing was significantly influenced by some of these other versions. In colonial times, for example, when African Caribbeans were brought to Bermuda as slaves or convicts to help build the British military installations on the island, they carried with them their own gombey traditions, which eventually combined with those that had already taken root in Bermuda. What's unique about the Bermudian version of gombey, however, is its use of the British snare drum, played with wooden sticks, as an accompaniment to the dancing.

A handful of gombey recordings are available, enabling you to hear the sounds of this African-based music, with its rhythmic chanting and rapid drumbeat. Among the recordings, the album Strictly Gombey Music (Edmar 1165), performed by four members of the Pickles Spencer Gombey Group, offers a good selection of gombey dances.

Aficionados of this art form, however, will argue that gombey's allure lies not so much in the music as in the feverish—almost trancelike—dancing that accompanies it, as well as in the colorful costumes of the dancers. For that reason, they say, audio recordings can't convey the full mesmerizing power of a gombey dance the way a videotape can. So, while you're in Bermuda, consider taping a gombey dance to show when you get back home, and perhaps remind yourself of some of the enchanting sounds and sights of the island.

Regrettably, there's no one place in Bermuda where you can always see gombey. Your best bet is to inquire at your hotel to see what events and performances might be staged during your visit. Sometimes hotels present gombey shows but follow no rigidly announced schedule.

THE BALLADEER TRADITION

Bermuda also has a strong balladeer tradition. Although its exponents are fewer than they used to be, local balladeers continue to enjoy considerable popularity among islanders and visitors alike. A wry, self-deprecating humor has always distinguished their compositions, and balladeers can strum a song for any occasion on their guitars. Today, many of their songs have to do with Bermuda's changing way of life.

By virtually everyone's estimate, the musical patriarch of Bermuda was Hubert Smith, who was the island's official greeter in song. A balladeer of formidable talent and originality, Smith composed and performed songs for the visits of nearly all the foreign heads of state who graced Bermuda's shores in recent memory. His performances for members of the British royal family included one of the most famous songs ever written about the island, "Bermuda Is Another World." The song is now the island's unofficial national anthem; it's included in the best-selling album *Bermuda Is Another World* (Edmar 1025).

6 Island of the Sunday Painter

Art in Bermuda has never reached the status enjoyed by such islands as Haiti and Jamaica. A critic once wrote that "Bermuda is the perfect place for the Sunday painter." Some serious art, however, is displayed at such places as the Masterworks Foundation Gallery at Bermuda House in the City of Hamilton (see chapter 9, "Shopping"). Still, a great deal of Bermuda art is of the watercolor variety, with idyllic landscapes and seascapes sold at various shops around the island.

Bermuda's earliest works of art were portraits painted by itinerant artists for the local gentry. Most of these were by the English-born Joseph Blackburn, whose brief visit to Bermuda in the mid-1700s led to requests by local landowners to have their portraits painted. Many of these portraits can be found today in the Tucker House Museum in St. George's. A handful of portraits from the same period were done by the American-born artist John Green. Also prized are a series of paintings from the mid–19th century depicting sailing ships; they're signed "Edward James," but the artist's real identity remains unknown.

During the 19th century, the traditions of the English landscape painters, particularly the Romantics, came into vogue in Bermuda. Constable, with his lush and evocative landscapes, became the model for many. Other than a few amateur artists, however, whose works showed great vitality but little sense of perspective, most of Bermuda's landscape paintings were executed by British military officers and their wives. Their body of work includes a blend of true-to-life landscapes with an occasional stylized rendering of the picturesque or Romantic tradition then in vogue in England. Among the most famous of the uniformed artists was Lt. E. G. Hallewell, a member of the Royal Engineers, whose illustrations of the island's topography were used for planning certain naval installations.

Another celebrated landscapist was Thomas Driver, who arrived as a member of the Royal Engineers in 1814 and remained on the island until 1836. Trained to reproduce detailed landscape observations as a means of assisting military and naval strategists, he later modified his style to become more elegant and evocative. He soon abandoned the military and became a full-time painter of Bermuda scenes. Because of Driver's attention to detail, his works are frequently reproduced by scholars and art historians, who hope to recapture the aesthetic and architectural elements of the island's earliest buildings.

Later in the 19th century, other artists depicted the flora of Bermuda. Lady Lefroy, whose husband was governor of the island between 1871 and 1877, painted the trees, shrubs, fish, flowers, and animals of the island in much detail. Later, at scattered intervals during their careers, such internationally known artists as Winslow Homer, Andrew Wyeth, George Ault, and French-born Impressionist and cubist Albert Gleizes all painted Bermudian scenes.

Today, Bermuda has the greatest number of artists painting and creating than it has ever had in its history. Among prominent Bermuda-born artists was Alfred Birdsey, who died in 1996. His watercolors represented some of the most elegiac visual odes to Bermuda ever produced. Birdsey's paintings, as well as those of other artists mentioned above, are on display in galleries around the island.

Other local favorites include Eric Amos, known for his illustrations of wild birds of Bermuda, which are sought by collectors all over the world. Captain Stephen J. Card has developed an international reputation by specializing in marine art. Vivienne Gardner is known not just for her paintings but for her sculpture, stained glass, and mosaics as well. Christine Phillips-Watlington has achieved an international reputation for her botanical paintings.

Protecting art works from climate damage is a constant problem on the island. As the administrator of one major art gallery explained, "Bermuda's climate is unquestionably the worst in the world for the toll it takes on works of art, with three elements—humidity, salt, and ultraviolet light—all playing their part." Some very valuable Bermudian paintings have been totally destroyed. As a result, more and more galleries and exhibition rooms on the island have installed air-conditioning.

In addition to its painters, Bermuda also boasts several noted sculptors, including Chelsey Trott, who produces cedarwood carvings, and Desmond Hale Fountain, who creates works in bronze. Fountain's life-size statues often show children in the act of reading or snoozing in the shade.

7 Prospero, a Lovesick Poet & Other Bermudian Literary Legacies

Bermuda has long been a haven for writers. It has figured in many works of literature, beginning with Shakespeare's *The Tempest*. Shakespeare never visited the island himself, but was inspired to set his play here by accounts he had read or heard of the island.

The Irish poet Thomas Moore (1779–1852), who visited Bermuda for several months in 1804, was moved by its beauty to write:

> *Oh! could you view the scenery dear*
> *That now beneath my window lies.*

Moore left more memories—literary and romantic—than any other writer who came to Bermuda. He once stayed at Hill Crest Guest House (now Aunt Nea's Inn at Hillcrest) in St. George's (see chapter 4, "Where to Stay") and soon became enamored of Nea Tucker, the adolescent bride of one of the most prominent men in town. "Sweet Nea! Let us roam no more," he once wrote of his beloved.

It's said that the lovesick poet would gaze for hours upon Nea's veranda, hoping that she'd appear. One day a jealous Mr. Tucker could tolerate this no more and banished the poet from his property. Moore was chased down a street that now bears the name Nea's Alley—to commemorate his unrequited romance.

Today, one of the most popular restaurants in Bermuda is Tom Moore's Tavern (see chapter 5, "Where to Dine"). The building was once the home of Samuel Trott, who constructed it in the 17th century. Unlike Mr. Tucker, the descendants of Samuel Trott befriended Moore, who often visited the house. Moore immortalized the calabash tree on the Trott estate in his writing; he liked to sit under it and write his verse there.

Following in Moore's footsteps, many famous writers visited Bermuda in later years. None, however, have left their mark on the island like Tom Moore.

For Americans, it was Mark Twain who helped make Bermuda a popular tourist destination. He published his impressions in *Atlantic Monthly* in 1877

Fun Fact   Royalty Comes to "Shangri-La"

The Irish poet Tom Moore and the American humorist Mark Twain publicized the glories of Bermuda, but—for the British, at least—the woman who put Bermuda on the tourist map was Princess Louise. The daughter of Queen Victoria, she spent several months in Bermuda in 1883. Her husband was the governor-general of Canada, so she traveled to Bermuda to escape the fierce northern cold. Although Bermuda hosted many royal visitors in the 20th century, including Queen Elizabeth II, Princess Louise was the first royal personage to set foot in the colony. When she returned to Canada, she told reporters that she'd found the Shangri-La of tourist destinations.

---

through 1878, and in his first book, *The Innocents Abroad.* He became so enamored of the island that, as he wrote many years later to a correspondent, he would fain choose it over heaven.

After Twain, Eugene O'Neill came to Bermuda in 1924, and returned several more times, at least through 1927. While here, he worked on *The Great God Brown, Lazarus Laughed,* and *Strange Interlude.* O'Neill was convinced that cold weather adversely affected his ability to write. He thought that Bermuda would "cure" him of alcoholism. At first, O'Neill and his family rented cottages on what is now Coral Beach Club property. Later, O'Neill bought the house "Spithead," in Warwick. In 1927, however, his marriage ended, and O'Neill left his family—and Bermuda.

During the 1930s, several eminent writers made their way to Bermuda, in hopes of finding idyllic surroundings and perhaps a little inspiration: Sinclair Lewis, who spent all his time cycling around "this gorgeous island"; Hervey Allen, who wrote *Anthony Adverse,* his best-selling novel, at Felicity Hall in Somerset; and James Ramsey Ullman, who wrote *The White Tower* on the island. James Thurber also made several trips during this time.

In 1956, Noël Coward came with his longtime companion, Graham Payn, to escape "the monstrously unjust tax situation in England." He was not, he said, "really mad about the place," yet he purchased "Spithead" in Warwick (O'Neill's former home) and stayed some 2 years, working on *London Mornings,* his only ballet, and the musical *Sail Away.* "Spithead" is now privately owned.

Other well-known authors who visited Bermuda over the years include Rudyard Kipling, C. S. Forester, Hugh Walpole, Edna Ferber, Anita Loos, John O'Hara, E. B. White, and Philip Wylie.

Bermuda's own writers include William S. Zuill—a former director of the Bermuda National Trust who wrote *The Story of Bermuda and Her People,* an excellent historical account—and Nellie Musson, Frank Manning, Eva Hodgson, and Dale Butler, who have written about the lives of African Bermudians.

Index

See also Accommodations and Restaurant indexes, below.

Frommer's
Portable Guides
Complete Guides for the Short-Term Traveler

FROMMER'S® COMPLETE TRAVEL GUIDES

Alaska
Alaska Cruises & Ports of Call
Amsterdam
Argentina & Chile
Arizona
Atlanta
Australia
Austria
Bahamas
Barcelona, Madrid & Seville
Beijing
Belgium, Holland & Luxembourg
Bermuda
Boston
Brazil
British Columbia & the Canadian
  Rockies
Budapest & the Best of Hungary
California
Canada
Cancún, Cozumel & the Yucatán
Cape Cod, Nantucket & Martha's
  Vineyard
Caribbean
Caribbean Cruises & Ports of Call
Caribbean Ports of Call
Carolinas & Georgia
Chicago
China
Colorado
Costa Rica
Denmark
Denver, Boulder & Colorado
  Springs
England
Europe
European Cruises & Ports of Call
Florida

France
Germany
Great Britain
Greece
Greek Islands
Hawaii
Hong Kong
Honolulu, Waikiki & Oahu
Ireland
Israel
Italy
Jamaica
Japan
Las Vegas
London
Los Angeles
Maryland & Delaware
Maui
Mexico
Montana & Wyoming
Montréal & Québec City
Munich & the Bavarian Alps
Nashville & Memphis
Nepal
New England
New Mexico
New Orleans
New York City
New Zealand
Northern Italy
Nova Scotia, New Brunswick &
  Prince Edward Island
Oregon
Paris
Philadelphia & the Amish Country
Portugal
Prague & the Best of the Czech
  Republic

Provence & the Riviera
Puerto Rico
Rome
San Antonio & Austin
San Diego
San Francisco
Santa Fe, Taos & Albuquerque
Scandinavia
Scotland
Seattle & Portland
Shanghai
Singapore & Malaysia
South Africa
South America
South Florida
South Pacific
Southeast Asia
Spain
Sweden
Switzerland
Texas
Thailand
Tokyo
Toronto
Tuscany & Umbria
USA
Utah
Vancouver & Victoria
Vermont, New Hampshire &
  Maine
Vienna & the Danube Valley
Virgin Islands
Virginia
Walt Disney World® & Orlando
Washington, D.C.
Washington State

FROMMER'S® DOLLAR-A-DAY GUIDES

Australia from $50 a Day
California from $70 a Day
Caribbean from $70 a Day
England from $75 a Day
Europe from $70 a Day

Florida from $70 a Day
Hawaii from $80 a Day
Ireland from $60 a Day
Italy from $70 a Day
London from $85 a Day

New York from $90 a Day
Paris from $80 a Day
San Francisco from $70 a Day
Washington, D.C. from $80 a Day

FROMMER'S® PORTABLE GUIDES

Acapulco, Ixtapa & Zihuatanejo
Amsterdam
Aruba
Australia's Great Barrier Reef
Bahamas
Berlin
Big Island of Hawaii
Boston
California Wine Country
Cancún
Charleston & Savannah
Chicago
Disneyland®
Dublin
Florence

Frankfurt
Hong Kong
Houston
Las Vegas
London
Los Angeles
Los Cabos & Baja
Maine Coast
Maui
Miami
New Orleans
New York City
Paris
Phoenix & Scottsdale

Portland
Puerto Rico
Puerto Vallarta, Manzanillo &
  Guadalajara
Rio de Janeiro
San Diego
San Francisco
Seattle
Sydney
Tampa & St. Petersburg
Vancouver
Venice
Virgin Islands
Washington, D.C.

FROMMER'S® NATIONAL PARK GUIDES

Banff & Jasper
Family Vacations in the National
  Parks
Grand Canyon

National Parks of the American
  West
Rocky Mountain

Yellowstone & Grand Teton
Yosemite & Sequoia/ Kings Canyon
Zion & Bryce Canyon

FROMMER'S® MEMORABLE WALKS

Chicago	New York	San Francisco
London	Paris	Washington, D.C.

FROMMER'S® GREAT OUTDOOR GUIDES

Arizona & New Mexico	Northern California	Vermont & New Hampshire
New England	Southern New England	

SUZY GERSHMAN'S BORN TO SHOP GUIDES

Born to Shop: France	Born to Shop: Italy	Born to Shop: New York
Born to Shop: Hong Kong,	Born to Shop: London	Born to Shop: Paris
Shanghai & Beijing		

FROMMER'S® IRREVERENT GUIDES

Amsterdam	Los Angeles	San Francisco
Boston	Manhattan	Seattle & Portland
Chicago	New Orleans	Vancouver
Las Vegas	Paris	Walt Disney World®
London	Rome	Washington, D.C.

FROMMER'S® BEST-LOVED DRIVING TOURS

Britain	Germany	Northern Italy
California	Ireland	Scotland
Florida	Italy	Spain
France	New England	Tuscany & Umbria

HANGING OUT™ GUIDES

Hanging Out in England	Hanging Out in France	Hanging Out in Italy
Hanging Out in Europe	Hanging Out in Ireland	Hanging Out in Spain

THE UNOFFICIAL GUIDES®

Bed & Breakfasts and Country	Southwest & South Central	Mid-Atlantic with Kids
Inns in:	Plains	Mini Las Vegas
California	U.S.A.	Mini-Mickey
Great Lakes States	Beyond Disney	New England and New York with
Mid-Atlantic	Branson, Missouri	Kids
New England	California with Kids	New Orleans
Northwest	Chicago	New York City
Rockies	Cruises	Paris
Southeast	Disneyland®	San Francisco
Southwest	Florida with Kids	Skiing in the West
Best RV & Tent Campgrounds in:	Golf Vacations in the Eastern U.S.	Southeast with Kids
California & the West	Great Smoky & Blue Ridge Region	Walt Disney World®
Florida & the Southeast	Inside Disney	Walt Disney World® for Grown-ups
Great Lakes States	Hawaii	Walt Disney World® with Kids
Mid-Atlantic	Las Vegas	Washington, D.C.
Northeast	London	World's Best Diving Vacations
Northwest & Central Plains		

SPECIAL-INTEREST TITLES

Frommer's Adventure Guide to Australia & New Zealand	Frommer's Italy's Best Bed & Breakfasts and Country Inns
Frommer's Adventure Guide to Central America	Frommer's New York City with Kids
Frommer's Adventure Guide to India & Pakistan	Frommer's Ottawa with Kids
Frommer's Adventure Guide to South America	Frommer's Road Atlas Britain
Frommer's Adventure Guide to Southeast Asia	Frommer's Road Atlas Europe
Frommer's Adventure Guide to Southern Africa	Frommer's Road Atlas France
Frommer's Britain's Best Bed & Breakfasts and Country Inns	Frommer's Toronto with Kids
Frommer's Caribbean Hideaways	Frommer's Vancouver with Kids
Frommer's Exploring America by RV	Frommer's Washington, D.C., with Kids
Frommer's Fly Safe, Fly Smart	Israel Past & Present
Frommer's France's Best Bed & Breakfasts and Country Inns	The New York Times' Guide to Unforgettable Weekends
Frommer's Gay & Lesbian Europe	Places Rated Almanac
	Retirement Places Rated

Fly.
Sleep.
Save.

Now you can book your flights and
hotels together, so you can get even better deals
than if you booked them separately.

Travelocity

**Visit www.travelocity.com
or call 1-888-TRAVELOCITY**